Full endorsements for *The Life and Thought of*

'Dr Peter Morden has already shown himself t. and theology of Andrew Fuller. In this further woiк ... understanding of Fuller as a pivotal figure within Baptist life and mission and establishes himself as one of the leading interpreters of his work.'
Nigel Wright, Principal Emeritus, Spurgeon's College, London

'Peter Morden has written what will now be the definitive biography of Andrew Fuller. When Fuller died in 1815, his powerful theological articulation of evangelical Calvinism had been accepted by most Particular Baptists in England. This volume not only does full justice to Fuller's theological development and contribution, but also to his local and wider ministries, his role in shaping the Baptist Missionary Society, his relationships with family and friends, and his spirituality. It is a rounded and thoroughly satisfying evaluation of a towering Baptist figure.'
Ian M. Randall, Senior Research Fellow, Spurgeon's College, London

'Peter Morden's scholarly yet highly readable work chronicles a fresh account of Andrew Fuller by utilizing a wealth of unpublished artifacts and archives. Based on mature research and objective historiography, Fuller the theologian, pastor, missiologist, father, and husband emerges as a complex figure. This book is the most definitive and illuminating biography of its subject written since the nineteenth century!'
Chris Chun, Associate Professor of Church History at Golden Gate Baptist Theological Seminary, San Francisco, CA

'Dr Morden has written a biography of Andrew Fuller that offers an immense amount of careful scholarship, and that will illuminate every reader in manifold ways. A model of historical scholarship.'
Steven R. Holmes, Senior Lecturer in Systematic Theology, University of St Andrews, Scotland

'One of Andrew Fuller's contemporaries once summed up his life and ministry thus: for God's people at that time, it was "so valuable a life". If such an estimate was true, and there is every reason to think that it was, it seems strange that a critical biographical study of his remarkable ministry among his own people, the Particular Baptists, and further afield has been lacking until now. With this fresh biography of Fuller, however, Peter Morden has more than ably filled this lacuna. He has produced a substantial study of this Baptist's career and thought that is marked by both critical insight and empathetic warmth. It has been a joy to be reminded afresh of the importance of Fuller's ministry and why reading Fuller is so vital for our day.'
Michael A.G. Haykin, Professor of Church History & Biblical Spirituality, Southern Baptist Theological Seminary, USA

Andrew Fuller in 1802
Taken from the *Life...of Andrew Fuller* by John Ryland Jr
From an engraving published by Wm. Button and Son in 1816, based on a painting by
Samuel Medley (1769–1857)

The Life and Thought of Andrew Fuller (1754-1815)

STUDIES IN EVANGELICAL HISTORY AND THOUGHT

Series Editors

David Bebbington, Professor of History, University of Stirling, Stirling, Scotland, UK

John H.Y. Briggs, Senior Research Fellow in Ecclesiastical History and Director of the Centre for Baptist History and Heritage, Regent's Park College, Oxford, UK

Timothy Larsen, McManis Professor Christian Thought, Wheaton College, Illinois, USA

Mark A. Noll, McAnaney Professor of History, University of Notre Dame, Notre Dame, Indiana, USA

Ian M. Randall, Senior Research Fellow at Spurgeon's College, London, UK, and International Baptist Theological Seminary, Prague, Czech Republic

Series Preface

The Evangelical movement has been marked by its union of four emphases: on the Bible, on the cross of Christ, on conversion as the entry to the Christian life and on the responsibility of the believer to be active. The present series is designed to publish scholarly studies of any aspect of this movement in Britain or overseas. Its volumes include social analysis as well as exploration of Evangelical ideas. The books in the series consider aspects of the movement shaped by the Evangelical Revival of the eighteenth century, when the impetus to mission began to turn the popular Protestantism of the British Isles and North America into a global phenomenon. The series aims to reap some of the rich harvest of academic research about those who, over the centuries, have believed that they had a gospel to tell to the nations.

The Life and Thought of Andrew Fuller (1754-1815)

Peter J. Morden

First published 2015 by Paternoster

Paternoster is an imprint of Authentic Media
52 Presley Way
Crownhill
Milton Keynes MK8 0ES

09 08 07 06 05 04 03   8 7 6 5 4 3 2 1

British Library Cataloguing in Publication Data
A catalogue record for this book is available from the British Library

ISBN 978-1-84227-817-8

Printed and bound in Great Britain
for Paternoster
by Lightning Source, Milton Keynes

To the Staff and Students of Spurgeon's College, London, England

Contents

Contents

Forewords

Dr Morden has written a biography of Andrew Fuller that offers an immense amount of careful scholarship, and that will illuminate every reader in manifold ways; it may also perplex some. A century or more ago, church historians were concerned with ideas, supremely: the history of Christianity was the history of ideas, specifically theological ideas, and the only way to understand the twists and turns of the story was to be deeply immersed in exegetical and dogmatic controversies.

Of course, such an exclusive focus on intellectual currents was wrong; the doctrine of the incarnation is enough evidence for this. In the twentieth century church historians repeatedly and rightly turned to the social, political, and economic history of Christianity. Pendulums that swing in scholarly fashion often swing too far, however; three generations of historical scholarship has narrated the history of the Christian church as if doctrine was irrelevant; the Reformation was the result of social, economic, and political shifts, not theological or exegetical ones. Luther may have been rather concerned about justification by faith alone, but those who wrote about him and his time were not.

The pendulum is swinging back, and church historians are rediscovering the role of doctrine. Dr Morden's work on Fuller belongs in this renewed, albeit chastened, concern for the effect of doctrinal development and dispute on scholarship. He offers an account of Fuller's life that is deeply aware of social, economic, and political realities, but which sees doctrine as the key driver. Andrew Fuller's life is more determined by theological ideas than almost any other figure I can think of in church history. Almost every theological question he engaged led to changed practice, for him, for his church, for other churches, for his Baptist denomination, and – in the case of theorising world mission – for the world. It is because of this his biography works when told theologically: theological developments and disputes drive changes in practice and in life.

Dr Morden is certainly aware of cultural context: he – rightly – reads Fuller's account of his own conversion against a cultural tradition of evangelical conversion narratives, for instance. Again, the shifting economic fortunes of Kettering are not irrelevant to his story, but he does not attempt to reduce Fuller's theological explorations to a response to such economic pressures; they are a backdrop against which Fuller's thought takes shape, driven far more by his reading of Edwards than by the economic decline of his community.

This, then, is a thoroughly theological biography; it reveals its subject, Fuller, as a powerful theologian – and it also shows its author to be more than capable in elucidating tight doctrinal disputes. Calvinist soteriology is famously complex, as authors struggle to affirm rightly both divine sovereignty and human responsibility; the debate Fuller had with Abraham Booth would seem to many writers a mere splitting of hairs. Dr Morden's clear and patient untangling of it is a model of historical scholarship, and demonstrates not just where the precise differences lay between the two men, but why each of them thought the questions worthy of their energies. Much in fact was at stake, and Dr Morden helps us to see it.

Andrew Fuller revitalised English Particular Baptist life in the eighteenth century, more than any other single figure. His influence is greater than this, however: his involvement with the founding and establishing of the first modern mission society places him at the start of a movement that changed world history decisively. This biography shows that at the heart of such a significant life was Christian doctrine, that the decisive ideas that led to such major historical events were carefully-worked solutions to some of the knottier problems of Calvinistic soteriology. We have much cause to be grateful to Dr Morden for giving us it.

Stephen R. Holmes
Senior Lecturer in Systematic Theology
University of St Andrews, Scotland

Andrew Fuller was the pioneering missionary statesman who was the founding secretary of the Baptist Missionary Society. That alone would have been enough to secure him a place in history, but he was also an outstanding theologian, an important apologist and missiologist, and a significant local church pastor. This new biography of Fuller, published to commemorate the bicentenary of his death, examines these different dimensions of his ministry in depth.

Like all good biographies, this book takes us below the surface and into an understanding of the context of Fuller's achievements. There is the historical context of course but also that of his family life and the theological environment in which he was one of the leading thinkers of his day.

The cost for Fuller was not insignificant. Physically, there were long periods when he was far from well. Alongside the physical ailments, and not entirely independent of them, there was the distress of seeing a number of children suffer and die, and also the death in distressing circumstances of his beloved first wife Sarah. There was another cost too of course, namely that of being attacked, sometimes viciously, by those who disagreed with his gradual but significant theological reorientation towards evangelical Calvinism.

It is true that today we might not stand entirely aligned with every aspect of Fuller's missiology. The primacy he gave to preaching the gospel was laudable and, he believed, entirely consistent with the ministry of Jesus who sought 'a moral revolution in the hearts of men'. But he was largely against any radical engagement in politics, even though during his lifetime the work of BMS colleagues in India included many expressions of engagement with issues of social justice. Let it be said, too, that his emphasis on evangelism and a call to conversion stands as a significant challenge today when the significance of those not 'in Christ' is not always considered the matter of urgency it once was.

The question I ask myself is whether Fuller would recognise the BMS that has grown and developed over the last two centuries as being consistent with the Society he and others formed those many years ago. I believe he would see in the sacrifice of lives laid down, especially in the nineteenth and early-twentieth centuries, the same level of commitment that he himself gave to his life and work. Though mercifully such events are far less common today, the graves of BMS missionaries – men, women and children – from India to Congo, China to Brazil, stand as a testimony of continuing willingness to lay down their lives for the cause of Christ. This must be said also of the long years of ministry that in many cases constituted lifelong service to the missionary task, shown by the example of Fuller's friend, William Carey.

I believe that Fuller would also see the same urgency in preaching Christ though, as in many expressions of evangelicalism today, a greater focus on the love and mercy of God has tempered somewhat the personal anguish even he experienced concerning the assurance of salvation.

He would, however, certainly see a greater emphasis on matters of justice as evangelicalism has embraced a concern for 'life before death' and not just 'life after'. I would like to believe he would approve of this, but that approval might not be immediately forthcoming as he would first enter into robust theological debate on the matter! But if I was optimistic, I believe he would see that just as his life, captured eloquently in this book, is cast in the motif of an unfolding journey, he would surely understand that in two centuries, the journey of the Baptist Missionary Society would also give rise to new insights and opportunities.

David Kerrigan
General Director
BMS World Mission

Preface and Acknowledgements

The publication of this new biography of Andrew Fuller is timed to coincide with the bicentenary its subject's death. It has been a privilege to write a new volume on Fuller's life and thought to commemorate such a significant occasion. I am most grateful to Mike Parsons at Paternoster for commissioning me to do so. Mike has been a sympathetic and thorough editor of this book. I am most grateful.

I have been writing about Fuller and the multi-faceted nature of his life and ministry for nearly twenty years. My interest in him began when I started working towards an MPhil degree examining his role in the revival of eighteenth-century Calvinistic Baptist life. This field of research was suggested by Ian Randall who became my supervisor and encouraged me in numerous different ways. I was also stimulated as I began research by reading Michael Haykin's *One Heart and One Soul: John Sutcliff of Olney, His Friends and His Times*. This groundbreaking book on eighteenth-century English Baptists includes an outstanding chapter on Fuller which provided a model for what I hoped to achieve. I still have my original well-thumbed copy of this book, which Professor Haykin signed for me on the occasion of our first face-to-face meeting in 2002. I remain profoundly grateful to Ian and to Michael for their early help and for their personal encouragement which continues to this day. Thank you.

The Life and Thought of Andrew Fuller is very much a new book, but at different points I have drawn from my previously published work. This includes my earlier book length study *Offering Christ to the World* (Carlisle: Paternoster, 2003) and my chapters from the edited volume *At The Pure Fountain of Thy Word* (Milton Keynes: Paternoster, 2004). I have reworked some material from a paper on Fuller's friend, Samuel Pearce, which I gave at the 2011 conference 'Andrew Fuller and his Friends' sponsored by the Andrew Fuller Center at Southern Baptist Theological Seminary, Louisville, Kentucky. The main talks from the conference will be published in due course and so I am especially grateful to Michael Haykin for permission to draw from my own paper here.

My research on Fuller has taken me to a number of different libraries and archives. I acknowledge the assistance I received from Michael Brealey of Bristol Baptist College, Debra Lyons of Cambridgeshire County Archives, David Milner of Fuller Baptist Church Kettering, Emma Walsh of The Angus Library and Archives, Regent's Park College, Oxford and Judy Powles and Annabel Haycraft of Spurgeon's College, London. Laura and Philip Staves and Geoff and Julia Pollard provided wonderful hospitality when I stayed over in Kettering and Bristol respectively. I am also grateful to Michael Haykin (again) for allowing me to access and draw from Fuller's recently rediscovered 1781 autograph manuscript, 'Thoughts on The Power of Men to do the Will of God' which is held at Southern Baptist Theological Seminary. Some of the illustrations that appear in *Life and Thought of Andrew Fuller* are photographs of material held in the archives at Bristol Baptist College and Fuller Baptist Church, Kettering and are used with permission.

I owe a special debt of gratitude to Ruth Broomhall, who was my study assistant as I worked on this project. Ruth did some archival research for me and transcribed a number of handwritten eighteenth-century documents with great speed and accuracy. She also read and commented on each of my chapters in draft as I produced them. Finally, she read a draft of the complete book. Her work – especially the judicious use of her red pen – has been invaluable! Thankyou. Ruth is a great, great niece of J. Hudson Taylor, the nineteenth-century cross-cultural missionary to China and founder of the China Inland Mission. So, she has a strong link to the so-called 'modern missionary movement' which Andrew Fuller did so much to pioneer. Others have read and commented on sections of the book or indeed the whole book, including Lindsay Caplen, Chris Chun, Anne Morden, Ian Randall and, of course, Mike Parsons. I am also grateful to David Kerrigan and Steven Holmes for agreeing to write Forewords to the book. Of course, I alone am responsible for all the opinions expressed in these pages and the errors that undoubtedly remain.

Much of this book was written during the Spring and Summer of 2014 when I was on research leave from my normal duties at Spurgeon's College. I am indebted to our Academic Board and to our Principal, Roger Standing, for granting me this time. I am also grateful to colleagues and friends who covered for me during my absence, only too aware of how this contributed to their own already considerable workloads. To my embarrassment there are rather too many of these people to list, but I especially want to thank Linda Campbell, David McLachlan, Philip Robinson and Joshua Searle. Spurgeon's has been my 'home' for over seven years now. It continues to be a special place for me and I receive much encouragement from staff and students alike. Accordingly, this book is dedicated to everyone who is part of the College community, with warm appreciation.

Finally, thankyou to my wonderful wife Anne and my two wonderful children, Rachel and Joseph. In different ways they each continue to be an inspiration to me. As a local church pastor and, more recently, a teacher and a writer, words have become part of my stock in trade. Yet I owe more to Anne, Rachel and Joe than I can ever say.

Peter J. Morden
Spurgeon's College, London
Autumn 2014

Leading Abbreviations

BAR	*Baptist Annual Register*
BQ	*Baptist Quarterly*
DEB	*Dictionary of Evangelical Biography*
HEB	*History of the English Baptists*

CHAPTER 1

Introduction

Fullerism

By the beginning of the nineteenth century, a new word had entered the vocabulary of English Calvinistic Baptists – 'Fullerism'. The term, used to describe the leading theological principles of Andrew Fuller (1754-1815), began to appear in print as early as 1804 in pamphlets with titles such as *A Blow at the Root of Fullerism* and *Fullerism Defended*.[1] It even became naturalised in the Welsh language as *Ffwleriaeth*.[2] Fuller himself protested at the use of the label, believing that the expansive, evangelical Calvinism he was contending for was nothing less than biblical Christianity. Moreover, he maintained his views were essentially the same as those held by a cluster of older Protestant and Reformed writers. It would be far better, he insisted, to call his theology 'Owenism' or 'Bunyanism' after the Puritan preachers and writers John Owen (1616-83) and John Bunyan (1628-88).[3] Having examined their writings, Fuller believed he was standing squarely in the tradition of these seventeenth-century men. Yet, despite his protests, the term 'Fullerism' stuck. As Geoffrey Nuttall points out, its coining and subsequent acceptance by friend and foe alike 'points to a remarkable achievement'.[4] Fuller was highly significant as a theologian during his lifetime, among Calvinistic Baptists and in the wider Christian world too. What is more, his work continued to shape people's thinking long into the nineteenth century and, indeed, beyond.

---

[1] Job Hupton, *A Blow Struck at the Root of Fullerism. In a Letter to a Friend* (London: L.J. Higham 1804); George Stonehouse, *Fullerism Defended; or Faith in Christ Asserted to be a Requirement of the Moral Law...* (Cranbrook, Kent: S. Waters, 1804).

[2] Richard Williams, *Y Pregethwr a'r Gwrandawr; sef, Calfinistiaeth a Ffwleriaeth yn Cael ei Hystyried, ar Ddull Ymddyddan Rhwng Dau Gyfaill* [The Preacher and the Listener: Namely Calvinism and Fullerism Considered, by Means of a Conversation between Two Friends] (Machynlleth: T. Hughes, 1840). Cf. Geoffrey F. Nuttall, 'Northamptonshire and the Modern Question', in Nuttall, *Studies in English Dissent* (Weston Rhyn: Quinta, 2002), 207. I am grateful to Robert Pope for translating the title of Williams's book for me.

[3] *Theological and Biblical Magazine* (London: Button & Son, London, 1804), 112. Fuller was reviewing Hupton's, *A Blow Struck at the Root of Fullerism*.

[4] Nuttall, 'Northants and the Modern Question', 207.

1

Fuller was not only known as a theologian. He spent the whole of his minis-terial career as a local church pastor, firstly at Soham, Cambridgeshire (from 1775 to 1782) and then at Kettering, Northamptonshire (from 1782 to 1815). As such he was immersed in the day-to-day demands of practical ministry. His pas-torates coincided with what Michael Haykin has termed a 'profound revitaliza-tion' of English Calvinistic (or 'Particular') Baptist life.[5] Fuller was a central figure in this revival, which was characterised by evangelical theological com-mitments, biblical exposition, lively friendships between like-minded ministers, a stress on corporate prayer and, finally, vigorous evangelism. Fuller and his friends had an overriding commitment to the spread of the gospel – at home and abroad. They preached and itinerated widely in order to reach out to people[6] and, in 1792, they formed the Baptist Missionary Society (BMS) to facilitate cross-cultural mission overseas.[7] Fuller became the indefatigable home secre-tary of the BMS, serving the Society in this capacity from its inception until his death in 1815, combining this work with his continuing duties at Kettering. As secretary he worked tirelessly to support those, like his close friend William Carey (1761-1834), who were serving in the field. As Brian Stanley has stated, the genesis of the BMS marked a 'new chapter', not only in the history of Chris-tianity, 'but also in the history of the relations between the Western and the non-Western world'. There were precedents for Protestant cross-cultural engage-ment, but the formation of the new Society was still 'a turning point in the histo-ry of Christian missionary endeavour'.[8] With his pivotal role, the Kettering pas-tor was involved in the beginnings of a movement which was to have immense global significance.

---

[5] Michael A.G. Haykin, 'A Habitation of God, through the Spirit: John Sutcliff (1752-1814) and the Revitalization of the Calvinistic Baptists in the Late-Eighteenth Centu-ry', *Baptist Quarterl* 34.7 (July 1992), 306. They were 'Particular' because they be-lieved in particular rather than general redemption. There were two streams of Bap-tist life in eighteenth-century England: General and Particular. At the risk of over-simplification, the 'Generals' were Arminian in their emphases, with a stress on hu-man choice and freedom. The 'Particulars' were Calvinistic with a stress on God's sovereignty. For the essential features of eighteenth-century Baptist life in its wider setting, see David W. Bebbington, *Baptists Through the Centuries* (Baylor UP: Wa-co, TX, 2010), 65-101.

[6] For Particular Baptist itinerancy, see Olin C. Robison, 'The Particular Baptists in England: 1760-1820' (unpublished DPhil thesis, University of Oxford, 1963), 95-106. For the wider context, see Deryck W. Lovegrove, *Established Church, Sectari-an People: Itinerancy and the Transformation of English Dissent, 1780-1830* (Cam-bridge: Cambridge University Press, 1988), *passim*.

[7] The Society's original full name was the 'Particular Baptist Society for Propagating the Gospel among the Heathen'.

[8] Brian Stanley, *The History of the Baptist Missionary Society, 1792-1992* (Edinburgh: T. and T. Clark, 1992), 1-2.

Fuller is, then, by any standards a figure of great importance, one whose story relates to a number of crucial shifts in Christian theology, Christian mission and world history. This new study of his life and thought, published to commemorate the bicentenary of his death, seeks to locate him in his immediate and wider context and show in detail why he was – and remains – such a noteworthy figure.

The Study of Fuller

For many years Fuller received remarkably little scholarly attention, despite the widespread availability of various editions of his multi-volume published works.[9] The studies from this rather barren period which do deserve special mention are those by Ernest Clipsham, published in different numbers of the *Baptist Quarterly* in 1963.[10] Clipsham's work on Fuller has been superseded by more recent treatments, but he still provides a good delineation of the principal features of his subject's thought. Apart from Clipsham's articles, the period stretching from about 1830 to 1980 offers slim pickings indeed, certainly as far as specialist studies on Fuller's life and thought are concerned. Thankfully, the situation has now changed, with a large number of books, articles and theses available. This resurgence of interest in Fuller began in the final two decades of the twentieth century and has gathered pace over the last few years.[11] Most of these studies add to an understanding of Fuller and his ministry and some of them are excellent. Michael Haykin did more than anyone to pioneer the renewed interest, especially through his chapter on Fuller in his book on the Kettering pastor's close friend John Sutcliff (1752-1814).[12] Professor Haykin has continued to write on Fuller, for example, editing and contributing to a volume

---

[9] For an excellent survey of Fullerite scholarship up to 2012, offering more detail than I have included here, see Nathan A. Finn, 'The Renaissance in Andrew Fuller Studies: A Bibliographic Essay', in *Southern Baptist Journal of Theology* 17.2 (Summer 2013), 44-61. The edition of Fuller's *Works* I have consistently used in this book is *The Complete Works of the Rev. Andrew Fuller, With a Memoir of his Life by the Rev. Andrew Gunton Fuller*, ed. by Andrew Gunton Fuller, rev. ed. by Joseph Belcher; 3 vols, 3rd edn (Harrisonburg, VA: Sprinkle Publications, 1988 [1845]).

[10] Ernest F. Clipsham, 'Andrew Fuller and Fullerism: A Study in Evangelical Calvinism', *BQ* 20.1-4 (1963); '1. The Development of a Doctrine'; 99-114; '2. Fuller and John Calvin', 147-54; '3. The Gospel Worthy of All Acceptation', 215-25; '4. Fuller as a Theologian', 269-76. See also his 'Andrew Fuller and the Baptist Mission', *Foundations* 10.1 (January 1967), 4-18.

[11] So, Finn, 'Renaissance in Andrew Fuller Studies', 45 and *passim*. Some earlier studies carry relevant material, as Finn points out. See, e.g., Ernest A. Payne, 'Andrew Fuller as Letter Writer', *BQ* 15.7 (July 1954), 290-96; and W. Reginald Ward, 'Baptists and the Transformation of the Church, 1780–1830', *BQ* 25.4 (1973), 167–84.

[12] Michael A.G. Haykin, *One Heart and One Soul: John Sutcliff of Olney, his friends and his times* (Durham: Evangelical Press, 1994), 133-52.

on his apologetic ministry[13] and editing a collection of his letters that especially relate to his spirituality.[14] In addition, a range of book-length studies are now available by other authors. Among the best of these works are Paul Brewster's on Fuller as a 'Pastor – Theologian',[15] Chris Chun's on the crucial connection between Fuller and the North American philosopher / theologian Jonathan Edwards (1703-58)[16] and Keith Grant's on Fuller's pastoral theology with special reference to his preaching.[17] Further books and articles are planned which are likely to advance our knowledge of Fuller considerably. Of particular significance is the initiative to publish modern critical editions of his writings which Michael Haykin is superintending through the 'Andrew Fuller Center' he established in 2007.[18] The 'Works of Andrew Fuller Project' aims to offer both definitive editions of Fuller's numerous books and pamphlets and also volumes covering a wealth of previously unpublished material. This endeavour will do much to open up the Kettering pastor's life and thought to wider readership.

There are also many unpublished PhD theses which relate to Fuller. Just three will be mentioned here. Pride of place goes to an excellent dissertation by J. Ryan West on William Carey and William Ward's (1769-1823) work among Muslims, which illuminates Fuller's relationship with these early BMS missionaries as never before.[19] Nigel Wheeler offers some detailed and helpful comment on the sermons Fuller preached at ordination services.[20] Finally, my own

---

[13] *At the Pure Fountain of Thy Word': Andrew Fuller as an Apologist*, ed. by Michael A.G. Haykin (Milton Keynes: Paternoster, 2004). In my judgement, the quality of the essays in this book is decidedly uneven. Haykin's own contributions are excellent. For another, important piece by Haykin, see his 'Particular Redemption in the Writings of Andrew Fuller (1754–1815)', in *The Gospel in the World: International Baptist Studies*, ed. by David W. Bebbington (Carlisle: Paternoster, 2002), 107-128.

[14] *The Armies of the Lamb: The Spirituality of Andrew Fuller*, ed. by Michael A.G. Haykin (Dundas, ON: Joshua Press, 2001).

[15] Paul Brewster, *Andrew Fuller: Model Pastor - Theologian* (Nashville, Tennessee: B. & H., 2010).

[16] Chris Chun, *The Legacy of Jonathan Edwards in the Theology of Andrew Fuller* (Leiden: Brill, 2012).

[17] Keith S. Grant, *Andrew Fuller and the Evangelical Renewal of Pastoral Theology* (Milton Keynes: Paternoster, 2013).

[18] For more detail, see Finn, 'Renaissance in Andrew Fuller Studies', 53-54. For the website of the Andrew Fuller Center, which is based at the Southern Baptist Theological Seminary, see http://www.andrewfullercenter.org/ [accessed 19 August 2014].

[19] J. Ryan West, 'Evangelizing Bengali Muslims, 1793-1813: William Carey, William Ward, and Islam' (unpublished PhD thesis, Southern Baptist Theological Seminary, Louisville, KY, 2014).

[20] Nigel D. Wheeler, 'Eminent Spirituality and Eminent Usefulness': Andrew Fuller's (1754-1815) Pastoral Theology in his Ordination Sermons (unpublished PhD thesis, Univ. of Pretoria, 2009).

PhD student, Richard Pollard, has done a fine job unpicking the debates between Fuller and the evangelical General Baptist, Dan Taylor (1738-1816).[21] The recent multiplication of published and as yet unpublished studies dealing with aspects of Fuller's life and ministry means the time is right for a major reassessment which engages with the best of these specialist works.

The primary sources available for a major study of Fuller are many and varied. Alongside his *Works* there is much additional printed material.[22] Of major importance are the two biographies which appeared immediately after his death. The first of these, by Fuller's longtime friend and *confidante* John Ryland Jr (1753-1825) is indispensable.[23] It contains much that is written by Fuller himself and Ryland's own commentary on his subject is invaluable. The second biography, by John Webster Morris (1763-1836) sheds much additional light.[24] Morris and Fuller knew each other well, but their friendship ceased when the former man became bankrupt in 1808 and, in Fuller's view, 'acted dishonourably towards his creditors'.[25] Morris's work was very much unofficial; indeed, by the time it was published he was regarded as *persona non grata* by most of the leading figures in Particular Baptist life.[26] Morris remained warm towards his former friend, yet he was more prepared than Ryland to be critical of his subject. Because he wrote as a former 'insider' who became detached from Fuller and his immediate circle, his interpretation of his subject's life and ministry forms a useful counterpoint to Ryland's. The other biography worth noticing here appeared in 1882 and is by Andrew Gunton Fuller (1799-1884), one of

---

[21] Richard Pollard, 'To Revive Experimental Religion or Primitive Christianity in Faith and Practice: The Pioneering Evangelicalism of Dan Taylor (1738-1816)' (unpublished PhD thesis, University of Wales / Spurgeon's College, 2014).

[22] The *Works* themselves are supplemented by Andrew Fuller, *Miscellaneous Pieces on Various Religious Subjects, being the last remains of the Rev. Andrew Fuller*, ed. by John Webster Morris (London: Wightman and Camp, 1826); and *The Last Remains of the Rev. Andrew Fuller: Sermons, Essays, Letters, and Other Miscellaneous Papers, Not Included in His Published Works*, ed. by Joseph Belcher (Philadelphia: American Baptist Publication Society, 1856).

[23] See John Ryland Jr, *The Work of Faith, the Labour of Love, and the Patience of Hope Illustrated in the Life and Death of the Rev. Andrew Fuller*, 1st edn (London: Button and Son, 1816), 2nd edn (London: Button and Son, 1818). Unless otherwise stated I always cite from the expanded 2nd edn.

[24] John Webster Morris, *Memoirs of the Life and Death of the Rev Andrew Fuller*, 1st edn (High Wycombe, 1816), 2nd edn (London: Wightman and Cramp, 1826).

[25] See Fuller to William R. Ward, 16 July 1809, 15 June 1810, Bound Volume of Andrew Fuller Letters to W. Carey, J. Marshman, W. Ward and other BMS Missionaries, 1795-1815, transcribed in India, with an index compiled by A. Gunton Fuller (3/170), Angus Library, Oxford. In these private letters to Ward, Fuller also spoke of Morris's 'pride and extravagance' and 'shocking failure'.

[26] See the terse note in the *Baptist Magazine*, 7, November 1815 (London: Button & Son, 1815), 477.

Fuller's sons from his second marriage. The son aimed to complement the earlier 'tombstone' biographies with a personal, family orientated portrait of his father.[27] Another, nineteenth-century work by one of Fuller's grandsons, Thomas Fuller, adds very little to these three and in any case is not, strictly speaking, a primary source.[28] Far more important than Thomas Fuller's work are periodicals such as the *Baptist Magazine* and the *Evangelical Magazine* which carry pieces by Fuller and much more that is relevant to him. These and other published sources from the eighteenth and nineteenth centuries constitute a rich seam for the researcher to mine.

As far as the unpublished sources are concerned, there is a large amount of material scattered among various archives. Important are the two boxes of typescript copies of various Fuller letters held in the Angus Library of Regent's Park College, Oxford.[29] Many of these are culled from published sources, but the Angus also holds much unpublished material, including correspondence between Fuller, Carey and other missionaries,[30] together with other original letters written by Fuller.[31] The Angus is an essential archive for the student of Fuller, but it is by no means the only one. The Cambridgeshire County Archive in Cambridge holds important material relevant to his pastorate in Soham.[32] Fuller Baptist Church, Kettering has the original Church Book for the period covering Fuller's ministry, as well as a number of letters[33] and many other relevant items. The 1781 autograph manuscript, 'Thoughts on The Power of Man to do the Will of God', held at Southern Baptist Theological Seminary, sheds much new light on Fuller's theological development in his early years of ministry. Moreover, there is a wealth of material at Bristol Baptist College, including Fuller's

---

[27] Andrew Gunton Fuller, *Men Worth Remembering: Andrew Fuller* (London: Hodder and Stoughton, 1882). Gunton Fuller also wrote the Memoir which was prefixed to his father's collected *Works*.

[28] Thomas E. Fuller, *A Memoir of the Life and Writings of Andrew Fuller: By His Grandson* (London: Heaton and Son, 1863). Thomas Fuller was one of Andrew Gunton Fuller's sons.

[29] Typescript Andrew Fuller Letters, transcribed by Joyce A. Booth, superintended by Ernest A. Payne, Angus Library, Regent's Park College, Oxford (4/5/1 and 4/5/2).

[30] For example, Letters of William Carey, William Ward, Joshua Marshman, and Others to the Baptist Missionary Society Committee, 1800-1827, Angus Library, Regent's Park College, Oxford (IN/21).

[31] For example, Andrew Fuller Letter to William Wilberforce, Angus Library, Regent's Park College, Oxford, 5 December 1801 (II/200).

[32] Especially, Andrew Fuller, A Narration of the dealings of God in a way of Providence with the Baptist Church at Soham from the year 1770 (NC/B - Soham R70/20).

[33] The Church Book of Kettering Baptist Church (The 'Little Meeting'), 1773-1815, Fuller Baptist Church Archive, Kettering.

diary from the years 1784-1801[34] and a 'Commonplace Book' in which he recorded various thoughts from 1798 onwards.[35] I only discovered the material at
Bristol when my previous study on Fuller, *Offering Christ to the World*, was
nearing completion.[36] Although I did draw from this archive, it did not have the
significant, shaping influence on my book that it might have done. I have sought
to put this right in this new theological biography. Even the best recent studies
on Fuller tend to focus on published primary material rather than unpublished.[37]
Utilizing the significant corpus of unpublished evidence allows new perspectives on Fuller's life and thought to be opened up.

In summary, although it is possible to sink under the weight of material, its
existence and availability makes it possible to trace the central aspects of
Fuller's life and thought with some precision. Also, a portrait of the man not
just in public but also in private can be drawn.

Still, is a new biography really necessary? Writing in 1993, Roger Hayden
lamented, 'it is a tragedy that no serious biography of [Fuller] has been written
since 1863'.[38] Hayden's reference is to Thomas Fuller's *Memoir* from 1863. He
appears to have missed Gunton Fuller's 1883 book, which certainly qualifies as
a 'serious biography' if the 1863 one does. Nevertheless, Hayden's essential
point is still valid. At the time he wrote there had been no 'serious biography' of
the Kettering pastor for many years; indeed, the only book I am aware of which
might qualify for the title of 'biography' at all is a slim volume by Gilbert Laws,
published in 1942.[39] Have things changed? As I have sought to show, since
1993 there has been a great resurgence in Fuller studies and the situation over
twenty years on is very different. Yet, despite the profusion of 'biographical
sketches',[40] there is still no full, modern biography of this highly significant

---

34 Andrew Fuller, Diary and Spiritual Thoughts [1784-1801], Bristol Baptist College
Library (G 95 b). The vast majority of entries are from the 1780s.
35 Andrew Fuller, Commonplace Book [first entry 22 June 1798], Bristol Baptist College Library (95 a).
36 Peter J. Morden, *Offering Christ to the World: Andrew Fuller (1754-1815) and the
Revival of Eighteenth Century Particular Baptist Life* (Carlisle: Paternoster, 2003).
37 The main exceptions are a number of Haykin's studies. Grant draws from some of the
unpublished autograph MS material relating to Fuller's two pastorates.
38 Roger L. Hayden, 'The Life and Influence of Andrew Fuller', in *The Kettering Connection: Northamptonshire Baptists and Overseas Mission*, ed. by Ronald L.
Greenall (Leicester: Department of Adult Education, University of Leicester, 1993),
12.
39 Gilbert Laws, *Andrew Fuller: Pastor, Theologian, Ropeholder* (London: Kingsgate
Press, 1942).
40 I have written a number of these myself, the most recent being '"So valuable a
life...": A Biographical Sketch of Andrew Fuller (1754-1815)', *Southern Baptist
Journal of Theology* 17.1 (Spring 2013), 4-14. For alternatives, see the *résumés* of
Fuller's life in Brewster, *Andrew Fuller*, 8-35, and Bart D. Box, *The Atonement in
the Thought of Andrew Fuller* (New Orleans: ProQuest, 2009), 34-45. This last

Baptist leader, still less one that seeks to draw from unpublished as well as published sources. Consequently, there is a need for such a work and this current study is an attempt to fill the gap.

The Structure and Aims of this Book

This book has a thematic structure rather than a strictly chronological one. This thematic approach does perhaps need a sentence of explanation as a reader might reasonably expect the story of a person's life to be told in the order that events occurred. I believe the structure I have adopted allows for greater analysis of central themes, particularly different dimensions of his theology, ministry and mission. Following this brief introductory chapter, chapter two examines Fuller's early life, including his evangelical conversion and call to pastoral ministry. Much that happened in this early period was formative and set the trajectory for later developments. Chapter three considers his ministry at Soham and his developing theology, charting his journey towards the writing of his most famous book, the *Gospel Worthy of All Acceptation*. This was the work which encapsulated the thinking that became known as 'Fullerism'. Chapter four covers his early ministry at Kettering and shows how he defended his theological system against the criticisms which came at him from a number of different quarters. Chapter five shows how his commitment to overseas mission grew and traces the steps that were taken towards the founding of the BMS, with Fuller accepting the mantle of secretary. This was a moment of great significance, yet the founding of the BMS was played out against the backdrop of much personal tragedy for Fuller and this pivotal chapter seeks to bring this out. Chapter six sets out some further theological controversies. Theology was vitally important to Fuller, hence the phrase 'theological biography' which has appeared once already in this introduction. Some of the theological debates are demanding, but we cannot understand Fuller properly unless we engage with them. Chapter seven evaluates his later ministry at Kettering and shows how his multidimensional work as secretary of the BMS developed. Chapter eight covers issues of spirituality and his last illness and death. The final, concluding chapter draws together the main threads of this study, before offering a brief assessment of his legacy.

Fuller's life was so extraordinary and so full that there are inevitably some gaps in my treatment of him. I have not surveyed everything he did and everything he wrote; indeed, there are some significant published works, for example, the *Gospel its Own Witness*, that are not considered.[41] The danger of trying to

---

named work is a PhD thesis from New Orleans Baptist Theological Seminary now available through ProQuest.

[41] On the *Gospel its Own Witness*, see Alan P.F. Sell, 'The Gospel its Own Witness: Deism, Thomas Paine and Andrew Fuller', in *"You Shall Be My Witnesses": A Festschrift in Honor of Reverend D. Allison A. Trites on the Occasion of his Retirement*,

be comprehensive is that the book becomes too large and unwieldy and consequently misses 'the wood for the trees'. Nevertheless, I give extended treatments to a number of his theological works and published sermons, as well as analysing an important example of his apologetic writing (the *Apology for Missions in India*) and his most significant more general work (the *Memoirs of Samuel Pearce*). Thus a representative sample of his published *corpus* is considered in a way which I hope gives insight into the whole.

As already stated, I have tried to portray Fuller as he was not just in public but also in private. More than that, I have sought to get to the heart of what drove him on. Bruce Hindmarsh comments on how difficult it is to write someone's story not just from the 'outside' but from the 'inside' as well. Few historians, he contends, manage to do this well.[42] I have tried (whilst doubtless falling far short) to write Fuller's story from the 'inside', appreciating what was important to him and seeking to understand, if you like, what 'made him tick'. This biography aims to uncover something of the personal, private Andrew Fuller so that a clearer picture of the real man can be seen. He emerges as a far more complex person than has sometimes been supposed and yet there was significant integration between the public figure and the private man. Fuller was a flawed character, but he was also a man of integrity who thought and felt deeply about life and faith and agonized over major decisions and issues.

The Historian as Interpreter

In undertaking the task of researching and writing I have sought to be as objective as possible. However, as another historian wisely observes, 'objectivity is not neutrality'.[43] I freely confess I am not neutral. As will already be apparent to those who have read my Preface and Acknowledgements I am a committed Christian. Furthermore, I am an evangelical Baptist minister who has been pastor of two churches (including one originally established as a result of the revival in which Fuller played so central a part).[44] I now teach in a confessional theological college which is evangelical and which trains Baptist pastors and other Christians for mission and ministry. Furthermore, I do find myself in sympathy with many (although not absolutely all) of Fuller's emphases. So I am biased, but then all historians are. This unavoidable bias does not make the task of history impossible, indeed, 'a historian frigid towards his theme can hardly ever

---

ed. by R. Glenn Wooden *et al* (Macon, GA: Mercer University Press, 2003), 188–229.

[42] In his foreword to Grant, *Andrew Fuller*, xiii.

[43] Thomas J. Haskell, *Objectivity is Not Neutrality: Explanatory Schemes in History* (Baltimore: John Hopkins University Press, 1998).

[44] This is Shirley Baptist Church, Solihull. The Baptist work in Shirley can be traced to 1797, when members at Cannon Street, Birmingham, the church pastored by Fuller's friend Samuel Pearce, started meetings in Shirley, which at the time was a tiny village.

write good history'.[45] George Marsden, in the Introduction to his magisterial biography of Jonathan Edwards (1703-58), not only sums up the situation faced by the historian, he also points the way forward. Marsden observes,

> Even the fairest observers have biases and blind spots. They have (and they ought to have) interests. The best way to deal with these universal phenomena is to acknowledge one's point of view rather than posing as a neutral observer. That way readers can take an author's viewpoint into account, discount it if they wish, and learn from it to the extent they can. At the same time, authors who are self-conscious about their points of view can use such self-knowledge to limit unintended or unfair warping of the evidence to fit their perspectives.[46]

I have sought to take these words as my guide, especially the final sentence. Throughout the process of researching and writing I have tried to be aware of my presuppositions and how these might shape my handling and interpretation of the evidence. I have been especially alert to the danger of distorting or limiting my presentation of the material, however subtly, for the purposes of edification or for polemical intent.[47]

Seeking to avoid such mistakes is most important for, much as I welcome the new upsurge in Fuller studies, I do believe that some recent writers have been too intent on co-opting the Kettering pastor to serve a predetermined polemical agenda. A few authors almost remake Fuller in their own image, effectively reshaping him so that he serves their concerns. I suspect much of this reshaping is inadvertently done. Because of the complexities of Fuller's thinking on, say, the extent of the atonement, it is all too easy to read a single quotation and believe this represents the totality of his view without taking into account the sweep of his thought or the subtlety of some of his approaches, still less the specific cultural and religious contexts which underpinned them. Yet the type of writing that leaps all too quickly to polemic without prior understanding is not only poor history, it also fails to serve the church well, leading as it does to badly informed debates about crucial issues. Such an approach, which so often generates more heat than light, is to be avoided. It is true that I myself believe that many of Fuller's emphases have much to say to the contemporary church. Yet only when Fuller is appreciated on his own terms can those challenges be correctly identified and a properly informed response be made. Consequently, my hope and indeed my prayer for this book is simply that it would enable us to understand Andrew Fuller better. This may seem a modest aim. Nevertheless, I believe the more we truly understand his life and thought, the deeper the challenges for the church of today will be.

---

[45] Owen Chadwick, *The Spirit of the Oxford Movement* (Cambridge: Cambridge University Press: 1990), 157.

[46] George M. Marsden, *Jonathan Edwards: A Life* (New Haven and London: Yale University Press, 2003), 5. Marsden also cites the title of Haskell's book.

[47] For similar comments, see Timothy Dudley Smith, *John Stott: The Making of a Leader* (Leicester: IVP, 1999), 17.

CHAPTER 2

Early Life

Like many other great and original characters, MR ANDREW FULLER arose out of obscurity...

John Webster Morris was not exaggerating when he stated that Andrew Fuller 'arose out of obscurity'.[1] Fuller was born on 6 February 1754 at Wicken, a village near Ely in Fenland Cambridgeshire, in a small, ramshackle farmhouse which was finally demolished in 1861.[2] He was the youngest son of Robert Fuller (d. 1781) and Philippa Gunton (d. 1816). Robert was a tenant farmer, making a living by renting a succession of small and, it appears, not especially profitable farmsteads. In 1761 the family moved to Soham, two and a half miles from Wicken. Both parents were Dissenters, although Robert was markedly less committed than his wife. Philippa became a member of the Particular Baptist church at Soham, and the whole family attended.[3] Her own mother, also called Philippa, had actually been one of the six founding members of the church.[4] In 1775 her son Andrew, despite a meager formal education, would become its pastor.

The evidence for this early period of Andrew Fuller's life is incomplete and fragmentary, partly because of the 'obscurity' noted by Morris. Yet sufficient information remains for the essential background to be sketched in and for a picture of important, formative influences to be drawn. Fuller's early experiences would be significant indeed for his future life and ministry.

---

[1] John Webster Morris, *Memoirs of the Life and Death of the Rev Andrew Fuller*, 2nd edn (London: Wightman and Cramp, 1826), 17.

[2] A hundred years after the Fuller family left it. It was painted by Andrew Fuller's son, Andrew Gunton Fuller, in the year it was demolished. The painting is held at Fuller Baptist church, Kettering.

[3] John Ryland Jr, *The Work of Faith, the Labour of Love, and the Patience of Hope Illustrated in the Life and Death of the Rev. Andrew Fuller*, 2nd edn (London: Button and Son, 1818), 8-10.

[4] Soham Baptist Church Book, 1752-1868, Cambridgehire County Archive (N/B - Soham), 1.

Family and Background

Andrew Fuller's parents came from families who had been based in the Soham / Wicken area for generations; on his father's side, his forbears had lived in Wicken itself 'from time immemorial'.[5] Also, both branches of the family were part of the English Nonconformist or Dissenting tradition, refusing to conform to the established state church, the Church of England. Ryland made much of this Dissenting lineage in the opening pages of his official biography. Andrew Fuller's paternal grandmother was Honour Hart, a 'pious woman' who was a member of the Independent (Congregational) church at Isleham before she became 'convinced of the propriety of believers' baptism' and – according to Ryland – joined the Baptist church at Soham.[6] Her father Robert Hart was, according to family tradition, converted through the preaching of Francis Holcroft (1629?-93). Holcroft was one of the early Nonconformists, a Puritan minister ejected from the Church of England in 1662 for refusing to accept the Act of Uniformity. As to doctrine, Holcroft was Calvinistic, having been taught by the famous Cambridge Puritan divine David Clarkson, a link Ryland duly noted.[7] Ryland also highlighted that Holcroft had been persecuted (he was imprisoned in Cambridge Castle in 1663 for preaching at an illegal meeting).[8] Holcroft, who was a committed Independent, was directly or indirectly responsible for founding the majority of Dissenting causes in Cambridgeshire.[9] To be connected with him – however tenuously – was an important sign of local Dissenting pedigree.

On Andrew Fuller's mother's side, as well as his devout Particular Baptist grandmother, Philippa, her Nonconformist parents, Friend Stevenson and Mary Malden were also singled out, with Mary in particular 'remarkable for her pie-

---

[5] Ryland, *Fuller*, 8; cf. Andrew Gunton Fuller, *Memoir*, in *The Complete Works of the Rev. Andrew Fuller, With a Memoir of his Life by the Rev. Andrew Gunton Fuller*, ed. by Andrew Gunton Fuller, rev. ed. by Joseph Belcher; 3 vols, 3rd edn (Harrisonburg, VA: Sprinkle Publications, 1988 [1845]), 1: 1.

[6] Ryland, *Fuller*, 9. I could not find her name in the Soham Baptist Church Book, 1770-1833, but the records of members may well be incomplete. Independent churches were committed to congregational church government alongside infant baptism. Baptists added believers' baptism to this commitment to congregational church polity.

[7] Ryland, *Fuller*, 9, n.

[8] Ryland, *Fuller*, 9; Ryland drew his information on Holcroft from Edmund Calamy and Samuel Palmer, *The Nonconformists' Memorial...* vol. 1 (London: W. Harris, 1775), 202-203.

[9] For more on Holcroft and the beginnings of Cambridgeshire Nonconformity, see Geoffrey F. Nuttall, 'Cambridge Nonconformity 1660-1710: From Holcroft to Hussey', in Nuttall, *Studies in English Dissent* (Weston Rhyn: Quinta, 2002), 161-80, esp. 161-72; 179-80. This chapter originally appeared as an article in the *Journal of the United Reformed Church History Society* in April 1977. For ease of reference I have cited this and other pieces by Nuttall from this later collection.

ty'.[10] Mary's parents – and Andrew Fuller's great, great grandparents – were John and Joan Malden. Living after the Puritan Commonwealth had ended and the monarchy had been restored, they had become 'objects of ridicule and persecution, on account of their nonconformity'.[11] Here too there was a connection with Holcroft, as the family held that John and Joan were friends with him and one of his principal lieutenants, Joseph Oddy. Little evidence for this connection is offered, although John and Joan were buried in the same graveyard as Holcroft and Oddy, at Oakington, just north of Cambridge.[12]

Thus, Ryland set a lineage of determined, principled Nonconformity before his readers. Links to the renowned Holcroft were highlighted, with hard evidence probably mixed with a measure of family lore. Congregationalism, Calvinistic theology and a willingness to endure persecution for the Dissenting cause were emphasised, together with examples of inner 'piety' – Ryland wanted to give due weight to personal faith and holiness alongside other elements of the Dissenting tradition. Recent conversions to the Baptist cause completed an impressive picture. This was the self-consciously Dissenting heritage Andrew Fuller was born into and which played an important role in moulding him. Andrew's two older brothers, Robert (1747-1829) and John (b. 1748) each made their own Christian commitments and became first members and then deacons of Particular Baptist churches, whilst following their father into farming.[13] Fuller and his family were steeped in a particular brand of Nonconformist Christianity. For Ryland this was a significant heritage, more important than other advantages of birth. Fuller may have been born in obscurity, but he was still part of a significant tradition, one which could be prized.

As well as recognising the Dissenting background, it is important to consider the Fenland location and the extent to which a sense of place might have shaped Fuller. The Fens had been mostly marshland before they were drained towards the end of the seventeenth century so they could be farmed. The area was characterised by an almost unrelenting flatness and, by the mid-eighteenth century, a complex network of ditches, drains, sluices and banks which combined to keep the water at bay.[14] The inhabitants of various Fenland districts were aware that the low dykes crisscrossing their land might one day be breached, causing a catastrophe. In heavy rain and driving winds they would band together to shore

---

[10] Ryland, *Fuller*, 9.

[11] Ryland, *Fuller*, 10. For persecution of Dissenters after the restoration, see Raymond Brown, *Spirituality in Adversity: English Nonconformity in a Period of Repression, 1660-1689* (Milton Keynes: Paternoster, 2012).

[12] Ryland, *Fuller*, 10. For Oddy, see Calamy and Palmer, *Nonconformists' Memorial*, 1: 1, 216.

[13] Ryland, *Fuller*, 9. The brothers' farms were at Isleham and Little Bentley in Essex respectively. Cf. Morris, *Fuller*, 2nd edn, 18.

[14] For detail, see Henry C. Darby, *The Draining of the Fens*, 2nd edn (Cambridge: Cambridge University Press, 1968), esp. 117-82.

up the defences, sometimes working through the night to defend their homes and their livelihoods. As already stated, Fuller's ancestors were deeply embedded in this setting, rarely travelling far from their home base on the Cambridgeshire / Suffolk border. Gilbert Laws describes Fuller as a 'son of the Fenland' and reflects on how the 'character of a country has an influence on the character of those who live in it'.[15] He makes a number of suggestions as to how this very specific rural context may have moulded his subject. So, Fuller's 'enduring energy' and 'the fearlessness and persistence of [his] character' are ascribed in part to this setting.[16] Laws further suggests that Fenland people in Fuller's day tended to incline towards Calvinistic theology, as becomes those who 'live close to nature and know the limits' of what humanity can do.[17] These comments can seem fanciful, but Andrew Gunton Fuller also wrote about the importance of his father's Fenland context, one characterised by 'danger' and strenuous physical activity. The son believed it 'exerted a strong influence' in forming his father's character.[18] Indeed, there must have been influence to a degree. Fuller's Fenland upbringing helps explain some of the imagery he used ('my hands hung down like a bulrush', he once wrote),[19] together with his enduring countryman's distrust of London. More importantly, his tenacious, determined spirit and a certain independence of thought can be attributed, in part, to his being a 'son of the Fens'.

Andrew Fuller helped his father in farming until Robert and Philippa moved in 1773 to take up the tenancy of farm in Bottisham, which was some eight miles south west of Soham. Fuller's time on the farm constituted his early 'education' more than any formal schooling. For a few years he attended a small 'free school' in Soham, but he received 'only the common rudiments of an English education'.[20] So, although he developed a 'taste for reading',[21] much of his childhood and youth was spent in physical activity: milking and tending cattle, dealing with other livestock, scything grass and threshing wheat. He also spent time talking with – and distracting – farm labourers.[22] As to character, the mature Fuller described his younger self as having had a 'daring spirit' to go alongside his 'athletic frame'.[23] He was especially drawn to bouts of wrestling,

---

[15] Gilbert Laws, *Andrew Fuller: Pastor, Theologian, Ropeholder* (London: Carey Press, 1942), 9-10.
[16] Laws, *Fuller*, 9, 12. Cf. Paul Brewster, *Andrew Fuller: Model Pastor – Theologian* (Nashville, Tennessee: B. & H., 2010), 9.
[17] Laws, *Fuller*, 12.
[18] Andrew Gunton Fuller, *Men Worth Remembering: Andrew Fuller* (London: Hodder and Stoughton, 1882), 16.
[19] Fuller letter to John Thomas, 16 May 1796, in Ryland, *Fuller*, 159.
[20] Morris, *Fuller*, 2nd edn, 17.
[21] Gunton Fuller, *Fuller*, 22.
[22] Gunton Fuller, *Fuller*, 16-18.
[23] Gunton Fuller, Memoir, in *Works*, 1: 4.

which he both used to watch and engage in himself.[24] He later testified that in his early teenage years he 'seldom thought of religion'.[25] This would change as he entered his mid-teens.

Immediate Church Context

Despite Fuller's avowed lack of early religious conviction, Soham Baptist Church had an important place in his early upbringing, one which would become even more central from 1769 onwards. The church was an offshoot from the aforementioned Independent meeting at Isleham. By the late 1740s some of the members of the Isleham fellowship who lived in the Soham area were becoming attracted to Baptist principles. A bitter dispute arose, with the Congregationalists refusing to countenance having a 'waterman' in the pulpit.[26] Soham Baptist Church was formed by Isleham members who believed they had no choice but to withdraw. The split happened in April 1752, two years before Fuller was born. Those who had come to Baptist convictions had been encouraged by Stone Yard Baptist Church in Cambridge and their minister, George Simson (d. 1763). Simson was described in the Stone Yard Church Book (although not until after he had left his post) as 'a good preacher, a rigid Baptist, of a violent temper, a Lord in his church, a tyrant in his family, a libertine in his life'.[27] Although the Stone Yard church 'greatly declined' during his pastorate,[28] for a short time he exercised considerable influence in villages around Cambridge.[29] A preacher from Stone Yard, John Eve (d.1782), a former sieve maker from nearby Chesterton, received a call to be pastor at Soham soon after the Baptist work there had begun.[30]

As to theology, Soham Baptist Church was staunchly Calvinistic. More specifically, it was strongly influenced by the theology known as 'hyper Calvinism' or, as Fuller would later call it, 'false Calvinism'.[31] A less pejorative term is

---

[24] Gunton Fuller, *Fuller*, 20.

[25] Gunton Fuller, *Memoir*, in *Works*, 1: 4.

[26] Soham Church Book, 2. Cf. *The Church Book of the Independent Church... Isleham 1693-1805*, ed. by Kenneth C. Parsons (Cambridge Antiquarian Records Society: Cambridge, 1984), 57.

[27] *Church Book: St Andrew's Street Baptist Church, Cambridge: 1720-1832* [typescript by Leonard G. Champion; Introduction by Len Addicott] (Didcot: Baptist Historical Society, 1991),18. Cf. Joseph Ivimey, *A History of the English Baptists(HEB)*, 4 vols (London: Hinton, Holdsworth & Ball, 1811-30), 4: 452.

[28] Ivimey, *HEB*, 4: 452.

[29] *Church Book: St Andrew's Street*, viii. Simson left both the church and the Cambridge area in 1756.

[30] Soham Church Book, 2-4. Eve was ordained on 26 Sept 1752. The *Church Book: St Andrew's Street Baptist Church*, 17, recorded that his ministerial abilities had been formally recognised by them on 2 April 1749.

[31] Ryland, *Fuller*, 11.

'high Calvinism' and this is the designation I have used throughout this book. Both Simson and Eve were high Calvinists, unsurprising since this theology and its accompanying practices were widespread among the Independents and the Baptists of the Fens.[32] High Calvinism is vitally important to Fuller's unfolding story and so a delineation of its leading features and personalities is helpful.

High Calvinism in Cambridgeshire and Northamptonshire

Put simply, high Calvinists exalted the sovereignty of God in salvation in ways which greatly minimised the importance of human response.[33] In particular, it was no one's 'duty' to repent and believe the gospel, since total depravity rendered such a response impossible. Building on these theological foundations, high Calvinists refused to 'offer' the gospel freely to all. As Fuller himself later put it, preachers said nothing to 'sinners...inviting them to apply to Christ for salvation.'[34] Such invitations to trust in Christ were, high Calvinists claimed, a nonsense since faith was not a 'duty' and God's 'elect' would come to believe anyway in God's good time. Furthermore, applied evangelistic preaching was dangerous because it encouraged false professions of faith which could sully the purity of the church. In summary, it was considered both theologically wrong and practically dangerous to 'offer' the gospel openly and freely to all. Invitational gospel preaching was rejected.

The first systematic exposition of high Calvinism was published in 1707 by Joseph Hussey, with the phrase 'No Offers of [God's] Grace' actually in the book's title.[35] Hussey had strong Cambridge connections and was influential in the surrounding area.[36] Even more important to the spread of high Calvinism in the Cambridgeshire / Fenland context was the ministry of Richard Davis (1658-1714), an Independent minister at Rothwell. Although Rothwell was in Northamptonshire, Davis itinerated widely and helped establish a number of Dissent-

---

[32] For Simson's high Calvinism, see Addicott, 'Introduction', *Church Book: St Andrew's Street*, viii. The Isleham Independents were also inclined to this theology.

[33] Keith S. Grant, *Andrew Fuller and the Evangelical Renewal of Pastoral Theology* (Milton Keynes: Paternoster, 2013), 28. Grant's brief survey of high Calvinism (26-28) is extremely well done. For an alternative and more detailed treatment, see Peter Toon, *The Emergence of Hyper Calvinism in English Nonconformity 1689-1765* (London: Olive Tree, 1967). High Calvinism was a departure from earlier, Puritan emphases which sought to hold divine sovereignty and human responsibility in more careful balance.

[34] Ryland, *Fuller*, 31-32.

[35] Joseph Hussey, *God's Operations of Grace, But No Offers of His Grace* (London: D. Bridge, 1707).

[36] Nuttall, 'Cambridge Nonconformity' in Nuttall, *Studies in English Dissent*, 170-73.

ing causes in Cambridgeshire.[37] Although he did not adopt the 'no offer' position until later in life, his network of churches was by then well established and did much to encourage high Calvinism's spread. Yet, important as these men were, by the mid-eighteenth century high Calvinism in Particular Baptist circles – both in the Fens and elsewhere – was especially associated with John Brine (1703-65) and John Gill (1697-1771).

Of these two men, Gill was the most significant.[38] Like Hussey, Gill also had links with Cambridge, although he was most closely associated with Northamptonshire. Gill was born in Kettering and had been converted through the preaching of William Wallis, the first minister of the Baptist congregation there. This was the church which Fuller would later pastor. As a young man Gill had known the elderly Richard Davis well, and had been taught by him.[39] Gill felt the call to pastoral ministry and moved to London, where he was pastor at Carter Lane in Southwark from 1719 until his death. For most of this time he was the leading figure on the London Baptist Board, a group of pastors who met regularly and were widely influential in national Particular Baptist affairs. Nevertheless, important as his preaching ministry and work for the London board was, his reputation largely rested on his voluminous published works, later memorably described by Robert Hall Jr (1764-1831) as a 'continent of mud'.[40] These included the *Cause of God and Truth*, originally published in four volumes (1735-38) and a nine volume *Exposition of the Holy Scriptures* (1746-66). Gill's work as a skilled Hebraist was recognised beyond Particular Baptist circles and formally acknowledged with the award of an Aberdeen DD in 1748. Still, it was in his own denomination that his writings were best known and his personal links with Northamptonshire and Cambridgeshire meant his books were perhaps especially treasured there.

Gill took the standard high Calvinistic position on the 'free offer' of the gospel.[41] In 1748 he wrote a Preface to the seventh edition of a collection of the

---

[37] For example, at Burwell and in Cambridge itself. See Geoffrey F. Nuttall, 'Northamptonshire and The Modern Question: A Turning Point in Eighteenth-Century Dissent', in Nuttall, *Studies in English Dissent*, 210.

[38] For biographical details of Gill, see John Rippon, *A Brief Memoir of the Life and Writings of the late Rev. John Gill, DD* (London: John Bennett, 1838). See also *The Life and Thought of John Gill (1697-1771): A Tercentennial Appreciation*, ed. by Michael A.G. Haykin (Leiden: Brill, 1997).

[39] See Geoffrey F. Nuttall, 'Northamptonshire and The Modern Question: A Turning Point in Eighteenth-Century Dissent', in Nuttall, *Studies in English Dissent*, 222.

[40] *The Works of Robert Hall*, ed. by Olinthus Gregory, vol. 6 (London, 1833), 155-56.

[41] George Ella seeks to defend Gill from the charge of high Calvinism, but his argument flies in the face of the evidence. See his 'John Gill and the Charge of Hyper-Calvinism', *BQ* 36.4 (October 1995), *passim*, e.g., 167. For a balanced appraisal of Gill's life and ministry, see Robert W. Oliver, 'John Gill (1697-1771)', in *The British Particular Baptists,* vol.1, ed. by Michael A.G. Haykin (Springfield, MO: Particular Baptist Press, 1998), 145-65.

hymns of his former mentor, Richard Davis. Commenting on Davis's occasional use of 'free offer' language in these hymns, Gill declared,

> I can affirm, upon good and sufficient testimony, that Mr Davis, before his death, changed his mind in this matter, and disused the phrase, as being improper, and being too bold and free for a minister of Christ to make use of. And though I have not thought fit to alter any words or phrases in the revision of these hymns, yet in the use of them in public service, those who think proper may substitute another phrase in its room more eligible.[42]

Gill carefully noted Davis's change of mind on the 'free offer' and approved of it. Elsewhere Gill declared that talk of 'gospel-commands, gospel-threatenings and gospel-duties' were a 'contradiction in terms' and smacked of 'loose and unguarded speech'.[43] John Eve was an avid reader of Gill and so it was no surprise that the Soham pastor had 'little or nothing to say to the unconverted', as Fuller later put it.[44] Eve agreed with Gill: it was wrong to offer the gospel to all. Such a practice was altogether too 'bold' and too 'free'.

Wider Church Context

Before returning to Fuller's own story, it is important to consider some issues relating to the wider ecclesial context. Four questions can be posed. Firstly, to what extent had the high Calvinism that was prevalent in the Fens impacted Particular Baptist life in the rest of England? Secondly, what was the state of the denomination as a whole, both numerically and spiritually? Thirdly, what were the reasons for the situation the Particular Baptists found themselves in? Fourthly, how did Calvinistic Baptists respond to the eighteenth-century Evangelical Revival which was a crucial dimension of the wider religious context? Answering these linked questions enables us to see English Particular Baptist life in its broader setting. It is this setting that forms the essential backdrop to Fuller's life and work.

---

[42] John Gill, 'Recommendatory Preface' to Richard Davis, *Hymns Composed on Several Subjects, and on Divers Occasions*, 7th edn (London: J. Ward, 1748), printed in George T. Streather, *Memorials of the Independent Chapel at Rothwell* (Rothwell: Rothwell United Reformed Church, 1994), 63-64. Cf. *Protestant Nonconformist Texts*, ed. Alan F. Sell *et al*; *Vol. 2: The Eighteenth Century;* ed. by Alan F. Sell *et al* (Aldershot: Ashgate, 2006), Doc IV.1 (c), 192.

[43] John Gill, *The Doctrines of God's Everlasting Love to His Elect... Stated and Defended. In a Letter to Dr Abraham Taylor* (London, 1732), 78. Cf. also the examples given by Ivimey of Gill and Brine's preaching, and his comments on them, *HEB*, 4: 22-24. Like Gill, Brine was from Kettering and he also became a prominent London minister.

[44] Ryland, *Fuller*, Letter I, 11.

High Calvinism in English Particular Baptist Life

First of all, to what degree had high-calvinism been embraced by the Particular Baptists? The view of Baptist historians of an older generation (William T. Whitley stands as an example) was that high Calvinism was almost all pervasive in Particular Baptist life for much of the eighteenth century and that, consequently, this was a period that was analogous to the 'dark ages' for Particular Baptists.[45] This strain of Baptist historiography has rightly been challenged by a number of more recent writers. In particular, Roger Hayden has shown that a much more expansive, evangelistically minded Calvinism was kept alive during the first half of the eighteenth century through the work of the Baptist Academy in Bristol.[46] Hayden's work is significant and he certainly shows that Particular Baptist churches in the south west were less affected by high Calvinism than those elsewhere in England. The view of eighteenth-century Particular Baptist life represented by Whitley has received a needed corrective.

Nevertheless, there is considerable evidence to suggest that high Calvinism was the ascendant theology in many Particular Baptist churches in England. Gill was widely read, as was Brine and other writers, such as Anne Dutton, who held similar views.[47] The broadly high Calvinistic London Board was consulted on a range of issues by churches far beyond the capital.[48] John Fawcett Jr wrote of high Calvinism's dominance in Particular Baptist churches in the 1760s in the north of England, declaring that Gill 'was read almost exclusively, to the neglect of other works on divinity'.[49] In Norfolk and Suffolk, closer to the Cambridgeshire / Northamptonshire epicentre of high Calvinism, it was perhaps even more dominant.[50] Commenting on the situation as it was in the mid-

---

[45] William T. Whitley, *A History of English Baptists* (London: Charles Griffin, 1923), 258, 'In the dark ages of the [mid-] eighteenth century there were not ten learned men by whose reputation the [Baptist] denomination might be redeemed.' See also Arnold H.J. Baines, 'The Pre-History of Regents Park College', *BQ* 36.4 (October 1995), 191.

[46] Roger Hayden, *Continuity and Change: Evangelical Calvinism Among Eighteenth-Century Baptist Ministers Trained at Bristol Academy, 1690-1791* (Didcot: Baptist Historical Society, 2006), *passim*. Cf. the comments of John H.Y. Briggs, *English Baptists of the Nineteenth Century* (Didcot, Baptist Historical Society, 1994), 98, 160.

[47] Dutton was a prolific author, who wrote on a wide range of subjects. Michael A.G. Haykin, *One Heart and One Soul: John Sutcliff of Olney, his friends and his times* (Durham: Evangelical Press, 1994), 295-96.

[48] For the minutes of the London Board see William T. Whitley, 'Baptist Board Minutes, 1750-1820', *Transactions of the Baptist Historical Society* 7 (1918-19), 72-127.

[49] John Fawcett Jr, *An Account of the Life, Ministry and Writings of the late Rev John Fawcett, DD* (London: Baldwin, Craddock and Joy, 1818), 97-102 (97).

[50] As shown, for example, by the opposition that Fuller faced from those counties when he later wrote against high Calvinism. See, e.g., Fuller letter to Thomas Steevens

eighteenth century, Ryland stated that, largely through the influence of Gill and Brine, the opinion had 'spread pretty much among the ministers of the Baptist denomination [that] it is not the duty of the unregenerate to believe in Christ'. Consequently, pastors were 'too much restrained from imitating our Lord and his apostles, in calling on sinners to repent and believe the gospel'.[51] Ryland had himself been strongly inclined towards high Calvinism as a young man, but had been weaned away from it through his friendship and correspondence with the evangelical clergyman John Newton (1725-1807).[52] But there were few who had access to such a mentor. To be sure, the situation in mid-eighteenth century Particular Baptist life was not uniform, but the high Calvinism that characterised Soham and underpinned Eve's preaching had an influence that was both broad and deep.

The Numerical and Spiritual State of Particular Baptist Life

So to the second question, what was the state of the Particular Baptist denomination? The short answer – admitted by many Particular Baptists themselves – was that they were in significant difficulties, indeed, they were declining both numerically and spiritually. The evidence for numerical decline during the first half of the eighteenth century is compelling.[53] The best source of statistical evidence for the number of Dissenting congregations at the beginning of the century is a list largely drawn up between 1715 and 1718 by Dr John Evans, a London Presbyterian minister. Probably the list is fairly accurate with regard to paedobaptist churches,[54] but Whitley was able to discover a number of Particular Baptist churches not on the Evans list. He suggested there were approximately 220 Calvinistic Baptist congregations in England and Wales in the years

---

[sic.] of Colchester, 18 May 1793, Typescript Andrew Fuller Letters, transcribed by Joyce A. Booth, superintended by Ernest A. Payne, Angus Library, Regent's Park College, Oxford (4/5/1 and 4/5/2) (4/5/1): 'I know the opposition made to "Andrew Fuller" in S[uffolk] and N[orfolk].'

[51] Ryland, *Fuller*, 8.

[52] See D. Bruce Hindmarsh, *John Newton and the English Evangelical Tradition: Between the Conversions of Wesley and Wilberforce* (Oxford: Clarendon Press, 1996), 142-49.

[53] Cf. the discussion in Michael A.G. Haykin, 'A Habitation of God, through the Spirit': John Sutcliff (1752-1814) and the revitalization of the Calvinistic Baptists in the late eighteenth century', *BQ* 34.7 (July 1992), 314-319.

[54] See the comprehensive discussion in Michael R. Watts, *The Dissenters. Vol 1: From the Reformation to the French Revolution* (Oxford: Clarendon Press, 1978), 267-71, 491-510. Watts' conclusion, 504, is 'that the Evans list is a largely reliable base from which to estimate the numerical strength of Dissent in the years 1715-18'. The MS of the Evans list is held in Dr Williams' Library, London.

between 1715 and 1718, statistics accepted by Michael Watts.[55] This can be compared with figures for the mid-eighteenth century, which are largely based on a survey from 1753 by John Collett Ryland (1723-1792), John Ryland Jr's father. Although, as with the Evans list, the survey is incomplete, it is evident that the number of congregations had fallen dramatically. Probably only about 150 remained.[56] Over a period of less than fifty years, then, the number of churches had decreased by approximately one-third. Many of those that did exist were, like Soham, small and experiencing serious difficulties. For example, when Robert Hall Sr (1728-91) became minister of Arnesby Baptist Church in Leicestershire in 1753 he took pastoral charge of a congregation that had been declining numerically for many years. At the time of his induction there were approximately twenty-six members, most of whom were elderly. To make matters worse, several of these resided some distance from Arnesby (with a number not even living in Leicestershire). Unsurprisingly, these members were unable to attend worship on a regular basis.[57] Churches like Soham and Arnesby were not untypical. The English Particular Baptists were in serious difficulties.

To speak of a corresponding spiritual decline alongside the numerical one is more subjective, but this is what many Particular Baptists themselves believed was happening. In 1746 Benjamin Wallin, pastor of Maze Pond in London, spoke of a 'decay of practical and vital godliness' within the denomination. Writing again in 1752, Wallin stated his belief that this was a 'melancholy' time in Particular Baptist life, with the situation getting steadily worse.[58] Despite Wallin's blanket assessment, the picture across England was not uniformly negative. There was a richness to some dimensions of Baptist life in some regions of the country which has not always been recognised.[59] In the west of England there was most cause for optimism. For instance, letters from Benjamin Beddome and his church at Bourton-on-the-Water in Gloucestershire provide evidence of considerable life and depth of spirituality.[60]

---

[55] William T. Whitley, 'The Baptist Interest under George I', *Transactions of the Baptist Historical Society* 2 (1910-11), 95-109; Watts, *Dissenters*, 1:498. The figures for Wales are most suspect.

[56] See Arthur S. Langley, 'Baptist Ministers in England About 1750 A.D.', *Transactions of the Baptist Historical Society*, 6 (1910-11), 138-57; cf. Whitley, *English Baptists*, 108.

[57] John Ryland Jr, *Memoirs of Robert Hall of Arnsby [sic.]. With a Brief History of the Baptist Church...* 2nd edn; rev. ed. J.A. Jones (London: James Paul, 1850), 12.

[58] Benjamin Wallin, *The Christian Life, In Divers of its Branches Described and Recommended* 2 vols (London: Ward, 1746), 2: ix; *Exhortations, Relating to Prayer and the Lord's Supper* (London: Ward, 1752), viii, x.

[59] On this see, e.g., the careful study by Karen Smith, 'The Community of Believers: A Study of Calvinistic Baptist Spirituality in Some Towns and Villages of Hampshire and the Borders of Wiltshire, c. 1730-1830' (unpublished DPhil thesis, University of Oxford, 1987).

[60] *Protestant Nonconformist Texts; Vol. 2: The Eighteenth Century*, 193-95.

Nevertheless, even in the west there were significant issues. The annual newsletters from the Western Association regularly bemoaned the low spiritual temperature in the Particular Baptist churches in their region.[61] The letter for 1740 urged readers to acknowledge their 'spiritual danger' and set aside four days for fasting and prayer, so that what had been written could be 'read publicly and pondered by the members'.[62] But twenty years later it appeared little had changed. In the 1761 letter Isaac Hann wrote that he and other concerned ministers were 'almost at a loss to know what we can say further for the stirring up of sleepy professors'. Those who read Hann's words were exhorted to take heed 'lest they sleep the sleep of death'. He pleaded with his readers, 'Look over the letters which of late years you have had from us...hearken to the counsel and advice of those who would not cease to warn every one with tears.'[63] There seemed to have been few ministers who would have disagreed with Daniel Turner of Abingdon in Oxfordshire, who, writing in 1769, expressed his view that the spiritual life of the Particular Baptists was markedly 'upon the decline'.[64]

Reasons for the State of Particular Baptist Life

If Particular Baptist life was characterised by decline, what were the reasons for this? The answer to this third question is complex. A number of interconnected factors are relevant.[65] One of the factors contributing to decline was the discrimination that all Dissenters faced. It is true that the 1689 Act of Toleration gave Baptists a real measure of freedom in common with other Nonconformists, including freedom to worship; yet, although eighteenth-century Nonconformists did not have to face the severe persecution that had been prevalent in Francis Holcroft's day, there were still many restrictions. Dissenters did not enjoy any-

---

[61] This was the new Western Baptist Association formed in 1773-74 with a clear Calvinistic basis. See Hayden, *Continuity and Change*, 30-36. Baptists in the west of England had a tradition of associating from before this date. The old Association had also drawn in Welsh churches and those of Arminian persuasion. See 12-30.

[62] Raymond Brown, *The English Baptists of the Eighteenth Century* (London: Baptist Historical Society, 1986), 77.

[63] John G. Fuller, *A Brief History of the Western Association* (Bristol, I. Hemmans, 1843), 44-45. The reference to 'professors' is to those who had professed faith in Christ.

[64] Daniel Turner letter to Samuel Stennett, 1769, cited in Ernest A. Payne, *Baptists of Berkshire: Through Three Centuries* (London: Carey Kingsgate Press, 1951), 79. Cf. the evidence cited by Geoffrey F. Nuttall, 'Methodism and the Old Dissent: Some Perspectives', in Nuttall, *Studies in English Dissent*, 265.

[65] So, Michael A.G. Haykin, '"Very affecting and evangelical": A Review of Keith S. Grant, Andrew Fuller and the Evangelical Renewal of Pastoral Theology', *Southern Baptist Journal of Theology* 17.1 (Spring 2013), 43.

thing like full civil rights[66] and even in the area of worship constraints remained. Only buildings registered as meeting houses with the local bishop or
justice of the peace could be used for worship and even then the door had to be
kept propped open as a safeguard against seditious activity.[67] Furthermore, although in theory there was freedom of worship, at a local level meetings could
still be disrupted, and often were. To cite just one example, Hall's services at
Arnesby were regularly interrupted by 'Lewd fellows of the baser sort'.[68] Administering believers' baptism in such circumstances was especially difficult.
Such services took place in rivers, as church buildings did not have purpose
built baptisteries. Such open air baptismal services could be scenes of much
disorder, with local mobs jeering, throwing stones at those in the water and generally seeking to wreak havoc. Soham experienced this widespread problem.
The Church Book recorded that baptism was often administered as 'early as 2
or 3 o'clock in the morning' because when baptismal services were held at more
convenient times 'the local populace behaved so ill'.[69] Fuller himself never saw
an act of believers' baptism until after he was converted, despite him being part
of the regular congregation as he grew up.[70] The sort of legal and social discrimination described in this paragraph discouraged active witness and made
Baptist congregations unattractive to potential new members.

The geographical isolation of a large number of Baptist causes did not help.
Many like Soham were situated in small villages with communication between
them difficult. This isolation was compounded, not only by the terrible state of
the early- to mid-eighteenth-century roads, but also by the traditional Baptist
stress on the autonomy and independence of the gathered congregation.[71] Association life – with the Western Association again a notable exception – was
generally either weak or non-existent. There was no national denominational

---

[66] As an example, Caleb Evans Birt (1795-1854), the son of Baptist minister Isaiah
Birt, studied law at Cambridge University but did not graduate because he refused to
subscribe to the 39 Articles of the Church of England. See *Baptist Autographs in the
John Rylands University Library of Manchester, 1741-1845*, trans. and ed. by Timothy Whelan (Macon, GA: Mercer UP, 2009), 356. This example helps show that discrimination continued on into the nineteenth century.

[67] *Protestant Nonconformist Texts: Vol. 1: 1550-1700*; ed. by R. Tudor Jones *et al*
(Aldershot: Ashgate, 2007), Doc VIII.1, 397. For other important clauses in this Act,
see 397-400.

[68] Ryland, *Robert Hall*, 2nd edn, 12. For numerous further examples of problems experienced by Baptists after the Act of Toleration, see Peter Naylor, *Picking up a Pin for
the Lord: English Particular Baptists from 1688 to the Early Nineteenth Century*
(Durham: Grace Publications Trust, 1992), 33-39.

[69] Soham Church Book, 9.

[70] Ryland, *Fuller*, 22

[71] Cf. Deryck W. Lovegrove, *Established Church, Sectarian People: Itinerancy and the
Transformation of English Dissent, 1780-1830* (Cambridge: Cambridge University
Press, 1988), 7.

structure and little support for struggling causes. Churches might receive help from those in neighbouring towns or villages, but this left them open to the influence of idiosyncratic preachers such as Simson in Cambridge. The lack of an educated ministry, with most pastors self-taught, compounded the problem. Once more, the west of England, with the Bristol Academy based around Broadmead Baptist Church, provided a different model. But Bristol alone could not solve the situation. Soham was an example of a Baptist work which was affected by a whole cluster of negative factors. Other churches found themselves in similar circumstances.

Important as these factors – social, legal and geographical – were, my contention is that high Calvinism was a significant cause of decline.[72] Most obviously, the belief that it was wrong to offer the gospel to all stifled active evangelism. There were exceptions to the dearth of invitational gospel preaching. Many ministers in the west, for example Caleb Evans, the lead tutor at the Bristol Academy, dealt in applied evangelism. Even in London, one of the bastions of high Calvinism, there were exceptions to the rule. These included Andrew Gifford (1700-84), who was the effective, evangelistically minded pastor of Eagle Street Baptist Church in Holborn from 1735 until his death. It was estimated that some 600 people were converted under his vigorous ministry, but significantly he was kept at arms length by the members of the London Board.[73] Despite the ministry of men like Gifford, the Baptist minister and historian Joseph Ivimey's (1773-1834) summary of the situation in the 1760s and 1770s is not unfair, 'Ministers were contending earnestly that they were an elect people, whom God would save through sanctification of the Spirit, and the belief of the truth, but without…bringing the sheep of Christ into his fold by going after the strayed and the lost.'[74] Maintenance rather than mission was the order of the day.

The quotation from Ivimey suggests that lack of evangelistic thrust was allied with an insular ecclesiology. Many Calvinistic Baptists proudly described themselves as 'a garden enclosed', language taken from one of their favourite texts (Song of Songs 4.12). According to Gill, the church, as 'a garden enclosed', is protected and 'encompassed with the power of God as a wall about it… It is so closely surrounded, that it is not to be seen nor known by the world; and indeed is not accessible to any but believers in Christ.'[75] Doubtless this insularity was

---

[72] Contra. Clive Jarvis, 'The Myth of High Calvinism?' in *Recycling the Past or Researching History?* ed. by Philip E. Thompson and Anthony R. Cross (Carlisle: Paternoster, 2005), 231–63.

[73] Robert W. Oliver, 'George Whitefield and the English Baptists', *Grace Magazine* 5 (October, 1970), 10-11; Raymond Brown, *English Baptists of the 18th Century* (London: Baptist Historical Society, 1986), 80-81.

[74] Ivimey, *HEB*, 3: 280.

[75] John Gill, *An Exposition of the Old Testament*, 4 vols (London: Matthews and Leigh, [1763-65] 1810), 4: 662.

fed by the discrimination that Baptists faced, but theology was also important. Gill himself recognised that the Particular Baptist cause was in decline;[76] he could hardly do otherwise. But the way to renewal for Gill and those who followed in his tradition was jealously to guard Calvinistic Baptist distinctives and maintain rigorous church discipline. This insularity, especially the overriding focus on maintaining the correctness and purity of congregational life, was a central reason determining Particular Baptist attitudes to developments in the wider Christian life of England. This leads on the fourth and final question to do with context, namely, what were Particular Baptist responses to the Evangelical Revival?

Particular Baptists and the Evangelical Revival

The Revival profoundly reshaped British religious life and gave birth to modern evangelicalism, described by David Bebbington as 'a popular Protestant movement that has existed in Britain since the 1730s'.[77] The Revival's two most important figures in England were George Whitefield (1714-70), who in 1737 began preaching to crowds in the open air exhorting them to seek the 'new birth', and John Wesley (1703-91). In 1738 Wesley felt his heart 'strangely warmed' as he trusted in 'Christ alone for salvation'[78] and a year later, encouraged by Whitefield, he began 'field preaching' himself. Whitefield, Wesley and other evangelical preachers pressed on their hearers the necessity of personal commitment. Formal religion was not enough, for it was essential that all people be born again. Many responded to the message. The Evangelical Revival was a trans-atlantic phenomenon, greatly facilitated by a religious print culture that was both sophisticated and international. Already in 1734 there had been an

---

[76] See Ivimey, *HEB*, 3: 277.

[77] David W. Bebbington, *Evangelicalism in Modern Britain: A History from the 1730s to the 1980s* (London: Unwin Hyman, 1989), 1. This understanding of evangelicalism has been contested, with a number of writers wanting to emphasise a fundamental continuity between earlier Reformed and Puritan movements and the later eighteenth-century Revival. See, esp., the majority of essays in *The Emergence of Evangelicalism: Exploring Historical Continuities*, ed. by Michael A.G. Haykin and Kenneth J. Stewart (Leicester: IVP, 2008). It is beyond the scope of this book to consider this debate in detail, but I find the objections to Bebbington's essential thesis unconvincing. On this, see his 'Response' to the essays in *The Emergence of Evangelicalism* on 417-32, in which he defends his thesis whilst making a few adjustments on points of detail. I have attempted a modest contribution to the debate, 'John Bunyan: A Seventeenth-Century Evangelical?', in *Grounded in Grace: Essays to Honour Ian M. Randall and Renewal Evangelicalism* ed. by Peter J. Lalleman, Peter J. Morden, Anthony R. Cross (London: Baptist Historical Society / Spurgeon's College, 2013), 33-52.

[78] John Wesley, Journal entry, 24 May 1738, *The Bicentennial Edition of the Works of John Wesley*, ed. by W. Reginald Ward and Richard Heitzenrater, vol. 18 (Nashville, TN: Abingdon, 1988), 250.

'awakening' in Northampton, Massachusetts, where Jonathan Edwards was minister of the Congregational church.[79] News of what had occurred spread to the British Isles and caused much excitement. What happened in 1734 was a precursor to the American 'Great Awakening' of 1740-42 in which Whitefield, making the first of his six visits to America, was the major figure. The results of the Evangelical Revival in both Britain and America were dramatic: a substantial increase in the number and intensity of new religious commitments with a concomitant increase in the zeal and passion of corporate religious life. Something new and dynamic was happening.

The distinguishing marks of the evangelicalism which flowed from the Revival are described by David Bebbington in his landmark *Evangelicalism in Modern Britain*. He speaks of a 'quadrilateral of priorities', namely 'conversionism', 'crucicentrism', 'biblicism' and 'activism'. Together, these four 'special marks' form the 'basis of Evangelicalism'.[80] In a later work he describes the quadrilateral more simply, speaking of a 'zeal for conversion', 'proclamation of the cross', 'devotion to the Bible' and 'unbounded activism'.[81] A few scholars have reacted against what one writer has described as the 'stark geometry' of Bebbington's quadrilateral.[82] Nevertheless, and as Timothy Larsen observes, the definition of evangelicalism Bebbington offers has become the 'standard one'.[83] It is this fourfold understanding of essential evangelical characteristics that I work with in this book. The evangelicalism spawned by the Revival had a powerful impact on eighteenth-century religious life from the 1730s onwards. Yet, up to at least the early 1770s, the majority of Particular Baptists stood aloof from this powerful revivifying force on the religious scene. So, the answer to the question – how did Calvinistic Baptists respond to the eighteenth-century Evangelical Revival? – is that the majority of them responded negatively. Why was this?

Questions of church order were crucial in determining most Particular Baptists' rejection of evangelicalism. The Revival leaders (for example, Wesley and

---

[79] Of the three central figures in the transatlantic eighteenth-century Evangelical Revival, Edwards is the most significant for this study. For his life, see George M. Marsden, *Jonathan Edwards: A Life* (New Haven and London: Yale University Press, 2003); for his theology, see Stephen R. Holmes, *God of Grace and God of Glory: An Account of the Theology of Jonathan Edwards* (Edinburgh: T. & T. Clark, 2000).

[80] Bebbington, *Evangelicalism*, 2-3. Cf. 5-17.

[81] David W. Bebbington, 'Towards an Evangelical Identity', in *For Such a Time as This*, ed. by Steve Brady and Harold H. Rowden (London: Scripture Union, 1996), 44.

[82] Peter S. Forsaith, Review of Doreen Rosman, *Evangelicals and Culture*, 2nd edn, in *Wesley and Methodist Studies* 4 (2012), 175.

[83] Timothy Larsen, 'The Reception given to *Evangelicalism in Modern Britain* since its Publication in 1989', in *The Emergence of Evangelicalism*, ed. by Haykin and Stewart, 24-29.

his brother Charles, George Whitefield and, in Wales, Howell Harris), were all members of the Church of England, which was regarded by Gill and those who followed him as apostate. Anglican ecclesiology was castigated by William Herbert, a Welsh Baptist, who wrote to Howell Harris in 1737 to make his views on this subject known. Herbert scathingly compared the Church of England to a public house which was 'open to all comers'. Did Harris not realise that the scriptures described the church as 'a garden inclosed [sic.], a spring shut up, a fountain sealed...separate from ye profane world?'[84] For Herbert, as well as for many other Particular Baptists, Harris and others like him belonged to a 'church' that was not worthy of the name, one that neglected crucial questions of order and discipline.

The invitational messages which characterised the Revival were an obvious further cause for hostility. The Wesleys' open rejection of Calvinism with a concomitant stress on human freedom and choice put them beyond the pale for Particular Baptists. In fact, Wesley and Gill engaged in a pamphlet war with no quarter given.[85] But Whitefield's more Calvinistic approach was also regarded as defective, with Particular Baptists doubting his avowed commitment to the divine decrees and speaking dismissively about his 'Arminian dialect'.[86] Evangelical preachers by definition offered the gospel to all. This on its own was enough to make them deeply suspect.

The dramatic style of delivery adopted by the Revival preachers and the emotional responses their messages often provoked – with people uttering loud cries and openly weeping in services – were further factors alienating Particular Baptists. Gill in his *Body of Divinity* stated that spiritual joy 'is not to be expressed by those who experience it; it is better experienced than expressed.'[87] In its historical context, this remark was almost certainly an implicit criticism of the perceived emotionalism of the Evangelical Revival.[88] The net result of these concerns was that people were excommunicated from Particular Baptist churches for associating with the Methodist Societies established by the Revival. There is no evidence that this happened at Soham – but then there is no evidence that the Revival ever touched the church there during Eve's pastorate. Churches like Soham where high Calvinism held sway would remain 'a garden inclosed', 'shut up' from any Revival influences.

To be sure, this opposition was not universal. The aforementioned Andrew Gifford was actually a friend of Whitefield and there were other Particular Bap-

---

[84] Cited by Haykin, *One Heart and Soul*, 27.
[85] For the debate, see *Protestant Nonconformist Texts; Vol. 2: The Eighteenth Century* 128-33.
[86] See Michael A.G. Haykin, 'The Baptist Identity: A View From the Eighteenth Century', *Evangelical Quarterly* 67.2 (1995), 141-43.
[87] John Gill, *A Complete Body of Doctrinal and Practical Divinity*, 1839 edn (London: repr. Paris, Arkansas: Baptist Standard Bearer, 1989), 781.
[88] Cf. Haykin, *One Heart and Soul*, 31.

tist ministers who were on good terms with the Revival preacher. A few even invited him into their pulpits and encouraged him to engage in field preaching in their areas.[89] But perhaps more importantly, as the century wore on, some men who owed their conversion and underlying theological and practical principles to the Revival entered Baptist pastoral ministry. Both Robert Robinson (1735-90) and John Fawcett (1740-1817) owed their conversions to Whitefield himself. Robinson first went to Whitefield's Tabernacle in Moorfields in 1752, 'pitying the poor deluded Methodists', but by the close of the service his views had changed and he 'went away envying their happiness'.[90] He started attending regularly and later wrote that he owed his 'love to real religion' to Whitefield.[91] Robinson was later baptised as a believer, becoming pastor of a reconstituted Stone Yard Baptist church in Cambridge in 1761. He brought with him an applied, evangelistic approach to preaching which was in marked contrast to Simson's high Calvinism. The church quickly grew as a result.[92] Fawcett first heard Whitefield in 1755. He experienced Christian conversion as a result and although he too became convinced of believers' baptism and became a Particular Baptist pastor in Yorkshire he never forgot his debt to Whitefield.[93] Ministers like these, together with some trained at Bristol, would be instrumental in changing the character of the denomination.

This change was in the future, however. In the 1750s and 1760s when Fuller was growing up the general picture of resistance to revival influences was not much altered by these exceptions. Those who regarded the Revival with deep suspicion tended to have minimal dealings with those who promoted its emphases. I have found no evidence of contact between Soham and Stone Yard in its new incarnation in the 1760s, despite their close geographical proximity.[94] Later, under Fuller's pastorate, this would change and a relationship with Robinson would be established, as will be seen in chapter three. Fuller would also become Fawcett's correspondent, but only much later, in 1792 as the BMS was being formed.[95] In the 1750s and 1760s Fuller's theological context was dominated by high Calvinism. Yet he did – after many years' conviction – experience Christian conversion. It is to this we now turn.

---

[89] This occurred as early as 1739. See Brown, *English Baptists*, 81.

[90] Luke Tyerman, *The Life of the Rev. George Whitefield*, 2nd edn, 2 vols (London: Hodder and Stoughton, 1890), 2: 408.

[91] *Church Book: St Andrew's Street*, 20.

[92] *Church Book: St Andrew's Street*, 18-20. The church was restarted in 1759 after the chaos caused by Simson's ministry. Robinson was unusual among Particular Baptists in that he became unorthodox on the Trinity later in life.

[93] Fawcett Jr, *John Fawcett*, 15-18.

[94] As well as very different theologies, Robinson's strong commitment to open communion (both paedo- and credo-baptists could be members) most likely kept a wedge between Stone Yard and Soham, with the latter church committed to closed communion and believers' baptism as an essential prerequisite for membership.

[95] Fawcett Jr, *John Fawcett*, 297.

Fuller's Conversion

The primary sources for Fuller's conversion are two letters reproduced by Ryland and made much use of by other early biographers.[96] These were written to a Scottish friend, Charles Stuart, and were originally published in the *Evangelical Magazine* in 1798, although Fuller was not then named as the writer.[97] Together the letters tell a powerful story of a tortuous progress towards conversion in a high Calvinistic context.

Fuller's Account of his Conversion

In his first letter to Stuart, Fuller spoke about Eve's preaching, which he and his family heard Sunday-by-Sunday as he was growing up. He made the comment already cited in this chapter that, as a high Calvinist, Eve had 'little or nothing to say to the unconverted'. In consequence, Fuller wrote, 'I…never considered myself as any way concerned in what I heard from the pulpit.' He experienced a measure of spiritual conviction when he was about fourteen years of age, but not as a result of his pastor's ministry. Instead, this occurred due to his own 'reading and reflection'.[98] Books he engaged with included John Bunyan's *Grace Abounding to the Chief of Sinners* (1666) and *The Pilgrim's Progress* (1678), which were staples of Nonconformist piety. The first named book was effectively Bunyan's own conversion narrative.[99] Fuller also mentioned the Scottish evangelical minister Ralph Erskine's *Gospel Sonnets: or, Spiritual Songs, in Six Parts*.[100] As he read from this last named book he wept; indeed, he said he 'was almost overcome with weeping', so 'interesting did the doctrine of eternal salvation' seem.[101] Despite this experience, his sense of spiritual conviction soon passed.

His feelings of concern did occasionally return. For instance, 'about the year 1767' he saw that his 'heart was wicked'. However he believed 'it was not in me to turn to God.'[102] A text from Scripture impressed itself on his mind, Romans 6.14, 'Sin shall not have dominion over you; for ye are not under law, but

---

[96] In what follows I cite the letters from Ryland. For Morris's use of these letters, see Morris, *Fuller*, 2nd edn, 18-26.

[97] Ryland, *Fuller*, 10, says they were in the magazine in 1788, but this is an error. For background on Charles Stuart, who had met Fuller in Scotland through the latter's tours on behalf of the BMS, see *The Armies of the Lamb: The Spirituality of Andrew Fuller* ed. by Michael A.G. Haykin (Dundas, Ontario: Joshua Press, 2001), 65, n. 1.

[98] Ryland, *Fuller*, Letter I, 11.

[99] Ryland, *Fuller*, Letter I, 11. I have analysed *Grace Abounding* in 'John Bunyan: A Seventeenth-Century Evangelical?', 33-52; esp. 41-46.

[100] For the text of what Fuller read, see *The Sermons and Other Practical Works of the Later Reverend Ralph Erskine, A.M. vol. 7* (London: Wm. Tegg, 1865), 255-59.

[101] Ryland, *Fuller*, Letter I, 13.

[102] Ryland, *Fuller*, Letter I, 13-14.

under grace.'[103] He briefly concluded that this meant 'he was in a state of salvation' and he was overcome with joy. This experience was deeply emotional for him, so that his face was 'swollen with weeping'. Yet before the day was over 'all was gone and forgotten'.[104] In the following year he had a similarly intense experience, but with similar results. It was not until 1769 that his concern regarding salvation returned. This time his consciousness of sin and guilt was not transient. Rather, it remained and steadily grew stronger. Fuller now had an overriding sense that he was under the judgement of God,

> The fire and brimstone of the bottomless pit seemed to burn within my bosom. I do not write in the language of exaggeration... I saw, that there was no truth in me. I saw, that God would be perfectly just in sending me to hell, and that to hell I must go, unless I were saved of mere grace, and as it were in spite of myself... I never before knew what it was to feel myself an odious, lost sinner, standing in need of both pardon and purification. Yet, although I needed these blessings, it seemed presumption to hope for them, after what I had done.

He was by now deeply and continually distressed, under a 'burden which [he] knew not how to bear'. He did not know how to respond to such feelings; in fact he was unsure there was anything he could do. This was in November 1769.[105]

Fuller did not believe he had a 'warrant' or 'qualification' to trust in God. What right did he have to come to Christ in repentance and ask for salvation?[106] His uncertainty and the language he used betray the influence of high Calvinism, as we will see. Eventually he was encouraged by the Old Testament examples of Esther, who went in to see the King without being invited (Esther 4.11; 5.1-2) and Job, who threw himself on God's mercy with the words, 'Though He slay me, yet will I trust him' (Job 13.15). Through the influence of these at first sight rather unlikely texts, Fuller finally found release from the agonies of conviction.

> I was determined to cast myself upon Christ, thinking, peradventure, he would save my soul; and if not, I could but be lost. In this way I continued above an hour, weeping, and supplicating mercy for the Saviour's sake: (my soul hath it still in remembrance, and is humbled in me!) and as the eye of the mind was more and more fixed upon him, my guilt and fears were gradually and insensibly removed.[107]

As Fuller drew his second letter to Stuart to a close, he wrote of the joy he had felt when he finally trusted Christ. He declared,

---

[103] Ryland, *Fuller*, Letter I, 14.
[104] Ryland, *Fuller*, Letter I, 14.
[105] Ryland, *Fuller*, Letter II, 17.
[106] Ryland, *Fuller*, Letter II, 18. Italics original.
[107] Ryland, *Fuller*, Letter II, 18-19.

I was now conscious of my being the subject of repentance, faith, and love. When I thought of my past life, I abhorred myself, and repented as in dust and ashes; and when I thought of the gospel way of salvation, I drank it in, as cold water is imbibed to a thirsty soul. My heart felt one with Christ, and dead to every other object around me. I had *thought* I had found the joys of salvation heretofore; but now I *knew* I had found them and was conscious I had passed from death unto life.

Fuller's joy was accompanied by a commitment 'to devote [his] future life' to God. This, he believed, was his moment of 'salvation'.[108] This conversion experience was pivotal for his life and thought.

Analysis: The 'Conversion Narrative'

It is important to take a step back and analyse Fuller's account of his conversion.[109] Although there is no compelling evidence to doubt the essential truthfulness of what Fuller narrates (indeed, the dating of his conversion is corroborated by a diary entry he made in 1780),[110] we need to remember he was writing in the late 1790s, some thirty years after the events he was describing. Consequently, he probably did not recall everything accurately, something he acknowledged himself.[111] Furthermore, we should be aware that he was writing according to the conventions of the evangelical 'conversion narrative'. By the time he composed his letters to Stuart, the conversion narrative was a well established genre of writing. As Bruce Hindmarsh has shown, it had its immediate antecedents in the popular Puritan conversion narratives of the early modern period, before the eighteenth-century Evangelical Revival ushered in a new era in 'the history of spiritual autobiography' with the proliferation of such accounts.[112] The conventions which shaped the literary genre were not fixed; indeed, within the evangelical tradition there were many variations. For example, different ecclesiologies shaped spiritual autobiography in particular ways.[113] But a number of standard features were usually present. These were, firstly,

---

[108] Ryland, *Fuller*, Letter II, 20.

[109] See also Keith Grant's reading of Fuller's conversion narrative in his *Andrew Fuller*, 23-50, esp. 23-43. Although I think his emphasis on 'pastoral theology' is overdone and he perhaps reads too much into some of Fuller's passing comments (for example, the brief reference to Erskine's *Gospel Sonnets*), this is still the best detailed analysis of Fuller's narrative to date, setting it in both its immediate and its wider context.

[110] Ryland, *Fuller*, 75.

[111] Fuller stated the account was marked with 'imperfections' given the 'lapse of many years'. Ryland, *Fuller*, Letter I, 11.

[112] D.B. Hindmarsh, *The Evangelical Conversion Narrative: Spiritual Autobiography in Early Modern England* (Oxford: Oxford University Press, 2005), 33-87 (61).

[113] Hindmarsh gives the conversion narrative of John Ryland Jr an extended treatment as an example of a narrative in the gathered church tradition. Hindmarsh, *Evangelical Conversion Narrative*, 301-315.

intense conviction of sin and guilt, often described in distressing detail; secondly, an experience of conversion which was frequently dramatic and immediate; and, thirdly, further intense feelings, this time of joy and release, regularly accompanied by desires for future usefulness in the cause of Christ.[114] Fuller's own narrative fits this basic pattern well, even though he was not converted in an evangelical setting. In other words, his mature understanding of his experience was refracted through the prism of his later commitment to evangelical theology and spirituality.

As a consequence, we should be aware that both the shape and content of the account is likely to have been moulded in significant degree by evangelical concerns.[115] Fuller sought to convey not only the outline facts of what he believed happened – the times he was under 'conviction', the Bible verses that were important to him, etc. – but also his mature theological understanding of what had taken place in his life. Moreover, he anticipated others would read his letters as well as Stuart and most likely expected them to be published. By the late 1790s Fuller was a well known pastor. He wanted his own experience to be a help to others who might be facing similar struggles,[116] as well as to bring glory to God.

In fact, Fuller's spiritual autobiography was shaped by evangelical emphases. The understanding of sin and guilt as a 'burden' was derived from *The Pilgrim's Progress*, a book which – perhaps above all other seventeenth-century works of Puritan spirituality – had become deeply embedded in the evangelical consciousness and was especially popular with Nonconformist evangelicals.[117] Fuller's early regard for Bunyan's book would have been confirmed by his later evangelical contacts. The way he focused on the cross as he described his conversion is significant. He found rest for his 'troubled soul in the cross of Christ', he said.[118] Crucicentrism, as already noted, is one of the defining characteristics of the evangelical movement. He also struck a confident note of assurance. When he trusted in Christ, he was 'conscious' he had passed from 'death to life'; indeed, he 'knew' this.[119] This was typical of evangelical assurance. The

---

[114] Cf. Bebbington, *Evangelicalism in Modern Britain*, 5, who writes of 'agony, guilt and intense relief'; and Grant, *Andrew Fuller*, 29-30.

[115] Cf. the work I have done on C.H. Spurgeon's mature account of his conversion, *'Communion with Christ and His People:' The Spirituality of C.H. Spurgeon* (Oxford: Regent's Park, 2010 / Eugene, OR: Wipf and Stock, 2014), 47-62. Spurgeon's conversion narrative developed over time, and he even misremembered some of its important details.

[116] See, esp. his comments in Ryland, *Fuller*, Letter II, 19.

[117] See Morden, 'John Bunyan: A Seventeenth-Century Evangelical?' *passim*. As Grant points out, Bunyan had also made use of the Esther image in *Grace Abounding*, with similar language to that later deployed by Fuller. See, Grant, *Andrew Fuller*, 39; *Grace Abounding to the Chief of Sinners*, ed. by W.R. Owens (London: Penguin, 1987), 64 (para 251).

[118] Ryland, *Fuller*, Letter II, 19-20.

[119] Ryland, *Fuller*, Letter II, 20.

way the mature Fuller wrote of his conversion shows how he had been decisively shaped by evangelicalism by the time he penned his narrative.

Fuller's narrative also shows the extent to which high Calvinism formed his religious context as a young man. Fuller highlights the fact that Eve did not challenge him from the pulpit. It was not that Eve and ministers like him rejected conversion. But the 'elect' would eventually be brought to realise their position by having an 'inner persuasion' they were one of God's chosen people. Often this inner witness took the form of an appropriate text of scripture which would come seemingly unbidden but with immediacy and power into their minds. This gave them the required 'warrant of faith', providing the grounds for them to trust in Christ. Fuller's comments about the need for a 'warrant' or 'qualification' need to be read against this background. Gunton Fuller is worth quoting at this point. His father, he said, was 'brought up in the very atmosphere of hyper-Calvinism'.[120]

In his letters to Stuart, Fuller was quite explicit about his unhappiness with high Calvinistic emphases as he experienced them in the 1760s. He reckoned he would have found 'rest' for his 'troubled soul' much sooner if he had not 'entertained the notion of having no warrant to come to Christ without some previous qualification'. This, he stated bluntly, constituted an 'erroneous' understanding of the gospel. His conversion narrative shows he had been immersed in high Calvinistic *milieu*; but it also demonstrates he later broke free from it, and discovered a different approach to Christian doctrine and practice.

From Convert to Pastor

The high Calvinistic John Eve may not have given Fuller any significant help during the young man's struggle with conviction, but at least he accepted him as a genuine convert, baptising him in April 1770. Fuller was sixteen years of age. Following baptism he became a member at Soham. Gunton Fuller, commenting on the 'straitness' and 'sluggishness' of the Soham church at this time, nevertheless noted one 'redeeming feature'. There was, he believed, a good family spirit of 'brotherly affection' within the small group of members.[121] But in 1771 even this was destroyed as the close-knit church was riven by a dispute which Fuller later referred to as the 'wormwood and gall of my youth'.[122] By his own admission it was to have a formative influence on his thought and was significant in his eventual journey into pastoral ministry.

---

[120] Gunton Fuller, *Fuller*, 38.

[121] Gunton Fuller, *Fuller*, 32-33.

[122] Ryland, *Fuller*, Letter III, 25. Ryland included three more of Fuller's letters describing his early experiences. Two of these chart his progress towards becoming pastor at Soham. One of the letters is dated 1809 and two, written to an unnamed friend in Liverpool, are dated 1815, the last year of Fuller's life.

Dispute at Soham

The conflict began in the autumn of 1770, when Fuller himself discovered that a fellow member (identified in the nineteenth-century transcription of the Church Book as James Levit)[123] had been guilty of excessive drinking. Fuller saw Levit and, with newly converted zeal, challenged him on 'the evils of his conduct'. Levit answered in a way that reveals the presence of antinomianism at Soham. Antinomianism was the belief that Christians were not obliged to obey the moral law. On a popular level, it was often used to justify licentious behaviour. With its diminished view of the importance of human responsibility it often accompanied high Calvinism.[124] To Fuller's consternation, Levit justified his behaviour by saying he could not help his drinking and did not have the power to keep himself from sin. Fuller considered this a 'base excuse'. Levit was told that 'he *could* keep himself' from sins such as these and that his way of talking was merely to excuse what was 'inexcusable'. The errant member's behaviour was promptly reported to the church by Fuller. The result was that Eve commended Fuller, whilst the church excluded Levit from membership. In the course of the dispute, however, Eve made a comment to the effect that, whilst people had no power in and of themselves to do anything spiritually good, they did have the power to obey the will of God 'as to outward acts'.[125] This seemingly innocuous statement was to open up a more general debate and set in train a series of events which would lead to Eve's resignation.

Some members of the church, including Joseph Diver (d. 1780), challenged Eve's assertion that a believer had the ability to do God's will. Fuller, who had also stated this view, was readily excused as a 'babe in religion', but the pastor 'should have known better'.[126] This group of members insisted that believers did not have the power to keep themselves from evil, for only God could do this. Scriptures that Eve was referred to included Jeremiah 10.23, 'The way of man is not in himself: it is not in him that walketh to direct his steps.' Fuller, in his later handwritten record of 'God's dealings' with the church at Soham, recorded that the matter was 'warmly debated' – a euphemism for a lacerating dispute.[127]

---

[123] Soham Church Book, 16.

[124] See Alan F. Sell, *The Great Debate: Calvinism, Arminianism and Salvation* (Worthing: H.E. Walter, 1982), 67-84, for antinomianism in its eighteenth-century context. Sell distinguishes between theoretical or doctrinal antinomianism, which he argues was rare (Gill, for example, wrote against it), and practical antinomianism, which was more common.

[125] See Ryland, *Fuller*, Letter III, 23-24, for these and other quotations in this paragraph.

[126] Ryland, *Fuller*, Letter III, 25-26.

[127] A Narration of the dealings of God in a way of Providence with the Baptist Church of Christ at Soham, from the year 1770..., Cambridgeshire County Archive (N/B - Soham R70/20), 5. The 'Narration' was mainly written by Fuller whilst he was pastor at Soham, and all the quotations in this chapter appear to be from him.

At the beginning of the conflict Fuller sided with his pastor, but as it escalated he found it increasingly difficult to answer Eve's opponents. Although Diver was an older man he had been baptised at the same time as Fuller and was close to him.[128] This may have influenced Fuller. Whether this was true or not he switched sides, although with great reluctance and obvious pain. Eve was determined not to give way, at one point accusing a deacon of holding 'abominable errors'. The earlier cited comment, that Eve's pastor at Stone Yard, George Simson, was a 'libertine in his life' suggests Simson was probably an antinomian. Had Eve seen the damage antinomianism could do at close hand and had this strengthened his determination to resist it at Soham? Whatever the reason, the relationship between the minister and many of the people completely broke down.[129] Eve felt compelled to resign, leaving to pastor a church in Wisbech in 1771. He left 'without requesting any [letter of] dismission' from Soham, a sure sign of the bad blood that now existed between him and the church.[130] Eve's high Calvinism had not been consistent enough for the majority of his church members.[131] For the dominant party at Soham, any talk of human responsibility was enough to arouse suspicion.

The dispute is revealing of the type of theology, attitudes and concerns prevalent at Soham. It is also significant because it caused the deeply sensitive Fuller much distress. In the 'Narration' of God's dealings with the church he lamented, 'our plowshares was [sic] converted into swords, and our pruning hooks into spears'.[132] Most importantly for his own unfolding story, the bitter and essentially unresolved argument had left him with a major theological problem. To what extent, and in what sense, was it a person's 'duty' to do the will of God? He was increasingly dissatisfied with high Calvinism, particularly its practical effects. Yet he was unable to articulate with any clarity what was wrong or discern what a credible alternative might be. As he later wrote, this early dispute 'had furnished me with some few principles inconsistent with [high Calvinism], yet I did not perceive their bearings at first.'[133]

Fuller's Early Preaching and Call to the Pastorate

Fuller was wrestling with important issues, but there was a more immediately pressing concern. The small fellowship was now without a minister and 'divided into parties'.[134] It seemed the church might have to be dissolved, thus becoming another negative statistic in the story of Particular Baptist decline. Fuller him-

---

[128] See Morris, *Fuller*, 2nd edn, 27.
[129] Narration of...the Baptist Church at Soham, 5.
[130] Narration of...the Baptist Church at Soham, 11.
[131] Cf. the comment of Watts, *Dissenters*, 1: 459-60.
[132] Narration of...the Baptist Church at Soham, 11. Cf. 'Our conversation was...little else but exclaimings against each other.' Also 11.
[133] Ryland, *Fuller*, Letter IV, 32; cf. Letter III, 28.
[134] Ryland, *Fuller*, Letter III, 28.

self seriously considered leaving.[135] They were unable to get any Particular Baptist ministers to help them, unsurprising given there were precious few close by. Assistance from Robinson and Stone Yard would probably have been considered unacceptable, even if it had been offered. After a time of fasting, a majority of the members decided to try and continue without a pastor, with Fuller among them. Joseph Diver was elected a deacon and became the leading figure in the church. In the absence of any pastor, he often gave a short exposition of scripture at Sunday meetings. Diver's prominence shows the church had not broken with high Calvinism.

Fuller was clearly an able young man. In November 1771 there was the possibility of him moving to London to learn a trade. His mother, in despair at the situation in the church, was pushing him in this direction. Yet he was reluctant. About this time Diver was unable to preach and Fuller stepped in, taking as his text Psalm 30.5, which he proceeded to expound, as he later remembered, with 'considerable freedom'. Suitably encouraged, he soon preached a second time, but on this occasion without the same 'liberty'.[136] Though frequently asked, he did not preach again for over a year. Early in 1773, when Diver was once more absent, Fuller was persuaded, speaking on Luke 19.10, 'The Son of Man came to seek and to save that which was lost.'[137] Not only did he personally feel the preaching went well, he found his message had a tangible effect, with several young people joining the church as a result. Suitably emboldened, he began to speak more often, with Fuller and Diver dividing the ministry between them.[138] All talk of moving to London to learn a trade appears to have been dropped.

In January 1774 an elderly lady from the church died having left a request: she wanted Fuller to preach at her funeral. This he duly did and it was the catalyst for the church seeking to call him as their pastor.[139] 26 January was designated a day of fasting and prayer, after which Fuller began to operate as the church's primary preacher. Several requests were made for him to accept the pastorate and on 19 February 1775 he finally agreed.[140] He was formally recognised as minister at a service later that year, on 3 May. A number of pastors attended on this occasion, with John Emery, of Little Staughton in Bedfordshire, preaching. Far more significant than Emery's involvement was the presence of Robert Hall Sr, whose Arnesby church had undergone an upturn in its fortunes under his ministry. Hall gave the 'charge' to the new minister, speaking

---

[135] Narration of...the Baptist Church at Soham, 14.

[136] Ryland, *Fuller*, Letter IV, 29-30.

[137] Ryland, *Fuller*, Letter IV, 30.

[138] Narration of...the Baptist Church at Soham, 15.

[139] Ryland, *Fuller*, Letter IV, 31.

[140] Requests were made on 17 July 1774, 28 October 1774, 15 Jan 1775, 12 Feb 1775. See Narration of...the Baptist Church at Soham, 20-23.

from Acts 20.28.[141] The isolation of the small Soham congregation can be judged by the distance the 'neighbouring' pastors had travelled for the service (Arnesby was some eighty miles away) and by the fact they were unaware of the reasons behind Eve's departure four years previously. Fuller sought to explain to them about Eve. Emery had high Calvinistic tendencies,[142] but Hall had turned away from high Calvinism and recommended the new pastor read a book that had helped him make this journey, namely Jonathan Edwards's *Freedom of the Will*.[143] This was a seminal moment.[144] Fuller's inherited high Calvinism was about to be decisively challenged.

Conclusion

The young Fuller was formed by a matrix of different factors. These included his Fenland upbringing, his church at Soham and the high Calvinism which had permeated not only Calvinistic Baptist life in his particular *locale*, but also the denomination more widely. His conversion experience and the way this came about were crucial in challenging some of his inherited assumptions. The dispute between Eve and the majority of Soham church members on whether people had the power to do the will of God's was also crucial. This dispute impacted his youthful sensibilities and set the trajectory for future theological exploration. On a practical level it also opened the pathway for him to become pastor at Soham in succession to Eve. His context and early experiences formed the seed bed out of which his future ministry would grow.

There is no evidence that Fuller was impacted by the Evangelical Revival before becoming pastor at Soham in 1775. However, the evangelicalism which by this date was beginning to flow into Particular Baptist life around the country would also renew his own theology and praxis in the early years of his pastorate. His own encounter with evangelicalism would in turn lead to a further reshaping of his denomination. The Particular Baptists had known years of decline but this was about to change, with Fuller himself rising from 'obscurity' to play a central role. Before this could happen, however, his high Calvinism would have to be overturned. How this happened is the subject of the next chapter.

---

[141] Narration of...the Baptist Church at Soham, 24; Ivimey, *HEB*, 4: 459; Ryland, *Fuller*, 42.
[142] Fuller letter to J. Ryland Jr, 22 March 1783, in Ryland, *Fuller*, 218.
[143] Morris, Fuller, 31.
[144] Ryland, *Fuller*, 27, Letter III, Jan 1815.

CHAPTER 3

Early Pastoral Ministry and Theological Development

Being now devoted to the ministry, I took a review of the doctrine I should preach...

Andrew Fuller was now, as he put it, 'devoted to the ministry'.[1] Nevertheless, he was understandably nervous as he began as pastor at Soham in May 1775. He was still only twenty-one and, what is more, had lived in the town since he was six years of age. Would he as a young pastor be respected by its inhabitants, especially given that many of them had known him from childhood? He had a further anxiety: what would he actually preach? He had been questioning central tenets of high Calvinism for a number of years and his doubts about this system had steadily grown. But if he were not to preach high Calvinism, what would he preach? In the early period of his ministry he spent many hours reading and reflecting as he examined high Calvinistic teaching and studied Christian doctrine more generally.[2] Initially the people of Soham respected him although later, at least in the church, he would be subject to much personal 're-proach'.[3] That reproach was linked in large measure to the results of his theological exploration, as we will see.

This chapter charts the course of Fuller's first pastorate at Soham, which lasted just over seven years. It also – and especially – maps out his journey from an inherited high Calvinism to a consciously adopted evangelical Calvinism, a journey which led to his writing the *Gospel Worthy of All Acceptation*. Although the *Gospel Worthy* was not published until 1785 by which time Fuller was resident in Kettering, it was all but ready in manuscript form by the time he left Soham; indeed, the work was essentially written as early as 1781.[4] Accord-

---

[1] John Ryland Jr, *The Work of Faith, the Labour of Love, and the Patience of Hope Illustrated in the Life and Death of the Rev. Andrew Fuller*, 2nd edn (London: Button and Son, 1818), Letter IV, 31.

[2] Ryland, *Fuller*, Letter IV, 31.

[3] A Narration of the dealings of God in a way of Providence with the Baptist Church of Christ at Soham, from the year 1770..., Cambridgeshire County Archives (N/B - Soham R70/20), 46. 'Reproach hath broken my heart'. Cf. Ryland, *Fuller*, 63.

[4] Andrew Fuller, Preface to the *Gospel Worthy of All Acceptation*, 1st edn, in *The Complete Works of the Rev. Andrew Fuller, With a Memoir of his Life by the Rev.*

ingly, this chapter summarises the central arguments of the first edition and sets out in some detail the major factors which led to his change of view. The shift that took place in his thinking and practice was significant indeed.

The Soham Pastorate to November 1779

Barely one month after the young pastor's induction the church made a decision which would greatly lessen its isolation. On 8 June 1775 it applied to join the Northamptonshire Association of Particular Baptist churches. Perhaps surprisingly given its tempestuous recent history, the application was made by 'unanimous consent' of the church.[5] This move was surely driven by Fuller himself, most likely with encouragement from Robert Hall who was a senior figure in Association life having been influential in its foundation. Soham of course was in Cambridgeshire, but the Northamptonshire Association included churches from outside the county (Hall's church was in Arnesby which, as noted in chapter two, was in Leicestershire). The wide geographical spread of member churches reflected the small number of Particular Baptist congregations existing at this time. In common with the churches that were already part of this group, Soham strongly affirmed its essential independency; indeed there is a comment to this effect in Fuller's 'Narration', made alongside his record of their application.[6] Yet, whilst guarding their autonomy as congregation, Fuller wanted Soham to be in active fellowship with other churches. The application was successful and they were duly accepted into the Association. It is unlikely either the congregation or indeed Fuller himself had any real idea the impact that becoming part of this wider body would have on their fellowship. The new Association had been formed in 1764 and was, as John Briggs states, the 'archetype of the new associations, born out of the Evangelical Revival'.[7] High Calvinists tended to be suspicious of such bodies and so have been described as 'classic

---

Andrew Gunton Fuller, ed. by Andrew Gunton Fuller, rev. ed. by Joseph Belcher; 3 vols, 3rd edn (Harrisonburg, VA: Sprinkle Publications, 1988 [1845]), 2: 328; John Webster Morris, *Memoirs of the Life and Death of the Rev Andrew Fuller*, 2nd edn (London: Wightman and Camp, 1826), 33. Fuller revised the work after he had moved to Kettering, but it was 'written chiefly' at Soham. See Morris, *Fuller*, 2nd edn, 41.

[5] Narration of...the Baptist Church at Soham, 25. The best study of the Association is still Thornton S.H. Elwyn, *The Northamptonshire Baptist Association* (London: Carey Kingsgate Press, 1964).

[6] Narration of...the Baptist Church at Soham, 24. Fuller was stating that the pastors involved in his ordination 'Disclaim'd all authority and superintendancy over or among us'. We maintain 'that form of church government called Independency', he declared.

[7] John H.Y. Briggs, *English Baptists of the Nineteenth Century* (Didcot: Baptist Historical Society, 1994), 203.

non-joiners'.[8] The existence and growth of the Northamptonshire Association was in and of itself an indication that Particular Baptist life was beginning to change. For the Soham church, a new era had begun.

Official meetings of the Association usually only took place once a year, in May or June, but through these Fuller came into contact with evangelical Baptist ministers and real friendships developed. In addition to Hall, the most significant of those he met were Ryland Jr, his future biographer who was then at Northampton, and John Sutcliff, who had recently settled at the Baptist church at Olney, Buckinghamshire. Both Ryland and Sutcliff are important figures for this study, and references to them will occur regularly, not least in this chapter.[9]

From the time they joined, Soham wrote annual letters to the Association, as was the custom for member churches. Each of these letters gave up-to-date membership statistics and a report on church life over the previous twelve months. The letters from Soham survive and are very helpful for gauging the state of the fellowship under Fuller's ministry, although we need to remember they were written for public consumption. Fuller composed most of them himself and, as the church's principal 'messenger' at each annual gathering, he would have delivered them in person.[10] His first Association meeting was at Olney on 28 May 1776 and it was probably there that he first met Sutcliff and Ryland.[11] Soham's 1776 letter stated that as a church they were 'not without complaints' because of their 'unfruitfulness in religion and proneness to evil'.

---

[8] See Sharon James, 'Revival and Renewal in Baptist Life: The Contribution of William Steadman (1764-1837)', *Baptist Quarterly* 37.6 (April 1998), 266, 281 n.

[9] Biographical detail on these two men will be given as this book unfolds. For more detail on Sutcliff, see Michael A.G. Haykin, *One Heart and Soul: John Sutcliff of Olney, his Friends and his Times* (Durham: Evangelical Press, 1994). Ryland lacks both a full 'tombstone' biography and a modern, critical study. The best sketch of his life is probably Grant Gordon, 'John Ryland, Jr. (1753-1825),' in *The British Particular Baptists, 1638-1910*, ed. by Michael A.G. Haykin (Springfield, Missouri: Particular Baptist Press, 2000), 2: 76-95. At the time of writing Chris Crocker is beginning doctoral studies on Ryland at Bristol Baptist College, a most welcome development.

[10] Annual Letters on the State of the Ch[urch] sent to the Association from the year 1776, Cambridgeshire County Archives (N/B - Soham R70/20). There are eight letters in all, covering the years 1779-83, inserted at the back of the 'Narration of...the Baptist Church at Soham'. The last letter was not composed by Fuller, but the others are in his handwriting.

[11] So Morris, *Fuller*, 2nd edn, 33-34. At the close of his life, Fuller wrote that he became 'acquainted' with Sutcliff first, then with Ryland 'soon after'. It may be that he got to know Sutcliff fairly well at the 1776 Association, but only spoke briefly to Ryland on that occasion. See Andrew Fuller Letter to 'My Dear Friend', Feb. 1815, Typescript Andrew Fuller Letters, transcribed by Joyce A. Booth, superintended by Ernest A. Payne, Angus Library, Regent's Park College, Oxford (4/5/1 and 4/5/2) (4/5/2).

Nevertheless, 'Sinners [had been] awakened and some of them, we trust, bro't to the knowledge of [Christ]'. The church was both 'increased' and 'built up'. In the course of the year, two members had died but six had joined, so the total membership stood at thirty-five.[12] The church was small but under Fuller's ministry it was growing. Unfortunately, the following year the news was less positive. The Association was informed that in the previous twelve months one member had been excluded from Soham and 'None added'.[13] They were able to report two better years numerically in 1778 and 1779, with more additions than deaths and with no one excluded or leaving for other reasons. By May 1779 the number of members had risen to forty-five.[14] However, this was as large as the membership would get during Fuller's pastorate.

Behind these headline figures, ministry at Soham was a struggle for the young pastor. The 1779 letter made mention of 'unhappy differences between individuals'.[15] The more detailed 'Narration' of 'God's dealings' with the church reveals that a range of behavioural issues were regularly brought before the monthly church meeting. For example, in 1776 a member was admonished for 'repeatedly...speaking falsehoods' and suspended from communion for a number of months.[16] In 1777 the same member was reprimanded for being repeatedly drunk and was excluded. Drunkenness, which we saw had been an issue during Eve's ministry, was a continuing problem. Also in 1777 another member was 'publicly examin'd' in respect of his heavy drinking. He confessed, expressed sorrow and explained he had been 'strangely overtaken'.[17] Such issues were not uncommon in Particular Baptist life in the eighteenth century and they were usually dealt with by the church meeting. Church minute books show that members could be censured for a variety of reasons, with Robert Robinson's growing and lively church in Cambridge no exception.[18] So the problems at Soham and the way these were handled were not unusual.[19] Nevertheless, the behaviour of some in the fellowship was dispiriting for Fuller,

---

[12] Annual Letters...of the Soham Church, Letter 1, May 1776 (Olney, Bucks).

[13] Annual Letters...of the Soham Church, Letter 2, May 1777 (Okeham, Rutland).

[14] Annual Letters...of the Soham Church, Letter 3, May 1778 (Leicester), six added, one died; Letter 4, May 1779 (Northampton), seven added, one died.

[15] Annual Letters...of the Soham Church, Letter 4, May 1779 (Northampton).

[16] Narration of...the Baptist Church at Soham, 26.

[17] Narration of...the Baptist Church at Soham, 27.

[18] *Church Book: St Andrew's Street Baptist Church, Cambridge: 1720-1832* [Typescript by Leonard G. Champion; Introduction by Len Addicott] (Didcot: Baptist Historical Society, 1991). See, e.g., entry for 18 Feb 1773, 50.

[19] Cf. *Protestant Nonconformist Texts*, ed. by Alan P.F. Sell and others; *Vol. 2: The Eighteenth Century* (Aldershot: Ashgate, 2006), 389, and the editorial comment that many eighteenth-century church books (both Independent and Baptist) 'devote a significant proportion of their space to disciplining matters'.

whose plain speaking and often bluff exterior masked a man of deep and 'sensitive feelings' who could be easily hurt.[20] In December 1776 Andrew Fuller had married Sarah Gardiner, a member at Soham. Morris described her as 'an amiable woman…greatly beloved by her connections'.[21] Andrew Gunton Fuller wrote in similar vein about his father's first wife, stating that she won 'the affections of all who knew her'.[22] Andrew and Sarah's relationship in these early years appears to have been strong, but their marriage was marked by tragedy. They had four children in the first four years of their marriage but three of them died very young.[23] Both parents were struck with grief at the loss of their children.[24] They also had serious financial concerns. Fuller's stipend from the church was a paltry £13 a year. He did receive an additional £5 from the Particular Baptist Fund in London and an extra £3 for preaching some sermons in a neighbouring village (probably Bottisham). Yet his yearly income was still inadequate. Attempts to supplement this, first by running a small shop and then a school, failed. The Fullers found it very difficult to manage and their situation looked as if it would be untenable long term.[25]

In the midst of these various struggles Andrew Fuller's theological explorations continued. More will be said later in the chapter about how his thinking developed; suffice to say here that his 'doubts' about high Calvinism were increasing year by year, with much accompanying anxiety.[26] However, he moved forward in his thinking with what he described as 'slow and trembling steps', aware that breaking decisively with high Calvinism would effect the 'whole tenor' of his preaching. As he began to form clearer views still he dared not 'address an invitation to the unconverted to come to Jesus'.[27] At last, towards the end of 1779, his mind was made up. In line with his unhappiness at dimensions of high Calvinism he determined that his public ministry would have to change.

---

[20] Andrew Gunton Fuller, *Men Worth Remembering: Andrew Fuller* (London: Hodder and Stoughton, 1882), 44.

[21] Morris, *Fuller*, 2nd edn, 34.

[22] Gunton Fuller, *Fuller*, 43.

[23] Ryland, *Fuller*, 44, 88. Cf. Morris, *Fuller*, 2nd edn, 34.

[24] Fuller evidently wrote about the death of these children, but Ryland did not reproduce the relevant diary extracts. Three children had died before January 1781. See Ryland, *Fuller*, 88. Fuller's diary for this period of his life appears not to have survived, but Ryland had it to hand and cited a number of extracts.

[25] Andrew Gunton Fuller, Memoir, in *Works*, 1: 1, 18-19; Ryland, *Fuller*, 44. According to Morris, *Fuller*, 2nd edn, 34, Fuller stopped running the school in April 1780.

[26] Preface to *Gospel Worthy*, 1st edn, in *Works*, 2: 329. Gunton Fuller, *Fuller*, 43.

[27] Ryland, *Fuller*, Letter IV, 32.

The Soham Pastorate from December 1779

Fuller introduced direct appeals to the unconverted into his preaching late in 1779. The result was, unsurprisingly, consternation and 'bitterness of spirit' at Soham,[28] although not all the members turned against him. Ryland wrote that, 'A tinge of false Calvinism infected some of the people, who were inclined to find fault with his ministry, as it became more searching and practical, and as he freely enforced the indefinite calls of the gospel.'[29] Fuller himself, as already noted, wrote of 'reproach' but added that this was true of 'some' rather than all.[30] Nevertheless, he found the personal nature of some the attacks on him very hard to deal with.[31] Probably we should think of strong opposition from a significant, vociferous minority of the members. A degree of antagonism was almost inevitable considering the views of John Eve and the disputes that had only recently divided the church. Ryland, working with free access to all Fuller's private papers, was able to date the beginning of the opposition precisely, to December 1779.[32] This was probably the month Fuller first appealed to his unconverted hearers, inviting them to put their trust in Christ.

A bound volume of Fuller's sermon outlines for this period survives,[33] but the vast majority of these are in his own style of shorthand and very brief.[34] Some outlines appear to contain just Bible texts and a few key words. Consequently, it is difficult to find hard evidence of Fuller's change of approach. Nevertheless, the five sermon books which make up the bound volume do con-

---

[28] Gunton Fuller, *Fuller*, 45.

[29] Ryland, *Fuller*, 44; cf. Morris, *Fuller*, 2nd edn, 34.

[30] In the Narration of...the Baptist Church at Soham, 47, Fuller referred to the 're-proach of some and the indifference of others'.

[31] 'Narration of...the Baptist Church at Soham', 46.

[32] Ryland, *Fuller*, 44.

[33] Shorthand Sermons by Andrew Fuller with some Meditations in Longhand, Books I-V, Bristol Baptist College (G 95 A). These were bound by Andrew Gunton Fuller and presented to Bristol by one of Gunton Fuller's sons in 1905.

[34] Fuller seems to have devised his own shorthand system, although he drew from elements of other schemes which were in common use. For example, there are some discernable traces of the system introduced by John Byrom at the beginning of the eighteenth century (for this, see Thomas Molyneux, *An Introduction to Byrom's Universal English Short-hand*, 4th edn [London: J. Wilson, 1813]). There is a 'key' to Fuller's shorthand inserted at the front of the bound volume of sermons. This was originally done by John G. Fuller and copied by Gunton Fuller. Unfortunately, the key is not especially helpful. It omits many symbols that Fuller used and does not seem to be particularly accurate with regards to those it does include. The inadequacy of the key and the poor state of many of the pages in the bound volume, together with Fuller's handwriting (which is not always easy to decipher in longhand), make it difficult to discern the meaning of his shorthand with any certainty.

tain a number of clues.[35] December 1779 is when Book III begins.[36] It may then be that Ryland was using this book to date Fuller's change to evangelical preaching (although it is likely he had other sources, especially since he could not personally read Fuller's shorthand).[37] Book III does give some hints about the ways Fuller was now preaching. In notes for a sermon on Deuteronomy 23.9, probably preached mid-1780, he made a long hand note, 'enforce & apply...' followed by a symbol which may well mean the cross.[38] Whatever his point was (and his text does not seem to relate to the cross in an especially obvious way) it does appear that he aimed to 'enforce' and 'apply' his message to the congregation. The word 'enforce' occurs again later on the same page[39] and further on in the book the words 'duty', 'trust' and 'venture' are grouped together.[40] Was Fuller telling unbelievers it was their 'duty' to 'trust' in Christ, before encouraging them to 'venture' all on him, appealing to Christ for mercy? Such terminology and general approach would certainly fit with his new theological commitments and it also carries echoes of how he would later write up his conversion narrative.

Probably we should not imagine an 'overnight' *volte-face* in Fuller's approach to preaching, with high Calvinism shaping his methodology one week and fully fledged appeals to the unconverted being given the next. It is more likely that his approach developed over a number of months. As 1780 wore on he was still worried his sermons were not searching and practical enough. He wrote in his diary for 29 July 1780, 'I find, by conversation today, with one seemingly in dying circumstances, that but little of my preaching has been suited to her case.' Fuller's conclusion was that an increased amount of time spent visiting the people of the town would make his sermons more 'experimental' and applied.[41] Yet still he struggled to break decisively from his past as far as his practical ministry was concerned.

Fuller's behaviour towards his father provides further evidence of this continuing struggle. By the close of January 1781 Robert Fuller was dying. He had never come into membership at Soham, remaining only a 'hearer' or regular attender. The son believed Robert was unconverted and agonised over his fa-

---

[35] The bound volume contains five original books which were assembled in one volume together by Gunton Fuller, with occasional notes added by him. Book I was begun by the preacher in 1778.

[36] The date 10 December 1779 is on page 1 of Book III. See also Gunton Fuller's note inserted in-between Books II and III.

[37] See Ryland, *Fuller*, 45.

[38] 'Shorthand Sermons...with some Meditations in Longhand, Book III, 33.

[39] Shorthand Sermons...with some Meditations in Longhand, Book III, 33. A word that may be 'Motives' appears immediately before 'enforce'. Fuller may have been setting out some 'motives' as to faith and obedience, before urging his hearers to respond.

[40] Shorthand Sermons...with some Meditations in Longhand, Book III, 119. The words are just visible at the top of the page.

[41] Ryland, *Fuller*, 77.

ther's 'eternal state'. Despite his new approach to ministry he was hesitant to speak evangelistically to Robert, although his heart was 'much drawn out' in prayer to God for him.[42] By 26 January, with his father's health clearly failing, the son plucked up some courage and the following conversation is recorded by Ryland, who was drawing from Fuller's diary,

> *Son.* 'Have you any outgoings of soul, father, to the Lord?' *Father.* 'Yes, my dear,
> I have.' *Son.* 'Well, father, the Lord is rich in mercy to all that call upon him. This
> is great encouragement.' *Father.* 'Yes, my child, so it is; and I know, if I be saved,
> it must be by him alone. I have nothing to recommend me to his favour... but my
> hopes are very small.'[43]

Fuller's words indicate that high Calvinism continued to have an influence over him. Especially suggestive is the opening comment, 'Have you any outgoings of soul...to the Lord?' with its focus on inner witness – the warrant of faith – rather than the gospel itself. True, he went on to say, '[T]he Lord is rich in mercy to all that call upon him' but, assuming this is where the conversation ended, there is no direct application of this truth to his father's personal situation and no explicit encouragement to trust in Christ. In fact there is really nothing in this exchange that could not have been said by a high Calvinist. Probably Fuller found it easier to put his new principles into practice in the pulpit than one-to-one and doubtless his hesitation here was due in some degree to a natural reticence in speaking with his father. Still, this still falls rather short of what we might have expected at this stage of his career and contrasts sharply with later examples of his evangelistic ministry, including with elderly and respected relatives.[44] Fuller did not initially find the break from high Calvinism easy.

Yet, step-by-step, his approach was changing. There are two particular indications of this. First of all, he was invited by the Baptist church at Kettering to consider their vacant pastorate. The initial invitation came before the close of 1779.[45] The church at Kettering was already committed to an evangelical Calvinism and gave every impression they would be personally supportive (as part of this support they would be able to provide an adequate stipend). Fuller initially rebuffed the approach, feeling he was committed to Soham. The second indication of his developing ministry was that by the early 1780s there were some conversions and baptisms and an increased number from the village and

---

[42] Ryland, *Fuller*, 87.
[43] Ryland, *Fuller*, 88.
[44] See, e.g., Fuller letter to 'An Elder Relative', Jan 1815, in Ryland, *Fuller*, 316-18, esp. 317.
[45] Gunton Fuller, *Fuller*, 45.

surrounding areas wanting to hear him.[46] Yet, alongside this success, Fuller's problems in Soham were growing.

As well as the opposition to his applied preaching, his perilous financial situation continued to be a grave cause of concern. The issues with behaviour at Soham showed no signs of abating either, with their Association letter for May 1781 speaking of much discouragement due to the 'disorderly walk' of a number.[47] In the 'Narration…' Fuller recorded that one member was 'admonished' for 'neglecting a church meeting, and being at an alehouse the chief part of the day'. After the May Association (which had been at Kettering) matters got worse, and on 9 September 1781 a man was 'excluded publickly, for Adultery!'[48] The exclamation mark in the 'Narration…' probably reflected the despair Fuller was feeling by this point. Diary entries for 1780 and 1781 reveal much unhappiness. A 'continual heaviness lies upon me,' he wrote.[49] Matters were coming to a head.

In the autumn of 1781 Kettering renewed their invitation to Fuller, inviting him again to consider their pastorate. As he wrestled with the situation and agonised over what to do he experienced so much 'mental distress' that he became physically unwell. For a time he was unable to leave the house.[50] Soham knew about their pastor's unhappiness and the approach from Kettering. By now they were in contact with Robert Robinson in Cambridge and the matter was referred to him. Robinson advised Fuller to stay at Soham for at least another year. Robinson further stated that Fuller's stipend should be raised to £26 per annum, something the Soham church had already agreed to in principle.[51] If they failed to meet this financial condition, then Fuller would be free to leave at the end of the twelve month period. Yet by now his financial position, precarious as it was, was not the primary issue. Indeed, it probably never had been.[52] A number of Fuller's friends, including Hall and Sutcliff, were disappointed with Robinson's advice.[53] Nevertheless, the Soham pastor wrote to the leading deacon at Ketter-

---

[46] Four were baptised in the period May 1780 to May 1781. See Annual Letters…of the Soham Church, Letter 6, May 1781 (Kettering, Northants). See Ryland, *Fuller*, 44, for the increased numbers attending.

[47] Annual Letters…of the Soham Church, Letter 6, May 1781 (Kettering, Northants).

[48] Narration of…the Baptist Church at Soham, 40.

[49] Ryland, *Fuller*, 45-47.

[50] Gunton Fuller, *Fuller*, 48.

[51] Ryland, *Fuller*, 51-52; cf. Fuller letter to John Sutcliff, 27 Sept 1782, in F.G. Hastings, 'Andrew Fuller and Ministerial Removals', *BQ* 8.1 (January 1936), 12-13. The original letter is held in the Isaac Mann Collection, Yale University.

[52] Fuller himself made this clear. Narration of…the Baptist Church at Soham, 48-49.

[53] For Hall's response, see Ryland, *Fuller*, 52. Cf. Robert Hall letter to Fuller, 15 Jan 1781, Fuller Chapel Letters [Letters to Andrew Fuller], vol. 1 (1-34), vol. 2 (35-71), Fuller Baptist Church, Kettering, 1.1. Even early in 1781, Hall was hinting to his young friend he should move, although he expressed himself with great care. For

ing, Beeby Wallis, to tell the church there he could not respond positively to their invitation to go for a year's trial.[54] Ryland recorded that this was a 'grievous disappointment' for the Kettering church.[55]

The matter was not at an end, however. It is unclear whether or not the Soham church kept its pledge to raise their pastor's income, but the other problems continued.[56] At last Fuller concluded he should leave, writing in the 'Narration' on 26 May 1782, 'my continuance [at Soham] would not be to my or their profit'.[57] Yet in the early summer of that year he was hesitating again. Finally, after an exchange of letters between him and Kettering, he agreed to move. The final break was made on 2 October 1782, when he and his family tore themselves away from Soham and set off with their belongings to establish a new home in Kettering. Fuller's account in the 'Narration…' is abruptly broken off and in its place there is a rather doleful entry in a different hand, 'Bro. Fuller left the church and went to a place called Kettering.'[58] The Soham Association letter for 1783 was more expressive, 'Surely Mr Fuller's leaving Soham was attended with many tears, some reflecting on themselves as having bin Instruments of Wo!'[59] There was, it appears, some repentance or at least regret. By the time these words were written, however, it was too late. Soham's young pastor and his family were gone.

So, after a number of difficulties and much inner turmoil Andrew Fuller, who had been so deeply embedded in the Cambridgeshire fens, uprooted himself and his family and were transplanted some sixty miles west in the neighbouring county of Northamptonshire. Important as this journey to a new place was, even more significant was the distance he had travelled in theology in his seven years as Soham pastor. It is to this theological journey we now turn.

The *Gospel Worthy of All Acceptation*

As the Fuller household moved to Kettering, amongst their belongings was the handwritten manuscript of the *Gospel Worthy*. Although this would be revised at Kettering,[60] the available evidence suggests it was not substantially changed

---

Sutcliff's views, see Fuller letters to John Sutcliff, 15 August 1781 and 27 September 1782, in Hastings, 'Andrew Fuller and Ministerial Removals', 13.

[54] Ryland, *Fuller*, 51-53.
[55] Ryland, *Fuller*, 54.
[56] Gunton Fuller, *Fuller*, 50.
[57] Narration of…the Baptist Church at Soham, 50.
[58] Narration of…the Baptist Church at Soham, 50.
[59] Annual Letters…of the Soham Church, Letter 8, 10 June 1783. As elsewhere in my quotations from the Church Book, the spelling is original.
[60] Fuller was sharing his MS with Ryland and Sutcliff and inviting comment. See Fuller letter to John Sutcliff, 27 September 1782, in Hastings, 'Andrew Fuller and Ministerial Removals', 13.

before publication. This, therefore, is an appropriate point to summarise this most important of all Fuller's works.

The opening arguments of the *Gospel Worthy* challenged the prevailing high Calvinist definition of faith.[61] High Calvinists set great store on a person's 'inner persuasion' of their 'interest' in Christ. For them, if someone felt this inner persuasion strongly enough and for long enough they might legitimately believe they had the all-important 'warrant of faith'. Only then might they reasonably conclude the Holy Spirit was drawing them and that they were one of the elect. This effectively made someone's subjective feelings that God was at work in their lives the focal point of faith. It was this high Calvinistic understanding of faith that Fuller attacked as deeply unbiblical. The scriptures, he insisted, represent faith as being focused, not on something subjective or 'within' a person, but on something objective or 'without', namely Christ himself. To establish this was extremely important to Fuller, because if faith was someone's belief that they were 'interested' in Christ, then it could not be the 'duty' of the unconverted to believe. Indeed, he stated, if the high Calvinistic understanding of faith was allowed to stand then 'the controversy [concerning whether faith is a 'duty' or not] is, or ought to be, at an end.' This was because it would mean 'none but real Christians have any warrant to believe; for it cannot be any man's duty to believe a lie.'[62] Fuller, however, was able to show that faith should be defined differently, as a belief in Christ and the gospel revealed in the scriptures.[63] Because biblical faith always focused on Christ and his gospel and not on inner feelings it could, he argued, be a person's duty to believe. Indeed, it *was* a duty, for, he insisted, if God has revealed and declared something, we are surely 'obliged' to believe it.[64]

Having laid this important foundation, Fuller marshaled further arguments to show that faith in Christ was the 'incumbent duty' of all who heard the gospel.[65] Most importantly, he was able to show that, in the scriptures, unconverted sinners were commanded to have faith. He was certain that in the New Testament, 'true saving faith [was] enjoined upon unregenerate sinners, as plain as words can express it'. Fuller cited a whole series of texts to support this contention, just one example being John 12.36, 'While ye have the light, believe in the light, that ye may be the children of light,' which he went on to expound,

> The persons to whom this was addressed were such, who though [Christ] had done so many miracles among them, yet believed not on him…it seems they were

---

[61] Andrew Fuller, *The Gospel Worthy of All Acceptation*, 1st edn (Northampton: Thomas Dicey, 1785). The 2nd edn is printed in *Fuller's Works*, 2: 328-416, in which the date of publication for the 1st edn is wrongly given as 1786.

[62] *Gospel Worthy*, 1st edn, 6.

[63] *Gospel Worthy*, 1st edn, 29, 10, in which Fuller refers to 2 Thess. 2.13. Cf. the Preface to *Gospel Worthy*, in *Works*, 2: 329.

[64] *Gospel Worthy*, 1st edn, 33.

[65] For the heart of the argument, see esp. *Gospel Worthy*, 1st edn, 37-49; 65-74.

given over to judicial blindness, and were finally lost. By the light they were commanded to believe in he undoubtedly meant himself…and what kind of faith it was that they were called upon to exercise is very plain, for that on their believing they would not have abode in darkness, but would have been the children of light, which is a character never bestowed on any but true believers.[66]

In other words, those who were not Christian believers (and in Fuller's view never became so), were commanded to have saving faith – by Christ himself. Surely to such a command it had been their 'duty' to respond, although in fact they had never done so.

A number of possible objections to Fuller's views, with a focus on those which might be raised by Particular Baptists, were stated and then demolished. For example, to say that faith was a duty was not inconsistent with particular redemption or election. God's commands, not his secret decrees, were to be our rule of conduct and God commanded all people everywhere to repent and believe the gospel. None of the central tenets of Calvinism were in dispute, as Fuller had immediately made clear in his Preface.[67] He explicitly argued he was standing in the tradition of older writers, particularly John Owen. His was not a 'new scheme', rather he was advocating a return to the 'good old way'. He declared,

> A great outcry has been raised of late respecting a *new scheme* which some ministers have adopted, and many insinuations thrown out as if they had forsaken the *good old way*. 'Tis wonderful indeed, to think how some things of modern date can lay claim to antiquity. The truth is, they have only returned to the good old way which all the servants of Christ walked in from age to age, till the present.[68]

Yet, despite these protests, there was a distinctive eighteenth-century dimension to his argument. As Fuller dealt with further objections he responded to the view that if faith really was the duty of all, it could not, at one and the same time, be a sovereign gift of God given to some and not to others. He was able to maintain that faith was both a duty and a gift by distinguishing between what he called 'natural' and 'moral' inability,[69] a distinction one will look for in vain amongst the Puritans. Fuller's use of these terms, and the basis for them, are explored in the second half of this chapter.

In his conclusion to the *Gospel Worthy*, Fuller came to the two crucial, practical outworkings of his thesis. The first was that there was 'free and full encouragement for any poor sinner to…venture his soul on the Lord Jesus Christ'. With pastoral concern for those anxious about salvation, Fuller averred that no one need hold back from coming to Christ because they lacked an 'inner persuasion' that God was at work in their lives. The gospel itself was all the 'war-

---

[66] *Gospel Worthy*, 1st edn, 40.
[67] Preface to *Gospel Worthy*, 1st edn, in *Works*, 2: 328-32 (330).
[68] *Gospel Worthy*, 1st edn, 138.
[69] See, e.g., *Gospel Worthy*, 152-53, 192.

rant' that was needed. Fuller's second conclusion flowed naturally from the first. Christians, especially gospel ministers, should exhort everyone without exception to believe in Christ. The pages of the New Testament were full of such open 'offers' of the gospel. 'Calls, warnings, invitations, expostulations, threatenings and exhortations, even to the unregenerate', were perfectly consistent with Calvinistic belief.[70] Thus Fuller struck, quite deliberately, at the two pillars of high Calvinist 'orthodoxy', contending that it was firstly, the duty of all to believe and secondly, the duty of ministers to offer the gospel to all. This argument was to have far reaching consequences, both for Fuller himself and for the Particular Baptist denomination.

Reasons for Fuller's Changed Theology

How had his thinking shifted so radically in the course of his Soham pastorate? To begin with, the vital importance of Fuller's conversion experience needs to be properly recognised. It was this that caused him to examine and question what he would come to believe were 'erroneous views of the gospel' which had kept him in 'darkness and despondency for so long'.[71] The dispute which led to Eve's resignation further fuelled his questioning; indeed, Fuller was quite explicit about this.[72] The title of his draft manuscript of the *Gospel Worthy*, namely, 'Thoughts on the Power of Men to do the Will of God' is strongly evocative of this earlier dispute.[73] His own early experiences, then, had provoked deep and prolonged theological reflection and set in train a process which would eventually lead to a sea-change in both doctrine and practice. These experiences, already covered in chapter two, were crucial to his change of views and this needs to be underlined. Yet a number of other factors were also important and these will now be considered in turn.

Biblicism

The first of these is – to use David Bebbington's term – 'biblicism'.[74] Fuller himself held that his commitment to the Bible, which he believed was God's revealed word, was central to his change of approach.[75] Of course, the high Calvinists maintained that it was they who were being biblical. Moreover, there were many in the eighteenth century propounding a wide range of views on a diverse array of subjects who similarly claimed to have the Bible on their side.

---

[70] *Gospel Worthy*, 1st edn, 162-63, 166.

[71] Gunton Fuller, *Fuller*, 28.

[72] Gunton Fuller, *Fuller*, 34.

[73] Andrew Fuller, Thoughts on the Power of Men to do the Will of God, Wrote [sic.] in 1777, or 1778, Southern Baptist Theological Seminary, Louisville, KY.

[74] David W. Bebbington, *Evangelicalism in Modern Britain: A History from the 1730s to the 1980s* (London: Unwin Hyman, 1989), 12-14.

[75] Preface, *Gospel Worthy*, in *Works*, 2: 328.

Therefore, Fuller's commitment – even though it was deeply held – should not simply be accepted at face value. Yet neither should it be quickly dismissed.

One of the reasons for taking the Bible seriously as a primary motor for Fuller's theological development is a private 'covenant' he wrote whilst at Soham, addressed directly to God. This was not intended for publication, or indeed to be seen by anyone except the author. It is inserted near the beginning of 'Book III' in the bound volume of Soham sermon outlines, and is dated 10 January 1780.[76] So it was written out at a crucial juncture in Fuller's life, when his practice of preaching was coming into line with his new theological commitments. At this time when so much was uncertain and in flux, his stated aim was to follow wherever the scriptures led. Significantly, he was acutely aware of how difficult a thoroughgoing biblicism is in practice. He reflected how there were many preachers and authors who professed 'to be searching after truth [and] to have Xt & the inspired writers on their side'. He was conscious of his own fallibility too, that he was 'as liable to err as other men'.[77] Yet he was determined to be as biblical as possible. At the heart of the covenant lies the following passage,

> O Let not the sleight of wicked men, who lie in wait to deceive, nor ev'n the pious character of good men (who yet may be under great mistakes), draw me aside.....Nor do thou suffer my own fancy to misguide me. Lord, thou hast given me a determination, to take up no principle at second hand; but to search for everything at the pure fountainhead, thy Word.[78]

The covenant is especially valuable for being heartfelt and private, and also because of the self-awareness and humility before God that it reveals. Fuller did not believe being biblical was easy and he was aware of some of the major pitfalls, for example, professing to search after the 'truth' of the scriptures, whilst in reality using the Bible to support opinions already arrived at by another route. Of course, an approach to scripture that is free of 'presuppositions' is not possible and I am not suggesting that Fuller achieved this. His reading of the Bible was influenced by his background, his times and his temperament. Yet, his avowed commitment to go back to the 'fountainhead' of the Bible needs to be taken seriously.

What is the evidence this personal, private commitment was worked out in public? More specifically, what are the indications biblicism shaped his journey towards his writing of the *Gospel Worthy*? One important piece of evidence comes from 1775. In this year Fuller visited London and discovered a pamphlet he later said was crucial in the development of his thought.[79] The tract was enti-

---

[76] Shorthand Sermons...with some Meditations in Longhand, Book III, 22-23. The date is inserted at the end of the covenant.
[77] Shorthand Sermons... with some Meditations in Longhand, Book III, 22-23.
[78] Shorthand Sermons...with some Meditations in Longhand, Book III, 23.
[79] Ryland, *Fuller*, Letter III, 34; Letter V, 37.

tled *The Modern Question* and it was written by an Independent minister, Abraham Taylor, although when it first appeared in 1742 it was published anonymously.[80] The 'Modern Question' which concerned Taylor was whether the unconverted have a duty to believe the gospel. Obviously relevant to Fuller's concerns, literature on the 'Modern Question' had begun to appear in 1737 with the publication of a pamphlet by Matthias Maurice, *A Modern Question Mostly Answer'd*.[81] According to Fuller, however, before coming across Taylor's tract 'he had never seen anything relative to this controversy before',[82] although, of course, he was only too aware of the fundamental issue at stake through his experiences at Soham.

Fuller read Taylor's tract carefully. The Congregationalist's abrasive style (he had been accused of promoting 'bigotry'),[83] was unlikely to endear him to Fuller. Indeed, by his own account he was 'but little impressed with [Taylor's] reasonings'. That was until he came to a passage in which the Independent cited a string of biblical texts, specifically some of those which show John the Baptist, the apostles and Christ himself directly addressing the unconverted. Taylor was able to show, in a way that Fuller was unable to answer, that New Testament figures repeatedly challenged the 'ungodly' to spiritual repentance and faith.[84] The impact on Fuller was great. In the following months he read and reread the relevant scripture passages. 'The more I read and thought', he said, 'the more I doubted the justice of my former views.'[85] He could not forget these texts, nor help feeling that they exposed his preaching as 'anti-scriptural and defective in many respects'.[86] The point is not so much that Taylor influenced Fuller, rather that the passages Taylor cited did.

The text of the *Gospel Worthy* itself carries much evidence of the foundational importance of the scriptures for Fuller. The book is full of biblical theology, with the author arguing his points from scripture. John 12.36 has already been mentioned as a text given an extended treatment. Psalm 2 is a further example. This was referred to in the Preface of the *Gospel Worthy* and then expounded in the main text. In the Psalm, Fuller averred, 'Kings who set themselves against the Lord and against his anointed are positively commanded to

---

[80] See Geoffrey F. Nuttall, 'Northamptonshire and the Modern Question', in Nuttall, *Studies in English Dissent* (Weston Rhyn: Quinta, 2002), 207-208.

[81] For the 'modern question', see Nuttall, 'Northamptonshire and the Modern Question', 207-30; Chris Chun, *The Legacy of Jonathan Edwards in the Theology of Andrew Fuller* (Leiden: Brill, 2012), 36-38. Matthias Morris was actually a successor of Richard Davis at the Independent church at Rothwell, so he was departing from the previous pastor's views.

[82] Ryland, *Fuller*, Letter V, 37.

[83] By the well-known Independent minister Philip Doddridge. See Nuttall, 'Northamptonshire and the Modern Question', 221.

[84] Ryland, *Fuller*, Letter V, 37. Cf. Gunton Fuller, *Fuller*, 42.

[85] Ryland, *Fuller*, Letter V, 37.

[86] Ryland, *Fuller*, Letter III, 34.

kiss the Son'.[87] He went on to expound the Psalm in the main body of the text, focusing on the way that it was used in Acts 4.25-27. In these verses the anointed one to be kissed is none other than the 'Holy child Jesus'. Fuller further made the point that the obedience required – 'serve the Lord with fear', 'kiss the son' – is surely an inward as well as an outward obedience. Putting all this together, Fuller argued that what is commanded of unregenerate sinners in Psalm 2 and Acts 4 is nothing less than 'a holy fear of Christ's majesty, and a humble confidence in his mercy'. In short, they were commanded to have saving faith. This close attention to the text of scripture as Fuller worked out his central arguments is typical of the *Gospel Worthy*.[88] My own conviction is that Fuller's biblicism was thoroughgoing and central to him, and we will need to return to it on a regular basis throughout this study. As far as his theological development at this stage of his career was concerned, he sought to be true to the biblical revelation.

Puritan Writers

Of course, Fuller was reading books other than the Bible, and these had a direct influence on him, as well as shaping the ways he interpreted the scriptures. As already noted, the young Fuller was reading books by John Bunyan alongside those by the ubiquitous Gill and Brine. As he did so he 'perceived...that the system of Bunyan was not the same as [Gill's]; for while he maintained the doctrines of election and predestination, he nevertheless held with the free offer of salvation to sinners without distinction.'[89] Fuller's initial thought was that Bunyan was not as consistent in his Calvinism as Gill, but he began to change his mind as a result of yet further reading. In particular he found that the sixteenth- and seventeenth-century Calvinist writers he was able to check seemed to agree with Bunyan. Morris commented that as Fuller became 'better acquainted' with the Puritans he 'found them to harmonize much more with [Bunyan] than with Dr Gill or Mr Brine'.[90]

In the text of the *Gospel Worthy*, Fuller would include quotations from a number of Puritan authors, for example Stephen Charnock and Thomas Goodwin.[91] These men were significant, but a close examination of the book suggests that the aforementioned John Owen was the most important Puritan for Fuller as he advocated a return to the 'good old way'. Owen's works were quoted extensively and with approval by Fuller in the first edition of the *Gospel Worthy*,[92]

---

[87] Preface to *Gospel Worthy*, 1st edn, in *Works*, 2: 328.
[88] *Gospel Worthy*, 1st edn, 37-38. This section is headed 'Faith in Christ is Commanded in the Scriptures to Unconverted Sinners'.
[89] Ryland, *Fuller*, Letter V, 36.
[90] Morris, *Fuller*, 2nd edn, 32.
[91] See *Gospel Worthy*, 1st edn, e.g. 9 n, for a reference to 'the great Charnock', and 161, for a quotation from Thomas Goodwin.
[92] See *Gospel Worthy*, 1st edn, 86-88 and 127, for lengthy quotations from Owen.

and there are no fewer than seven separate mentions of his name in the 1777/78 draft of the book – more than any other writer – and much quotation.[93] When Fuller was later accused by an opponent, who had seen the manuscript of the *Gospel Worthy* prior to publication, of 'disrespect to Drs Gill and Owen', Fuller replied concerning Owen, 'I know of no writer for whom I have so great an esteem; it would be a faint expression for me to say I approve his principles – I admire them.'[94] Fuller's response was unsurprising as he was convinced that on the main points at issue the seventeenth-century Puritan divine was on his side. The fact that he had drawn heavily from Owen as he worked out his arguments for the *Gospel Worthy* came to be widely recognised.[95]

An assessment of the importance of Puritan writers for the development of Fuller's thought needs to be carefully balanced, however. Bunyan was significant at a particular stage in Fuller's life, but he was hardly referred to in the text of the *Gospel Worthy* and leaves little obvious imprint on Fuller's theology of salvation.[96] In assessing the importance of other Puritans, a central issue is the extent to which they were *formative* for Fuller. Excepting Owen, there are no explicit references to Puritan authors in the 1777/78 manuscript. This suggests that Fuller's engagement with them may have come later in his thought processes and that they were more important in confirming his growing convictions than they were in shaping them. With his target readership of Particular Baptists, Puritan authors were especially useful in the final text of the *Gospel Worthy*. His use of them showed he had not departed from the old Calvinistic paths; rather it was the high Calvinists who had done so. This to a degree explains the frequency of quotation in the published book.

Owen is the exception. Given the number of times he is cited in the early manuscript and the importance of some of the quotations to the first edition of the book,[97] Owen's influence on Fuller should be given more weight than I allowed in *Offering Christ to the World*.[98] Moreover, there was a continuing influence, with Fuller quoting more from the seventeenth-century Puritan in the

---

[93] Thoughts on the Power of Men to do the Will of God, 18-20, 24-25, 35-39, 48-50, 49.

[94] Gunton Fuller, Memoir, in *Works*, 1: 39.

[95] Morris, *Fuller*, 2nd edn, 32; James Bennett and David Bogue, *The History of Dissenters During the Last Thirty Years: from 1808 to 1838* (London: Hamilton and Adams, 1839), 472, 'By reading the works of Dr John Owen [Fuller] found that there was one who harmonized with Bunyan in invitations to sinners, rather than with Gill and Brine.'

[96] Although there is a reference in the *Gospel Worthy*, 2nd edn, *Works*, 2: 388.

[97] *Gospel Worthy*, 1st edn, 138. Here Fuller sought to show that Owen held it was the duty of sinners to believe.

[98] Peter J. Morden, *Offering Christ to the World: Andrew Fuller (1754-1815) and the Revival of Eighteenth Century Particular Baptist Life* (Carlisle: Paternoster, 2003), 30-33.

second edition of the *Gospel Worthy* than in the first.[99] Still, Owen was not mentioned in the Preface of *The Gospel Worthy*, in which Fuller listed a number of authors who had been important to him. Nor is he mentioned in the five letters reprinted by Ryland in which he described his early religious experience and subsequent theological formation. And a significant comment occurs in the 1777/78 manuscript in respect of Owen. Fuller declared his commitment 'not to rely on <u>Dr Owen</u> nor any other human testimony'; rather, he wanted to attend primarily 'to what the unerring standard of truth says'.[100] Unsurprisingly, this was a reference to the scriptures. Fuller's commitment to go back to what he regarded as the pure 'fountainhead', expressed in his 1780 covenant, was already being worked out as he drafted this early version of the *Gospel Worthy*.

The Possible Influence of John Calvin

Before moving on from early modern Calvinistic authors it is important to consider the influence John Calvin himself may have had on Fuller. That Calvin's writings were important was argued by Arthur Kirkby in an unpublished PhD dissertation on Fuller. Ernest Clipsham in one of his articles in the *Baptist Quarterly* graciously but firmly disagreed. In *Offering Christ to the World* I sided with Clipsham. Fuller only quotes from Calvin once in the first edition of the *Gospel Worthy* itself, on the necessity of the work of the Holy Spirit in conversion, something that was hardly in dispute among Calvinists.[101] In fact, I declared that, 'there is no firm evidence that [Fuller] directly read Calvin during the 1770s, and it is not impossible that the quotation he deployed in the 1785 edition of the *Gospel Worthy* was passed on to him by someone else.'[102] But in the newly discovered 1777/78 manuscript Calvin is explicitly mentioned twice. What is more, there are accompanying, detailed references to the *Institutes* and on the second occasion he is cited there is a lengthy quotation.[103] Fuller had access to the *Institutes* in the 1770s and was studying the work carefully, footnoting a number of pages. So the conclusion I reached regarding the influence of Calvin on Fuller in *Offering Christ for the World* needs to be revised. Fuller had certainly read Calvin by 1777 and was wrestling with the Genevan Reformer's *magnum opus* as he worked on the manuscript of what became the *Gospel Worthy*.[104]

---

[99] See the *Gospel Worthy*, 2nd edn, *Works*, 2: 353, for a quotation from Owen in the 2nd edn which was not included in the 1st edn.

[100] *Thoughts on the Power of Men to do the Will of God*, 25.

[101] *Gospel Worthy*, 1st edn, 145.

[102] Morden, *Offering Christ to the World*, 35.

[103] *Thoughts on the Power of Men to do the Will of God*, 3, 28.

[104] Calvin's *Institutes* are included in Fuller's list of his books which he made on 28 August 1798. See Book of Miscellaneous Writings [including Fuller's "List of Books" from 1798, and a "Meditation" by Ann Fuller] (G 95 b). The *Institutes* are no. 14 on Fuller's main list. In 1798 he also had 'Calvin on the Acts' and Calvin on

Having said this, it does not follow that Calvin was especially formative for Fuller. In fact, the balance of evidence still suggests that he was not. Fuller's description of Calvin as 'that morning star of the Reformation', an ascription often used of John Wycliffe but rarely of the Genevan Reformer, indicates he was not especially conversant with Reformation thinking at this early stage of his life. The long quotation in the 1777/78 manuscript is on the work of the Spirit, the subject on which Fuller cited Calvin in 1785,[105] and is simply not central to Fuller's argument. Although my section on Calvin and Fuller in *Offering Christ to the World* was wrong in some respects, I still stand by much of my critique of Kirkby's thesis. For example, I believe my strictures on the ways he draws parallels between Calvin's writing and some of Fuller's statements are sound.[106] Overall, Fuller believed Calvin's views on the 'will' were not inconsistent with those he was developing himself,[107] yet for his central arguments he turned elsewhere.

Association Life

If Fuller was working out his arguments with various books at his side, he also now had sympathetic friends to turn to. Fuller wrote that in the ministers of the Northampton Association, especially Hall, Ryland and Sutcliff, he found 'familiar and faithful brethren' who had all rejected high Calvinism as a system.[108] As noted in chapter two, Ryland had been helped in his adoption of evangelical Calvinism by his friendship with John Newton, which was largely carried on through correspondence.[109] Sutcliff had trained for the ministry at Bristol Baptist Academy, the College which had remained committed to an older Calvinism, more expansive and less dependent on high Calvinist theology. He shared what he had learnt from Bristol with Fuller, and a long quotation from the Bristol Principal, Caleb Evans, is included in the first edition of the *Gospel Worthy* (and this on the crucial distinction between natural and moral inability).[110] As

---

the Gospels'. See nos 126 and 127 respectively. 'Calvin on the Psalms' was listed under 'books missing'.

[105] Thoughts on the Power of Men to do the Will of God, 28.

[106] Morden, *Offering Christ to the World*, 33-35. Similarly, I continue to hold to my arguments about Calvin's lack of direct influence made later in the book on 87-89.

[107] Thoughts on the Power of Men to do the Will of God, 3

[108] Ryland, *Fuller*, Letter IV, 35.

[109] *Wise Counsel: John Newton's Letters to John Ryland Jr*, ed. by Grant Gordon (Edinburgh: Banner of Truth, 2009).

[110] *Gospel Worthy*, 1st edn, 183-85. Roger Hayden, 'Evangelical Calvinism Among Eighteenth Century Particular Baptists with Particular Reference to Bernard Foskett, Hugh and Caleb Evans and the Bristol Baptist Academy 1690-1791' (unpublished PhD thesis, Keele University, 1991), 217, exaggerates the importance of Evans for Fuller, however. The quotation, on 183-85 of the *Gospel Worthy*, 1st edn, was dropped from the 2nd edn. For the regard Evans had for Edwards, see Caleb Evans

already seen Fuller's initial contact with Sutcliff and Ryland developed into strong friendship; indeed, his friendship with them would become one of the mainstays of his life. As transport and communication links gradually improved in the late-eighteenth century, regular and meaningful contact between these ministers became increasingly possible. Yet it is important not to over-emphasise either the extent to which the transport infrastructure improved or the degree of influence men like Sutcliff and Ryland had over Fuller's theological formation. Fuller wrote, 'As I lived sixty or seventy miles from them, I seldom saw them, and did not correspond upon the subject. I therefore pursued my enquiries by myself, and wrote out the substance of what I afterwards published under the title of *The Gospel Worthy of all Acceptation.*'[111]

Therefore, Fuller's friends in the Northamptonshire Association may have had less personal input into the development of his ideas than might be supposed, helping him most as he revised his manuscript after it had been largely completed, and then encouraging him to publish.[112] Nevertheless, and in spite of Fuller's comments, the knowledge that there were others who were thinking along the same lines as him would have been important as he hammered out his own ideas. And it was through Hall, Ryland and Sutcliff that Fuller was able to obtain works from American evangelicals, most importantly those of Jonathan Edwards. This was crucial and the importance to Fuller of Edwards and other New England authors deserves an extended treatment.

Jonathan Edwards and the Transatlantic Evangelical Network

Jonathan Edwards is a significant figure for this study and so some biographical detail is in order.[113] He was born on 5 October 1703 in Windsor, Connecticut and became pastor of the Congregational church at Northampton, Massachusetts in 1729 after a period as assistant. As already noted, in 1734 and 1735 he was involved in a remarkable Revival at Northampton, with over 300 people apparently converted over a six month period. Edwards subsequently described what had happened in *A Faithful Narrative of Surprising Conversions*, originally published in 1737. From 1740-42 he was an important figure in the 'Great Awakening', that extraordinary period in American religious and cultural histo-

---

letter to Fuller, 7 November 1787, Fuller Chapel Letters, 2.35, 'I have just been reading Edwards on virtue…what precision, what modesty, what sublimity!'

[111] Ryland, *Fuller*, Letter IV, 35. Morris, *Andrew Fuller*, 2nd edn, 41, stated, 'He [Fuller] had to explore his path…unaided and alone.' But this is an exaggeration.

[112] It is possible Hall did not see the MS until late 1780 / early 1781. In a PS to his letter to Fuller, 15 Jan 1781, Fuller Chapel Letters, 1.1, he wrote, 'I greatly approve of your thoughts which by your leave I [pocketed?] at Kettering.'

[113] For these and further details, see George M. Marsden, *Jonathan Edwards: A Life* (New Haven and London: Yale University Press, 2003); *Dictionary of Evangelical Biography 1730-1860(DEB)*, ed. by Donald M. Lewis, 2 vols (Oxford: Blackwell, 1995), 1: 345-46.

ry that is especially associated with Edwards's friend, George Whitefield. After a controversy regarding the conditions for communicant church membership, Edwards was dismissed from the pastorate at Northampton in 1750, later accepting a call to a small frontier church at Stockbridge. Edwards was a philosopher and theologian of the very first rank. His period at Stockbridge, when he had lighter pastoral duties, was particularly fruitful in terms of writing. He died in 1758 following an unsuccessful smallpox vaccination, shortly after he had accepted the presidency of the College of New Jersey (Princeton).

Fuller's discovery of Edwards and other New England writers needs to be seen in context. The eighteenth century had seen the establishment of strong links between evangelicals on different sides of the Atlantic (the friendship between Edwards and George Whitefield being a prime example). Susan O'Brien states that 'through an exchange of ideas and materials Calvinist revivalists...built a "community of saints" that cut across physical barriers.'[114] In addition to the regular exchange of letters there was, from the 1740s onwards, a shared literature which included Revival narratives and theological books and booklets. Through this transatlantic network – initially indirectly – Ryland and Sutcliff received a steady stream of evangelical works that originated in America, which they in turn shared with other ministers in their circle. John Newton was most likely their most important early source of such literature and it was directly from him that Ryland received a pamphlet containing two printed sermons by a New England minister, John Smalley (1734-1820), in 1776.[115] These were passed on to Robert Hall, but not before Ryland had carefully transcribed them.[116] Smalley's pamphlet was essentially a distillation, in more popular form, of Edwards's *Freedom of the Will*, a work Hall had already received some years earlier, most likely from the same source.[117] It may have been Newton who put Ryland in direct contact with John Erskine (1721-1803) of Edinburgh, a Church of Scotland clergyman and a central figure in the transatlantic evangelical network.[118] Erskine became a fruitful source of evangelical literature for Ryland,

---

[114] Susan [Durden] O'Brien, 'A Transatlantic Community of Saints: The Great Awakening and the First Evangelical Network, 1735-1755', *American Historical Review* 91 (1986), 813.

[115] See D. Bruce Hindmarsh, *John Newton and the English Evangelical Tradition* (Oxford: Clarendon Press, 1996), 149-55, for Newton's friendship with Ryland, including the loan of Smalley's book, *The Consistency of the Sinner's Inability to comply with the Gospel... illustrated and confirmed in two discourses, on John VIth, 44th* (1769).

[116] Ryland, *Fuller*, 6 n.

[117] Smalley was actually converted through reading the *Freedom of the Will*. See *DEB*, 2: 1021.

[118] For Erskine's importance to the evangelical letter writing network, see O'Brien, 'Transatlantic Community of Saints', 819.

Sutcliff and other Northamptonshire Association men.[119] As a young minister in the Kirk, Erskine had been a correspondent of Edwards,[120] and through his influence many American works had been published in Scottish editions. These included Edwards's *Life of David Brainerd*, a book that was explicitly mentioned by Fuller as being important to the development of his views. Brainerd (1718-47) had been a pioneering cross-cultural missionary among native Americans and had been engaged to one of Edward's daughters, Jerusha, at the time of his death at the age of thirty-two.[121] Fuller read Brainerd's life and a work by Robert Millar which detailed the exploits of some (including John Eliot) who had engaged in similar activity.[122] In the Preface of the *Gospel Worthy*, Fuller, referring to himself in the third person, commented directly on the influence these books had on him,

> Reading the lives of such men as Elliot, Brainerd, and several others, who preached Christ with so much success to the American Indians, had an effect on him. Their work, like that of the apostles, seemed to be plain before them. They appeared to him, in their addresses to those poor benighted heathens, to have none of those difficulties with which he felt himself encumbered. These things led him to the throne of grace, to implore instruction and resolution.[123]

---

[119] For Erskine's correspondence with Ryland, see Jonathan Yeager, 'The Letters of John Erskine to the Rylands', *Eusebia* 9 (Spring 2008), 183-95. There are 91 extant letters to John Ryland Jr and his father, John Collett Ryland, held in the Edinburgh University Library special collections (E.99.14). The first of these, written to the father, is dated 1 November 1779. Cf. Jonathan M. Yeager, *Enlightened Evangelicalism: The Life and Thought of John Erskine* (Oxford: Oxford University Press, 2011), e.g., 11. Erskine and Sutcliff were also correspondents. See Chun, *Legacy of Jonathan Edwards*, 42, n 39.

[120] For the friendship between Erskine and Edwards, see Christopher W. Mitchell, 'Jonathan Edwards's Scottish Connection and the Eighteenth-Century Scottish Evangelical Revival, 1735-1750' (unpublished PhD thesis, University of St Andrews, 1997), 120, 212, 220-23.

[121] For biographical detail, see John A. Grigg, *The Lives of David Brainerd: the Making of an American Evangelical Icon* (Oxford: Oxford University Press, 2009), 3-127. For the text of Edwards's book, see *The Life of David Brainerd*, in *The Works of Jonathan Edwards*, vol. 7, ed. by Norman Pettit (New Haven: Yale University Press, 1985 [1749]).

[122] See Fuller's diary, 30 Aug. 1780, in Ryland, *Fuller*, 90. Millar's book was *The History of the Propagation of Christianity...* (Edinburgh, 1723). 2nd and 3rd edns appeared in London in 1726 and 1731 respectively. See Ronald E. Davis, 'Robert Millar – An Eighteenth-Century Scottish Latourette', *Evangelical Quarterly* 62.2 (1990), 144. John Elliot engaged in missionary work amongst native Americans in seventeenth-century New England. His efforts were celebrated by later generations because they were exceptional for his time, not because they were the norm.

[123] Preface, *Gospel Worthy*, in *Works*, 2: 329; cf. Ryland, *Fuller*, 90.

Fuller had access to these works by the early 1780s.[124] He was greatly impressed by the practical vitality of the men he was reading about and was deeply moved by their sacrificial efforts as well.[125] Further reflection convinced him that what men like Elliot and Brainerd had done was biblical and that they were indeed standing in the tradition of the apostles by freely offering the gospel whilst he himself was 'encumbered' in his own preaching. Thus his changing theological stance was influenced by works that told the story of those who were urging men and women to put their faith in Christ in especially challenging, pioneering circumstances.

The strong likelihood is that John Smalley's *Two Discourses* were also significant. In 1794 the *Evangelical Magazine* would carry an anonymous, appreciative review of a new 1793 edition of Smalley's book, almost certainly written by Fuller himself, although not included in his *Works*.[126] This does not prove that Fuller had read Smalley in the 1770s, although this is surely likely given that the work was freely circulating amongst the Northamptonshire men. Yet – assuming he had read Smalley – his importance would have been similar to that of Caleb Evans's. Both men were popularisers of Edwards's thought, specifically as it was expressed in the *Freedom of the Will*.[127] As will be shown, it was Edwards's book that was crucial to the formation of Fuller's theological thought and vital to the writing of the *Gospel Worthy*.

Edwards's Freedom of the Will

So we return to Robert Hall's 1775 recommendation to the newly inducted Andrew Fuller, noted at the end of chapter two: the young pastor should read 'Edwards on the Will'. Fuller wasted no time in following up on Hall's advice, but initially obtained the wrong book, *Veritas Redux* by an English Anglican minister, John Edwards.[128] Although Fuller appreciated this work, which was solidly

---

[124] Fuller had read of Elliot's life by late-1780 and possibly earlier. He probably read Edwards's *Life of Brainerd* in early- to mid-1781. See Fuller letter to John Sutcliff, 28 January 1781, Fuller Letters (4/5/1), 'I cannot tell how you come to think of my having had Brainerd's life. I have never seen it.' Sutcliff surely remedied the situation for his friend. In the Book of Miscellaneous Writings [including Fuller's "List of Books" from 1798...] 'Brainerd's Life' is no. 69 on the main list.

[125] For Fuller's mature reflections on these men, esp. Elliot, see his *Calvinistic and Socinian Systems Examined and Compared* (Market Harborough: Harrod and Button, 1793), in *Works*, 2: 127-28.

[126] For the text of the review and comments see Arthur H. Kirkby, 'Theology of Andrew Fuller in its relation to Calvinism' (unpublished PhD thesis, University of Edinburgh, 1956), Appendix C, 279-84.

[127] See the similar point made by Chun, *Legacy of Jonathan Edwards*, 44-45. There are no explicit references to Brainerd or Smalley in Fuller's MS, Thoughts on the Power of Men to do the Will of God.

[128] John Edwards, *Veritas Redux* (London: Jonathan Robinson *et al*, 1707).

Calvinistic, it said nothing regarding 'the power of man to do the will of God'. Fuller was puzzled. It was not until 1777 that he discovered his mistake and obtained the right book, possibly from Ryland, although he does not say.[129] This unfortunate misunderstanding and the time it took for him to realise what had happened is further evidence that, in the early years of his ministry, Fuller pursued his studies some steps removed from his friends.

What was the book that, in 1777, Fuller at last held in his hands? Edwards's *A Careful and Strict Enquiry into the Modern Prevailing Notions of the Freedom of Will* was largely philosophical rather than theological (the first reference to Jesus Christ does not occur for 175 pages, taking the text from the Yale critical edition).[130] Doubtless in part because of this, Edwards's publishers thought it necessary to raise subscriptions for the work prior to printing, so to insure themselves against serious financial loss. Significantly, forty-two of the original 298 subscribers were from Scotland.[131] Edwards's argument was that 'the freedom human beings possess, when properly understood, is not inconsistent with our actions being predictable or indeed necessitated – not incompatible fundamentally with predestination.'[132] The will 'is simply that by which the mind chooses anything' and these choices are always determined by the strongest motive 'in view of the mind'.[133] Stephen Holmes explains by using an image of some traditional balancing scales. We have a series of inducements to act one way or another and what we judge to be the strongest set of inducements will *inevitably* determine which way the scales will tip (i.e. what choices we make). The will itself, therefore, is not free, because (contrary to what Arminians believed or implied) it has no self-determining power. Put another way, although a person may correctly be described as 'free' because they possess a will, the will itself is not free because it does not possess a 'will' of its own. Something always causes an act of the will.

It was in expanding on his notion of cause and effect that Edwards developed a distinction between what he termed 'natural' and 'moral' inability. The most relevant pages of Edwards's work are Part 1, Section 4, headed 'Of the distinc-

---

[129] Ryland, *Fuller*, Letter V, 36.

[130] As noted by Stephen R. Holmes, *God of Grace and God of Glory: An Account of the Theology of Jonathan Edwards* (Edinburgh: T. & T. Clark, 2000), 153. The distinction between theology and philosophy was less sharply drawn in Edwards's day. For the text, see Jonathan Edwards, *Freedom of the Will*, in *The Works of Jonathan Edwards*, vol. 1, ed. by Paul Ramsey (New Haven: Yale University Press, 1985 [1754]), 135-440.

[131] Iain H. Murray, *Jonathan Edwards: A New Biography* (Edinburgh: Banner of Truth, 1987), 425.

[132] Holmes, *God of Grace*, 151. See 151-54 for Holmes's reading of Edwards's work, from which I have drawn. For an alternative, complementary reading, see Chun, *Legacy of Jonathan Edwards*, 10-31.

[133] Edwards, *Freedom of the Will*, 137.

tion of Natural and Moral Necessity and Inability'.[134] No one could respond to the gospel without the electing grace of God and the regenerating work of the Holy Spirit. But this helplessness was not because of a lack of any 'natural' powers. Rather a person's inability was wholly of the 'moral' or 'criminal' kind. They could not respond because they did not have a 'mind' to. To return to the image of the scales, there were not enough inducements (as far as the unregenerate mind was concerned) to tip the balance in favour of a positive response. All had the natural powers to respond, but they refused to do so. Anyone who did not respond was, therefore, criminally culpable.

Edwards's work had been vitally important for Robert Hall. In 1779 he preached to the Northamptonshire Association a sermon which was later published in expanded form with the title *Help to Zion's Travellers*.[135] Hall wanted to remove 'various stumbling blocks' from the path of those who wanted to follow Christ. In a wide-ranging address, he contended, amongst other things 'that the way to Jesus is graciously open for everyone who chooses to come to him'. As he expanded this point, Hall made use of arguments derived from Edwards's *Freedom of the Will*, defending 'Scriptural exhortations to repentance and faith' on the basis of the Edwardsean distinction between 'natural', and 'moral inability'.[136] There is surprisingly little direct evidence that *Help to Zion's Travellers* or the sermon that preceded it were particularly formative for Fuller in themselves, although he does refer to Hall's book once in the first edition of the *Gospel Worthy*.[137] Possibly this lack of discernible influence is because Hall did not go into the arguments in any depth. However, the influence of Edwards on Hall's *Help to Zion's Travellers* certainly finds a parallel in Fuller's *Gospel Worthy*.

It is not difficult to establish the importance of the *Freedom of the Will* for Fuller. In his 1777/78 manuscript, 'Thoughts on the Power of Man to do the Will of God', he declared, on the third page, 'Largely and ably is this subject handled by Mr <u>Jonathan Edwards</u> in his <u>masterly Enquiry into the Freedom of the Will</u>.'[138] Later on in the manuscript Fuller included two long quotations from Edwards's work, which address his central concerns.[139] In the Preface to the published *Gospel Worthy*, the author was explicit concerning his debt to the New England man. Speaking of himself, he declared,

---

[134] Edwards, *Freedom of the Will*, 156-62.

[135] Hall Sr, *Complete Works*, 47-199, contains the 2nd edn. The sermon was originally preached at the 1779 Association meeting at Northampton.

[136] Hall Sr, *Complete Works*, 200. See 183-87 for the section on 'Natural and Moral Inability Distinguished'.

[137] *Gospel Worthy*, 1st edn, 163. Hall is not explicitly mentioned in Thoughts on the Power of Men to do the Will of God.

[138] Thoughts on the Power of Men to do the Will of God, 3.

[139] Thoughts on the Power of Men to do the Will of God, 51-52.

He had read and considered, as well as he was able, President Edwards's Inquiry into the Freedom of the Will, with some other performances on the difference between natural and moral inability. He found much satisfaction in the distinction; as it appeared to him to carry with it its own evidence – to be clearly and fully contained in the Scriptures... The more he examined the Scriptures, the more he was convinced that all the inability ascribed to man, with respect to believing, arises from the aversion of his heart.[140]

The references to the scriptures should not be missed or merely glossed over. Fuller maintained he was not following Edwards slavishly. Rather, he had tested what he had discovered in Edwards at what he had privately called the 'fountainhead', the Bible. The comment about 'other performances' is important too. He could have had in mind Smalley's *Two Discourses* and Caleb Evans's *An Address to Serious and Candid Professors of Christianity* at this point.[141] A further possibility was that some works by Joseph Bellamy (1719-90) may have been important. Bellamy was another American theologian mentioned by name in the text of the *Gospel Worthy*. Bellamy had been close to Edwards and was shaped by him. He would become increasingly important for Fuller in the years following 1785. Yet it is Edwards whom Fuller mentions explicitly and, crucially, Hall, Smalley, Evans and Bellamy were all deriving their arguments on natural and moral inability directly from the *Freedom of the Will*.

Moreover, although frequency of quotation is relevant in establishing the importance of one author for another, and acknowledgement of indebtedness even more so, the way a text is shaped by another writer's ideas is more important still. Fuller's writing is demonstrably indebted to Edwards's *Freedom of the Will* and especially the distinction between natural and moral inability. The 1777/78 manuscript shows Fuller leaning on Edwards early. In its opening pages he posed what was his fundamental question, 'How far must we go in acknowledging the power of men, & where must we stop?' before continuing,

> I cannot but think the Distinction made by some Divines between Natural & Moral Ability, self-sufficient to determine this Difficulty. By the former, I understand, and think they understand, the enjoyment & exercise of the faculties of our souls, & the Members of our Bodies. By the latter, An Inclination, or Disposition of Mind to exercise these Natural Powers, to good or Holy Purposes. Or thus, Natural Power is simply a power of acting, Moral is a power of acting well....In this sense, be it observed, I would be all along understood...When I ascribe power to men I mean mere natural power, When I deny power to men, I mean moral power, both as above defined.[142]

---

[140] Preface to *Gospel Worthy*, 1st edn, *Works*, 2: 330.
[141] Published in Bristol, 1772.
[142] Thoughts on the Power of Men to do the Will of God, 2.

The references to 'some Divines' and 'they' again shows he was not reading Edwards alone. Nevertheless, the imprint of Edwards's thought on Fuller's own would – I submit – have been established by this extract, even if Edwards had not been explicitly acknowledged on the next page of the manuscript. The terms Fuller used and the definitions of them were Edwards's. Moreover, the long quotation just cited was a foundational statement for the whole manuscript and for its central argument.

Furthermore, the *Freedom of the Will* demonstrably shaped the published *Gospel Worthy*. This is not just true in the chapter, 'General Observations on Natural and Moral Inability', but in many other places too. For example, Fuller dealt with one objection to his view of 'duty faith', namely that people have 'no power to believe', by saying that,

> Men want power to do this [i.e. believe in Christ] no more than they want power to do everything else that is really good, even so much as to think a good thought. But if this be not the duty of men, then the Almighty had no reason to complain as he did, when he looked down upon the children of men, that none of them did good, no not one. Moreover, I wish what has, or may be said on the subject of natural and moral inability, to be taken as an answer to this objection.[143]

This is typical of Fuller pursuing an argument to its logical conclusion. Granted people had no moral power in and of themselves to do any 'really good' thing, yet it was still their 'duty' to do good. Otherwise, God would not have been just when he condemned sin in sinful humanity (the scriptural allusions in the penultimate sentence of the extract are to Psalm 14.3 and Romans 3.12). The scriptural argument is primary, but it is buttressed with the reference to Edwards's distinction. It was true that all humanity did not have the moral power to do good, but all did have the natural power. Consequently, sinners were guilty and God was just in condemning them.[144] When Fuller drove home his main practical conclusions, he also made heavy use of Edwards's distinction.[145] The *Gospel Worthy* was shaped by the *Freedom of the Will*.

Did Edwards's distinction between natural and moral inability open the door to Arminianism? Some thought so and accused Fuller of giving ammunition to Arminians, as will be shown in chapter four. Yet Fuller thought differently; indeed, he believed the opposite was true. He held that Edwards's work safeguarded Calvinism. Towards the end of the treatise he declared,

> For want of knowing better, some people have suspected this distinction [i.e. between natural and moral inability] to be friendly to Arminianism, a sort of frag-

---

[143] *Gospel Worthy*, 1st edn, 152-53.

[144] For yet further evidence of Edwards's direct influence on Fuller in the period before the *Gospel Worthy* was published, see Fuller letter to John Ryland, 22 March, 1783, Fuller Letters (4/5/1).

[145] *Gospel Worthy*, 1st edn, 172-84, esp. 186.

ment, as they suppose, of the old idol free will, whereas nothing is better calculated to destroy that system. It is abundantly improved for this purpose by PRESIDENT EDWARDS, in his Inquiry into the Freedom of the Will.[146]

Edwards's distinction allowed Fuller to hold together strict Calvinism (people were morally unable to come without the regenerating work of the Holy Spirit) and invitational evangelistic preaching (even though they were *morally* unable, all had the *natural* powers to respond). Because people's inability was not natural, it was their duty to believe and, crucially, the duty of ministers like him to exhort them to repentance and faith. This line of argument is absolutely fundamental to the *Gospel Worthy*. If Fuller had not been reading 'Edwards on the Will', together with other writers who derived their arguments from this work, it is hard to see how the *Gospel Worthy* could have been written. I agree, therefore, with Ernest Clipsham who concluded that Edwards was 'the most powerful and important extra biblical influence' on Fuller.[147]

Does this mean that Fuller merely copied Edwards, or popularized him? Such is not the case. Chris Chun declares,

[E]ven though Fuller does not give a detailed rendering of natural and moral inability, as did Edwards, yet Fuller's distinctions are more inclined to be practically as well as soteriologically focused. It is as if the results of the complex mathematical formula solved by Edwards [i.e. establishing the distinction between natural and moral inability] were taken to their maximum potential by Fuller and applied to the formulation of a precise theology.[148]

The comment about the practical focus of Fuller's work is important. He understood Edwards well and drew out some practical implications of Edwards's 'formula' in ways the New England theologian had not.[149] Whether men and women had a duty to believe was not an issue in New England. It was simply assumed that they did. Edwards's *Freedom of the Will* was actually written to combat Arminianism. This was the context in which Edwards hammered out his ideas on natural and moral inability. Fuller took this thinking and creatively reapplied it to issues the English Particular Baptists were facing. Fuller, at this early stage in his career, was showing himself to be an outstanding applied theologian.

---

[146] *Gospel Worthy*, 1st edn, 192. Morris, *Fuller*, 2nd edn, 383, was reflecting his subject's own views when he described 'Edwards on the Will' as 'that bulwark of the Calvinistic system'.

[147] Ernest F. Clipsham, 'Andrew Fuller and Fullerism: A Study in Evangelical Calvinism', *BQ* 20.1-4 (1963); '1. The Development of a Doctrine', 110-11.

[148] Chun, *Legacy of Jonathan Edwards*, 58.

[149] For the argument that Fuller understood Edwards's complex reasoning, see Chun, *Legacy of Jonathan Edwards*, 50-57, esp. the comment at the foot of 57.

Biblicism Revisited

Clipsham's comment, that Edwards was 'the most powerful and important extra biblical influence' on the Kettering pastor invites further analysis. His caveat – that Edwards was the foremost 'extra biblical' influence – is a vital one. At the risk of being accused of repetition, I want to insist that Fuller genuinely believed that the scriptures were primary. He was determined to have his theology and praxis shaped by the biblical witness. He knew he was fallible and would fall short of this aim. Of course, he read the scriptures in a particular context. Indeed, to understand the importance of context we need only return to Fuller's private covenant from 1780.

Fuller's writing of the covenant – in which he affirmed his commitment to follow wherever the Bible led – was actually prompted by his reading of another book. At the close of the covenant, he wrote, 'The above was occasioned by reading a passage or two of Fletcher's Vindication of Wesley's Ministry'.[150] This was almost certainly Jonathan Fletcher's *A Vindication of the Rev. Mr Wesley's Minutes* published in Bristol in 1771.[151] Fletcher of Madeley was an Arminian Methodist and close *confidante* of John Wesley. He was defending evangelical Arminian principles against attacks from evangelical Calvinists, seeking to be biblical but (to Fuller's mind) failing. Ryland's belief was that the debate between the two sides 'was not very ably nor fairly conducted' by either party and this may have reflected Fuller's own views.[152] This particular context is reflected in his comments that many were arguing about 'religion', all professing to be 'searching after truth' and to have Christ and the scriptures 'on their side'.[153] So the context of eighteenth-century Arminian / Calvinist polemic was informing Fuller's reflections.

There are further points to be made about context. It should be evident by now that by the late 1770s Fuller was engaging with a range of evangelical literature. He was reading scripture alongside these evangelical works and through the lens of a growing evangelicalism. The Bible was not being engaged with in a vacuum. His context, including his recent discovery of new authors, was shaping him.

There were many other presuppositions that he brought to his reading of scripture as well. His background (rural, dissenting, Baptist, Calvinistic) was important, as was his temperament. There were cultural presuppositions too. Edward's *Freedom of the Will* was shot through with Enlightenment thinking and this influenced Fuller.[154] Indeed, the 'covenant' itself shows the influence of

---

[150] Shorthand Sermons…with some Meditations in Longhand, Book III, 23.
[151] Jonathan Fletcher, *A Vindication of the Rev. Mr Wesley's Minutes* (Bristol: Pine, 1771).
[152] Ryland, *Fuller*, 129.
[153] Shorthand Sermons…with some Meditations in Longhand, Book III, 22-23.
[154] Edwards attention to epistemology, that is the theory of knowledge, was typical of the enlightened spirit of the age. Crucial to his argument is that God does not compel

the Enlightenment. Fuller wrote of his commitment to the 'simplicity of ye gospel' and asked God to 'illumine my Understanding, Teach my Reason Reason, my Will Rectitude, and let every feeling of wh[ich] I am possess'd be kept within the Bound of thy Service.'[155] These words and phrases reveal that enlightened patterns of thinking were shaping him, particularly in his emphases on simplicity and reason. A more detailed discussion of what it meant to be 'enlightened' and how Fuller was shaped by this cultural movement will be given in the next chapter. The effect of the Enlightenment is noted here to show that Fuller was moulded by cultural as well as well as other commitments as he approached scripture.

Nevertheless, after all these necessary qualifiers have been made, Fuller had a deep desire to be faithful to what the Bible revealed. No text is approached without presuppositions. Edwards, Owen, Bunyan *et al* were also read in context and in the light of Fuller's temperament, experiences, and shifting commitments. Yet for him the Bible was the primary text. His encounter with the verses presented by Abraham Taylor is just one example of an occasion when his reading of the Bible challenged his inherited views, setting him on the road to a reshaped theology and praxis. Consequently, I believe there is much evidence to support the conclusion that – as important as Edwards was for Fuller – there was another source that was even more important, namely the Bible.

Conclusion

If this chapter has described Fuller's physical 'uprooting' and 'replanting', namely his move from Soham to Kettering, it has also set out a parallel process, one which led to significant uprooting and replanting in his theology and practical ministry. To be sure, there was much continuity as well. Fuller remained committed to Calvinism and to the Particular Baptists; in fact he would argue his allegiance to essential Calvinistic tenets had deepened in his years at Soham. Yet there had been much change alongside these important elements of continuity. High Calvinism was now, for him, 'false Calvinism'; Gill and Brine would never again be his theologians of choice; and, crucially, he had 'unshackled' himself as far as direct appeals to the unconverted were concerned. By the time he had moved to Kettering, Fuller had become an evangelical – a particular type of evangelical, Dissenting, Baptist, Calvinistic – but an evangelical nonetheless.

---

people to behave in a manner contrary to their wills. David Bebbington summarises, 'Free acts are not forced though they are caused. This was to contend that human beings are part of an ordered universe, but to hold that nevertheless they are responsible for what they do. Edwards was reinterpreting the sovereignty of God as an expression of the law of cause and effect.' See Bebbington, *Evangelicalism in Modern Britain*, 64. Consequently the *Gospel Worthy*, leaning as it did on these ideas, was also marked by aspects of the cultural mood and intellectual climate of the Enlightenment.

[155] Shorthand Sermons…with some Meditations in Longhand, Book III, 22-23.

As his ministry in Northamptonshire commenced, he was determined to put his new found principles into practice.

CHAPTER 4

Kettering and Responses to the *Gospel Worthy*

[I]t is the duty of every minister of Christ...to preach the gospel to all

Andrew Fuller arrived in Kettering in 1782 with the manuscript of the *Gospel Worthy* amongst his belongings and a renewed theology and approach to practical ministry. A new era in his life and ministry had begun. Yet still his heart was torn as he thought of Soham – the place and the people he had left behind. In a letter to an unnamed member at Soham, dated 4 December 1782, he wrote of a 'union of affection' that still existed between him and the Soham church. Nothing in 'time' or 'eternity' would ever 'dissolve' this, he believed. As he thought of his former church, now without a pastor, he was distraught. '[A]las my poor people!' he lamented, 'they are destitute! Oh! this, after all, wounds me.'[1] However, in the personal statement of circumstances he gave at his induction in Kettering some months later he expressed himself somewhat differently. His heart had been 'broken' by the attacks he had endured at Soham, to the extent that the 'bond of affection' between him and the people there *had* been 'dissolved'. He no longer felt 'a union of spirit' with his Soham members and so, he declared, it had been impossible for him to continue as their pastor.[2] Fuller's thoughts and feelings as he thought of his 'removal' from his old church were not stable and his statements about it were not always consistent. Nevertheless, he was sure he had made the right decision, painful as this was.[3] He had prayed that a 'door' to 'greater usefulness in Christ's cause' would open before him and he believed his call to Kettering was God's answer to this prayer.[4] He was determined to make the most of the opportunities his new post afforded.

The first half of this chapter considers the early years of Fuller's Kettering pastorate, together with aspects of his developing wider ministry. The second half of the chapter looks at some of the ways Fuller responded to criticisms of

---

[1] Fuller to Soham member, 4 Dec 1782, in John Ryland Jr, *The Work of Faith, the Labour of Love, and the Patience of Hope Illustrated in the Life and Death of the Rev. Andrew Fuller*, 2nd edn, (London: Button and Son, 1818), 59.
[2] Personal Statement, delivered 7 October 1783, in Ryland, *Fuller*, 63.
[3] Fuller letter to Soham member, 4 Dec 1782, in Ryland, *Fuller*, 59-60; Personal Statement, delivered 7 October 1783, in Ryland, *Fuller*, 63.
[4] Fuller to letter Beeby Wallis, 20 August 1782, in Ryland, *Fuller*, 52.

the *Gospel Worthy* after it had been published in 1785. Fuller would come to believe – not unreasonably – that God had answered his prayers for 'greater usefulness'. However, this increased 'usefulness' would go hand-in-hand with significant opposition.

Kettering and the 'Little Meeting'

Andrew and Sarah Fuller had moved to a small market town with a population of approximately 3500 people.[5] Kettering was the centre of the Northampton-shire wool trade and this industry was vital to the prosperity of the town. Weaving and woolcombing (mainly for the men) and spinning (mainly for the women) were important occupations, with many manufacturers based along the turnpike road that ran through the town.[6] The wool trade in Kettering declined steadily from 1785 onwards, with the small manufacturers unable to compete with the big new textile factories in the north of England. Shoemaking was an alternative means of employment, but for this trade it was Northampton that was the acknowledged centre for the area. Kettering experienced considerable economic difficulties during the first ten years of Fuller's ministry there and the number of inhabitants fell to just over 3000.[7] Life in the town and the immediate surrounding area at the end of the eighteenth century was difficult for many.

In contrast to the economic struggles, the religious life of Kettering was strong, with Dissent very much in the ascendancy. The 'graceful tower and spire of the parish church' may have been the 'admiration of the district',[8] but it was the Independent chapel – known by Fuller's day as the 'Great Meeting' – that housed the best known congregation in the town. Its first minister was John Maidwell (d. 1692) who had been rector at Kettering before his ejection from the Church of England in 1662.[9] The Baptist church – the 'Little Meeting' – was formed by seven people who seceded from this Independent congregation in 1696. The first pastor of the new Baptist cause was William Wallis (the great

---

[5] Andrew Gunton Fuller, *Men Worth Remembering: Andrew Fuller* (London: Hodder and Stoughton, 1882), 52.

[6] That is, a toll road administered by a turnpike trust. At their height in the 1830s there were over a 1000 such trusts in the British Isles.

[7] For details in this paragraph, see Keith Sugden, 'The Occupational and Organizational Structures of the Northamptonshire Worsted and Shoemaking Trades, circa 1750-1821' (unpublished MA thesis, University of Cambridge, 2011), 1-69, esp. 6, 20, 31. The year-on-year decline in the number of apprenticed weavers points to the increasingly depressed state of the worsted industry. The town experienced some moderate growth in the early nineteenth century. It had 3242 inhabitants in at the beginning of 1816 according to Ryland, *Fuller*, 383.

[8] Gunton Fuller, *Fuller*, 52.

[9] Geoffrey F. Nuttall, 'Northamptonshire and *The Modern Question*', in Nuttall, *Studies in English Dissent* (Weston Rhyn: Quinta, 2002), 209. Maidwell's name was sometimes spelt Maydwell or Medwell.

grandfather of Beeby Wallis, the deacon who had been instrumental in bringing Fuller to Kettering).[10] Alongside William Wallis, two other prominent early members were Edward and Elizabeth Gill (née Walker), the parents of John Gill. By the 1780s both the Independent church and its Baptist offshoot had adopted evangelical principles. The pastor of the Great Meeting since 1776, Thomas Northcote Toller, preached 'evangelical truth' and was a man of 'piety'.[11] The Little Meeting, despite its early association with the name of Gill, became committed to an evangelical Calvinism. There was also a Methodist chapel in the town, yet further evidence of the impact of the Evangelical Revival.[12] Unsurprisingly, Kettering, in contrast to Soham, would prove to be fertile ground for Fuller's evangelical preaching.

Induction Service and Fuller's 'Statement of Principles'

Although in Fuller's case it was little more than a formality, a twelve month trial period for the prospective pastor was observed. Consequently, he was not inducted until 7 October 1783. A number of Fuller's friends took part in the service, with Ryland preaching from Acts 20.31 and Sutcliff leading in prayer.[13] As he had done at Soham, Robert Hall was to give the 'charge' to the new minister. However, due to what Ryland described as an 'excess of modesty' on account of Hall's 'high respect for his younger brother', he only felt able to express a 'wish': 'The Lord Jesus Christ be with thy Spirit'.[14] The personal 'statement of circumstances' which Fuller read to the congregation has already been referred to. As the new pastor brought this statement to a close he declared that the focus for his ministry would be on Christ and the 'welfare of Christ's Kingdom'. The circumstances of his move from Soham continued to cast a shadow and Fuller also referred to this. 'I must own,' he declared, that 'the pleasure of this day is marred to me, because a union with the one church cannot be effected but by a disunion with another.'[15] The heart that had been 'broken' by recent events would take some time to heal.

At the service, to complement his 'statement of circumstances', Fuller also read out a corresponding 'statement of principles'. This set out his theology and ecclesiology, as well as saying something about his approach to practical minis-

---

[10] Remaining page of Wallis Church Book, Fuller Baptist Church, Kettering.

[11] Thomas Coleman, *Facts and Incidents in the Life and Ministry of the late Rev. Thomas Northcote Toller* (London: John Snow, 1865), 153. Thomas N. Toller's ministry began in 1776 and ended with his death in 1821, at which point his son, also called Thomas, succeeded him.

[12] See Gunton Fuller, *Fuller*, 52, for the Methodist chapel.

[13] Ryland, *Fuller*, 61. Acts 20.31, 'Therefore watch, and remember, that by the space of three years I ceased not to warn every one night and day with tears.'

[14] 2 Tim. 4.22. Ryland, *Fuller*, 61.

[15] Ryland, *Fuller*, 63.

try. This was an important declaration of his views made at a watershed moment in his life and it is worth pausing to note some of the central points.

Firstly, the statement of principles included a strong commitment to the Bible, which was nothing less than a 'divine volume', a 'perfect rule of faith and practice'.[16] Fuller's biblicism can again be seen. Secondly, the statement was Trinitarian. Fuller believed the Bible revealed God to be both 'one' and 'three'. Avowing belief in the Trinity was important in an age in which an increasing number of people, including some Dissenters, were embracing Unitarianism. In this context the Kettering pastor insisted that although the Trinity was 'above' reason, it was not 'contrary' to it.[17] Thirdly, the statement was Calvinistic. Predestination, election and the final perseverance of the saints were all affirmed[18] and Arminianism explicitly rejected.[19] It is true that Fuller hesitated to speak of double predestination and this set him apart, not only from high Calvinists but also from some seventeenth-century Calvinists such as John Owen. Fuller declared, 'What has been usually, but, perhaps improperly, called the *decree of reprobation*, I consider as nothing more than *the divine determination to punish sin, in certain cases, in the person of the sinner*.'[20] Just because salvation was foreordained by God, it did not mean that reprobation was foreordained in exactly the same way. So, Fuller distanced himself from what Stephen Wright has called the 'fiercer elements of predestinarian teaching'.[21] Yet, he was still comfortably within the bounds of accepted Calvinistic teaching; indeed, the signatories of the landmark 1644 London Particular Baptist Confession had also hesitated to declare that reprobation was the logical corollary of predestination and election.[22] Thus, Fuller's views were congruent with a confession of impeccable Calvinistic orthodoxy.

Fifthly and finally, the statement bore the imprint of the Kettering pastor's conversion to 'Edwardsean' evangelicalism. As far as this was concerned, Clause XV is the most relevant of the twenty separate clauses. In this Fuller stated,

> I believe it is the duty of every minister of Christ plainly and faithfully to preach the gospel to all who will hear it; and, as I believe the inability of men to spiritual

---

[16] Ryland, *Fuller*, Clauses II, III and X, 64, 66 (64).

[17] Ryland, *Fuller*, Clauses III and IV, 64.

[18] Ryland, *Fuller*, Clause VIII, 66; XIV, 68.

[19] Ryland, *Fuller*, Clause VII, 65-66.

[20] Ryland, *Fuller*, Clause VIII, 66.

[21] Stephen Wright, *The Early English Baptists, 1603-1649* (Woodbridge: Boydell, 2006), 134.

[22] 1644 *London Confession*, Clauses XXI and XXII, in *Baptist Confessions of Faith*, ed. by William L. Lumpkin (Valley Forge: Judson Press, 1969), 162-63. Cf. Peter J. Morden, 'Nonconformists and the Work of Christ: A Study in Particular Baptist Thought', in *T. & T. Clark Companion to Nonconformity*, ed. by Robert Pope (Edinburgh: T. & T. Clark, 2013), 186-87.

things to be wholly of the moral, and therefore of the criminal kind – and that it is their duty to love the Lord Jesus Christ, and trust in him for salvation, though they do not; I therefore believe free and solemn addresses, invitations, calls, and warnings to them, to be not only consistent, but directly adapted as means, in the hand of the Spirit of God, to bring them to Christ. I consider it as part of my duty that I could not omit without being guilty of the blood of souls.[23]

In many ways this reads like a summary of the main points of the *Gospel Worthy*, still two years away from publication. People were unable to respond to 'spiritual things' apart from the saving grace of God, but this inability was 'wholly' moral. As he put it in an earlier clause, if people were possessed of 'a right disposition of mind, there [was] nothing…in the law of God…they could not perform.'[24] People had the natural ability to respond and this made them criminally culpable. As he would later state in the *Gospel Worthy*, it was their 'duty' to believe and, it followed, the duty of pastors like him to preach to them. Alongside the threefold repetition of 'duty' in Clause XV, the word 'means' is also crucial and this deserves some comment. Fuller believed wholeheartedly in God's sovereignty, but he also believed God used human 'means' to bring his sovereign will to pass. The means Fuller especially had in view here were 'free and solemn addresses' delivered by pastors to the unconverted. God would bring about the salvation of his people through human evangelistic activity, especially preaching. Consequently, the belief that God would save all he had chosen was not a disincentive to evangelism ('why bother, since God will save all those he wants to anyway?'), but an incentive ('God is going to save people and he will use my applied, invitational preaching to accomplish this'). This belief – that God uses human 'means' to fulfill his sovereign will – was most important for Fuller and we will return to it at various points in this book.

Early Ministry as Kettering Pastor

Ministry in the Town

The newly inducted Kettering pastor threw himself into ministry. This involved much prayer. He often commented on his prayer life in his diary. In the diary volume held by Bristol Baptist College the very first entry, which is dated 11 April 1784, includes the following, 'A tender forenoon, in publick prayer. My heart ach[e]s for the congregation, young and old; especially for some who seem to be under concern. O that Christ may be formed in them!'[25] This was a reference to corporate intercessory prayer in the context of a church service and

---

[23] Ryland *Fuller*, Clause XV, 68.
[24] Ryland, *Fuller*, Clause VII, 65.
[25] Diary and Spiritual Thoughts [1784-1801], Bristol Baptist College (G 95 b), 11 April 1784. Cf. 29 August 1784, 3 July 1785, 8 January 1786.

such prayer was most important for Fuller.[26] But he was also committed to leading daily family prayers and to personal private prayer, as is attested by a range of diary entries.[27] As well as intercession he engaged in other dimensions of prayer, such as praise, confession and thanksgiving. Reflections on scripture, with prayer and Bible reading blended together, were an evident feature of his devotional life.[28] Taken together, prayer and the scriptures were crucial to Fuller's understanding of his ministry. It is unsurprising that, in a 'charge' he gave to Robert Fawkner at his ordination in 1787, he urged the new minister, 'Give yourself up to the word of God, and to prayer'.[29] This was essential advice and something he sought to practice himself.[30]

Fuller aimed to prioritise his own relationship with God, but it was vital to him that he also gave himself to active service; indeed, the activism which characterised evangelicalism was very much in evidence in his early years at Kettering.[31] This activism – at this stage of his ministry – included much pastoral visiting around the town. He saw church members such as his leading deacon, Beeby Wallis and his wife, Martha,[32] as well as a host of others.[33] Fuller kept a notebook entitled 'Families that attend at the Meeting' in which details of members and some regular attenders – their names, families and 'particular cases' – were recorded.[34] He had a marked concern for the poor, of whom there were many in his congregation and in the wider community.[35] On 21 June 1784 he recorded in his diary, 'Much affected to-day in visiting some poor friends to see a little boy, of 7 to 8 years old, in a decline not likely to continue long. My heart

---

[26] Diary and Spiritual Thoughts, e.g., 3 October 1785.
[27] Diary and Spiritual Thoughts, e.g., 23 August 1784 (family prayer); 5 August 1784, 11 January 1785, 22 February 1785 (personal, private prayer).
[28] Diary and Spiritual Thoughts, e.g., 19 February 1785, 4 March 1785.
[29] 'The Qualification and Encouragement of a Faithful Minister Illustrated by the Character and Success of Barnabas', in *The Complete Works of the Rev. Andrew Fuller, With a Memoir of his Life by the Rev. Andrew Gunton Fuller*, ed. by Andrew Gunton Fuller, rev. ed. by Joseph Belcher; 3 vols, 3rd edn (Harrisonburg, VA: Sprinkle Publications, 1988 [1845]), 1: 137. This was originally published together with a sermon by Ryland preached on the same occasion, *The Qualifications and Encouragement of a Faithful Minister: Illustrated by the Character and Success of Barnabas; And, Paul's Charge to the Corinthians Respecting Their Treatment of Timothy... Being the Substance of Two Discourses ...* (London: J. Buckland, 1787).
[30] Diary and Spiritual Thoughts, 30 March 1785.
[31] For evangelical activism, see David W. Bebbington, *Evangelicalism in Modern Britain: A History from the 1730s to the 1980s* (London: Unwin Hyman, 1989), 10-12.
[32] Diary and Spiritual Thoughts, 25 March 1785 (Beeby Wallis), 22-29 November 1785 (Martha Wallis).
[33] See Diary and Spiritual Thoughts, 20 April 1785, 27 July 1785, for references to Fuller's pastoral visiting.
[34] Ryland, *Fuller*, 381. The book was dated August 1788. It appears not to be extant.
[35] Diary and Spiritual Thoughts, 3 and 4 August 1785.

felt for his everlasting state. Conversed with him a little...'[36] Fuller was moved by the plight of the child and visited him on a number of occasions. When the boy died the young pastor was asked to take the funeral, which was on a Saturday. An emotional man, he found this an extremely draining experience and was still deeply affected by it the following day as he engaged in Sunday ministry.[37]

Significant as visiting was, the focus of Fuller's public ministry was preaching. This included speaking at funerals such as the young boy's and also giving messages from scripture on other occasions during the week, for example at monthly church members' meetings.[38] But it was the Sunday services that were most important. The Kettering church had Sunday meetings in the morning, afternoon and evening.[39] As the pastor Fuller would usually preach at each of these and lead the services as well. All-in-all, there is plenty of evidence that he was heavily engaged in work in his home town in his early years as a pastor there.

Wider Ministry

Nevertheless, one of the striking features of his ministry between 1782 and 1792 is the amount of time he spent away from his home base. Morris stated that when Fuller moved to Kettering, he came into much more regular contact with Hall, Ryland and Sutcliff.[40] This contention is certainly borne out by his diary. He continued to attend the yearly Association gatherings, but, in addition to these, he met up with his friends informally at other times and these meetings took place with increasing regularity.[41] In 1784 the group of friends agreed to set aside the second Tuesday of every other month for fasting and prayer 'for the revival of religion', and soon monthly prayer meetings were started in their respective congregations, with the same revival focus.[42] The background to these meetings and their importance to Fuller's story – as well as the wider story of Particular Baptist renewal – will be dealt with in chapter five. What is important to note here is the way spiritual friendships with like-minded ministers were developing. Fuller had become 'greatly attached' to Hall, Ryland and Sutcliff and by 1785 was getting to know a number of others in the Association

---

[36] Diary and Spiritual Thoughts, 21 June 1784. For another reference to visits to 'poor friends', see 3 and 4 August 1785.

[37] Diary and Spiritual Thoughts, 18 July 1784.

[38] Diary and Spiritual Thoughts, 22 July 1784, 28 July 1785.

[39] Diary and Spiritual Thoughts, 25 April 1784, 5 September 1784.

[40] John Webster Morris, *Memoirs of the Life and Death of the Rev Andrew Fuller*, 1st edn (High Wycombe, 1816) 2nd edn (London: Wightman and Camp, 1826), 2nd edn, 40.

[41] See, e.g., Diary and Spiritual Thoughts, 31 October 1785, 15 Jan 1786.

[42] Morris, *Fuller*, 2nd edn, 41.

well, such as Morris.[43] These men were increasingly influencing his ministry, as indeed he was influencing theirs.

Partly due to his contact with these men, Fuller's 'labours took on a wider range'.[44] He received many invitations to preach elsewhere,[45] with the number of engagements away from Kettering increasing after the publication of the *Gospel Worthy*.[46] His diary entry for 21 November 1785 recorded he had just returned from a demanding preaching tour,

> For above a fortnight past, I have been chiefly out, in journies to Bedford, Arnsby, Bosworth, Eltington, Guilsborough, and Spratton. Preached at each of these places, with more or less earnestness. Came home, on Friday, and spoke, with some tenderness, from 'Hold thou me up, and I shall be safe [Psalm 119.117].' On Lord's-day, I preached on the evil tendency of mental departures from God, from Prov. xiv. 14. Also, on soul-prosperity, from 3 John 2. Had a tender and earnest mind.[47]

Fuller had returned to Kettering at the end of the fortnight so as to be ready for the Friday meeting and his Sunday preaching in what was now his home town. His work amongst his own people was crucial to him and he did not want to neglect it. Yet his November itinerary had taken in three counties, Bedfordshire (Bedford), Leicestershire (Arnesby, Bosworth) and, on the return leg of the journey, Northamptonshire (Eltington [Elkington], Guilsborough and Spratton). If this was not enough, he was soon away from Kettering again, preaching at Burton (probably Burton Latimer) before the month was out.[48] On occasion he found his hectic schedule difficult: 'I am weary of being out from home so much', he confided to his dairy on 13 June 1784. He had found some return visits to Soham so painful he determined in May 1785 he would not preach there again.[49] Mostly, though, he found his wider ministry encouraging and invigorating, especially when he was able to combine preaching and meeting with friends.[50] Together with Ryland and Sutcliff, he was involved in establishing a new church at 'Winnick' (Winwick, Northamptonshire). On this occasion both Ryland and Fuller preached and, after the three men had listened to testimonies

---

[43] Diary and Spiritual Thoughts, 20 June 1785: 'Visited this morning by Mr. Morris, a young minister just come out of Norfolk to Clipsham…'

[44] Morris, *Fuller*, 2nd edn, 40.

[45] In addition to the evidence cited elsewhere in this paragraph, see, e.g., Diary and Spiritual Thoughts, 28 April 1784, 3 May 1784, 5 October 1785. This last entry recorded that his preaching at Corby on 22 January 1784 had led to the conversion of at least one individual.

[46] See, e.g., Diary and Spiritual Thoughts, 5 – 7 October 1785. On these days Fuller preached at Corby, Spratton and Northampton.

[47] Diary and Spiritual Thoughts, 21 November 1785.

[48] Diary and Spiritual Thoughts, 29 November 1785.

[49] See, e.g., Diary and Spiritual Thoughts, 31 May 1785.

[50] See, e.g., Diary and Spiritual Thoughts, 18 May 1785, 28 and 30 September 1785.

of conversions, Sutcliff baptised seven people.[51] This was exciting work for Fuller and he thrived on it. Moreover, a collaborative church planting initiative such as this was a sign that, as Fuller's own ministry developed, the fortunes of the Particular Baptists were also on the rise.

Early Publications

What was Fuller preaching, at Kettering and further afield? Some of his pulpit notes survive but, as was the case for his Soham ministry, these are mainly in shorthand and very brief. But two messages from the 1780s are available in printed form and are included in his published *Works*. One of these, the ordination 'charge' given to Robert Fawkner in 1787 at Thorn in Bedfordshire, has already been referred to. The other message was an earlier one, based on the text 2 Corinthians 5.7, 'We walk by faith, not by sight'. This was preached at the Association meeting on 2 June 1784 at Nottingham and, at the request of his friends, printed later that year as *The Nature and Importance of Walking by Faith*.[52] This was in fact Fuller's first major published work.[53] Although it was preached at an Association meeting, it appears he had already given the message, or something like it, at Kettering.[54] Consequently, it provides a good surviving example of his preaching from the 1780s.

A Fuller Sermon: The Nature and Importance of Walking by Faith

Fuller probably only decided on his text and theme for the Association meeting as he travelled to get there. As he headed to Nottingham on horseback he encountered a flooded road. He urged his horse forward into the water but, as its level steadily rose, he was reluctant to proceed. A local man who was watching on told Fuller he would be safe and so the traveller continued to press ahead. But when the water reached his horse's saddle he hesitated again. 'Go on, sir,' the man exclaimed, 'all is right'. Fuller kept going. He found the flood became no deeper and he was able to reach dry ground safely and continue on his journey. He had taken the man at his word and found him to be trustworthy. At this point or soon after it seems Fuller determined he would rework his earlier 'walking by faith' sermon for the Association.[55]

---

[51] Diary and Spiritual Thoughts, 19 and 20 October 1784.

[52] Andrew Fuller, *The Nature and Importance of Walking by Faith...To which [is] Added, a Few Persuasives to a General Union in Prayer for the Revival of Real Religion* (Northampton: T. Dicey, 1784), in *Works*, 1: 117-34.

[53] He had written the Annual Association Letter to the churches in 1782, which was published as *The Excellency and Utility of the Grace of Hope*. For the text of the letter, see *Works*, 3: 308-17.

[54] Diary and Spiritual Thoughts, 25 April 1784, 'a very good forenoon...preaching on walking by faith'.

[55] *Walking by Faith* in *Works*, 1: 117, n. The anecdote seems to have been inserted as a footnote by Joseph Belcher, who revised the *Works* for republication in 1845.

As Fuller began his message he sought to establish that a person's faith should be focused on God and his word, rather than on subjective inner feelings. We should not be concentrating so much on ourselves, but on Christ, he insisted.[56] This was congruent with what he had said about faith in the as yet unpublished manuscript of the *Gospel Worthy*. Over and against the pervasive high Calvinist stress on analysing and trusting inner feelings, Fuller insisted that faith should be fixed on Christ and on the promises God gave in the gospel. Thus focused, the Christian would be able to 'go forward in the ways of godliness', trusting in the invisible realities of which the Bible speaks whatever their feelings might be.[57]

In the heart of his message, Fuller made four practical points about true faith. Firstly, he declared that a Christian is called to trust God and his word in the 'many *dark seasons*' of life.[58] He illustrated this point by referring to a number of Bible characters whose children had died. His examples included the Shunammite woman of 1 Kings 4, who said, '*it is well*' even after she had lost her son. Fuller observed approvingly, 'This is believing when we cannot see, taking God at his word, against all the rebellion of sense and feeling.'[59] He and his hearers were called to do the same, trusting God as they went through their own times of darkness. Fuller did not refer explicitly to the deaths of his and Sarah's own children, yet these tragic events surely underlie his comments. He was preaching to the assembled congregation and also to himself.

Secondly, Fuller insisted that faith, as he had defined it, was crucial if believers were to grow in '*fellowship with Christ*'. Trusting in the promises of God's word, which were a 'rock', gave Christians the assurance their relationship with him was secure. Thus assured, they could approach God in prayer with confidence, believing they would be welcomed. And as they prayed in this way their relationship with Christ would develop. Again, the preacher set his point about trusting in God in direct contrast with trust in feelings. 'I know, were I to consult nothing but my feelings, and only to fix my eyes on the enormity of my sin, I should utterly despair; but encouraged by HIS WORD, I will go forward; I will walk by faith, not by sight.'[60] In this way Fuller challenged high Calvinism once again. He sought to apply the scriptures to his hearers (and later to his readers) in a way that was suited to their context, with high Calvinistic spirituality often a significant force even in churches which preached an evangelical Calvinism.

As he made his third practical point, Fuller began by highlighting the call for Christians to deny themselves and take up their cross. 'Self-denial,' he declared, 'is one of the initial laws of Christ's kingdom.' 'We have to *give up many pre-*

---

[56] *Walking by Faith* in *Works*, 1: 119.
[57] *Walking by Faith* in *Works*, 1: 123. In the original, the quotation is all in upper case.
[58] *Walking by Faith* in *Works*, 1: 125.
[59] *Walking by Faith* in *Works*, 1: 126. For the quotation 'it is well', see 1 Kings 4.26.
[60] *Walking by Faith* in *Works*, 1: 128.

sent enjoyments, for Christ's sake,' without any *'visible* prospect of recompense'. This was a vital challenge, but how was it to be done? Fuller insisted it was impossible to respond to this call to self-denial and sacrifice without a robust biblical faith. A life of cross-bearing could only be sustained by a deep trust in the promises of God, specifically those which speak of 'invisible enjoyments' and future reward.[61] The life of true discipleship was nothing less than a journey of faith for every individual who embarked on it.

Fourthly and finally, Fuller applied the challenge of faith to the church as a whole. 'There are many low and distressing seasons to which the *church of God* is subject', he said, with 'little or no *visible* ground of encouragement' apart from that which 'arises from *the promises of God'.*[62] As an individual believer was called to journey with God through dark times, so the church as a body was called to walk by faith through difficult periods in her life, continuing to engage in ministry and 'looking forward...hoping for better days.'[63] 1784 was the year Fuller and his friends began praying for revival regularly and this was most likely in his mind. Yet even if the hoped for revival did not appear, still the church was to press onward in faith. The preacher closed his message with a stirring appeal to action,

> Christians, ministers, brethren, all of us! let us realize the subject. Let us pray, and preach, and hear, and do every thing we do with eternity in view! Let us deal much with Christ and invisible realities. Let us, whenever called, freely deny ourselves for his sake, and trust him to make up the loss. Let us not faint under present difficulties, but consider them as opportunities afforded us to glorify God. Let us be ashamed that we derive our happiness so much from things below, and so little from things above. In one word, let us fight the good fight of faith, and lay hold of eternal life![64]

Some of Fuller's evident power in the pulpit survives its transfer onto the printed page, despite the rather clumsy final sentence, 'In one word, let us fight...' The practical thrust, with the six-fold repetition of 'Let us' and its warm, urgent tone is especially evident. Here was a call to focus on Christ and eternal realities in a way which transformed life in the present. 'Everything' was to be done with eternity in view.

The Publication of the Gospel Worthy

Although *Walking by Faith* was Fuller's first published work, the *Gospel Worthy* had, of course, been basically ready at least three years before the Association sermon appeared in print. He was now under increasing pressure from his

---

[61] *Walking by Faith* in *Works*, 1: 128. For the biblical challenge to self-denial and cross-bearing, see Mark 8.34-38 and parallels.
[62] *Walking by Faith* in *Works*, 1: 129.
[63] *Walking by Faith* in *Works*, 1: 131.
[64] *Walking by Faith* in *Works*, 1: 134.

friends to allow the *Gospel Worthy* to appear in print as well.[65] As 1784 drew to a close he was at last willing for his manuscript to be published. On 21 October he wrote in his diary,

> I feel some pain in the thought of being about to publish on the <u>obligations of men to believe in Christ</u>, fearing I shall hereby expose myself to…plenty of abuse, which is disagreeable to the flesh. Had I not the satisfaction that 'tis the cause of <u>God and truth</u>, I would drop all thoughts of printing. The Lord keep me meek and lowly of heart.[66]

A month later Fuller travelled the fifteen or so miles from Kettering to a printers in Northampton. As he did so he offered up prayer 'that God would bless that about which I am going namely, the printing of my manuscript on the duty of sinners to believe in Christ.'[67] Fuller's use of the phrase 'the cause of God and truth' in his diary was almost certainly a conscious echo of Gill's major treatise of the same name. The *Gospel Worthy* would in fact outstrip even Gill's work in terms of importance and influence and Fuller would come to believe that his prayers for God's 'blessing' had indeed been answered.

Some were delighted with the *Gospel Worthy*. Caleb Evans, for example, obtained multiple copies of the work with a view to giving it away to others and wrote to Robert Hall to express his pleasure at Fuller's 'performance'.[68] However, not all would give the *Gospel Worthy* such a welcome. Fuller had correctly foreseen that some readers would respond negatively. In the wake of publication, Ryland recorded that Fuller had to contend with many 'ignorant people' who 'began to raise an outcry against the book and its author; charging him and his friends with having forsaken the doctrines of grace, and having left the good old way'.[69] This comment refers in the main to high Calvinist opponents from within the Particular Baptist denomination, but there were also others in the wider Christian world who thought that Fuller had not gone far enough in modifying his theology. As a result of his decision to go to print, Fuller would be engaged in controversy for the rest of his life. As Morris vividly put it, the Kettering pastor found himself, 'between two fires; the Hyper-Calvinists on the

---

[65] Ryland, *Fuller*, 144.
[66] Diary and Spiritual Thoughts, 21 October 1784.
[67] Diary and Spiritual Thoughts, 22 November 1784.
[68] Robert Hall letter to Fuller, 22 December 1786, Fuller Chapel Letters [Letters to Andrew Fuller], vol. 1 (1-34), vol. 2 (35-71), Fuller Baptist Church, Kettering, 1.2. Hall was passing on Evans's thoughts to Fuller. 'He says the performance is much admired by those who have read it. But people will not buy as the controversy is not in those parts, but he has given many away and perhaps can get through them all in time, which he will try if you do not want them.'
[69] Ryland, *Fuller*, 132.

hills and the Arminians in the vallies [sic.]'.[70] Opposition from high Calvinists will be treated first.

Opposition from High Calvinists

Some of the antagonism that came from this quarter was both petty and personal. Pride of place goes to Rushden Baptist Church and its elderly pastor, William Knowles. Fuller had encountered Knowles prior to 1785, and recorded in his diary that the Rushden pastor was 'deeply tinged with false Calvinism'.[71] One of Knowles's members, a Mrs Wright, had moved to Weekly, a village immediately to the north of Kettering, from which time she started to attend the 'Little Meeting'. However, when she asked to come into membership in 1785, Rushden refused to provide the normal letter of transfer because, in Knowles's view, 'the church at Kettering had gone off from their former principles'.[72] The deacons at Kettering wrote to Rushden on 7 August 1785, protesting 'that we know of no one principle relating to the doctrines of grace which we feel in the least inclined to give up'. They asked the church at Rushden to 'consider the matter again'.[73] Two months later they had received no reply, prompting them to write once more, this time in stronger terms.[74] The Rushden Baptists eventually responded in December. They again refused to provide a letter of transfer for the unfortunate Mrs Wright and accused the Kettering church of 'lording it' over them.[75] The real problem was only too clear to the church at Kettering. The following entry was written into the Church Book,

> That there are differences in sentiment between us and the church at Rushden, is true. We consider the doctrines of grace as entirely consistent with a free address to every sinner, and with an universal obligation on all men where the gospel is preached to repent of their sins, and turn to God through Jesus Christ. They think otherwise, and it is simply on account of this difference that they have disowned communion with us.

Described as 'a timid character', Mrs Wright was reluctant to transfer membership without a formal dismissal from Rushden, despite the 'Little Meeting' now being ready to receive her without this. Astonishingly, it was not until 1796, two years after the death of Knowles, that a letter of transfer was provided. Morris mentioned a congregation close to Kettering which refused to have any dealings with Fuller, or 'allow any of their members to have fellowship with his church'

---

[70] Morris, *Fuller*, 2nd edn, 223-24.
[71] Diary and Spiritual Thoughts, 16 July 1784.
[72] The Church Book of Kettering Baptist Church (The 'Little Meeting'), 1773-1815, Fuller Baptist Church, Kettering, 28 July 1785.
[73] Church Book, Kettering Baptist Church, 7 August 1785.
[74] Church Book, Kettering Baptist Church, 6 November 1785.
[75] Church Book, Kettering Baptist Church, 22 December 1785.

for seven years.[76] Probably he was referring to Rushden, which was twelve miles to the south east of Kettering. Doubtless, though, there were other candidates.

Some of the published replies to the *Gospel Worthy* were replete with personal abuse of the Kettering pastor. Fuller was anxious when he read advertisements concerning a forthcoming work by a certain Dr Withers, who promised to reduce the *Gospel Worthy* to 'dust'.[77] According to Ryland, Withers was a man 'deeply tinged with antinomianism' whose book was full of 'extravagant crudities'.[78] When Fuller received a copy of Withers's work he was deeply shocked by its violent language. 'What horrid sentiments does he advance!' he wrote in his diary.[79] He determined not to dignify Withers's book with any published response. The *Gospel Worthy* was also the target of a series of three intemperate pamphlets published between 1788 and 1791 by a London Particular Baptist pastor, John Martin.[80] Morris described Martin's efforts as a 'ponderous load of polemics' and wrote of the contempt that Fuller expressed in private for 'such a writer'.[81] The Kettering pastor did publish a defence against Martin's first pamphlet, but did not respond to the subsequent ones.[82] The attacks of Withers and Martin and the dispute with the Rushden church serve as examples of the sort of opposition that would dog Fuller for the rest of his life. Yet there was also a more measured response to the *Gospel Worthy* from a high Calvinist perspective, published by a respected London Particular Baptist, William Button (1754-1821).

Button was pastor at Dean Street, Southwark, from 1774 until his resignation due to financial difficulties in 1813. He was, in the words of Robert Oliver, 'a representative of those London churches which still revered the memory of John Gill'.[83] Dean Street was in fact an offshoot from Gill's old church in Carter Lane, where Button's father had been a deacon. It was created by a minority of

---

[76] Morris, *Fuller*, 2nd edn, 271.

[77] Diary and Spiritual Thoughts, 8 August 1785.

[78] Ryland, *Fuller*, 132. Withers's treatise was entitled *Philanthropos, or a Letter to the Revd. Fuller in reply to his Treatise on Damnation* (London, 1786). A copy of this work has not been traced, but there are quotations from it in *Works*, 2: 418-19.

[79] Diary and Spiritual Thoughts, 29 January 1786.

[80] John Martin, *Thoughts On The Duty Of Man Relative To Faith In Jesus Christ, In Which Mr Andrew Fuller's Leading Propositions On This Subject Are Considered* (London: W. Smith, 1788-91).

[81] Morris, *Fuller*, 1st edn, 269, 303.

[82] Andrew Fuller, *Remarks on Mr Martin's Publication Entitled 'Thoughts on the Duty of Man...to Faith in Jesus Christ...'* (Clipstone: J.W. Morris, 1788), in *Works*, 2: 716-36.

[83] Robert W. Oliver, 'The Emergence of a Strict and Particular Baptist Community Among the English Calvinistic Baptists, 1770-1850' (unpublished DPhil thesis, CNAA [London Bible College], 1986), 87. The financial difficulties Button experienced were in connection with a bookselling business he had set up for his two sons.

members who opposed the appointment of the Bristol Academy student John Rippon (1750-1836) as Gill's successor in 1773. Button's *Remarks on a Treatise entitled The Gospel Worthy of All Acceptation* appeared in London in 1785, prompting a rejoinder from Fuller, *A Defence of a Treatise...*, which was published two years later.[84] Personal relations between the two men remained reasonably good and Button later became a supporter of the Baptist Missionary Society.[85] Button's work and Fuller's response merit a more detailed treatment.

William Button's Remarks on...the Gospel Worthy

In his *Remarks*, Button predictably attacked Fuller's leading argument, that faith in Christ was the duty of all who heard the gospel. According to him, it was impossible for faith to be a duty, since no one could respond without the electing grace of God. It was just as absurd to talk of someone who was unregenerate having a 'duty' to believe as it was to call the blind to look, the deaf to hear or the dead to rise. Therefore, 'calls, invitations and exhortations to special faith and spiritual acts' should not be issued by preachers.[86] The carefully worked out distinction between natural and moral inability was meant to undercut this sort of argument, but Button could not accept it. He struggled to follow Fuller's line of reasoning and, it appears, failed to grasp the meaning of the Edwardsean terms. For example, he consistently confused Fuller's use of the term 'natural' with the 'natural man'. What he could not understand was how it was possible to maintain on the one hand that someone's inability to believe was total, and on the other say that that inability was not natural, but moral. 'All I contend for,' he complained, 'is for the total inability of man to believe. Mr F says this is what he never denied, and yet fills up 196 pages which tend to the contrary. How he can clear up this inconsistency I am at a loss to determine. I must leave it to himself.'[87]

---

[84] Andrew Fuller, *A Defence of a Treatise, entitled, The Gospel of Christ Worthy of All Acceptation: Containing a Reply to Mr Button's Remarks and the Observations of Philanthropos* (Clipstone: J.W. Morris, 1787). See *Works*, 2: 421-511. The 'Philanthropos' in question was not Withers but, as we shall see, the New Connexion General Baptist Dan Taylor. Button and Fuller appear to have corresponded on the subject of the *Gospel Worthy* before Button's *Remarks* appeared. There is a reference to a letter from 'Mr. B. of London' in connection with the *Gospel Worthy* in Diary and Spiritual Thoughts, 24 June 1785.

[85] As Fuller was later to write, Fuller to William R. Ward, 7 Jan 1813, Typescript Andrew Fuller Letters, transcribed by Joyce A. Booth, superintended by Ernest A. Payne, Angus Library, Regent's Park College, Oxford (4/5/1 and 4/5/2) (4/5/1), 'Our High Calvinist Brethren are coming nearer; the mission attracts them, as well as the General Baptists; and we endeavour not to counteract its salutary influence by our behaviour in either case.'

[86] Button, *Remarks*, 99.

[87] Button, *Remarks*, 56-58.

Button further complained that Arminians were saying that Fuller's work would 'cure some of their Gillism and Brineism'. For this reason alone the Kettering pastor's arguments were suspect.[88] In the *Gospel Worthy* Fuller had admitted that some Calvinistic ministers who had preached in an invitational manner had subsequently gone on to 'to dabble in Arminianism'. Button quoted this passage back to Fuller (as indeed did Martin), seizing on it as evidence that the Kettering pastor was surely wrong to argue as he did.[89] Invitational preaching, Button declared, might be the slippery slope to Arminianism; was it not self-evident, therefore, that such preaching should be avoided? Despite a rather baffling assertion that invitational preaching was 'inconsistent with Scripture',[90] Button's *Remarks* betray a fundamental and overriding attachment to high Calvinism as a system. That is to say, an *a priori* commitment to the principles of high Calvinism, over and against the dread spectre of Arminianism, exercised a controlling influence over his work. Because of this commitment he remained firmly wedded to what Ivimey described, not unfairly, as the 'non-invitation, non-application scheme'.[91]

Fuller's Reply to Button

Button's arguments failed to engage adequately with the *Gospel Worthy*. The verdict of Caleb Evans, expressed privately to Fuller, was scathing. Surely Button and Edwards could not be of the same 'species,' he said. A 'snail and a tortoise are not so distant'.[92] Hall's verdict, also expressed by letter, was more measured but still critical of Button.[93] Both of Fuller's correspondents believed the author of the *Gospel Worthy* had nothing to fear from the London high Calvinist's pamphlet. Fuller too believed Button's attacks had left the *Gospel Worthy* 'unshaken'.[94] In his reply to Button he believed he really only had to restate his main themes whilst interacting with his opponent.[95] This he did with vigour. The difference between natural and moral inability was explained again, at

---

[88] Button, *Remarks*, v.
[89] Button, *Remarks*, i-ii and 100; Martin, *Thoughts*, 77. The quotation in question is from the *Gospel Worthy*, 1st edn, 167.
[90] Button, *Remarks*, 99.
[91] Joseph Ivimey, *A History of the English Baptists (HEB)* 4 vols (London: Hinton, Holdsworth & Ball, 1811-30), 3: 272-73.
[92] Fuller Chapel Letters, Caleb Evans letter to Fuller, 7 November 1787, 2.35. Did he perhaps mean to say a 'hare and a tortoise'?
[93] Fuller Chapel Letters, Robert Hall letter to Fuller, 22 December 1786, 1.2.
[94] Fuller, *Defence of a Treatise*, in *Works*, 2: 418; cf. 420.
[95] Fuller confided to his Diary and Spiritual Thoughts, 7 December 1785, that he believed Button had included 'an abundance of things...very foreign to the point, and very little evidence.'

some length and with considerable care.[96] The charge that his theology necessarily led to Arminianism was addressed. Fuller declared that this accusation
was no more valid than the one, made sometimes by Arminians that Calvinism
necessarily led to antinomianism.[97] He was also adamant that Gill and Brine
should not be set up as infallible 'standards of orthodoxy', something Button
appeared to do.[98] Rather, he urged, people should be free to examine the scriptures and think for themselves. When arguing a particular point in reply to Button, who had cited Gill, Fuller stated, 'What was Dr Gill's meaning I cannot
tell, nor is it worth while to dispute about it, as the opinion of the greatest unin-
spired writer is not decisive.'[99] For Fuller, adherence to a system or a human
author was far less important than a commitment to the Bible and a spirit of free
enquiry. Scriptures were nonetheless true for having been quoted by Arminians,
and it was the Bible rather than John Gill's writings which should be the primary text for Particular Baptists.

Fuller concluded the part of his *Defence* which dealt with Button with a stirring appeal, specifically addressed to the individual reader. He declared,

> [L]et me entreat [the reader] to put one serious question to his own soul, 'Dost
> *thou* believe on the Son of God?' Let him remember that nothing less than his
> eternal salvation or destruction hangs upon the answer; that the question *must* be
> answered, sooner or later; that there is no medium between being Christ's friend
> or enemy; and that it is not taking this or the other side of a dispute that will de-
> nominate any man a Christian. Neither let him evade the question by answering
> that he has already been acknowledged as a believer in Christ, is a member of a
> Christian church, perhaps a preacher of the gospel, and has long been in the habit
> of taking the matter for granted, and of sitting in judgment upon other men and
> other things. All this may be true; and yet things may issue in a dreadful disap-
> pointment![100]

This was bold indeed, despite being couched in the third person. Fuller's appeal
provides a good example of how he must have been preaching at this stage of
his career. The message of eternal salvation in Christ was pressed home to the
reader, as it might have been to someone listening to a sermon. Fuller had re-
stated his foundational principles in his reply to Button; now he was showing
what those principles looked like when put into practice. His readers – many of
whom would have been high Calvinists – found themselves directly challenged.
Whatever their theology was, it would not save them; neither would their role
within a Christian church (even if they were preachers!). Salvation would only

---

[96] *Defence of a Treatise*, in *Works*, 2, esp. Section VIII, 443-46 and Section IX, 446-49.

[97] *Defence of a Treatise*, in *Works*, 2: 456.

[98] *Defence of a Treatise*, in *Works*, 2: 421.

[99] *Defence of a Treatise*, in *Works*, 2: 442.

[100] *Defence of a Treatise*, in *Works*, 2: 458. The Bible quotation is from John 9.35.

come, Fuller insisted, through the exercise of faith in the Son of God. The words show his growing confidence, as well as an evangelical focus on simplicity, a dislike of disputing for its own sake and, above all, evangelistic passion. Books could be 'means' that God used to bring about conversions as well as preaching. He was determined, in the words of the 'statement of principles' he had given at his induction at Kettering, not to be 'guilty of the blood of souls' by neglecting an evangelistic opportunity.

Opposition from Arminians

As already stated, it was not only high Calvinists who responded to the *Gospel Worthy*. Coupled with Fuller's response to Button was one to Dan Taylor (1738-1816), the leader of the New Connexion of General Baptists. Fuller received a copy of Taylor's *Observations on the Rev Andrew Fuller's late pamphlet entitled The Gospel of Christ Worthy of All Acceptation* in February 1786, immediately after it had been published. He wrote in his diary that he had 're-ceived another treatise written against me', with his underlining of 'another' suggesting his weariness and – perhaps – frustration at the attacks on his work. However, after he had read Taylor's short book the tone of the diary entries changed. 'The author [i.e. Taylor] discovers an amiable spirit and there is a good deal of plausibility in some things which he maintains,' Fuller wrote. A few days later he added, 'My mind has been much employed all the week in thinking on the above piece, the more I examine it, the more I perceive it is (though ingeniously wrought together) capable of a solid reply.'[101]

Taylor was an energetic Baptist denominational leader and a prolific author who hailed from the north of England. He had impeccable evangelical credentials. Thoroughly indebted to the Revival, as a youth he had regularly trekked across the Yorkshire Moors to hear Whitefield and the Wesleys on the occasions they had preached in the area. Following Taylor's conversion he became involved in Wesleyan Methodist Societies around Halifax but became unhappy with certain features of Methodism as practised in the West Riding. In 1762 he withdrew from the movement. By 1763, whilst remaining strongly committed to Arminianism, he had become convinced that believers' baptism by immersion was biblical and that he should submit to the rite himself. No local Particular Baptist minister would baptise him, so together with a friend he walked to the Nottinghamshire village of Gamston where he was baptised by a General Baptist minister in February 1763.[102] He formed the New Connexion of General

---

[101] Diary and Spiritual Thoughts, 5 – 12 Feb 1786. Fuller made his comments relating to these days in a single entry.

[102] For biographical details of Taylor and the early history of the New Connexion see Adam Taylor, *Memoirs of the Rev. Dan Taylor* (London: Baynes and Son, 1820), *passim*. There are now two good modern studies available. For the New Connexion, see Frank W. Rinaldi, *The Tribe of Dan: The New Connexion of General Baptists, 1770-1891* (Carlisle: Paternoster, 2008). For Taylor's theology and general approach

Baptists in 1770 after he had become disillusioned by the doctrinal drift and internal wrangling that characterised the existing English General Baptists.[103] The New Connexion was organised along unashamedly evangelical lines, but was also Arminian. All the ministers of the Connexion were required to subscribe to six articles of faith (which rejected both Unitarianism and Calvinism) and give an account of their religious experience. There was a strong commitment to churches associating together and they 'were much more alive to the needs of the time than the old Assembly', engaging in vigorous outreach work.[104]

By the time his dispute with Fuller began Taylor was an established and respected figure in the evangelical world,[105] a respect that was shared by Fuller himself, as will be shown. Taylor published his *Observations on the...Gospel of Christ Worthy* under the pseudonym 'Philanthropos', the *nom de plume* that had earlier been adopted by Withers (although Taylor was almost certainly unaware of this). The controversy did not end with Fuller's response. Taylor dropped his use of 'Philanthropos' for two further pamphlets, published under his own name in 1787 and 1790 respectively. Curiously Fuller did the reverse, adopting a pseudonym of his own, 'Agnostos', in replying to Taylor's second tract in 1788.[106]

The Arguments of Dan Taylor and Fuller

Throughout the dispute Taylor maintained that 'the universal calls and invitations' of the gospel could only be based on the 'universality of Divine love, and

---

to ministry, see Richard Pollard, 'To Revive Experimental Religion or Primitive Christianity in Faith and Practice: The Pioneering Evangelicalism of Dan Taylor (1738-1816)' (unpublished PhD thesis, University of Wales / Spurgeon's College, 2014).

[103] For a summary of the state of the older General Baptists and reasons for their decline, see Ian M. Randall, 'The Low Condition of the Churches': Difficulties faced by General Baptists in England – the 1680s to the 1760s', *Pacific Journal of Baptist Research* 1.1 (October 2005), 3-19.

[104] Kenneth R. Hylson-Smith, *The Churches in England from Elizabeth I to Elizabeth II. Vol. 2: 1689-1833* (London: SCM Press, 1997), 107.

[105] Ryland, *Fuller*, 132.

[106] 'Philanthropos'[Dan Taylor], *Observations on the Rev Andrew Fuller's late pamphlet entitled The Gospel of Christ Worthy of All Acceptation* (London: J. Buckland, 1788); Dan Taylor, *Observations on the Rev Andrew Fuller's Reply to Philanthropos* (St Ives, Cambridgeshire: T. Bloom, 1788); *The Friendly Conclusion Occasioned by the Letters of 'Agnostos'* (London: W. Ash, 1790). The first book is especially rare, but one is held in Spurgeon's College Library, bound in between the two later pamphlets in one volume. Fuller's *The Reality and Efficacy of Divine Grace* (originally published as 'by Agnostos') is found in *Works*, 2: 512-60.

the death of Jesus Christ, as the propitiation for the sins of the whole world'.[107] That universal offers of the gospel should be made, in preaching and other evangelistic work, was not a matter of dispute between Taylor and Fuller. It was the grounds that underpinned such invitations to believe that were the focus of the debate. The distinction between natural and moral inability was again important as the arguments unfolded, although this time the issues were different. Taylor had a more optimistic view of human nature than Fuller. He believed there was no inability of any kind stopping people trusting in Christ. If Fuller's definition of moral inability was allowed to stand, Taylor argued, then people would be blameless and God would be guilty of injustice and cruelty in punishing any who did not embrace the gospel. Indeed, said Taylor, God would be a 'merciless tyrant'.[108] 'If men could never avoid [moral inability], and cannot deliver themselves from it, and the blessed God will not deliver them, surely they ought not to be punished for it, or for any of its necessary effects'.[109] Fuller's argument – according to Taylor – made God appear unjust.

This charge was one the Kettering pastor took very seriously and he devoted a significant section of his *Defence of a Treatise* to refuting it.[110] To combat Taylor, he insisted that people's moral inability to believe was the result of sin having 'dominion in their heart[s]'.[111] Sin was nothing less than willful rebellion against God. Therefore people who were morally unable to believe were still guilty before God, who was just in punishing them. Taylor was unconvinced, but Fuller held his ground. He was sure that his arguments, far from making God out to be unfair, showed him to be entirely just in his commitment to punish sin in unbelievers.[112]

Taylor further argued that Christ died not only for the elect, but for the whole world.[113] In saying this, he was not espousing universalism, for only those who responded to the gospel would be saved. But he was sure the atonement was general and not particular. There was, he insisted, potential provision in the death of Christ for all people, not just for the elect. He declared that the scriptures, 'never give us any intimation…that Christ died for some and not for others.'[114] Taylor made this an important part of the debate as a whole because he

---

[107] See the title pages of both Taylor, *Observations on the…Gospel of Christ Worthy* and *Observations on the Reply to Philanthropos*.

[108] Taylor, *Observations on the…Gospel of Christ Worthy*, 88.

[109] Taylor, *Observations on the…Gospel of Christ Worthy*, 67. Fuller cites Taylor's words, *Reply to Philanthropos*, in *Works*, 2: 472.

[110] *Defence of a Treatise*, in *Works*, 2: 477-83.

[111] *Defence of a Treatise*, in *Works*, 2: 477. Cf. Fuller letter to John Ryland, 22 March 1783, Fuller Letters (4/5/1).

[112] *Defence of a Treatise*, in *Works*, 2: 481.

[113] Taylor, *Observations on the…Gospel of Christ Worthy*, 70-88.

[114] Taylor, *Observations on the…Gospel of Christ Worthy*, 29; cf. 29-30, 'Christ died for all men, as the Scripture positively asserts'. Texts that Taylor cited included 2 Cor. 5.14-15 and 1 Tim. 2.6, 'Christ Jesus…gave himself as a ransom for all.'

argued that universal invitations for sinners to believe the gospel could only be properly grounded in a universal provision in the death of Christ. It was quite inconsistent to hold to a limited provision and plead for universal offers, because the preacher would be commanding something that, for many, would not only be 'morally' impossible, but 'naturally' impossible as well. Fuller and Taylor were both in agreement that no one could be saved unless Christ had died for them. Yet the New Connexion leader was able to argue that in Fuller's scheme, although a man could not say with certainty he was excluded from Christ's death, 'yet he must, in the exercise of reason say, that if he be excluded, his salvation is utterly impossible'. And, Taylor continued, 'It is certain that God could never command a thing which is naturally impossible.'[115] In short, Fuller's view was both unscriptural and unreasonable.

On this point – the extent of the atonement – Fuller did not now feel as sure of the arguments he had put forward in the *Gospel Worthy*. He considered Taylor's points carefully and evidently felt the force of them. The New Connexion leader's case was tightly argued. His insistence that it was 'naturally impossible' for the non-elect to believe if Christ had not in some sense died for them carried considerable weight with Fuller.[116] Elsewhere, the Kettering pastor was unimpressed with Taylor's comments on natural and moral inability, believing that his opponent's strictures lacked clarity and consistency.[117] However, on the extent of the atonement it seemed Taylor had an unanswerable point. He later confessed, 'I tried to answer my opponent...but I could not. I found not merely his reasonings, but the Scriptures themselves, standing in my way.'[118] By the time he published his *Defence of a Treatise*, a significant change in his views had taken place.

In his new work, Fuller argued that the particularity of redemption consisted 'not in the degree of Christ's suffering (as though he must have suffered more if more had been finally saved)...but in the sovereign purpose and design of the Father and the Son.' The sufferings of Christ, he continued, 'are of infinite value, sufficient to have saved all the world, and a thousand worlds, if it had pleased God...to have made them effectual to this end.'[119] Fuller was now locat-

---

[115] Taylor, *Observations on the...Gospel of Christ Worthy*, 31.

[116] Taylor further commented, 'it appears to be naturally impossible for any man to trust in one whom he does not know or believe to be his friend. Christ is not the friend of any for whom he did not die. How then can any man rationally trust in him, as a Saviour, before he understand that he died for him?' *Observations on the...Gospel of Christ Worthy*, 31-32.

[117] *Defence of a Treatise*, in *Works*, 2: 472. The evidence suggests Taylor had not actually read Edwards's *Freedom of the Will* first hand. On this, see Pollard, 'To Revive Experimental Religion... The Pioneering Evangelicalism of Dan Taylor (1738-1816)'.

[118] Andrew Fuller, 'Six Letters to Dr Ryland respecting the Controversy with the Rev. A. Booth', in *Works*, 2: 709-10. The six letters were all written in January 1803.

[119] *Defence of a Treatise*, in *Works*, 2: 488-89.

ing the particularity of redemption in the application of the atonement, or more precisely 'in the design of the Father and the Son, respecting the persons to whom it shall be applied'.[120] This enabled him to continue to speak of a 'special design' in the death of Christ, because those to whom the atonement would be applied had been decided in the purposes of God before time, not because God had foreseen that people would believe, but because 'God eternally purposed in himself that they should believe and be saved'.[121] It is important to emphasise this. He remained fully committed to particular redemption and did not become an Arminian. Nevertheless, his view of the atonement was at least in part now 'general'. As he stated, 'if all the inhabitants of the globe could be persuaded to return to God in Christ's name, they would undoubtedly be accepted by him.'[122]

Fuller had come to this view as a result of the dispute with Taylor, by reflecting on his opponent's arguments and by engaging afresh with the Bible. But he most likely had some help from the writings of Jonathan Edwards once again, for the view that Fuller was now espousing was basically Edwards's own. Moreover Edwards's approach was set out in the all important *Freedom of the Will*. The relevant passage stated,

> However Christ in some sense might be said to die for all, and to redeem all visible Christians, yea, the whole world by his death; yet there must be something particular in the design of his death with respect to such as be saved thereby. God has the actual salvation or redemption of a certain number in his proper absolute design, and of a certain number only; and, therefore, such a design can only be prosecuted in any thing God does in order to the salvation of men.[123]

Edwards held that the atonement was general (he died for the 'whole world'), yet redemption was still particular or specific (there was a 'particular...design' regarding the death of Christ). This was the position Fuller adopted. Almost all of the passage just quoted from the *Freedom of the Will* would be cited by Fuller, in his own Preface to the English edition of Joseph Bellamy's *True Religion Delineated*.[124] It is hard not to believe it was relevant to his change of views.[125]

---

[120] From a 'Conversation with a friend at Edinburgh, on the subject of Particular Redemption, in 1805', in Morris, *Fuller*, 2nd edn, 311.

[121] *Defence of a Treatise*, in *Works*, 2: 490-95 (493).

[122] *Defence of a Treatise*, in *Works*, 2: 506. Cf. *The Reality and Efficacy of Divine Grace*, in *Works*, 2: 541.

[123] Jonathan Edwards, *Freedom of the Will*, in *The Works of Jonathan Edwards*, vol. 1, ed. by Paul Ramsey (New Haven: Yale University Press, 1985 [1754]), 435.

[124] Andrew Fuller, 'Recommendatory Preface' to Joseph Bellamy, *True Religion Delineated; or, Experimental Religion... Set in a Scriptural and Rational Light*, 3rd edn (London: T. Hamilton, 1809), vii.

[125] See also Chris Chun, *The Legacy of Jonathan Edwards in the Theology of Andrew Fuller* (Leiden: Brill, 2012), 153, 176-82.

Taylor was unimpressed with this modification on the extent of the atonement, believing the inconsistencies he had highlighted in Fuller's earlier position still remained.[126] Nevertheless, it represented a significant shift for Fuller; a change from his earlier published stance that must have taken some courage. In the first edition of the *Gospel Worthy* he had stated that Christ only died 'for some of the human race'.[127] He now held to a more nuanced view. The particularity of redemption was located not in the extent of the atonement but in God's purposes in election. Indeed, particular redemption he now considered to be 'a branch of election'.[128] People were still unable to respond to the gospel without the electing, regenerating grace of God, but there was an objective provision for everyone in the atonement, whether they believed or not.[129] Fuller considered that in saying this, he had safeguarded the basis upon which the all-important universal calls to repentance and faith could be made. In terms of natural ability everyone could respond, because they had the natural powers to do so and because there was provision for them in the death of Christ. Their inability to respond was entirely moral and therefore criminal. Their 'cannot', as Fuller had always expressed it, was still nothing more than a 'will not'.

He was to make yet further modifications to his views in the course of the debate. In his *Reply to Philanthropos* he stated that terms such as ransom and propitiation were only ever applied in the Bible to those who were finally saved.[130] But in the *Reality and Efficacy of Divine Grace*, his pseudonymous reply to Taylor's second work, he declared he had been mistaken. These terms, he now said, were 'applicable to all mankind in general...conveying an indefinite, but not universal idea'.[131] That the *Reality and Efficacy of Divine Grace* was by Fuller is confirmed by comments in his biographies and especially by its inclusion in his *Works* with an explanatory 'Advertisement'.[132] To publish anonymously when engaged in controversy was, as Ivimey noted, unlike Fuller's usual 'manly daring'.[133] Ryland may have been right when he stated that this was because of a desire on his friend's part not to prolong the dispute,[134] but it is also possible that the Kettering pastor was becoming a little uncomfortable with the modifications he was having to make to his views. These modifications were considerable.

---

[126] Taylor, *Observations on Fuller's reply to Philanthropos*, 78-134, esp. 78-89.

[127] *Gospel Worthy*, 1st edn, 106. This comment was quoted and challenged by Taylor, *Observations on the...Gospel of Christ Worthy*, 30.

[128] 'Conversation with a friend at Edinburgh', in Morris, *Fuller*, 2nd edn, 311.

[129] Cf. Fuller letter to Robert Aked and Isaac Mann, 2 September 1806, Fuller Letters (4/5/2).

[130] *Defence of a Treatise*, in *Works*, 2: 496.

[131] *Reality and Efficacy of Divine Grace*, in *Works*, 2: 550.

[132] *Works*, 2: 512.

[133] Ivimey, *HEB*, 4: 87 n.

[134] Ryland, *Fuller*, 134.

Fuller, Taylor and Enlightenment Thinking

Before drawing this chapter to a close, it is worth commenting on the extent to which the dispute between Fuller and Taylor reveals their shared debt to the Enlightenment.[135] That Fuller was in some sense 'enlightened' has already been suggested in this book at the close of chapter three. In considering this further, it is vital to recognise that the Enlightenment was a complex and diverse phenomenon.[136] Many scholars argue it is better to speak of different 'enlightenments'.[137] It is indeed important to recognise there were many variations and that we are not talking about a monolithic, unified movement.[138] For example, the Scottish, English and French Enlightenments were not the same. To highlight just one area of difference, the movement tended to be more irreligious in France than it was in England or Scotland.[139] Nevertheless, there were certain core characteristics which crossed national boundaries and for this reason I refer in this book to 'Enlightenment' with an upper case 'E'. Central to these core characteristics was a confident belief in 'the ability of human reason to discover truth'.[140] Also important was the theory that all knowledge is derived from sense experience – what is known as 'empiricism'. Allied with Enlightenment rationalism and empiricism was a commitment to a spirit of free enquiry. Inherited opinions should not be taken on trust; rather they should be rigorously examined and, if found wanting, revised or even jettisoned. Further Enlightenment

---

[135] Especially as this dimension of Fuller and Taylor's debate was missed by Clint Sheehan, 'Great and Sovereign Grace: Fuller's Defence of the Gospel Against Arminianism', in *'At the Pure Fountain of Thy Word': Andrew Fuller as an Apologist*, ed. by Michael A.G. Haykin (Milton Keynes: Paternoster, 2004), 83-121. By contrast, the influence of the Enlightenment on the two men is set out in some detail by Pollard, 'To Revive Experimental Religion... The Pioneering Evangelicalism of Dan Taylor'.

[136] See, e.g., Bruce K. Ward, *Redeeming the Enlightenment: Christianity and the Liberal Virtues* (Grand Rapids: Eerdmans, 2010), 2-3.

[137] John G.A. Pocock, 'Historiography and Enlightenment: A View of their History', *Modern Intellectual History* 5.1 (April 2008), 83-96 (83).

[138] Roy Porter, *Enlightenment: Britain and the Creation of the Modern World* (London: Penguin, 2000), e.g., 11; Charles W.J. Withers, *Placing the Enlightenment: Thinking Geographically about the Age of Reason* (Chicago, IL: The University of Chicago Press, 2004), e.g., 4. As well as geographical differences, there were variations in respect of religion too. On this, see David Sorkin, *The Religious Enlightenment: Protestants, Jews, and Catholics from London to Vienna* (Princeton, NJ, and Oxford: Princeton University Press, 2008), e.g., 3-5.

[139] David W. Bebbington, *Holiness in Nineteenth-Century England* (Carlisle: Paternoster, 2000), 33; cf. *Baptists Through the Centuries*, 66.

[140] Bebbington, *Holiness in Nineteenth-Century England*, 33, 35.

characteristics included the importance of free public discussion and emphases on justice, tolerance, benevolence, pragmatism and progress.[141]

In considering the ways Fuller and Taylor were enlightened, it is worth noting first of all the eirenic manner in which their debate was conducted, particularly when compared with Fuller's parallel controversies with high Calvinist opponents. The opposition from a church like Rushden Baptist was mean-spirited and personal; the language used by Withers and Martin was often immoderate. At one point, Martin accused Fuller of being 'a very *obscure, inconsistent, erroneous, ignorant, artful, vain, hypocritical* kind of writer'.[142] By contrast, one of the most striking aspects of the dispute between Fuller and Taylor is the respectful tone both adopted from the outset. 'I love many things contained in Mr F's pamphlet', Taylor stated, 'and I love him for his work's sake'.[143] He was at pains to emphasise his 'Cordial love and esteem for Mr. F.'[144] What is more, he warmly welcomed the main thrust of the *Gospel Worthy* and conceded that Fuller had written with 'perspicuity' (a judgment Fuller himself contrasted with Martin's accusation of 'obscurity').[145] The Kettering pastor responded in similar vein. 'If I have, in any instance, mistaken his meaning,' Fuller said, 'I hope he will excuse it', and he was quick to acknowledge that Taylor had treated him 'with candour and respect'.[146] This careful, conciliatory tone, in marked contrast to Fuller's clash with Martin and even the more civilized dispute with Button, was maintained by both writers right to the end of the debate. Fuller would remain on good terms with the leader of the New Connexion and preached for him in London on at least two occasions in 1806 and 1807, to 'convince the world that perfect cordiality subsists between [Taylor] and myself'.[147] The commitment to distinguish between principles and personalities and the overall tone of the debate were alike informed by a tolerant, enlightened spirit.

---

[141] Alexander Brodie writes of the 'concept of Enlightenment' as 'a process in which reason is exercised in free public debate'. He further states, 'if reason leads one might expect real progress'. See his 'Introduction – What was the Scottish Enlightenment?' in *The Scottish Enlightenment: An Anthology*, ed. by Alexander Brodie (Edinburgh: Canongate, 1997), 17.

[142] *Remarks on Mr Martin's Publication* in *Works*, 2: 716.

[143] Taylor, *Observations on the…Gospel of Christ Worthy*, 6.

[144] Taylor, *Observations on the…Gospel of Christ Worthy*, 'Advertisement to the Reader'.

[145] Taylor, *Observations on the…Gospel of Christ Worthy*, 63; Fuller, *Remarks on Mr Martin's Publication* in *Works*, 2: 719.

[146] *Defence of a Treatise*, in *Works*, 2: 510, 459.

[147] Taylor, *Dan Taylor*, 177 n. Fuller's friend, Samuel Pearce, also preached at least once for Taylor in London in the late summer of 1795. See Ernest A. Payne, 'Some Samuel Pearce Documents', *BQ* 18.1 (January 1959), 30.

Secondly, Taylor and Fuller shared a commitment to a particular methodology as they argued their respective cases. Taylor's own commitment to a careful weighing of the evidence was explicitly stated,

> It is the glory of Christianity, that it imposes nothing upon man, without evidence; but appeals to our reason, understanding and conscience, for the truth and importance of what it recommends to our faith and practice... One excellency of [Fuller's] performance is the unreservedness with which he declares his sentiments, and intimates his desire to have them sincerely examined; and that one reason why his friends advised the publication of it was 'to invite a spirit of impartial enquiry'. This is speaking and acting like a man who wishes truth to be discovered.[148]

Here was Taylor emphasising the importance of 'reason' and commending Fuller for encouraging 'impartial' public 'enquiry' in the pursuit of 'truth'. He followed up this statement by carefully examining and weighing all the evidence relative to the dispute. For his part Fuller, in a *Defence of a Treatise*, stated, '[Taylor] has examined with freedom what I have advanced [and] I respect him for so doing. I can, with the less fear of offence, use a like freedom in return.'[149] The two men shared a commitment to the pursuit of truth through impartial enquiry ('let us remember, truth itself is of the greatest importance') and their approach was a 'scientific' one, in which 'hypotheses' could be exposed to all sorts of tests to examine their truthfulness ('neither of us ought to take his own hypothesis for granted').[150] This, again, smacked of enlightened thinking.

Thirdly, Fuller and Taylor displayed a common concern for 'practical' religion. Their mutual hatred of controversy for its own sake and their commitment to gospel ministry and to invitational evangelistic preaching regularly surfaced. These emphases were allied with a significant degree of pragmatism in religious matters. Taylor argued that the 'success...which has generally attended [the] free manner of addressing sinners' was a sure sign that this was the right approach. Indeed, it was 'a proof in fact, which nothing in theory [could] withstand, that God approves of, and owns this method of preaching; and is glorified by it'.[151] In other words, because 'gospel invitations' worked, that was good evidence they were right. In Fuller's reply to 'Philanthropos' he stated that he did not believe that success on its own could be proof 'of the goodness of a doctrine', although he allowed that it should be given considerable weight. He then proceeded to argue that those Taylor termed 'inconsistent Calvinists', namely Calvinists who 'offered Christ' in their preaching, were at least as successful in

---

[148] Taylor, *Observations on the...Gospel of Christ Worthy*, 8. Cf. 12, 'The pious and candid spirit with which he appears to submit his performance to public examination, greatly endears him to me.'

[149] *Defence of a Treatise*, in *Works*, 2: 459.

[150] Both these quotations are from *Defence of a Treatise*, in *Works*, 2: 481, 511.

[151] Taylor, *Observations on the...Gospel of Christ Worthy*, 4-5.

gospel ministry, if not more so, than Arminians![152] It hardly needs stating that this line of argument would have been anathema to both Button and Martin, indeed to all high Calvinists.

In a 1963 DPhil thesis Olin C. Robison analyses the differences between Gill and 'those in his tradition' on the one hand, and the eighteenth-century evangelical Particular Baptists on the other. Gill was a 'scholastic' and a 'systematizer'. 'He felt that God's laws...could be put down in orderly statements and in this effort he spent the major part of his time, both in pulpit and study.' By contrast, the evangelical Calvinists were far more concerned with 'practical piety', with the call to repentance and 'with truth primarily as an instrument to lead men to God'. It was not so much the 'reasons for God's actions' but 'what God did in the lives of men' that was important. Moreover, if Gill 'had moved in a theological world which owed more than it realized to the medieval scholastics', the eighteenth-century evangelical Calvinists, with their conception of religious truths as 'few, simple in their form and essentially practical in their application', owed more 'than perhaps they cared to concede' to the Enlightenment.[153]

This is extremely perceptive, not least because Robison made these comments at a time when making connections between religious and cultural movements was less common than it is today. Moreover, when Robison was writing evangelicalism was often regarded as a reaction against the Enlightenment, rather than a movement that was embedded in it. David Bebbington in his *Evangelicalism in Modern Britain* has now shown at length that eighteenth-century evangelicals were influenced by certain Enlightenment traits.[154] Fuller is – I submit – a particularly good illustration of that Enlightenment influence. He leant on Jonathan Edwards's *Freedom of the Will*, as shown in chapter three and, as discussed briefly there, this work was shot through with Enlightenment thinking. Moreover, his debate with Taylor, who must also be considered as 'enlightened', further illuminates his indebtedness to the prevailing cultural mood. Fuller's approach to theology was moulded by various Enlightenment presuppositions and ways of arguing.

Yet before concluding we need to return again to the overarching commitment to scripture which was characteristic of Fuller. Taylor shared this commitment. A comment from the New Connexion leader regarding the use of quotations from 'great men' to prove a point (that 'how great soever they were, their writings are not Scripture') entirely mirrored Fuller's own views. It was, Taylor insisted (and again Fuller agreed), the 'infallible book' that counted.[155] Both men wanted to maintain a thoroughgoing biblicism, and comments like the

---

[152] *Defence of a Treatise*, in *Works*, 2: 509.
[153] Olin C. Robison, 'The Particular Baptists in England: 1760-1820' (unpublished DPhil thesis, University of Oxford, 1963), 35-36.
[154] Bebbington, *Evangelicalism in Modern Britain*, 51-74.
[155] Taylor, *Observations on the...Gospel of Christ Worthy*, 35. Cf. Fuller's comments, *Defence of a Treatise*, in *Works*, 2, 421, 442, 456-57.

ones cited in this paragraph pepper both their works. Such a commitment is not anti-Enlightenment; indeed, going back to the Bible rather than relying on quotations from 'great men' was, in many ways, enlightened thinking. But the desire to be biblical transcended the Enlightenment and this was primary for Fuller. He was influenced by cultural trends, but he sought, first and foremost, to be true to the biblical witness. Of course, Fuller and Taylor could not agree on what the biblical witness actually was. Yet for both of them, examining the scriptures was primary.

Conclusion

Following his move to Kettering, Fuller's ministry developed significantly. Being pastor of the 'Little Meeting' opened a pathway to 'greater usefulness', especially providing a context in which he could engage fully in evangelical ministry, both in Kettering and further afield. His theology continued to develop alongside his preaching. His thinking 'did not remain static' after 1785, but carried on developing as he modified his views on the extent of the atonement in debate with Dan Taylor.[156] As he developed as a theologian he was influenced by the Enlightenment. Morris declared of Fuller,

> He burst asunder the enslaving fetters of human dogmas, emancipated himself from their paralysing influence on his researches after truth, and taking the word of God alone for his guide, he determined to call no man master upon earth, but to follow, with a firm and cautious step, the dictates of an enlightened understanding.[157]

The language is overblown but it is also perceptive. Fuller threw off the 'dogma' of high Calvinism and pursued the truth with an 'enlightened understanding'. However, he never forgot his avowed commitment to take the 'word of God' as his guide.

---

[156] Robert W. Oliver, 'Andrew Fuller and Abraham Booth', in *'At The Pure Fountain of Thy Word'*, 203.
[157] Morris, *Fuller*, 1st edn, 270-71.

CHAPTER 5

Suffering and Service: The Journey to the Founding of the BMS

It is well...

The period 1782-92 was crucial to Fuller's life and career. As we have seen, during these years he developed his ministry as an evangelical local church pastor and became well known and respected among the churches of the Northamptonshire Association. He also established a significant reputation as a writer, publishing the seminal *Gospel Worthy of All Acceptation* and defending its leading ideas against high Calvinists on the one side and Arminians on the other. By 1792 he was the leading advocate for evangelical Calvinism in the Particular Baptist denomination and his ability as a theologian was increasingly recognised by Christians in other groupings too.

Yet more needs to be said, for the period in question also saw Fuller and his friends become increasingly committed to the spread of the gospel around the globe. This commitment was fed by wider reading and manifested itself firstly in prayer and then in action. The 'Particular Baptist Society for Propagating the Gospel Among the Heathen' (henceforth the BMS) was founded in Kettering, on 2 October 1792. This was a development of huge significance.[1] This chapter covers the beginnings of the BMS and analyses Fuller's vital role in the setting up of the new society. It also considers some aspects of his first year as BMS secretary.

Alongside this larger story, the chapter also deals with some more personal issues. One of the avowed aims of this book is to tell its subject's story from the 'inside' as well the 'outside'. Some of Fuller's inner struggles have already been highlighted: his distress under conviction of sin prior to his conversion, the agonies he went through in his final years at Soham and the pain he felt at some of the more intemperate attacks on the *Gospel Worthy*. As already noted, behind the blunt, plain speaking, rather 'stern' exterior lay a deeply sensitive man.[2]

---

[1]   Brian Stanley, *The History of the Baptist Missionary Society, 1792-1992* (Edinburgh: T. & T. Clark, 1992), 1.

[2]   Cf. John Webster Morris, *Memoirs of the Life and Death of the Rev Andrew Fuller*, 2nd edn (London: Wightman and Camp, 1826), 43.

Already shaken by the death of his father (whom he believed had been unconverted) and of three of his children, he would have to face yet further family illness and bereavement. His diary entries indicate that he found these new family tragedies extremely difficult to deal with; in fact, he was almost shattered by them. For a number of years he went through much personal turmoil and passed through a period of profound spiritual depression and, I want to argue, clinical depression too. This chapter, then, goes both wider (the formation of the BMS) and deeper (his own family circumstances, his spirituality and his state of mind). The different dimensions of his personal difficulties will be dealt with first.

Personal Life

Family Illness and Bereavements

Two tragedies especially impacted Fuller between 1782 and 1792. The first of these was the death of a daughter, Sarah, affectionately known as Sally. Sally and her brother, Robert, had survived infancy and the father was deeply attached to them both.[3] On Friday 17 December 1785 he recorded in his diary that his daughter, who had been staying in Northampton at the invitation of Ryland, was 'ill with the measels[sic.]'. Fuller added, 'I think if God should take either of my children from me...I could scarcely sustain it. On this account I have many fears.'[4] At this stage Sally was six years old. Initially, she appeared to recover and in Fuller's entry for 19 December his relief is palpable, 'Bless the Lord, my child is revived tonight!'[5] But his joy was short lived. Sally became unwell again and in the early months of 1786 her condition steadily worsened.[6] Fuller was concerned not only about her physical health but also with her spiritual state and he agonised over whether or not this was secure.[7] Many diary entries could be adduced to show his deep distress at what he correctly guessed

---

3 See John Ryland Jr, *The Work of Faith, the Labour of Love, and the Patience of Hope Illustrated in the Life and Death of the Rev. Andrew Fuller*, 2nd edn (London: Button and Son, 1818), 118, 270, for the two different names for the same daughter. Sally's brother Robert was known as Bobby when he was young. See Diary and Spiritual Thoughts, 31 December 1784. In this account I have used the name Sally for the daughter, to distinguish her from her mother.

4 Diary and Spiritual Thoughts [1784-1801] (Bristol Baptist College) (G 95 b), 17 December 1785. I have constructed this account mainly from Fuller's contemporaneous diary entries. For an alternative, more measured description written after the events described, see Fuller's 'narrative' of Sally's life and death drawn up by Fuller and included in Ryland, *Fuller*, 270-75.

5 Diary and Spiritual Thoughts, 19 December 1785.

6 See, e.g., Diary and Spiritual Thoughts, and the entries headed, 1 – 8 January, 29 January – 5 February, 12 March – 16 April 1786.

7 Diary and Spiritual Thoughts, 28 April 1786.

was a terminal decline, from the frequent references to the failing health of his 'dear little girl'[8] to a simple but poignant, 'Lord help me!'[9] At one point he threw himself on the floor and 'wept exceedingly', crying desperately to God in prayer.[10] With his daughter close to death he himself became ill with what Morris described as 'an agony of grief'. In this state he contracted a fever that 'confined him to bed for several days.'[11] Watching his beloved daughter wasting away had weakened him to the extent he had become physically ill himself.

Sally finally died on the morning of 30 May 1786. In his diary Fuller wrote of the moment he heard the news,

> I heard as I lay very ill in bed in another room I heard [sic.] a whispering – I enquired...and all were silent...all were silent! but all is well! I feel reconciled to God! I called my family around my bed – I sat up & prayed as well as I could – I bowed my head and worshipped, and blessed a taking as well as a giving God.[12]

The shaky grammar and the repetition of 'I heard' conveys a little of his state of mind. His worship of a 'taking as well as a giving God' says something powerful about his Christianity and his determination – in the words of his 1784 Association sermon – to 'walk by faith' whatever the circumstances. Nevertheless, one almost senses he was trying to convince himself as he wrote 'all is well' in a shaky hand. There would be many times in the ensuing months when his diary would convey a rather different picture, with phrases such as 'all is well' conspicuous by their absence.

Sally's funeral took place on 1 June, with Ryland travelling from Northampton to preach. He spoke from 2 Kings 4.26 and the words of the Shunamite woman who had lost her son, 'It is well'. The phrase echoes the 'all is well' of Fuller's 30 May diary entry and it is possible the Kettering pastor asked his friend to preach on them, although I have not found direct evidence for this. Alternatively, Ryland may have deemed them appropriate as the Shunamite woman was one of the models of exemplary trust in God Fuller had cited in his 'Walking by Faith' message.[13] Whatever the truth of the matter, Ryland's choice of text was apposite, although Fuller almost missed hearing it expounded: he was so struck with illness and grief he was 'scarcely able' to attend the funeral.[14] Yet, as he continued to wrestle with his feelings he believed he was

---

[8] Diary and Spiritual Thoughts, 12 – 19 February 1786.
[9] Diary and Spiritual Thoughts, 12 March – 16 April 1786. Cf. his reference to 'heart-rending grief', Ryland, *Fuller*, 273.
[10] Ryland, *Fuller*, 274.
[11] Morris, *Fuller*, 2nd edn, 42; Ryland, *Fuller*, 274.
[12] Diary and Spiritual Thoughts, 30 May 1786.
[13] Diary and Spiritual Thoughts, 1 June 1786.
[14] Andrew Gunton Fuller, *Men Worth Remembering: Andrew Fuller* (London: Hodder and Stoughton, 1882), 64.

attaining a measure of calm,[15] not least because he had gained some assurance about his daughter's 'soul'. On that score at least he believed that all really was 'well'. On 3 June he wrote some lines which articulate that assurance, whilst also speaking of his ongoing struggle and grief.

> Surely her sorrows now to joy are turned,
> Yes, sure her infant cries were heard and sped,
> Her tender hopes, to blest fruition changed,
> And all her fears in disappointment fled.
>
> But must we part? – and, can I bid farewel[sic.]?
> We must – I can – I have – I kissed her dust –
> I kissed the clay-cold corpse, and bid farewel,
> Until the resurrection of the just.[16]

Fuller believed that Sally's cries had been 'heard' by God and he further believed he would see her again at 'the resurrection of the just'. This hope provided strength and comfort. Yet his distress, most obviously invoked in the image of him kissing her 'clay cold corpse', is clear enough, as it had been earlier in the poem when he spoke of receiving a 'wound' too 'deep for earth to cure'.[17] Elsewhere he recorded that seeing her in the open coffin had been 'almost too much' for him in his 'weak and afflicted state'.[18] Fuller would try to look to God as his source of healing, yet the death of his 'beloved' Sally would cast a shadow over his life for many years to come.

There were other bereavements that affected Fuller. In March 1791 he lost his friend and mentor, Robert Hall. The Kettering pastor delivered the funeral oration at the graveside, with his address full of the 'deepest emotion'.[19] The death of Beeby Wallis on 2 April 1792 was another severe blow. Wallis, as Gunton Fuller stated, 'had been the principle means of introducing...Fuller to Kettering'.[20] These men were not family in the strict sense, but they were father figures to whom the Kettering pastor was greatly attached.[21] Neither Hall nor Wallis wavered in their commitment to their younger friend. With their passing two of Fuller's most important props had been taken away, leaving him feeling

---

[15] Morris, *Fuller*, 2nd edn, 42.

[16] Morris, *Fuller*, 2nd edn, 43. For the date of composition, see Diary and Spiritual Thoughts, 3 June 1786.

[17] Morris, *Fuller*, 2nd edn, 43.

[18] Ryland, *Fuller*, 275.

[19] Gunton Fuller, *Fuller*, 65.

[20] Gunton Fuller, *Fuller*, 66. Cf. Morris, *Fuller*, 2nd edn, 45.

[21] The sermon Fuller preached at Wallis's funeral was published as *The Blessedness of the Dead who Die in the Lord...* (London: Dilly, 1792) and is printed in *The Complete Works of the Rev. Andrew Fuller, With a Memoir of his Life by the Rev. Andrew Gunton Fuller*, ed. by Andrew Gunton Fuller, rev. ed. by Joseph Belcher; 3 vols, 3rd edn (Harrisonburg, VA: Sprinkle Publications, 1988 [1845]), 1: 152-60.

decidedly unsteady. From this point on Ryland and Sutcliff would become even more important as people to lean on. But, significant as the deaths of these older friends were, there was a severer trial yet to come.

On 10 July 1792 Fuller recorded in his diary that his wife, his 'dear companion', was very ill.[22] There were physical problems brought on by multiple pregnancies and at this stage Sarah was pregnant yet again. But the main symptoms described denote severe mental illness. Although most of the material relating to this focuses on 1792, Ryland wrote of her 'frequent afflictions' and it is likely she had struggled with issues of mental health, at least periodically, for a number of years.[23] On 9 July 1792 Fuller wrote to Ryland of Sarah's 'hysterical complaints' observing that through the night she had been 'as destitute of reason as an infant'. At this point he hoped his wife's 'derangement' was 'temporary' but still feared for the immediate future. He wrote to Ryland saying he felt a 'habitual calmness' despite the situation,[24] but the reader of his diary entries might conclude otherwise. The next few months would be exceedingly difficult.

A letter Fuller sent to Sarah's father gives some distressing detail on her illness. She thought she would lose her remaining children and perhaps her husband too. Fuller stated that,

> For one whole day, she hung about my neck, weeping, for that I was going to die, and leave her. The next morning, she still retained the same persuasion; but, instead of weeping for it, she rejoiced with exceeding joy. – 'My husband (said she,) is going to heaven…and all is well!...I shall be provided for &c… Till very lately she has been so desirous of my company, that it has been with much difficulty that I have stolen away from her…[25]

Fuller himself became unwell, as he had been during their daughter's illness, writing to Ryland of severe chest pains. He was 'bled', a treatment still in use in the eighteenth century to 'draw out' a disease or illness.[26] Then Sarah's illness took an even more distressing turn. In his letter to her father Fuller wrote that, from late July,

> She…considered me as an imposter, who had entered the house, and taken possession of the keys of every place, and of all that belonged to her and her husband! She has been fully persuaded, that she was *not at home*; but had wandered somewhere from it, had lost herself, and fallen among strangers! She constantly

---

[22] Diary and Spiritual Thoughts, 10 July 1792.
[23] Ryland, *Fuller*, 285. Sarah's final illness appears to have begun in late May 1792. See 'Fuller letter to Mr Gardiner (Sarah's father)', 25 August 1792, in Ryland, *Fuller*, 286.
[24] Fuller letter to John Ryland, 9 July 1792, in Ryland, *Fuller*, 286.
[25] Fuller letter to Mr Gardiner, 25 August 1792, in Ryland, *Fuller*, 287. The same letter is included in Andrew Gunton Fuller, 'Memoir', in *Works*, 1: 59-61.
[26] Fuller letter to John Ryland, 9 July 1792, in Ryland, *Fuller*, 286. The 'treatment' was either useless or harmful in almost every case.

wanted to make her escape; on which account we were obliged to keep the doors locked, and to take away the keys. 'No! (she would say to me with a countenance full of inexpressible anguish) This is not my home...you are not my husband...these are not my children. Once, I had a good home...and a husband who loved me...and dear children...[27]

She walked from room to room in a desperately agitated state, moaning and wringing her hands. Sarah was suffering from serious mental illness in an era when this was little understood. The lack of security afforded to women in the late-eighteenth century, hinted at by her fear of losing her husband and being left destitute, was surely a factor, and the ravages of childbirth and the deaths of many of her children were other obvious contributing causes. Although she did not seem to know her living children, she had a 'lively remembrance' of those she had lost.[28] On one occasion she escaped from the house and was found by the family servant in the church's graveyard, looking in anguish at her children's graves, scraping frantically and obsessively at the inscriptions to wipe away grass and dirt.[29] The fears of what would become of her unborn child as her pregnancy progressed can scarcely be imagined. Some of the words her husband used as he wrote of his wife's illness – 'hysterical affections', 'deprived of her senses', 'wild despair'[30] – could grate on modern readers who are used to using different terms to describe mental illness, but the evidence suggests Fuller loved his wife and sought to care for her as best he knew. The couple were granted one brief interlude during which she was more rational. Fuller recorded an occasion when Sarah was in tears as she tried to obtain the keys to the house by force in order to escape. Andrew started crying too. Then,

> The sight of my tears seemed to awaken her recollections. With her eyes fixed upon me, she said,... 'Why are you *indeed* my husband?' 'Indeed, my dear, I am! 'O! if I thought you were, I could give you a thousand kisses! *Indeed*, my dear, I am your own dear husband! She then seated herself on my knee, and kissed me several times. My heart dissolved, with a mixture of grief and joy. Her senses were restored, and she talked rationally as ever. I then persuaded her to go to rest, and she slept well.[31]

For a twelve hour period there were further good conversations, both with Fuller himself and with Robert, their son. But soon, Fuller stated, her 'senses were gone' again.[32] On 23 August she gave birth to her child, a daughter who was named Bathoni. Physically and mentally exhausted, she died later that same

---

[27] Fuller letter to Mr Gardiner, 25 August 1792, in Ryland, *Fuller*, 287-88.
[28] Fuller letter to Mr Gardiner, 25 August 1792, in Ryland, *Fuller*, 288.
[29] Fuller letter to Mr Gardiner, 25 August 1792, in Ryland, *Fuller*, 288.
[30] Fuller letter to Mr Gardiner, 25 August 1792, in Ryland, *Fuller*, 287-88.
[31] Fuller letter to Mr Gardiner, 25 August 1792, in Ryland, *Fuller*, 288-89.
[32] Fuller letter to Mr Gardiner, 25 August 1792, in Ryland, *Fuller*, 289.

day, with her husband witnessing her final convulsions.[33] The girl had been born alive but survived only for three weeks, bringing the remaining family much further grief.[34]

Such a catalogue of illness and death was not unusual for lower-middle class English families at the end of the eighteenth century, but this broader context does not diminish the tragedy of the situation and should not lessen our sympathy for Sarah, who had endured numerous pregnancies and the death of most of her children. Moreover, it appears she had to cope with her husband's almost complete collapse at the time of Sally's death and, as we shall see, his subsequent depression. What would Sarah's account of her experiences have been, had she left one? In a recent article Matthew Haste helpfully probes dimensions of Fuller's family life, but I do not believe his comment that Fuller was as 'exemplary in his domestic life as he was in his better-known public ministry' stands scrutiny.[35] True, Fuller appears to have been a 'devoted father' and husband,[36] just as Sarah appears to have been a devoted mother and wife, her breakdown notwithstanding. Yet the evidence of life in the Kettering manse is too incomplete and fragmentary for confident judgments to be made about its 'exemplary' nature. Moreover, the evidence that is available points to a far more complex situation than Haste allows. What can be affirmed is that Fuller sought to live out his Christian faith in private as well as in public, and he tried to do his best for his wife and daughter whilst frequently failing (by his own testimony) in that aim. What can also be said is that his life was deeply marked by personal tragedy. In the previous chapter it was Fuller the influential preacher, theologian and Christian leader who was predominantly in view. What we see from this more personal material is that his progress as a minister took place through the midst of much suffering.

Inner Struggles

To complete the picture of his suffering during this period of his life, it is important to grasp the extent to which Fuller despaired internally in the early years of his Kettering ministry. His personal diary paints a bleak picture. Whilst at Soham he had sometimes questioned his own salvation. He wrote on 12 September 1780,

> Very much in doubt respecting my being in a state of grace... The Lord have mercy on me, for I know not how it is with me. One thing I know, that if I be a Christian at all, real Christianity in me is inexpressibly small in degree. O what a vast distance is there between what I ought to be, and what I am! If I am a saint at all, I

---

[33] Gunton Fuller, *Fuller*, 67.

[34] Ryland, *Fuller*, 291.

[35] Matthew Haste, 'Marriage and Family Life of Andrew Fuller', *Southern Baptist Journal of Theology* 17.1 (2013), 28.

[36] Haste, 'Marriage and Family Life of Andrew Fuller', 28-30 (28).

know I am one of the least of all saints. I mean, that the workings of real grace in my soul are so feeble, that I hardly think they can be feebler in any true Christian... I think of late, I cannot in prayer consider myself as a Christian, but as a sinner casting myself at Christ's feet for mercy.[37]

The first and final sentences of this extract express significant doubt as to his eternal security. It is perhaps not surprising that he had these thoughts at Soham as he wrestled with high Calvinistic theology with its tendency to lack of assurance, yet the diary gives ample evidence that doubt and struggle remained keynotes of his inner life at Kettering too. He does not explicitly doubt his salvation in the diary entries from 1784 onwards (at least in those which survive), but he does come very close on a number of occasions and is repeatedly negative about his own spirituality.[38] On 29 November 1784 he wrote,

Much dispirited, on account of my carnal-mindedness and perpetual propensity to depart from God. My life seems to have been one continued series of departures from God... The sins of my life are many; but the sin of my nature seems to be but one – one continual disposition to do evil, and aversion to draw near to God.[39]

At the turn of 1784 / 1785 his comments were briefer but, if anything, the language was stronger. 'What good I have done I scarcely know. Great has been my sin against God. I feel myself a vile wretch!'[40] A series of entries made between 3 and 6 June show him very 'low' and 'depressed' over a period of days. He felt 'guilty' because of his 'vain wandering heart'; 'O I tremble at myself!' he exclaimed.[41] 'Darkness and confusion of mind' overwhelmed him[42] and his 'sorrow of heart' was so great he began to feel physically ill.[43] It appears that on many occasions his mental stress was so great it manifested itself in physical illness, with Fuller experiencing chest pains, fevers and vomiting. There were many disturbed nights. He confided in his diary that he had terrible nightmares, dreaming, for example, that he had 'fallen into some great wickedness' following which he had been publicly exposed as a terrible sinner, his life and ministry irrevocably ruined.[44] His final surviving diary entry for 1786 was made on Sunday 11 June, at which point the diary abruptly breaks off. The next entry is dated 3 October 1789, over three years later. Ryland recorded that between sixteen to eighteen leaves had been torn out of the original volume (presumably by

[37] Ryland, *Fuller*, 78.
[38] For example, see Diary and Spiritual Thoughts, 8 June 1784, 'feel myself a poor, barren stupid wretch'; 26 June 1784, 'I find a great deal of sluggishness... Have gone thro' the day with very little if any spirituality!'
[39] Diary and Spiritual Thoughts, 29 November 1784.
[40] Diary and Spiritual Thoughts, 1 January 1785.
[41] Diary and Spiritual Thoughts, 3 June 1785.
[42] Diary and Spiritual Thoughts, 6 June 1785.
[43] Diary and Spiritual Thoughts, 5 June 1785. Cf. 6 June 1785.
[44] Diary and Spiritual Thoughts, 31 October 1785.

Fuller himself),[45] but in his 3 October 1789 entry the Kettering pastor also confessed to have written nothing for 'upwards of a year and a half'. The reason for this, he said, was that 'it seemed to me that my life was not worth writing', characterised as it was by 'lukewarmness' and 'carnality'.[46] Looking back on this period eight years later, in a letter sent to John Thomas (1757-1801) in India, he wrote of 'a deep dejection' that had gripped him, which, although he 'strove to throw it off in company', soon returned when he was in private.[47]

It is important to be aware that his diary does not necessarily give a totally rounded picture of his spiritual life. Bruce Hindmarsh, in his study of John Newton, comments that because his subject's diary was used as a means of 'disciplined self examination' in the Puritan tradition, its confessional and sometimes 'self recriminatory' tone may not have been reflective of his spirituality as a whole.[48] In other words, taken on its own, the diary is likely to be a distortion of Newton's spiritual life, a distortion created by the medium itself. The same is probably true for Fuller and Hindmarsh's words of caution need to be born in mind. Most likely the Kettering pastor's state of mind was sometimes brighter than the extracts above, and others like them, would lead one to believe. Nevertheless his letter to Thomas written years later confirms the impression given by the diary. There seems little reason to doubt that in the years 1782-92, whilst his public ministry flourished, Fuller was often struggling in his Christian faith. Furthermore, from the middle of 1786 for three years he experienced spiritual depression, a 'dark night of the soul'.[49] The evidence also indicates he was suffering from some form of clinical depression during this three year period. That evidence includes terrible dreams, bouts of insomnia, dramatic mood swings, frequent tears and despair that was so deep and pervasive it led to physical illness. Spiritual depression and clinical depression were closely intertwined in Fuller and it is hard to treat them separately. Consequently, the following analysis considers reasons for his depression, with spiritual and clinical aspects taken together.

---

[45] Ryland, *Fuller*, 119. This is not apparent from the rebound Diary and Spiritual Thoughts.

[46] Diary and Spiritual Thoughts, 3 October 1789.

[47] Fuller Letter to John Thomas, 16 May 1796, in Ryland, *Fuller*, 159. Thomas was, like Fuller, prone to depression. As we will see, he and William Carey were the first missionaries to be sent out by the BMS. For Thomas's life, see Charles B. Lewis, *The Life of John Thomas* (London: MacMillan, 1873).

[48] *John Newton and the English Evangelical Tradition: Between the Conversions of Wesley and Wilberforce* (Oxford: Clarenden Press, 1996), 222.

[49] The phrase, 'Dark night of the soul' is from John of the Cross. For a classic treatment of spiritual depression from an evangelical perspective, see D. Martyn Lloyd Jones, *Spiritual Depression: its Causes and Cures* (Glasgow: Pickering & Inglis, 1965).

Reasons for his Depression

Why did Fuller feel this way about himself and his relationship with God? As we might expect, the evidence of the diary suggests that the various illnesses and deaths of close family and friends were a primary factor. In particular, the death of his daughter in 1786 was a trigger for his period of deepest depression and his sense of distance from God. Fuller comes close to recognising this himself, saying that it was after Sally died that his heart began 'wretchedly to degenerate from God'.[50] His wife's failing health also triggered deep despair. On 25 July 1792 he wrote in his diary,

> O my God, my soul is cast down within me! The afflictions in my family seem too heavy for me. O Lord, I am oppressed, undertake for me! My thoughts are broken off, and all my prospects seem to be perished! I feel however some support, from such Scriptures as these 'All things work together for good, &c. God, even our own God, shall bless us. It is of the Lord's mercies that we are not consumed.' One of my friends observed, yesterday, that it was difficult, in many cases, to know <u>wherefore</u> God contended with us. But I tho't that was no difficulty of this kind with me! I have sinned against the Lord; and it is not a little affliction that will lay hold of me… Those words have impressed me of late, 'It was in my heart to chastise them.'[51]

The opening words of Fuller's extract are redolent of some of the so-called imprecatory Psalms, such as Psalm 88. Fuller expressed himself in strong terms as he bewailed his family's multiple 'afflictions', which were the stated cause of his desperate cries to God. Because of a series of calamities he felt 'oppressed' and without hope. He found some 'support' from scripture, but the verse he ended with is not one of the verses of comfort and encouragement he cited, for example, 'God, even our own God, shall bless us',[52] but the sterner, 'It was in my heart to chastise them'.[53] Fuller believed God was 'chastising' him for his sins by bringing illness and death on his family. True, he did not openly doubt his own salvation and he did not believe God had abandoned him or those closest to him; yet he was sure God was sending illness and difficulty because of his sin, which deserved 'not a little affliction'. It appears his spirituality at this stage of his life was a factor feeding his depression. The series of family tragedies combined with the way he related to God to pile agony upon agony.

What were the influences on Fuller's personal spirituality? Sixteenth- and seventeenth-century Puritanism was important. As has already been noted, Fuller's habit of keeping a confessional diary was rooted in the Puritan soil from which the English Particular Baptists had sprung. For the Puritans, the confessional diary was an important tool helping the 'godly' to engage in de-

---

[50] Diary and Spiritual Thoughts, 3 October 1789.
[51] Diary and Spiritual Thoughts, 25 July 1792.
[52] Psalm 67.6. Fuller also cited Romans 8.28 and Lamentations 3.22.
[53] Probably Hosea 10.10, 'It is in my desire that I should chastise them…'

tailed, rigorous self-examination. People who had made professions of faith were encouraged to examine themselves for evidence they were truly part of the elect, recording their reflections in their journals. Such self-examination would most likely be hard work, with a positive outcome as far as assurance was concerned far from certain. According to the Puritan divine Thomas Brooks, the Christian who wanted to attain assurance of salvation 'must work, and sweat and weep... He must not only dig, but he must dig deep before he can come to the golden mine. Assurance is such precious gold, that a man must win it before he can wear it.'[54] Some of the classic expressions of the Puritan struggle for assurance are found in the writings of John Bunyan, for example in *Grace Abounding to the Chief of Sinners*, which Fuller had read.[55] Even if assurance was at last attained, continued self-examination was encouraged in order to sustain growth in godliness. Fuller's diary provides ample evidence of his own commitment to protracted self-examination.[56] He looked inside himself for evidence of growth in godliness and believed there was very little; rather his self-examination seemed to suggest he was a vile sinner, repeatedly and habitually rebelling against God.

Fuller was never really specific in his diary about what his sins might have been. Most often he wrote about feeling 'cold' towards God, although he also mentioned a tendency to make an idol of his daughter and to have his head turned by his growing fame as a writer. It is easy for many twenty-first century readers to dismiss these thoughts as trivial and even ridiculous, but Fuller believed that his strong sense of sin and its consequences was embedded in the Bible's own thought world. Moreover, an awareness of what Jeremiah Burroughs called the 'exceeding sinfulness of sin' was an important dimension of Puritan spirituality that had carried over into Particular Baptist life.[57] Fuller was sure he had sinned and that God was chastising him for this. These beliefs and feelings fed both his 'dark night' experience and his clinical depression. Some dimensions of Puritan spirituality – as he interpreted them – fused with other factors to contribute to his depression.

However, we need to consider high Calvinism if we are to understand more completely Fuller's spirituality and the way it contributed to his state of mind. This is because it is a high Calvinistic mutation of Puritan themes that his diary

---

54 Thomas Brooks, *Heaven on Earth* (London: Banner of Truth, 1961 [1654]), 139. Cf. the discussion in David W. Bebbington, *Evangelicalism in Modern Britain: A history from the 1730s to the 1980s* (London: Unwin Hyman, 1989), 42-47.
55 John Bunyan, *Grace Abounding to the Chief of Sinners* (Harmondsworth, Middlesex: Penguin, 1987 [1666]), paragraphs 59-61, 19; paragraph 78, 23.
56 Systematically at the beginning of every new year, although at many other times too. See Diary and Spiritual Thoughts, 1 January 1784, 1 January 1785, 1 January 1786. Many other entries already cited in this chapter are also relevant.
57 Jeremiah Burroughs, *Evil of Evils; or, the Exceeding Sinfulness of Sin* (London: Goodwin, Nye *et al*, 1654).

most often reveals. It is true that by the mid-1780s he had broken with high Calvinistic theology and its accompanying 'non-invitation, non-application' approach to preaching. Yet, as the Kettering pastor took his leave of high Calvinism, it was the spirituality associated with it that he found hardest to shake off. High Calvinism had taken a number of the Puritan emphases and developed them in ways that would have distressed most of the seventeenth-century godly. The balance and pastoral concern which characterised the best of Puritan spirituality was lost. Puritans contended for 'experiential' spirituality and so feelings were important, but feelings were to be grounded on the objective truths of scripture. In high Calvinism, the subjective tended to overpower the objective. Considerable importance was attached to dreams and this, as we have seen, was the case with Fuller. The overriding stress he placed on feelings as a barometer by which spirituality is measured is one of the most striking features of Fuller's diary when it is viewed in the round. If he felt some 'tenderness' in preaching or in administering the Lord's supper, that was recorded as a positive sign of spiritual life;[58] if he felt 'cold', that was noted as a negative and taken as a sure sign of spiritual deadness.[59] The cold feelings engendered further negative reflections about his spiritual life and were the cause of much self-recrimination. They locked Fuller into a downward spiral from which – for a time – he found it impossible to escape.

Fuller's own temperament is important as well. He was a deep thinker who also felt with a real intensity. As has been noted at different points in the narrative, behind the phlegmatic exterior was a man of tender conscience and strong emotions. Sometimes these emotions broke out into the open, for example on the occasions he wept in the pulpit. But most often they were hidden from all but his closest friends. His feelings in the 1780s sometimes swung from one extreme to another in the course of a few days, with joy and despair both passionately felt. Even his better days were emotionally charged and most likely exhausting. Sunday 26 June 1785 was, he confided in his diary, one of the best days he had experienced for 'years'. In the morning service he preached on the grace of God from Acts 4.33, 'Great grace was upon them all'. His feeling that God was with him was so overwhelming he wept copiously during his message, so much so that it was only with great difficulty that he finished his sermon.[60] Such ecstasy came with a price however and, fairly predictably, by the following Wednesday he was 'very low and unhappy' again.[61] Such mood swings were not untypical, although in the period following 1786 it appears his darker feelings almost completely eclipsed any sense of joy.

The material in the previous paragraph, together with other material in this chapter, suggests Fuller had an inbuilt tendency to depression. Depression can

---

[58] *Diary and Spiritual Thoughts*, 23 September 1784.
[59] *Diary and Spiritual Thoughts*, 12 October 1784.
[60] *Diary and Spiritual Thoughts*, 26 June 1785.
[61] *Diary and Spiritual Thoughts*, 29 June 1785.

be reactive, when circumstances become too much for a person. Such depression is transient and when circumstances change the suffering lifts. The second form of depressive illness is endogenous (that is, from the inside), with the root cause an imbalance of brain chemicals. Although it can be brought on by a tragic event and exacerbated by other traumas, endogenous depression is likely to remain even when these trigger factors are removed. I find the evidence that Fuller suffered from a form of endogenous depression compelling. Although his 1786 illness was triggered by Sally's death, it remained for many years. Thinking of him as someone who battled endogenous depression sheds new light on the man and his ministry.[62]

To sum up, Fuller's dark night experience and struggles with depression were made up of a number of strands that became closely interwoven in his experience. These included traumatic family tragedies which were intensely felt and which drained both his emotional and physical energy. In particular, the illness and death of his daughter, Sally, was a specific trigger for a subsequent period of depression. Personal temperament was another strand and this temperament included – I contend – a predisposition to clinical depression. Spirituality was also important. He turned to his faith for comfort and instead found 'chastisement'; he focused on his own feelings as a litmus test of his relationship with God rather than looking to the promises of God and the gospel. This was a high Calvinistic spirituality, rooted in the Puritan spirituality of an earlier era though significantly different from mainstream Puritanism. As a result of the coming together of these different factors the years 1782-92 were very difficult for Fuller personally, with the period 1786-89 especially miserable. To consider that against this background he played such a prominent role in church ministry, in Association life and as a published author is little short of astonishing. Probably he found his work a release and – to a degree – was therapeutic. Certainly he found his growing interest in world mission gave him another focus. It is to this last development that we now turn.

Fuller and the Founding of the BMS

Fuller had a crucial role in generating the momentum which resulted in the BMS being founded. He was not, however, the most important figure in the genesis of the Society. This position belongs to William Carey, as both Ryland[63] and Fuller himself freely acknowledged. 'The origins of the society', the Kettering pastor said, 'will be found in the workings of our brother Carey's mind.'[64] Carey and Fuller first met at the 1782 Northamptonshire Association

---

[62] Cf. my very similar comments in respect of Charles Haddon Spurgeon, Peter J. Morden, *'Communion with Christ and His People:' The Spirituality of C.H. Spurgeon* (Oxford: Regent's Park, 2010 / Eugene, OR: Wipf and Stock, 2014), 261-62.

[63] Ryland, *Fuller*, 147-48.

[64] *Periodical Accounts Relative to the Baptist Missionary Society*, vol. 1 (Clipstone: J.W. Morris, 1800 [1794]), 1. See also Ernest F. Clipsham, 'Andrew Fuller and the

meeting at Olney, when Carey was only twenty-one years old and 'still feeling his way to the Baptist position'.[65] Evidence that Fuller had a particularly important role in the theological formation of the younger man is lacking. It was Robert Hall's *Help to Zion's Travellers* which was the crucial extra-biblical work that shaped Carey's own evangelical Calvinism. 'I do not remember ever to have read a book with such raptures,' he said, and years later he was to inform Fuller that 'its doctrines are the choice of my heart to this day'.[66] So, by the time the *Gospel Worthy* was published, Carey had already imbibed the warm evangelical Calvinism by then prevalent amongst the leading figures of the Northamptonshire Association. Nevertheless, Fuller did make a significant theological contribution to the formation of the BMS and he was an important figure in other ways in the run up to 1792. His theological contribution will be considered first.

Fuller's Theological Contribution to the Foundation of the BMS

Fuller was central in shaping the theological climate which enabled the seed thoughts about overseas mission to fall on fertile soil. The shift that had taken place in Particular Baptist life in Fuller's own county, Northamptonshire, can be taken as an example of a trend that was also impacting the denomination elsewhere. By the mid- to late-1780s Particular Baptist life in Northamptonshire was generally marked by a vigorous and evangelistically minded evangelical Calvinism, significantly different to the high Calvinistic theology which has been in the ascendant only thirty years previously. Evidence for this change comes from a letter by Fuller detailing 'the state of religion in Northamptonshire'. Although this was written in 1793, it reflected trends in Northamptonshire Particular Baptist life that had been established earlier.[67] This letter indicated that Fuller's own brand of Evangelical Calvinism had all but triumphed in the county. Out of 21 Particular Baptist churches, there were still 4 or 5 which embraced 'what is called the High Calvinist scheme'. These included the Rushden church pastored by William Knowles, the fellowship who opposed Fuller soon after the *Gospel Worthy* was first published. But the majority, according to Fuller, made 'no scruple' about openly 'exhorting' people to believe

---

Baptist Mission', *Foundations*, 10.1 (January, 1967), 4. Clipsham attempts what he terms a 'tentative appraisal' of Fuller's role in the BMS in this brief, but suggestive study.

[65] Ernest A. Payne, *The Prayer Call of 1784* (London: Kingsgate Press, 1941), 4.
[66] Eustace Carey, *Memoir of William Carey, DD* (London: Jackson and Walford, 1836), 15-16. Carey probably read *Help to Zion's Travellers* in 1782-3.
[67] Geoffrey F. Nuttall, 'The State of Religion in Northamptonshire (1793) by Andrew Fuller', *BQ* 29.4 (October 1981), 177-79. All quotations and information in this paragraph and the next are from Fuller's letter and Nuttall's introductory remarks. Fuller was writing here of the churches within the county of Northamptonshire, not the Northamptonshire Association as a whole.

the gospel. The county once associated with the names of Richard Davis and John Gill had come down decisively on the 'affirmative side' of the 'Modern Question'.

The letter also indicated that churches which had embraced what Fuller here termed 'Moderate Calvinism' were growing.[68] Its author wrote of a 'readiness discovered in many parts of the county for hearing the gospel' and of a 'considerable increase' among the churches. Indeed he could be more specific, stating that, 'Seven or eight new churches have been raised amongst [us] within the last 20 years.' There is no reason to doubt the figures Fuller gave, particularly as he expected his correspondent, possibly a General Baptist layman, to publish them. The statistics indicate that something highly significant was occurring. Particular Baptist churches in Northamptonshire were offering the gospel indiscriminately to all and they were increasingly imbued with an expansive evangelistic spirit. In 1793 they were ready to support a risky evangelistic venture such as the BMS. Churches in other counties and cities were ready to do the same. Bristol and the west of England were also ready to lend support. As we will see, so were Particular Baptist churches in the north of England, especially those in the orbit of John Fawcett, the Particular Baptist minister who had been converted under Whitefield's preaching. The time was right for this new and daring venture in Baptist life.

That the theological climate was conducive to the formation and progress of the BMS was obviously not due to Fuller and the *Gospel Worthy* alone. Even if Northamptonshire is considered in isolation, a complex cluster of factors was at work and these factors multiply once the picture is broadened to include the rest of England. There were many others who were promoting views similar to the Kettering pastor's, not least his friends Ryland and Sutcliff and, up to 1791, his mentor Hall. There was also the younger generation represented by Carey. The Bristol tradition represented by Caleb Evans must always be remembered too. Yet Fuller's work was vitally important. The *Gospel Worthy* was the denomination's most developed statement of Edwardsean evangelical Calvinism and it was this theology which underpinned moves towards the formation of the BMS, moves which took place in the Northamptonshire Association. Fuller's theological contribution was significant indeed.

The Prayer Call of 1784

Fuller also played a crucial role in the so-called 'Prayer Call of 1784'. The issuing of this call was an important step towards the founding of the BMS.[69] As already noted, in 1784 ministers of the Northamptonshire Association started

---

[68]   On other occasions he described his own system as 'strict Calvinism'.

[69]   Morris, *Fuller*, 2nd edn, 95-98; Stanley, *History of the BMS*, 4-6. For more detail on the call, see Ernest A. Payne, *The Prayer Call of 1784* (London: Kingsgate Press, 1941); Michael A.G. Haykin, *One Heart and Soul: John Sutcliff of Olney, his Friends and his Times* (Durham: Evangelical Press, 1994), 153-71.

setting aside the second Tuesday of every other month for prayer and fasting. The focus was on prayer for the spread of the gospel around the world. Soon the 'call' was given to churches and monthly prayer meetings were established in many places.

What had prompted Fuller and other ministers of the Association to establish such meetings? A book by Jonathan Edwards is once again essential background. In April 1784 John Ryland received another parcel of evangelical literature from John Erskine in Edinburgh. Amongst the various books and tracts was a treatise written by Edwards entitled *An Humble Attempt to Promote Explicit Agreement and Visible Union of God's People in Extraordinary Prayer*, which had originally been published in 1748.[70] Edwards's *Humble Attempt* was rooted in the movement to establish regular prayer meetings for Revival which had begun in the 1740s and subsequently criss-crossed the Atlantic.[71] The 'Concert of Prayer' actually began in Scotland, where a number of ministers who were part of the growing transatlantic evangelical network along with Edwards, such as John McLaurin of Glasgow and William McCullough of Cambuslang, had committed themselves and their churches to pray for Revival.[72] Edwards sought to set up something similar in New England, and a sermon he preached on the subject in 1747 was later revised, expanded and published as the *Humble Attempt*. Ryland was deeply impressed by what he read and lost no time sending the work to Sutcliff and Fuller.[73]

In the *Humble Attempt* Edwards urged the establishment of regular prayer meetings at which 'fervent and constant' prayer would be offered for the pouring out of the Holy Spirit and the rapid extension of God's Kingdom around the world.[74] He sought to ground his appeal in scripture, but he also referred in detail to his eighteenth-century context. Edwards viewed his age as exhibiting both 'great apostasy' and many 'wonderful works of God'. Examples of 'spiritual calamities' included the persecution of the Huguenots in France and what

---

[70] *The Works of Jonathan Edwards*, ed. by Edward Hickman, 2 vols (Edinburgh: Banner of Truth, 1974 [1834]), 2: 280-312.

[71] On this, see Michael J. Crawford, *Seasons of Grace, Colonial New England's Revival Tradition in its British Context* (Oxford: Oxford University Press, 1991), 229-31.

[72] See Susan O'Brien, 'Eighteenth Century Publishing in Transatlantic Evangelicalism', in *Evangelicalism: Comparative Studies in Popular Protestantism in North America, The British Isles and Beyond, 1700-1990*, ed. by Mark A. Noll, David W. Bebbington and George A. Rawlyk (Oxford: Oxford University Press, 1994), 41, 45, for the transatlantic Evangelical network. Cf. W. Reginald Ward, 'Baptists and the Transformation of the Church, 1780-1830', *BQ* 25.4 (October 1973), 170-71, who refers to what he terms 'the literary freemasonry' of the Revival.

[73] Ryland, *Fuller*, 98 n. The *Memoir* of Edwards by Sereno Dwight, written in 1830, contains a letter from Edwards to Erskine in which he promises to send him a copy of the *Humble Attempt*. See, *Edwards's Works* (Hickman), 2: xcv.

[74] Edwards, *Humble Attempt*, in *Edwards's Works* (Hickman) 2: 312. All the following quotations from the *Humble Attempt* are from 280-312 of this edn.

he saw as a general 'deluge of vice and immorality'; instances of God's works of 'power and mercy' included the British defeat of French forces in North America and, especially, the spiritual Revivals which had occurred in both Europe and the New World. Edwards believed that these 'remarkable religious awakenings...[should] justly encourage us in prayer for the promised glorious and universal outpourings of the Spirit of God.' The balance between divine sovereignty (God sending his Spirit) and human responsibility (the need to appropriate God's blessing through prayer) was typical of Edwards. Yet it is important to underscore how his argument was tied not only to biblical theology but also to his reading of the 'signs of the times'. The *Humble Attempt* was rooted in the cultural, political and ecclesiastical context of the eighteenth century.

A phrase such as 'the promised glorious and universal outpourings of the Spirit of God' is suggestive of Edwards's optimistic post-millennial eschatology, with its accompanying belief in the imminence of 'the latter day glory'. This was allied with some decidedly speculative interpretations of biblical prophecy. According to Edwards, the purity of the Protestant church would be restored between 1750 and 1800, Roman Catholics would come to embrace the gospel between 1800 and 1850 and Christ's millennial reign might well begin round about the year 2000.[75] The Northamptonshire men wanted to distance themselves from these aspects of Edwards's thinking. When Sutcliff brought out an English edition of the *Humble Attempt* in 1789, he took the opportunity to make this explicit. 'As to the author's ingenious observations on the prophecies', he declared, 'we entirely leave them to the reader's judgement'.[76] This is another indication of the independence and, indeed, discernment of Fuller, Ryland and Sutcliff. Nevertheless, broadly speaking they shared Edwards's eschatology. Fuller's own commitment to postmillennialism is shown in his published expositions of Revelation[77] and his postmillennial thinking shows the impress of Edwards's own views.[78] This optimistic Edwardsean postmillennial eschatology proved a great motivation to prayer and action.

Fired by their reading of the *Humble Attempt*, the Association's leading figures were determined to act. They met together on 11 May, a meeting that

---

[75] Edwards, *Humble Attempt*, in *Edwards's Works* (Hickman), e.g., 2: 306. For a detailed discussion of Edwards's millennial views see James A. De Jong, *As The Waters Cover the Sea, Millennial Expectations in the Rise of Anglo-American Missions, 1640-1810* (Kampen: J.H. Kok, 1970), 124-37.

[76] John Sutcliff, Preface to the *Humble Attempt* (1789) in *Edwards's Works* (Hickman), 2: 278-79.

[77] Andrew Fuller's, *Expository Discourses on the Apocalypse, Interspersed with Practical Reflections* were published in 1815. For the text, see *Works*, 3: 201-307.

[78] See Fuller, *Expository Discourses on the Apocalypse* in *Works*, 3: 251, for an explicit reference to the *Humble Attempt*. Edwards's influence of Fuller's eschatology is set out in some detail by Chris Chun, *The Legacy of Jonathan Edwards in the Theology of Andrew Fuller* (Leiden: Brill, 2012), 66-83.

Fuller recorded in his diary thus, 'This day I have devoted to fasting & prayer in conjunction with several other ministers, who have agreed each at home by himself to fast & pray the second Tuesday of every other month, to seek the revival of real religion and the extension of Christ's kingdom in the world.'[79] The real breakthrough, however, came at the annual Association meeting which took place at Nottingham on the 2 and 3 June. This was the Association at which Fuller preached his sermon on *Walking by Faith*.[80] The challenge to prayer he gave has already been considered in chapter four. What has not been mentioned is the way a major part of that challenge related explicitly to prayer for revival,

> Let us take much encouragement, in the present day of small things, by looking forward, and hoping for better days. Let us pray much for an outpouring of God's Spirit upon our ministers and churches, and not upon those only of our own connexion and denomination, but upon all that in every place call upon the name of Jesus Christ our Lord, both theirs and ours![81]

This extract nicely illustrates some of the central themes of the call to prayer. Firstly, there was postmillennialism in the reference to looking forward and 'hoping for better days'. This might be a 'day of small things' but there was no need to despair, for God would surely do great things in the future. Secondly, there was the world vision evident in the reference to 'every place'. Thirdly, Fuller exhibited a certain evangelical 'catholicity' as he urged prayer for those who were not Particular Baptists. Fourthly, there was an urgency in the way the call to prayer was issued. Edwards's earlier appeal to ministers and churches was being vigorously renewed.

The following day Sutcliff officially launched the Association's own 'Prayer Concert'.[82] Less than two months had passed between Ryland receiving the *Humble Attempt* and the 'Call' being issued. As already noted, Fuller quickly set up a monthly meeting at Kettering along the lines of the Association proposal. For at least the first few of these meetings he sought to stir up those who had come by reading passages from the *Humble Attempt*; at other times he would bring a message of his own. There was also some sung worship. But greatest amount of time on these Monday evenings was given over to extempore prayer, with a concentration on the over-arching theme of Revival. There are a number of references to these meetings in his diary, and it appears that Fuller found these times to be both a challenge and an encouragement. On 6 December 1784 he recorded that they had had an 'affecting meeting of prayer' for the 're-vival of real religion'. On this occasion he found 'much pleasure in singing' and

---

[79] Diary and Spiritual Thoughts, 11 May 1784.
[80] Andrew Fuller, *The Nature and Importance of Walking by Faith* (Northampton: T. Dicey, 1784), in *Works*, 1: 117-34.
[81] Fuller, *Walking by Faith*, in *Works*, 1: 131.
[82] For detail, see Haykin, *One Heart and Soul*, 163-66.

also 'freedom to God in prayer'.[83] On 7 March 1785 he wrote that he 'enjoyed Divine assistance at the monthly prayer meeting, in speaking on continuing in prayer, and in going to prayer, though I felt wretchedly cold before I began'.[84] These meetings also broadened his horizons. In the light of future events a diary entry for 3 September 1784 is significant. 'Engaged all day to day nearly in searching Paul's journies into <u>Asia</u>, <u>Macedonia</u> and <u>Greece</u>. O that I might enter into the spirit of that great man of God! Felt much pleasure in this day's work.'[85] The years following would indeed see Fuller seeking to enter into the missionary spirit of the apostle Paul.

'The Instances, Evil, And Tendency of Delay, in the Concerns of Religion'

The prayer meetings for revival continued throughout the 1780s and spread beyond the boundaries of the Northamptonshire Association. For example, in 1786 it was taken up by Particular Baptist churches in Warwickshire and in 1790 by those in the Western Association. The re-igniting of the 'Concert of Prayer' had led to a dynamic and growing movement. It was yet another sign of the life and vigour that was increasingly characterising the English Particular Baptists.[86] By the early 1790s significant momentum had been created, and there were a number of discussions taking place about the possibility of Particular Baptists actually engaging in mission work overseas. The Northamptonshire Association meetings were a vital context for such discussions. One of Fuller's sermons preached before the Association was particularly important in moving the debate forward. This was an address given on 27 April 1791 at Clipstone, when the church pastored by John Morris was hosting the meeting. The original title of Fuller's message was 'The Instances, Evil, And Tendency of Delay, in the Concerns of Religion',[87] and in the course of his address Fuller had some points to make to those who said that 'the time has not yet come' for world mission.[88] He boldly declared that it was because of the prevailing 'procrastinating spirit' that 'so few and so feeble efforts had been made for the propagation of the gospel in the world'.[89] The argument which followed was powerful and had a profound effect on many of those who heard him and on many others who later read the message in its printed form. Referring to the 'great commission' of Matthew 28.19-20, Fuller stated,

---

[83] Diary and Spiritual Thoughts, 6 December 1784.
[84] Diary and Spiritual Thoughts, 7 March 1785.
[85] Diary and Spiritual Thoughts, 3 September 1784.
[86] Ryland, *Fuller*, 98; Payne, *Prayer Call of 1784*, 11.
[87] It was later published as the *Pernicious Consequences of Delay in Religious Concerns* (Clipstone: J.W. Morris, 1791). For the text, see *Works*, 1: 145-51.
[88] Fuller's text was Haggai 1.2, in which God's people said, 'The time is not yet come' for the temple to be rebuilt. See *Pernicious Consequences of Delay* in *Works*, 1: 145.
[89] *Pernicious Consequences of Delay* in *Works*, 1: 147.

When the Lord Jesus commissioned his apostles, he commanded them to go and teach 'all nations' and preach the gospel to 'every creature'; and that notwithstanding the difficulties and oppositions that would lie in their way. The apostles executed their commission with assiduity and fidelity; but, since their days, we seem to sit down half contented that the greater part of the world should remain in ignorance and idolatry. Some noble efforts have indeed been made; but they are small in number, when compared with the magnitude of the object.

Fuller had just stopped short of saying that Matthew 28.19-20 was binding on all believers in every age, although it could be argued that this was implicit in the point he was making. The apostles had taken the gospel to 'all nations'; Fuller was increasingly convinced of the need for similar action in his own day. He continued,

Are the souls of men of less value than heretofore? No. Is Christianity less true or less important than in former ages? This will not be pretended. Are there no opportunities for societies, or individuals, in Christian nations, to convey the gospel to the heathen? This cannot be pleaded as long as opportunities are found to trade with them, yea, and (what is a disgrace to the name of Christians) to buy them, and sell them, and treat them with worse than savage barbarity? We have opportunities in abundance; the improvement of navigation, the maritime and commercial turn of this country, furnish us with these; and it deserves to be considered whether this is not a circumstance that renders it a duty peculiarly binding on us.[90]

Fuller's appeal was predicated on the eternal truth, relevance and power of the gospel, but it was also shaped by the circumstances of the age in which he and his hearers lived. He believed that real opportunities had opened up, making gospel work overseas a real possibility. Also worth noting at this point are Carey's words, that it was the accounts of Captain Cook's voyages to Australia and the South Seas that were 'the first thing that engaged [his] mind to think of missions'.[91] The 'disgrace' of the slave trade was a further motivating factor. Thus, the founding of the BMS can only be understood properly if viewed in its late-eighteenth century context. The word 'duty' of course carried much theological freight. It was the duty of all to believe, the duty of all pastors to preach invitational sermons and – Fuller's point here – a duty, given the particular opportunities their situation afforded, to engage in world mission.[92] The argument of the

---

[90] *Pernicious Consequences of Delay* in *Works*, 1: 147.

[91] Eustace Carey, *William Carey*, 18; Stanley, *History of the BMS*, 8. Probably these were the accounts of Cook's second and third voyages, published in 1784.

[92] Fuller would later extend this argument to include believers in North America. Writing in 1806 to a Philadelphia ship owner, Robert Ralston, he stated, 'Of all the nations upon earth, I think it is the duty of Britain and North America to disseminate the gospel. We have more commerce with mankind, more gospel knowledge, more liberty and more wealth, than perhaps any other nation', *The Last Remains of Andrew Fuller: Sermons, Essays, Letters, and Other Miscellaneous Papers, not includ-*

Gospel Worthy was being pressed to its logical conclusion. With an allusion to the 1784 Prayer Call, Fuller further drove home his appeal for action,

> We *pray* for the conversion and salvation of the world, and yet neglect the ordinary *means* by which those ends have been used to be accomplished. It pleased God, heretofore, by the foolishness of preaching, to save them that believed; and there is reason to think it will still please God to work by that distinguished means. Ought we not then at least to try by some means to convey more of the good news of salvation to the world around us than has hitherto been conveyed? The encouragement to the heathen is still in force, *"Whoever shall call upon the name of the Lord shall be saved:* but how shall they call on him in whom they have not believed? and how shall they believe in him whom they have not heard? and how shall they hear without a preacher? and how shall they preach except they be sent?"[93]

The appeal was scriptural with the long quotation from Romans 10.14-15 and the characteristic balance between God's sovereignty (it was God who would 'work') and human responsibility (the importance of preaching and preachers). If the word 'duty' was central in the previous extract, 'means' was a vital one here. The 'good news of salvation' was conveyed by God's appointed means of preaching. This was as true in respect of overseas work as it was of evangelism at home. Fuller was by this point ready at least to try to do something. As he was later to write to John Fawcett, 'we now think we ought to do something more than pray'.[94] Many of those who heard his Association sermon were likewise ready to act.

The importance of Fuller's Clipstone message for the founding of the BMS is brought out in all the major accounts,[95] as is that of a sermon by John Sutcliff, *Jealousy for the Lord of Hosts Illustrated*, that was preached on the same day.[96] After dinner that evening Carey proposed that something should be done, immediately, to set up a mission society. The fact that this did not happen there and then has been portrayed by some of Carey's biographers as evidence the leading Northamptonshire ministers, including Fuller, were dragging their feet. Indeed, 'they would not rise and build the Lord's house,' according to Samuel

---

ed in his Published Works (Philadelphia: American Baptist Publication Society, 1856), 287-88.

[93] *Pernicious Consequences of Delay* in *Works*, 1: 148.

[94] Fuller Letter to John Fawcett, 28 January 1793, in John Fawcett, Jr, *An Account of the Life, Ministry and Writings of the Late Rev John Fawcett, DD* (London: Baldwin, Craddock and Joy, 1818), 294.

[95] See e.g. Morris, *Fuller*, 2nd edn, 103; Ryland, *Fuller*, 149.

[96] This appears to be Sutcliff's only extant sermon. See Haykin, *One Heart and Soul*, 206-10, where the full text of Sutcliff's message is included in an appendix, 355-65. For the impact of Sutcliff's message, as originally preached, see Ryland, *Fuller*, 149.

Pearce Carey.[97] However, as Stanley points out, this is inherently unlikely in view of what had just been preached.[98] The delay was almost certainly due more to practical considerations, although Carey was surely frustrated by it. After the Clipstone meeting another key moment came in May 1792 when, following the active encouragement of Fuller, Ryland and Sutcliff, Carey was ready to publish something himself on the subject of world mission.

Fuller, Carey and Carey's Enquiry

Carey's famous pamphlet, *An Enquiry into the Obligations of Christians to use Means for the Conversion of the Heathens*, was published on 12 May 1792.[99] The words 'obligations' and 'means' in the title capture the thrust of his argument.[100] Christians were 'obligated' (he might have said it was their 'duty') to use 'means' to take the gospel to those who had never heard it. Carey had imbibed the language and the concepts of the Edwardsean evangelical Calvinism which was the hallmark of the Northamptonshire Association. Fuller, Ryland and Sutcliff had earlier urged Carey to publish on this theme and had read and approved what the younger man had written.[101] Stanley states that some of Carey's language 'corresponded closely to a passage in Fuller's April 1791 sermon on the dangerous tendency of delay'.[102] The particular example of this that Stanley notes is on page eight of the *Enquiry*. Carey stated that 'the work (of world mission) has not been taken up or prosecuted of late years, except by a few individuals, with the zeal and perseverance with which the primitive Christians went about it'. He continued,

> It seems as if many thought the commission [i.e. the 'great commission', Matthew 28.19] was sufficiently put in execution by what the apostles and others have done; that we have enough to do to attend to the salvation of our own countrymen; and that, if God intends the salvation of the heathen, he will some way or other bring them to the gospel, or the gospel to them. It is thus that multitudes sit at ease, and give themselves no concern about the greater part of their fellow sin-

---

[97] Samuel Pearce Carey, *Memoir of William Carey, DD* (London: Hodder and Stoughton, 1923), 69.

[98] See the discussion in Stanley, *History of the BMS*, 10-11.

[99] William Carey, *An Enquiry into the Obligations for Christians to use Means for the Conversion of the Heathens* (London: Kingsgate Press, 1961 [1792]). The text is also reproduced in Timothy George, *Faithful Witness: The Life and Mission of William Carey* (Leicester: IVP, 1991), E.1-57. Subsequent references are from the London edn.

[100] Cf. Stanley, *History of the BMS*, 12.

[101] Ryland, *Fuller*, 238-39; Francis A. Cox, *History of the Baptist Missionary Society from 1792 to 1842*, 2 vols (London: T. Ward and G. & J. Dyer, 1842), 1: 7-8.

[102] Stanley, *History of the BMS*, 12.

ners, who, to this day, are lost in ignorance and idolatry.[103]

Fuller in the *Instances, Evil, And Tendency of Delay* had similarly spoken of 'the few and feeble efforts [that] have been made for the propagation of the gospel in the world', referred to the work of the apostles and the 'great commission', and spoke scathingly of those who put things off to 'another time'.[104] There are a number of other similarities too, all within the space of a few pages. Was Carey copying Fuller? That Carey was drawing from Fuller's Clipstone sermon is, in fact, by no means certain. Indeed, it is possible that Fuller had borrowed from Carey rather than *vice versa*, given that Fuller had seen and critiqued the draft manuscript of the *Enquiry* before he had preached at Clipstone.[105] Moreover, Carey daringly argued that the 'great commission' was still 'binding' on present day disciples and did so at length.[106] This was not usual in Particular Baptist circles at this time even among evangelical Calvinists and it was a theme Fuller had not developed in his Clipstone sermon.[107] The *Enquiry* was very much Carey's own work. Nevertheless, on balance it is probable that Carey drew on Fuller's sermon at least to some extent (note especially Carey's critical comment, 'It has been said that some learned divines have proved from Scripture that the time is not yet come that the heathen should be converted...').[108] Fuller's influence can again be discerned.

The Founding of the BMS

Carey went on to preach his celebrated sermon on Isaiah 54.2-3 at the Association meeting held at Friar Lane, Nottingham, on Wednesday 30 May 1792. His motto has passed into Baptist folklore as 'Expect great things from God; Attempt great things for God,' but probably the shorter title, 'Expect great things; Attempt great things'[109] is strictly accurate.[110] At the business meeting the fol-

---

[103] Carey, *Enquiry*, 8.
[104] *Pernicious Consequences of Delay* in *Works*, 1: 147-48. For further parallels, see Carey's *Enquiry*, 12-13.
[105] Cf. Stanley, *History of the BMS*, 12.
[106] Carey, *Enquiry*, 6-13.
[107] For the background, see Ronald E. Davis, 'The Great Commission from Christ to Carey', *Evangel* 14.2 (1996), 46-49.
[108] Carey, *Enquiry*, 12.
[109] Cf. Fuller letter to John Fawcett, 30 August 1793, Typescript Andrew Fuller Letters, transcribed by Joyce A. Booth, superintended by Ernest A. Payne, Angus Library, Regent's Park College, Oxford (4/5/1 and 4/5/2), (4/5/1), in which Fuller recorded Carey's headings as: '1. Let us *expect* great things; II. Let us *attempt* great things.' He continued, 'I feel the use of his sermon to this day. Let us pray much, hope much, expect much, labour much; an eternal weight of glory awaits us!'
[110] See Ernest A. Payne, 'John Dyer's Memoir of Carey', *BQ* 22.6 (April 1968), 326-27; A. Christopher Smith, 'The Spirit and Letter of Carey's Catalytic Watchword: A Study in the Transmission of Baptist Tradition', *BQ* 33.5 (January 1990), 226-37,

lowing morning it seemed once again that no firm proposal to form a society would be made. But, with Carey's prompting, it was Fuller who submitted the following resolution, 'that a plan be prepared against the next ministers' meeting at Kettering, for forming a 'Baptist society for propagating the Gospel among the Heathen.'[111]

So it was that, when the BMS was finally formed on 2 October 1792, the founding meeting took place in Fuller's own town.[112] At least fourteen men crammed themselves (the dimensions of the room were twelve feet by ten), into the back parlour of the home of Martha Wallis, widow of the recently deceased Beeby. Of the fourteen, thirteen pledged an annual subscription. The only one who did not was in fact the greatest enthusiast for overseas mission present, William Carey. Probably the minimum subscription required (half a guinea) was beyond Carey's limited financial means.[113] Fuller was appointed as the Society's first secretary at this meeting. Carey and John Thomas were to become the Society's first missionaries, arriving in India aboard the Danish East Indiaman the Kron Princessa Maria on 7 November 1793. Fuller's part in the formation of the BMS had been a significant one; his role in its early history would be greater still.

The First Year as Secretary of the BMS

Fuller's work as the secretary of the BMS will be dealt with in detail in chapter seven, but some points regarding his first year in post can be included here. One of his first duties was to try and raise some funds. Given that the subscriptions and promises of money, collected in Fuller's snuffbox, amounted to £13 2s 6d, this was his most pressing task.[114] One of a number of letters he wrote in January 1793 to promote the work was to John Fawcett. Fuller had never met Fawcett, but this did not stop him making a strong appeal for support, 'Any sums of money conveyed...will be thankfully received. The sooner the better, as the time is short.' Carey was still in the country at this stage and Fuller wrote that the prospective missionary would actually be in Yorkshire within the next few weeks to 'visit a relation'. If Fawcett were to 'hear him preach,' Fuller assured him, he would certainly 'give him a collection'. He concluded his letter by offering to come to Yorkshire to preach himself. 'I feel that willingness to exert

---

although Ryland, *Fuller*, 150, has the longer title. Rather surprisingly (and, for historians of this period, most unfortunately), the full text of Carey's sermon has not been preserved.

[111] *The Baptist Annual Register*, ed. by John Rippon, vol. I (London: Dilly, Button and Thomas, 1793), 375, 419. See also Stanley, *History of the BMS*, 14.

[112] See *Periodical Accounts Relative to the Baptist Missionary Society*, vol. 1 (Clipstone: J.W. Morris, 1800 [1794]), 3-4, for details of this meeting and the text of the resolutions passed.

[113] *Periodical Accounts*, 1: 3-4; S. Pearce Carey, *William Carey*, 88-93.

[114] Ryland, *Fuller*, 150.

myself,' he said, so that if an 'excursion of two to three weeks' would promote the cause of the mission, 'I would cheerfully engage in it'.[115] Fawcett responded with enthusiasm, collecting £200 from churches in his area, including some Independent congregations.[116] Fundraising for the BMS was underway.

Fuller had already been away from Kettering on behalf of the society, for example, visiting London in late 1792. He called at the homes of various evangelical clergymen to get donations. Those he visited included the biblical commentator Thomas Scott[117] and Richard Cecil, the future biographer of John Newton. Scott was warmly supportive, but Cecil initially refused to give any money and spoke in 'slighting terms' of the Particular Baptist denomination. He was prepared, however, to make an exception regarding the writer of the theological treatise the *Gospel Worthy of All Acceptation*. This he described, without knowing he was speaking to its author, as 'one of the most masterly productions I know'. When Fuller replied that this was in fact his own work, Cecil 'rose from his chair, expressed the most eager apologies and earnestly pressed a subscription'. But the visitor had been stung and to begin with refused to accept it. 'You do not give in faith!' he protested. In concluding his account of this incident, Andrew Gunton Fuller recorded that 'it was not without considerable persuasion that the perhaps too sensitive collector could be induced to receive the money'.[118]

At least the meeting with Cecil ended positively. Many London Particular Baptists were still wedded to high Calvinism and refused to give at all. A meeting of London Baptist ministers chaired by Samuel Stennett decided they should not commit themselves to the new venture. The theological changes that had taken place in Northamptonshire and elsewhere had not yet taken sufficient hold in London. Some London Particular Baptists, most notably Abraham Booth, the pastor of Little Prescott Street broke ranks and were more positive. Yet the indifference of the majority rankled with Fuller all his life, even though more support came later. Stanley suggests their initial coldness had something to do with a metropolitan distrust of the 'provincial' origins of the venture as well as to the continuing influence of high Calvinism.[119] This may be true. In return, Fuller's 'provincial' distrust of London was confirmed.

Despite this less than enthusiastic reaction in the capital, enough funds were raised from around the country to send Carey, Thomas and their families to In-

---

[115] Fuller Letter to John Fawcett, n.d. but between February and April 1793, in Fawcett Jr, *John Fawcett*, 296.

[116] John Fawcett letter to Fuller, 22 March 1793, Fuller Chapel Letters [Letters to Andrew Fuller], vol. 1 (1-34), vol. 2 (35-71), Fuller Baptist Church, Kettering, 1.4, 'Inclosed you have a bill value two-hundred pounds for the Mission collected from various churches.'

[117] John Scott, *The Life of Thomas Scott* (London: Seeley, 1836), 115.

[118] Gunton Fuller, *Fuller*, 112.

[119] Stanley, *History of the BMS*, 17.

dia. When they finally embarked on their Danish ship Fuller could not contain his joy. He wrote to John Saffery, a Particular Baptist pastor in Salisbury, Wiltshire and a keen supporter of the Society, in the following terms,

> O brother! Tears of joyful adoration are but a small tribute for such mercies! All is well! ... Carey's heart is happy... He will live and die in the midst of hundreds of millions of heathens, for whose salvation he is ready to sacrifice his life, and a thousand lives if he had them.[120]

Is it too fanciful to suggest the 'All is well!' comment echoed the 'It is well' of the Shunamite woman? Sacrificing his life for those who had not yet heard the gospel was the way to happiness for Carey and, although Fuller would never travel to India or to any country in which the BMS had missionaries, he shared his young friend's priorities. He would give himself in sacrificial service to the cause of the BMS at home and this service would be the path for happiness for him too. Given the inner turmoil Fuller had endured through much of the previous ten years and his depressive temperament, this may come as a surprise, yet it is the testimony of his diary. On 18 July 1794 he wrote,

> Within the last year or two, we have formed a Mission Society; and have been enabled to send out two of our brethren to the East Indies. My heart has been greatly interested in this work. Surely I never felt more genuine love to God and to his cause in my life – I bless God that this work has been a good means of reviving my soul. If nothing else comes of it; I and many more have obtained a spiritual advantage.[121]

Six months earlier he had written to Ryland, 'I have found the more I do for Christ, the better it is with me. I never enjoyed so much the pleasures of religion, as I have within the last two years, since we have engaged in the Mission business. Mr Whitfield [sic] used to say, "The more a man does for God, the more he may".'[122] Both these extracts tie Fuller's changing mood and shift in spirituality to his work for the BMS. As he gave himself in activity for the new cause, his love for God increased, his soul was 'revived' and he enjoyed the 'pleasures of religion' to a new degree. Perhaps the key phrase is the opening one in the letter to Ryland, 'I have found the more I do for Christ, the better it is with me.' The ecstasy of his letter to Saffery would not always be maintained and he would have many anxious moments in his service of the BMS. Nevertheless, the sort of evangelical activism that had been exemplified by Whitefield was the key that unlocked the door to greater happiness for Fuller. He would

---

[120] Fuller Letter to John Saffery, 30 May 1793, as cited in Doyle L. Young, 'The Place of Andrew Fuller in the Developing Modern Missions Movement' (unpublished PhD thesis, Southwestern Baptist Theological Seminary, 1981), 202.

[121] Diary and Spiritual Thoughts, 18 July 1794. Fuller used the symbol ♥ for the word 'heart'.

[122] Fuller Letter to John Ryland, 3 December 1793, in Ryland, *Fuller*, 226.

not go through a period comparable to the darkness and despair of 1782-92 again. The foundation and early progress of the BMS is an event of huge significance in the history of world mission; it was also transformative for the Society's first secretary.

Conclusion

The years 1782-92 were very difficult years for Fuller personally. He experienced two highly traumatic family tragedies; for most of the period he felt low spiritually; and, from 1786 to 1789 he was in my view both spiritually and clinically depressed. Yet this was also a period in which he became established as a respected local church pastor with a significant translocal ministry which included preaching and especially writing, as was shown in chapter four. It was also the period in which the Northamptonshire Particular Baptists became increasingly interested in cross-cultural mission overseas. Moves towards the formation of what became known as the BMS gathered momentum from 1790 onwards, but the foundations had already been laid in the previous decade, particularly through the Call to Prayer. Fuller was closely involved in the developments which led to the Particular Baptists deciding they were being called to 'do more' than just pray. Setting the account of Fuller's personal struggles alongside that of BMS's formation enables us to see his commitment to world mission in a new light. The BMS was born out of a context which included much suffering. The story of the Society may have been one of triumph, but it was not one of triumphalism.

In the first year of the BMS's existence the two halves of our chapter come together. Through his work as the Society's secretary Fuller found a focus for his spirituality that was more conducive to his temperament than morbid introspection; and through missional activity his love for God increased and he found a greater and more settled degree of happiness than hitherto. He had found a cause, one to which he would be increasingly devoted. He would remain the very active secretary of the BMS for the rest of his life.

A nineteenth century print showing significant English Baptist ministers from the late- eighteenth and early-nineteenth centuries. From left to right, standing: Joshua Marshman, William Ward, William Knibb, Thomas Burchell, John Rippon, Dan Taylor, Robert Hall Jr, John G. Pike, William Steadman and Samuel Pearce; seated: William Carey, Joseph Kinghorn, John Ryland Jr, Andrew Fuller and John Foster. Many of the men pictured here were significant in Fuller's story. Image from a picture held by Spurgeon's College, used with permission.

Above: The opening words of Fuller's private 'Covenant', written on 10 January 1780. Image courtesy of Mike Brealey and Bristol Baptist College, used with permission.

Andrew Fuller's signature on the reverse of his map of London. Image courtesy of David Milner, Fuller Baptist Church. Used with permission.

The first page of Fuller's autograph manuscript, 'Thoughts on the Power of Men to do the Will of God'. Image courtesy of Michael A.G. Haykin, Southern Baptist Theological Seminary, Louisville, KY, used with permission.

Jonathan Edwards. The New England Theologian's writings had a great impact on Fuller's theology and practice. Image from *The Works of Jonathan Edwards*, vol. 1, ed. by Edward Hickman (London: Westley and Davis, 1834).

Three of Fuller's Friends. Clockwise: John Sutcliff (in silhouette), John
Ryland Jr and Samuel Pearce. Images from the *Baptist Magazine*, 1815, 1826,
and Fuller's *Memoirs of Samuel Pearce* (Clipstone: J.W. Morris, 1800)

Three of Fuller's Opponents. Above: William Button; below, from left to right: Dan Taylor and Abraham Booth. Image of Button from the *Baptist Magazine*, 1822; images of Taylor and Booth from pictures held by Spurgeon's College, used with permission.

Martha Wallis's house in Kettering, where the BMS was founded.

Andrew Fuller's snuffbox. The box was used to collect the first subscriptions to the BMS. The detail on the lid depicts the Apostle Paul's conversion. Images courtesy of David Milner, Fuller Baptist Church, Kettering, used with permission.

from the Author to Colonel Lana... James/81

AN

APOLOGY

FOR THE LATE

Christian Missions to India:

PART THE FIRST.

COMPRISING

An ADDRESS *to the* CHAIRMAN

OF THE EAST INDIA COMPANY;

In answer to

MR. TWINING;

And

STRICTURES on the PREFACE of a PAMPHLET,

BY

MAJOR SCOTT WARING;

With an

APPENDIX,

CONTAINING AUTHORITIES, PRINCIPALLY TAKEN FROM THE REPORT OF THE SOCIETY FOR PROMOTING CHRISTIAN KNOWLEDGE.

BY ANDREW FULLER.

SECRETARY TO THE BAPTIST MISSIONARY SOCIETY.

—>>◉<<—

Second Edition.

There are no such things done as thou sayest; but thou feignest them out of thine own heart.
NEHEMIAH.

And now, I say unto you, refrain from these men, and let them alone; for if this counsel, or this work, be of men, it will come to nought: but if it be of GOD, ye cannot overthrow it, lest haply ye be found even to fight against GOD. GAMALIEL.

Sold by BURDITT, 60, and BUTTON 24, Paternoster Row; also by WILLIAMS and SMITH, Stationer's Court, LONDON.

Printed by J. W. Morris, Dunstable.

1808.

Title page of Fuller's *Apology for the Late Christian Missions to India*, inscribed by the author. Image courtesy of David Milner, Fuller Baptist Church, Kettering, used with permission.

The Serampore Trio: Joshua Marshman, William Carey and William Ward. Image courtesy of Spurgeon's College, used with permission.

The Baptist missionary premises at Serampore, India. Image from the *Baptist Magazine*, 1825.

An image of Andrew Fuller later in life: from John W. Morris, *Memoirs of…Fuller* (London: Wightman and Cramp, 1826).

CHAPTER 6

Further Controversy

...clear and accurate views of evangelical truth[1]

The formation of the BMS was a watershed moment in Fuller's life and ministry. In his role as secretary he gave himself unstintingly to the work of the Society and, although he continued as a local church pastor, it is arguable that the BMS increasingly came to dominate his ministry. Yet he also continued to write books and pamphlets after 1792, only a minority of which related to overseas mission directly. Most were concerned with wider theological issues or were apologetic in intent. One of Fuller's apologetic works will be examined as part of chapter seven. This present chapter considers some of the theological debates Fuller was involved in post 1792, with the focus on two disputes with the London Particular Baptist minister, Abraham Booth, the first on the relationship between regeneration and faith, the second on the atonement. These controversies especially highlight the influence some American theologians of the so-called 'New Divinity school' had on Fuller. These New Divinity men were important for the Kettering pastor, although, as we have seen with other thinkers, he did not engage with their work uncritically.

Only a small proportion of Fuller's vast corpus of theological writings can be sampled in this chapter. Nevertheless, I believe this sampling is sufficient to show his importance as a theologian, certainly when taken together with the material already surveyed in chapters three and four. Bruce Hindmarsh has stated, 'it is one of the most serious indictments of the English Evangelical Revival that it produced so few theologians of stature'.[2] Fuller was one of the exceptions – an evangelical writer who was a theological 'heavyweight'. His 'stature' was recognised by his contemporaries, both inside and outside the Particular Baptist denomination, as will be shown.

---

[1] Review of the Rev. Thomas Scott's 'Warrant and Nature of Faith,' etc., in *The Complete Works of the Rev. Andrew Fuller, With a Memoir of his Life by the Rev. Andrew Gunton Fuller*, ed. by Andrew Gunton Fuller, rev. ed. by Joseph Belcher; 3 vols, 3rd edn (Harrisonburg, VA: Sprinkle Publications, 1988 [1845]), 3: 750.

[2] D. Bruce Hindmarsh, 'The Politically Correct Evangelicalism of John Newton', in *Amazing Grace, Evangelicalism in Australia, Britain, Canada and the United States*, ed. by George A. Rawlyk and Mark A. Noll (Grand Rapids: Baker, 1993), 53.

The Dispute Between Fuller and Booth on Regeneration and Faith

As already stated, Fuller's protagonist in both the disputes covered in this chapter was Abraham Booth. Fuller's opponent was born in 1734 in Derbyshire in the East Midlands of England.[3] He came to faith among the General Baptists and was baptised by immersion in 1755. He began preaching and pastoring in their churches but sometime in the mid-1760s, as a result of private study and 'many prayers', he became convinced of Calvinistic principles.[4] These he went on to expound in a book entitled the *Reign of Grace*, published in 1768.[5] The *Reign of Grace* was both Calvinistic and evangelical. He was certain that the gospel itself was all the warrant sinners needed to trust in Christ[6] and his book delighted the evangelical Anglican clergyman Henry Venn, who invited him to preach in his home. Through this book Booth came to the notice of the Particular Baptist church at Little Prescott Street in London. He became their pastor in 1769 and remained there until his death in 1806.[7] During his time at Little Prescott Street his reputation grew and he published works on a variety of subjects. Ivimey described him as a 'star of the first magnitude...and one of the brightest ornaments of the Baptist denomination to which he belonged'.[8] As noted in the

---

[3] Unlike many of the other important figures in Fuller's life, Booth has been the subject of a number of studies. For an introduction, see Raymond A. Coppenger, *A Messenger of Grace: A Study of the Life and Thought of Abraham Booth* (Joshua Press: Dundas, ON, 2009). The best modern studies are by Robert W. Oliver. See, e.g., 'The Emergence of a Strict and Particular Baptist Community Among the English Calvinistic Baptists, 1770-1850' (unpublished PhD thesis, CNAA [London Bible College], 1986); 'Andrew Fuller and Abraham Booth', in *At the Pure Fountain of Thy Word': Andrew Fuller as an Apologist*, ed. by Michael A.G. Haykin (Carlisle: Paternoster, 2004), 203-22. Bart D. Box, *The Atonement in the Thought of Andrew Fuller* (New Orleans: ProQuest, 2009), includes a section on Booth and the atonement, 68-79, which, whilst not being especially incisive, is a responsible survey.

[4] [Anon.], 'Memoir' in *The Works of Abraham Booth... With Some Account of his Life and Writings*, 3 vols (London: W. Button and Son, 1813), 1: xxiii. The *Oxford Dictionary of National Biography* mistakenly asserts the 'change took place at the same time [Booth] was in contact with ministers from the Northamptonshire Association such as Sutcliff, Fuller, Ryland, and the younger Hall.' No evidence is brought forward to support this assertion and, given the date of Booth's shift from Arminianism to Calvinism, it is impossible. Robert Hall Jr was only born in 1764. John Westby-Gibson, 'Booth, Abraham (1734–1806)', rev. Ernest F. Clipsham, *Oxford Dictionary of National Biography*, Oxford University Press, 2004 [http://www.oxforddnb.com/view/article/2871, accessed 17 July 2014].

[5] For the text of the 9th edn, see *The Reign of Grace from its Rise to its Consummation* in *Booth's Works*, 1: 1-327.

[6] See, e.g., *Reign of Grace*, in *Booth's Works*, 1: 89-91.

[7] For biographical details, see 'Memoir', in *Booth's Works*, 1: xvii-xxvii.

[8] Joseph Ivimey, *A History of the English Baptists (HEB)* 4 vols (London: Hinton, Holdsworth & Ball, 1811-30), 4: 375.

previous chapter, Booth was one of the few London Particular Baptist pastors to support the BMS from its inception. Fuller himself, writing in 1803, described Booth as 'aged and respected'.[9] Partly because of the London man's standing within the denomination, the Kettering pastor found his disagreements with him extremely difficult.

The Course of the Dispute

The dispute concerning the relationship between regeneration and saving faith began when the London minister published *Glad Tidings to Perishing Sinners; or, The Genuine Gospel a Complete Warrant to Believe in Jesus* in 1796.[10] It seemed from the title and subtitle of *Glad Tidings* that Booth was giving warm support to Fuller's own position. In line with his previous book, the *Reign of Grace*, he contended that the gospel itself was a 'complete warrant for the most ungodly person to believe in Jesus'.[11] And yet Fuller was far from happy. The problem was that in *Glad Tidings* Booth argued that a 'holy disposition in the heart of a sinner' was unnecessary for anyone prior to their believing in Christ.[12] Booth associated the view he was challenging with the New England theologian Samuel Hopkins (1721-1803), but Fuller was not convinced Hopkins was the real target. Fuller had a deep respect for the New England thinker and their views on the subject under discussion were essentially the same. Fuller's conclusion, which he expressed in a letter to William Carey in India, was 'that it was [Booth's] intent to oppose our sentiments, and that he chose to attack us under Hopkins's name.'[13]

Fuller had guessed Booth's intention correctly. The two men had a series of private meetings in an attempt to resolve their differences, but these were unsuccessful and their disagreement became public knowledge. Hopkins was

---

[9] See Andrew Fuller, *Six Letters to Dr. Ryland Respecting the Controversy with the Rev A. Booth* in *Works*, 2: 699.

[10] Abraham Booth, *Glad Tidings to Perishing Sinners or The Genuine Gospel a Complete Warrant to Believe in Jesus*, 2nd edn, in *Booth's Works*, 2: 2-202. Fuller had known as early as 1795 that privately Booth was unhappy with some of his statements, see Fuller letter to John Ryland, 28 August 1795, in John Ryland Jr, *The Work of Faith, the Labour of Love, and the Patience of Hope Illustrated in the Life and Death of the Rev. Andrew Fuller*, 2nd edn (London: Button and Son, 1818), 227-29.

[11] Booth, *Glad Tidings*, in *Booth's Works*, 2: 24

[12] Booth, *Glad Tidings*, in *Booth's Works*, 2: 11; 67-232 (11).

[13] Fuller letter to William Carey, 6 Sept 1797, Typescript Andrew Fuller Letters, transcribed by Joyce A. Booth, superintended by Ernest A. Payne, Angus Library, Regent's Park College, Oxford (4/5/1 and 4/5/2) (4/5/1). Cf. Fuller letter to Carey, 22 August 1798, Fuller Letters (4/5/1). Fuller's views are set out in his *A Defence of a Treatise, entitled, The Gospel of Christ Worthy of All Acceptation: Containing a Reply to Mr Button's Remarks and the Observations of Philanthropos* (Clipstone: J.W. Morris, 1787), in *Works*, 2: 461-71.

made aware of Booth's work by Fuller and Ryland, with Ryland sending a copy of *Glad Tidings* to New England.[14] The New Divinity man's views of it can be judged by some comments he made in a letter to Ryland: *Glad Tidings* was full of 'inconsistencies' and 'absurdities'; indeed, Booth was 'perverting the gospel'.[15] Hopkins wrote a reply to Booth and sent it to Fuller and Ryland, with permission to publish it. Out of deference to Booth they decided not to do so.[16] If the language in Hopkins's letter to Ryland was reflective of what he said in his reply to Booth – the New Divinity man labelled one passage from *Glad Tidings* 'senseless, evasive, and contradictory' – they were surely wise to hold back.[17] Fuller and Ryland did lend Hopkins's manuscript to Booth, however. Fuller reported to Carey that since Booth had read it, the pastor of Little Prescott Street 'was rigidly set against everything from America'.[18] With the dispute still unresolved, Fuller finally defended himself in print, doing so in a lengthy appendix to the second edition of the *Gospel Worthy*, which was published in 1801.[19]

The Main Points of the Dispute

The issues at stake are not obvious at first sight, but the heart of the debate turned on the temporal relationship between the saving faith exercised by a sinner coming to Christ and regeneration, that is, the inner renewal by the Holy Spirit or 'new birth' described in Titus 3.5, John 3.3 and 1 Peter 1.3. Which came first? Did regeneration precede faith, or did faith precede regeneration? Fuller had written on this issue in his dispute with Dan Taylor. For saving faith

---

[14] Samuel Hopkins letter to John Ryland, 24 November 1797, in *The Works of Samuel Hopkins, DD...With a Memoir* [by Edwards Amasa Park] *of his Life and Character*, 3 vols (Boston: Doctrinal Tract and Book Society, 1852), 748-52. Hopkins also became a correspondent of Fuller. See, e.g., Samuel Hopkins letter to Fuller, 15 October 1799, in 'Memoir', *Hopkins's Works*, 1: 236-237. Cf. Joseph A. Conforti, *Samuel Hopkins and the New Divinity Movement* (Grand Rapids: Eerdmans, 1981), 179.

[15] Samuel Hopkins letter to John Ryland, 24 November 1797, in *Hopkins's Works*, 2: 749.

[16] Park, 'Memoir', in *Hopkins's Works*, 1: 223.

[17] Samuel Hopkins letter to John Ryland, 24 November 1797, in *Hopkins's Works*, 2: 751. Hopkins wrote to Fuller that he could not consider Booth 'a divine of a clear or orthodox head', Samuel Hopkins letter to Fuller, 12 October 1798, in Park, 'Memoir', in *Hopkins's Works*, 1: 224.

[18] Fuller letter to William Carey, 22 Aug 1798, Fuller Letters (4/5/1).

[19] Appendix to the *Gospel Worthy*, 2nd edn, in *Works*, 2: 393-416. In the appendix Booth's views were coupled with those of a Scotch Baptist, Archibald MacLean. For MacLean, see *Dictionary of Scottish Church History and Theology*, ed. by Nigel M. de S. Cameron (Edinburgh: T & T Clark, 1993), 528. For MacLean's views, often described as 'Sandemanianism', see chapter seven and Michael A.G. Haykin, 'Andrew Fuller and the Sandemanian Controversy', in *'At the Pure Fountain of Thy Word'*, 228.

to be exercised, prior regeneration by the Spirit was necessary, although only in the sense that 'a cause is prior to an effect that immediately follows'.[20] Sinners putting their faith in Christ would be unaware regeneration had taken place; only when they reflected on their conversion later would they perceive God had been at work savingly in their lives before they believed.[21] Nevertheless, Fuller and Hopkins insisted people only trusted in Jesus because they had first experienced regeneration.[22] As good Calvinists, what both men wanted to safeguard was the sovereignty of God in salvation. Men and women could only exercise faith in Christ because God had worked in their hearts by the regenerating power of the Spirit.

Surprisingly, given his own avowed Calvinism, Booth disagreed. He argued there was no 'priority or posterity' with regard to regeneration and faith. What is more, he directly attacked Hopkins and Fuller, although only Hopkins was named. Booth somehow maintained that Hopkins's (and Fuller's) position was tantamount to saying that a subjective 'warrant of faith' was necessary for someone to believe in Christ.[23] According to Booth, Hopkins's view – that regeneration was necessary for faith – was equivalent to him saying that 'pious affections toward God, and a cordial inclination to keep his commands...must be our state and character before we believe in Jesus!'[24] Hopkins and Fuller, of course, were saying no such thing. In the *Gospel Worthy* Fuller had insisted the opposite: no subjective warrant was necessary for someone to come to Christ. This was certainly what Hopkins believed too. Booth had misunderstood and misrepresented their position and understandably the Kettering pastor was horrified.

What had happened? As Robert Oliver shows in his survey of this dispute, 'two distinct controversies had [been] confused' by Booth. In England the issue that had been hotly debated was whether unbelievers needed a subjective warrant to look for salvation, but in New England this had never been a matter of great contention. There, 'Edwards and his successors [such as Hopkins] had tried to guard against some careless evangelistic preaching' which almost suggested that people could save themselves.[25] Against this background, Hopkins emphasised the importance and priority of God's work in salvation, hence the stress that regeneration was necessary if someone were to exercise saving faith. Booth, it seems, misunderstood (at least in part) because he was not aware of the context in which Hopkins was writing. This was in fact recognised at the time by Thomas Scott, the evangelical clergyman who, like Booth, was an early

[20] Fuller, *Defence of a Treatise*, in *Works*, 2: 461-71.
[21] Cf. Robert W. Oliver, *History of the Calvinistic English Baptists, 1771-1892* (Edinburgh: Banner of Truth, 2006), 156.
[22] For Hopkins's views, see *Hopkins's Works*, 1: 454.
[23] Appendix to the *Gospel Worthy*, 2nd edn, in *Works*, 2: 397-400.
[24] Booth, *Glad Tidings*, in *Booth's Works*, 2: 77.
[25] Oliver, 'Emergence of a Strict and Particular Baptist Community', 105-106.

supporter of the BMS. Scott published on the controversy himself, effectively supporting Fuller's and Hopkins's position.

Scott's book, the *Warrant and Nature of Faith in Christ Considered*, first appeared in 1797.[26] Fuller wrote an appreciative review of this work in the *Evangelical Magazine* although, anxious as he was to take the heat out of the debate, he published it anonymously.[27] Scott did accept that some of Hopkins's comments were unfortunate, particularly when they were read outside their immediate New England context. Booth had been especially unhappy about a statement of Hopkins, 'that a hearty submission to, and acquiescence and delight in, the law of God, rightly understood, and so a true hatred of sin, must take place IN ORDER to any degree of true approbation of the Gospel, and FAITH AND TRUST in Christ'.[28] It was writing like this that enabled Booth to represent Hopkins as saying that 'pious affections toward God' were necessary before someone could believe in Christ. Scott agreed the quotation from the New England man highlighted by Booth was unhelpful, running the risk of implying more than regeneration (such comments do not appear in Fuller's writings). But on the main point at issue Scott had no doubt that saving faith was the result of regeneration.[29] Booth wanted to safeguard what for evangelical Particular Baptists was an essential truth: no subjective warrant was necessary before someone could trust in Christ. Yet he ended up effectively denying his own Calvinism. The logic of Booth's position was that someone could exercise saving faith without the regenerating work of the Holy Spirit. Fuller asserted in a communication to Morris that Booth's view was 'worse than Arminianism itself, which admits at least some kind of divine influence. Here Mr Booth would dissent: but why should he? It is an argument arising from his own principles.'[30] The content of this particular controversy seems obscure and difficult, with little wider interest or importance. Yet it was significant at the time and highlights some real contrasts between the two Particular Baptists.

The Significance of the Dispute

A letter the Kettering pastor wrote to Hopkins in 1798 is especially helpful in illuminating the differences between Fuller and Booth. Fuller began by thanking

---

[26] Thomas Scott, *Warrant and Nature of Faith in Christ Considered...* 2nd edn (Buckingham: J. Seeley, 1801 [1797]).

[27] *Evangelical Magazine*, 7 (London: Thomas Chapman, 1799), 199-202. Although the review was anonymous, Booth was aware Fuller was its author. The review was later included in Fuller's *Works*, 3: 749-52.

[28] As quoted in Booth, *Glad Tidings*, in *Booth's Works*, 2: 77. Booth's emphases.

[29] Scott, *Warrant and Nature of Faith*, 48. Regeneration was the 'immediate cause' of someone having faith in Christ. Cf. 50.

[30] John Webster Morris, *Memoirs of the Life and Death of the Rev Andrew Fuller*, 1st edn (High Wycombe, 1816), 2nd edn (London: Wightman and Camp, 1826), 2nd edn, 300-301.

his American friend for his 'remarks on Mr Booth's performance' (the work he and Ryland in the end decided not to publish). He then apologised for the London pastor's 'manner of writing', which had annoyed Hopkins.[31] Then he proceeded to make a number of points about Booth and his conduct in the dispute. Firstly, he noted his fellow Particular Baptist's 'seeming contempt for contemporary authors' and sought to explain. 'Mr B...is a generation older than Sutcliff, Pearce, or myself; and perhaps it may be owing to this that he is less attentive to anything we write.' Furthermore he believed Booth was guilty of insularity and a certain amount of 'British pride' in his attitude to American writers.[32] Secondly, Fuller commented on the extremely heavy use of quotation in *Glad Tidings*, which Hopkins had found especially irritating. The majority of Booth's quotations were from John Owen, often covering whole pages of his work.[33] Fuller wrote that Booth 'is a great admirer of Owen, Vitringa, Venema etc.; and seems to suppose that they have gone to the *ne plus ultra* of discovery,' an interesting comment given the warm appreciation of Owen Fuller had expressed earlier in his ministry. To these comments Fuller added that Booth had 'got into such a habit of quotation' that he seemed 'unable to write half a dozen pages without it'.[34]

These observations are important and based, of course, on personal knowledge of Booth as well as on his published works. Although admittedly made by his opponent, I believe they are astute in their assessment of Booth. The dispute with Fuller had revealed Booth as an older man, less open to new authors (particularly if they were American) and with a reliance on quoting the great Calvinistic divines of the past that was surprisingly reminiscent, at least in style, of the high Calvinist authors considered in chapter three. The London scene was still permeated with high Calvinism and was certainly a bastion of an older Calvinism which, although not 'high' in the accepted sense of the term, was resistant to many of the newer evangelical emphases. Ivimey commented that Booth 'in some particulars [approached] what is called High-Calvinism'.[35] Had the older man been influenced by his many years at the heart of London Particular Baptist life? The evidence suggests this was indeed the case.

---

[31] Fuller letter to Samuel Hopkins, March 17 1798, in Morris, *Fuller*, 2nd edn, 294.

[32] Fuller letter to Samuel Hopkins, March 17 1798, in Morris, *Fuller*, 2nd edn, 294-95. Hopkins had also used the phrase 'British pride' when writing to Ryland about Booth. See Samuel Hopkins letter to John Ryland, 24 November 1797, in *Hopkins's Works*, 2: 752.

[33] Booth, *Glad Tidings*, in *Booth's Works*, e.g., 2: 201. In some sections the quotations nearly take over, see, e.g., 103-109.

[34] Fuller letter to Samuel Hopkins, March 17 1798, in Morris, *Fuller*, 2nd edn, 294-95. Campegius Vitringa Sr was a Reformed Dutch theologian and Hebraist who died in 1722. Herman Venema was one of his most important students.

[35] Ivimey, *HEB*, 4: 375.

By contrast, the dispute between the two men reveals more of Fuller's evangelicalism, for example, in his attempt to argue from scripture rather than relying on quotation from older authors. Also relevant is his strong stress on regeneration. In respect of this last point, eighteenth-century evangelicals tended to emphasise regeneration more than justification, whereas the sixteenth-century Reformers had tended to stress the latter more than the former.[36] The vital importance of a direct impression of the Holy Spirit, which brought rebirth and renewal, was a key note of evangelical preaching and writing.[37] In a private communication to Booth, Fuller contended that 'the powerful motives furnished by the gospel are...no motives to an unrenewed mind. But if the Lord open the heart, we attend to the things that are spoken.' Fuller pleaded, in biblical language, that nothing less than a new heart, a heart not of 'stone' but of 'flesh', was necessary.[38] Booth may have been giving away more than he realised when he accused Hopkins and Fuller of 'enthusiasm', the epithet so often hurled at evangelicals for their emphases on experience and 'the new birth'.[39] For Fuller, as for eighteenth-century evangelicals in general, it was vital to emphasise regeneration.[40] The dispute between Booth and Fuller on this issue was never properly settled although after 1801 it did fizzle out, largely because the two protagonists had moved on to another area of disagreement, namely, the atonement.

The Dispute Between Fuller and Booth on the Atonement

The 1801 edition of the *Gospel Worthy* was to draw Fuller into even more painful controversy with Booth.[41] Fuller reworked the part of the book which dealt with particular redemption. In the second edition of his *magnum opus* he wrote of his shift from a strictly limited understanding of the atonement, bringing the *Gospel Worthy* into line with what he had said in the course of his debate with

---

[36] See, e.g., Harry S. Stout, *The Divine Dramatist: George Whitefield and the Rise of Modern Evangelicalism* (Grand Rapids: Eerdmans, 1991), xx, 3, 251-52; Mark A. Noll, *Turning Points, Decisive Moments in the History of Christianity* (Leicester: IVP, 1997), 232.

[37] Including, of course, the preaching and writing of Jonathan Edwards. Fuller noted that 'President Edwards' was with him and Hopkins on the point at hand in his review of Scott's *Warrant and Nature of Faith* in the *Evangelical Magazine*, 7: 200. The relevant footnote references were not included in the version of the review that appears in Fuller's *Works*.

[38] Morris, *Fuller*, 1st edn, 302. Ezekiel 36.26. Fuller also cited Jeremiah 31.33.

[39] Morris, *Fuller*, 1st edn, 302. Booth made this comment in response to Fuller's use of the 'heart of stone / heart of flesh' verse. In the context of the eighteenth century, enthusiasm was a term of abuse.

[40] So Morris, *Fuller*, 1st edn, 321.

[41] For an alternative survey of this dispute, see Michael A.G. Haykin, 'Particular Redemption in the Writings of Andrew Fuller', in *Gospel in the World: International Baptist Studies*, ed. by David W. Bebbington (Carlisle: Paternoster, 2002), 107-128.

Dan Taylor. Christ's atonement was 'in itself equal to the salvation of the world, were the world to embrace it', he insisted.[42] There were some other changes too. Fuller now argued that the atonement did not proceed on the basis of 'commercial, but of moral justice'. Indeed, its 'grand object [was] to express the Divine displeasure against sin'.[43] In a later publication he expanded on what he meant, 'Sin is a debt only in a metaphorical sense; properly speaking it is a crime, and a satisfaction for it requires to be made, not on pecuniary, but on moral principles.'[44]

Fuller was rejecting what has been termed a 'quasi-quantitative' understanding of the atonement, one which made the atonement sound like a commercial transaction, with humankind as the debtor and God as the creditor.[45] If the commercial view were allowed to stand then, according to Fuller,

> The sufferings of Christ would require to be exactly proportioned to the nature and number of the sins which were laid upon him; and if more sinners had been saved or those who had been saved had been greater sinners than they are, he must have borne a proportional increase in suffering. To correspond with pecuniary satisfactions, this must undoubtedly be the case. I do not know that any writer has so stated things; but am persuaded that such ideas are at the foundation of a large part of the reasonings on that side of the subject.[46]

This view of the atonement, which proceeded on 'the principle of debtor and creditor', was held by the high Calvinist Tobias Crisp and also by John Gill. Fuller was sure it could not be sustained.[47]

In place of seeing the atonement as a *quid pro quo* payment of a debt, Fuller deployed what was known as 'moral government' language to help him describe

---

[42] *Gospel Worthy*, 2nd edn, in *Works*, 2: 372-73.

[43] *Gospel Worthy*, 2nd edn, in *Works*, 2: 372-73. Cf. the *Gospel its Own Witness*, in *Works*, 2, 80-81 which was published in 1799. For examples of governmental language in Fuller's preaching, see the sermons 'The Reception of Christ the Turning Point of Salvation' (n.d.), *Works*, 1: 273-74, and 'Christianity the Antidote to Presumption and Despair' (n.d.), *Works*, 1: 322.

[44] Andrew Fuller, *Three Conversations on Imputation, Substitution and Particular Redemption* (London, 1806), in *Works*, 2: 680-9 (688). As we will see, this was written in the course of his dispute with Booth. Although *Three Conversations* did not appear until 1806, the year of Booth's death, it was written three years earlier.

[45] Haykin, 'Particular Redemption in the Writings of Andrew Fuller', 126. For the use of the term 'quasi quantitative' in respect of the atonement, see Alan P.F. Sell, *The Great Debate: Calvinism, Arminianism and Salvation* (Worthing: H.E. Walter, 1982), 87.

[46] *Three Conversations*, in *Works*, 2: 690; cf. *Gospel Worthy*, 2nd edn, in *Works*, 2: 373.

[47] *Six Letters to Dr Ryland*, in *Works*, 2: 699 (see 699 n for Fuller's comments on Gill). For Crisp's views, see Haykin, 'Particular Redemption in the Writings of Andrew Fuller', 114-15.

how the atonement worked. He held that God should be viewed as the wise and good 'moral governor' of the universe. On the cross, Christ was not so much 'putting to rest' God's wrath against sin as 'putting to right' God's sense of moral justice.[48] In the 'moral government' theory of the atonement God punishes sin primarily because, as the moral governor of the universe, his good governance must be upheld. On the cross, Christ dies to display God's holy hatred of sin and his determination to punish it. Through the cross sinners are pardoned in a way that upholds God's justice and brings glory to God.[49] It was Fuller's use of terms, concepts and approaches associated with the moral government understanding of the cross that especially led to this further dispute with Booth.

The Course of the Dispute

The conflict followed a pattern similar to the previous one. Fuller, having heard privately what he regarded as Booth's 'serious and heavy charges' against him, was keen to avoid the dispute spilling out into public controversy. As in the debate concerning regeneration and faith, he believed he had been misrepresented by the older man. In May 1802 he visited Booth in an attempt to come to an understanding. Yet despite a number of such meetings, Booth remained adamant that Fuller had departed from Calvinistic orthodoxy. The situation deteriorated rapidly. From the summer of 1802 reports, presumably emanating from Booth or those close to him, were circulated in London and Northamptonshire that Fuller had privately admitted he was now an Arminian. Booth wrote to Ryland to complain about Fuller and so, between 3 and 22 January 1803, the Kettering pastor wrote 'Six letters to Dr Ryland' to defend himself, although he decided not to make these public.[50]

In fact, it was Booth who was the first of the two men to go into print on the issues which divided them. In September 1803 he preached a sermon in London which was a thinly veiled attack on Fuller's views on the atonement. The Kettering pastor wrote to Booth to protest; once more he insisted he had been misrepresented.[51] The London man's response was to escalate matters by publishing his sermon. *Divine Justice Essential to the Divine Character* appeared within months of it having been preached, replete with an appendix in which Booth tackled the Kettering pastor's views directly, although he drew back from actu-

48 *Gospel Worthy*, 2nd edn, in *Works*, 2: 373-74.
49 Cf. Haykin, 'Particular Redemption in the Writings of Andrew Fuller', 120.
50 *Six Letters to Dr Ryland*, in *Works*, 2: 699-715. These were not in fact published until 1831, when they appeared in an early edition of Fuller's *Works*. The account of the course of this controversy is largely taken from the first letter (699-702), in which Fuller gives Ryland his own version of the dispute.
51 Fuller letter to Abraham Booth, 19 October 1803, in Morris, *Fuller*, 2nd edn, 306.

ally naming his opponent.[52] It was Fuller who fired the final shot in what Morris despairingly termed 'this hopeless piece of business',[53] publishing his *Three Conversations on Imputation, Substitution and Particular Redemption*. These appeared in 1806, the year of Booth's death. The *Three Conversations* take the form of a dialogue between John (Ryland), Peter (Booth) and James (Fuller), and a feature of them is that 'Peter' regularly apologises to 'James' for having misunderstood and misrepresented him.[54] Evidence from the actual dispute does little to suggest this was any more than wishful thinking on Fuller's part. *Divine Justice* proved a popular work and was reprinted in 1813.[55] Even after his opponent had gone to the grave, the shock waves from the dispute continued to be felt.

Imputation and Substitution

During the course of the controversy Fuller was further drawn out regarding the views he now held regarding imputation and substitution. These views flowed in part from his adoption of moral government language and approaches and his concern for an explanation of the atonement that did not make God appear somehow unjust.

Regarding imputation, Fuller sought to show how a person's sin was imputed (i.e. ascribed) to Christ and how Christ's righteousness was imputed to that person. In his *Six Letters* he argued for a 'figurative' rather than a 'proper' or 'real' imputation. Christ, he wrote, 'was accounted in the Divine Administration AS IF HE WERE, OR HAD BEEN, the sinner; that those who believe on him might be accounted AS IF THEY WERE, OR HAD BEEN, righteous.' Flowing from this, the Kettering pastor was hesitant to treat Christ's sufferings as punishment because Jesus was not, in any real sense, criminal or guilty. Someone who was not guilty could suffer but they could not, properly speaking, be punished. Fuller's view was carefully nuanced. He could still speak of Christ's sufferings being 'penal', just as he could of 'our salvation' being a 'reward'. Nevertheless, he reasoned, 'as [our salvation] is not a reward to us, so I question whether [his sufferings] can properly be said to be a punishment to him'.[56]

---

[52] Abraham Booth, *Divine Justice Essential to the Divine Character: a Sermon Preached in Mr. Timothy Thomas's Meeting-house near Devonshire-Square at the Baptist Monthly Meeting, September 22, 1803* (London: T. Whittingham, 1803) in *Booth's Works*, 3: 3-95. The appendix, *Relative to the Doctrine of Atonement by Jesus Christ*, is on 78-95.

[53] Morris, *Fuller*, 2nd edn, 309.

[54] *Three Conversations*, in *Works*, 2: 692.

[55] (London: J. Haddon, 1813).

[56] *Six Letters to Dr Ryland*, in *Works*, 2: 703-704. Fuller's emphases. See also, 'On Imputation and Original Sin', 7 March 1799, in Fuller's Commonplace book, [first entry 22 June 1798], Bristol Baptist College Library (95a), 5-10, which shows his views were shifting decisively by this point.

Booth was adamant in rejecting this, insisting that Christ had indeed been punished by God on the cross. Picking up on Galatians 3.13, in which the apostle Paul states that Christ became 'a curse for us', he commented, 'If, therefore Jesus was made a curse, he was PUNISHED – in a REAL and PROPER sense PUNISHED: for scarcely any words can convey the idea of punishment more forcibly than that of the apostle.'[57] Booth and Fuller were both Calvinists with an avowed commitment to the divine decrees and both believed the death of Christ was the fulcrum of God's saving work. They were unable, however, to agree on the 'mechanism' of atonement – how Christ's death actually 'worked' to save sinners. Booth believed that on the cross Christ was properly 'punished' by God; Fuller drew back from this because Christ was not guilty of any crime. And how could God punish an innocent man without being unjust?

Fuller and Penal Substitutionary Atonement

Booth believed that Fuller's views on the atonement, especially regarding imputation and substitution, were a departure from those that had been current in English Particular Baptist life up to his time. More recently it has been argued that Fuller's views on imputation and substitution are incompatible with the understanding of the cross known as penal substitutionary atonement. Stephen Holmes states that Fuller 'criticised' penal substitution. 'I don't think Fuller realised he was changing the doctrine', he continues, 'but he believed that guilt cannot be transferred from one person to another – and if you believe this, then you cannot talk about Jesus taking our guilt and suffering for us.'[58] Holmes further comments that the Kettering pastor was the 'first evangelical' he has been able to find who took this line.[59] So, did Fuller depart from belief in penal substitutionary atonement?

Three points can be made in response. All of them need to be recognised and borne in mind if the question posed is to be properly answered. Firstly, it does seem that Fuller was saying something new, not only in the context of Particular Baptist life but also in the context of British evangelical life. Holmes has not been able to find a British evangelical who rejected the idea of a literal transfer of guilt and I have not been able to find an example either.[60] It should be noted that eighteenth-century evangelicals such as the Wesleys and Edwards Sr did

---

[57] Booth, *Divine Justice*, in *Booth's Works*, 3: 52. Booth's emphases.

[58] Stephen R. Holmes, *The Wondrous Cross: Atonement and Penal Substitution in the Bible and History* (Paternoster: Milton Keynes, 2007), 66. Cf. Stephen R. Holmes, 'Ransomed, Healed, Restored, Forgiven: Evangelical Accounts of the Atonement', in *The Atonement Debate*, ed. by Derek Tidball, David Hilborn and Justin Thacker (Grand Rapids: Zondervan, 2008), 271.

[59] Holmes, *Wondrous Cross*, 66. Holmes is using the term 'evangelical' in the same way I deploy it in this book, to denote the evangelicalism that flowed from the eighteenth-century Revival.

[60] Of course, this does not mean one does not exist.

not only understand the cross in terms of penal substitution; they had a range of ways of talking about the atonement. Nevertheless, they held to an unambiguous understanding of penal substitutionary atonement and did not reject the idea that guilt could be transferred from one person to another. In Calvinistic Baptist life specifically, guilt transfer was accepted. The typical approach was exemplified in the work of Anne Steele. The influential poet and hymnwriter wrote that Christ, the 'spotless, bleeding, dying Lamb', experienced God's 'avenging justice' as he died on the cross. It was through the assuaging of this 'avenging justice' that 'guilty souls' were rescued from hell.[61] This is a straightforward statement of penal substitution and, to use Booth's terms, it assumes a 'real' and 'proper' punishment rather than a figurative one. This was the standard approach. The first point to note, therefore, is that Booth correctly identified that Fuller's views, as expressed in debate with him, represented a departure from this standard position.

Yet, secondly, we need to note that Fuller continued to refer to Christ's death in terms that were both 'penal' and 'substitutionary', allowing statements that quadrated with this understanding to remain in his writings. So, in one of his books we find the following,

> We believe that Christ, in laying down his life for us, actually *died as our substitute*; endured the curse of the Divine law, that we might escape it; was delivered for our offences, that we might be delivered from the wrath to come; and all the while we were yet enemies.[62]

This was in the *Calvinistic and Socinian Systems...Compared*. Admittedly this was first published in 1793, a number of years before Fuller's debate on the atonement with Booth. But this book, which was extremely popular, continued to be reprinted in new and corrected editions, with additional material added by its author. By 1810 it had gone through six editions, with the statement cited above consistently retained.[63] Its author never repudiated the views he expressed in the statement on the atonement from the *Calvinistic and Socinian Systems...Compared*. True, he does not state there that on the cross Christ was punished by God or that he bore our guilt. Yet he does say that Christ died as

---

[61] Anne Steele, 'Redemption by Christ Alone', Hymn 71, in John R. Broome, *A Bruised Reed: The Life and Times of Anne Steele* (Harpenden: Gospel Standard Trust, 2007), Part 2, 'Hymns of Anne Steele', 284.

[62] *The Calvinistic and Socinian Systems Examined and Compared as to their Moral Tendency*, in *Works*, 2: 217. Italics original.

[63] *Calvinistic and Socinian Systems Examined and Compared* was first published (Market Harborough: Harrod and Button, 1793). Important edns were the 2nd (London: Button & Son, 1794) from which the first American edn (Philadelphia: Lang and Ustick, 1796) was printed, and the 1802 edn (London: T. Gardiner / Button & Son, 1802) which was a 'new and corrected edn' with additional material added as a postscript. The 6th edn (London: Gardiner, Hamilton *et al*, 1810), 315-16, includes the passage cited.

our 'substitute' and 'endured the curse of the Divine law' that 'we might be delivered from the wrath to come' and there is nothing in the quotation or its immediate context to indicate this language is figurative. Moreover, this statement from the *Calvinistic and Socinian Systems...Compared* is not an isolated one. For example, in a letter to Ryland, dated 6 March 1803, Fuller declared that he believed that the 'full penalty of the law' due to us was borne by a 'substitute', namely Christ.[64] Again, there is nothing about the transfer of guilt, yet Christ bore the 'penalty' that was rightfully due to us. In the statements I have cited in this paragraph – by most definitions – Fuller is affirming penal substitution.[65]

Thirdly, the strength of the figurative or metaphorical language Fuller used in his dispute with Booth should not be underestimated. Chris Chun analyses the debate between the two men and addresses some of the theological issues it raises, drawing from work by the twentieth-century theologian Colin Gunton on the power of metaphor to convey truth.[66] Booth's argument was that the figurative language Fuller deployed to describe imputation and substitution stripped the doctrines of their ontological reality. For him, only literal language could convey ontological truth. This is the point that Chun contests. He cites Gunton, 'The truth of a claim about the world does not depend upon whether it is expressed in literal or metaphorical terms, but upon whether language of whatever kind expresses human interaction with reality successfully (truthfully) or not.'[67] We use metaphorical language all the time, but that language has been so 'successful' in conveying the reality of which it speaks we are unaware we are actually using a metaphor.[68] Working from this basis, Chun argues that Fuller's 'figurative rendering' of imputation conveys just as much reality as Booth's 'literal' account.[69] Granted, Fuller argued that guilt could not be 'properly' transferred from a guilty to an innocent person and, by return, punishment could not be 'properly' transferred from a guilty person to an innocent one. This transfer could only happen figuratively. Yet his figurative account is still a powerful one.

---

[64] See Fuller letter to John Ryland, 6 March 1803, in *Ryland*, 239.

[65] See also *The Deity of Christ Essential to Atonement* (London, 1802) in *Works*, 3: 693-97, esp. 693-94.

[66] Chris Chun, *The Legacy of Jonathan Edwards in the Theology of Andrew Fuller* (Leiden: Brill, 2012), 205-208.

[67] Colin Gunton, *The Actuality of the Atonement: A Study of Metaphor, Rationality and the Christian Tradition* (Edinburgh: T. & T. Clark, 1988), 35. Cf. Chun, *Legacy of Edwards in the Theology of Fuller*, 207.

[68] Gunton uses the illustration of the Latin word *musculus* from which the word 'muscle' is derived. *Musculus* literally means 'little mouse' and so it is a metaphor used to describe part of the human body. But the metaphor has become so successful it has effectively 'lost its metaphorical status', so effectively does it convey the reality of which it speaks. See Chun, *Legacy of Edwards in the Theology of Fuller*, 207.

[69] Chun, *Legacy of Edwards in the Theology of Fuller*, 208.

So did Fuller abandon penal substitution? Given the three points just considered, the answer must be carefully nuanced. In one sense, assuming a strict definition of penal substitution is applied, with the guilt and punishment rightfully due to the sinner being actually transferred to Christ on the cross, the answer is yes. Although his metaphorical understanding of imputation and substitution is indeed powerful, it remains true that some of Fuller's statements in his debate with Booth do not quadrate with a strict understanding of penal substitutionary atonement.[70] Yet in another and I think deeper sense the answer to the question is no. This is because he continued to make statements which spoke of Christ's death as both 'penal' and 'substitutionary'. Moreover, he brought these two concepts together, declaring that Christ endured the curse of the 'Divine law' on our behalf that we might be delivered from God's wrath. I would attempt to sum up in this way: Fuller made some statements which do not conform to a strict understanding of penal substitution, but he did not abandon penal substitution because statements that corresponded with that understanding of the atonement continued to take their place in his writings.[71]

Before moving on to consider the influences on Fuller's views on the atonement, it ought to be said that his contention – that one person's guilt cannot be transferred to another – is open to challenge. Later in the nineteenth century the Princeton theologian Charles Hodge (1797-1878) recognised the problem Fuller was wrestling with as a real one and proposed a solution. Hodge helpfully differentiated between two senses of the word guilt. On the one hand guilt could mean 'the psychological consciousness of having done wrong'.[72] It is impossible, Hodge argued, for guilt understood in this sense to be transferred.[73] Up to this point Hodge and Fuller are agreed. However, 'the psychological consciousness of having done wrong' is not the only way of understanding guilt; it could also mean 'the legal liability to punishment'.[74] The Princeton man argued that, when understood in the second sense, as 'the obligation of the sinner to satisfy divine justice', guilt could be removed from one person and transferred to an-

---

[70] Hence my conclusion in, 'Nonconformists and the Work of Christ: A Study in Particular Baptist Thought', in *T. & T. Clark Companion to Nonconformity*, ed. by Robert Pope (Edinburgh: T. & T. Clark, 2013), 192.

[71] Consequently, I would now nuance my brief comments in 'Nonconformists and the Work of Christ', 192-93. Although what I said on those pages is strictly speaking correct, it is not the only thing to be said about Fuller and penal substitution. I wish what I have said in this present paragraph *in toto* to be taken as expressing my views on Fuller and penal substitution.

[72] Holmes, *Wondrous Cross*, 66, from whom I am drawing in this paragraph. For Charles Hodge's account, see his *Systematic Theology*, 3 vols (London: James Clarke & Co., 1960 [1865]), 2: 476-77.

[73] Guilt understood in this sense 'cannot be transferred from one person to another'. Hodge, *Systematic Theology*, 2: 476.

[74] Holmes, *Wondrous Cross*, 66.

other, or assumed by 'one [person] in the place of another.'[75] Both understandings of guilt were legitimate, but it was in the second sense of the word that guilt transference occurred in the atonement. Hodge was making the sort of careful, subtle distinction Fuller (and of course, before him, Edwards) had made regarding the different types of human inability – moral and natural. Hodge shows how it is possible to speak of guilt transference – thus safeguarding a strict understanding of penal substitution – whilst at the same time dealing with Fuller's objections.

What Fuller would have thought of Hodge's argument is of course unknown and it is no disgrace to this outstanding, creative theologian that he did not anticipate this later approach. The man who had been attracted to wrestling in his youth grappled long and hard with the issues, as the false starts and frequent crossings out in the relevant entries in his Commonplace Book show.[76] Fuller believed that his own arguments had the support of scripture. Verses that he appealed to included Romans 3.25 and also Romans 8.3, which were relevant because of their implication that it was *sins* that were being punished and condemned on the cross rather than Christ himself. Fuller was sure that in the New Testament 'what Christ underwent [was] commonly expressed by the term *sufferings*.' When the terms 'chastisement' or 'punishment' were used the focus was on the fact that he 'bore *our* punishment', not that Christ *himself* was being punished. Following prolonged reflection on the relevant passages Fuller believed there was 'great accuracy in the scripture phraseology on this subject' and that this phraseology pointed to his metaphorical understanding.[77] Booth was equally sure, of course, that scripture was on his side. A thoroughgoing commitment to the Bible as God's word was no guarantee of agreement on its message.

Influences on Fuller's Views

What were the influences on Fuller's adoption of moral government language and his views of imputation and substitution? The 'moral government' theory of the atonement had been originally propounded in the seventeenth century by the Dutch Jurist Hugo Grotius (1583-1645).[78] No evidence that Fuller read Grotius directly has been discovered. Jonathan Edwards did read him, however, and moral government language appeared in some of the American divine's writ-

---

[75] Hodge, *Systematic Theology*, 2: 476.
[76] Commonplace Book, 5-10, 13. See esp. 13.
[77] *Six Letters to Dr Ryland*, in *Works*, 2: 705.
[78] See *New Dictionary of Theology*, ed. by Sinclair Ferguson and David F. Wright (Leicester: IVP, 1988), 284-85, for details on Grotius, the Dutch 'jurist, publicist, statesman and theologian.' Grotius' *Works* were in the library of Yale College by at least 1733. See Frank H. Foster, *A Genetic History of the New England Theology* (Chicago: Univ. Chicago Press, 1907), 114.

ings.[79] So Fuller could have imbibed some of the Grotian language and concepts directly from Edwards. Yet, as far as moral government thinking was concerned, the influence of the New Divinity theologians must be taken into particular account. The key figures were Hopkins himself, Stephen West (1735-1818)[80] and especially Jonathan Edwards's son, Jonathan Edwards Jr (1745-1801).[81] It was Edwards Jr who, of the different New Divinity men, gave the moral government theory 'its first elaborate statement'.[82] Hopkins's own views were set out in his *System of Doctrines Contained in Divine Revelation* (1793).[83]

During the 1790s, when Fuller's views on these matters were forming, he was reading most of the relevant works by these men. Ryland continued to be an increasingly fruitful source of a wide range of transatlantic publications. Fuller received a copy of Edwards Jr on *Free Grace and Atonement* in 1794 with 'great pleasure'. Writing to thank Ryland he said, 'I suppose I read it some time ago; but I never relished it so well before.' On opening another parcel of pamphlets he was disappointed not to find 'West on the atonement', a work he told Ryland he 'very much longed for'.[84] Presumably his friend was able to satisfy Fuller's wish, as only three weeks later Fuller wrote to Sutcliff describing Stephen West's *The Scripture Doctrine of The Atonement Proposed to Careful Examination* (1785) as a book 'for wh[ich] I w[oul]d not take 1/1 [one guinea]'.[85] That Fuller had been reading relevant works by Hopkins for some time is attested to by a wide range of sources.[86]

---

[79] See the evidence cited by Chun, *Legacy of Edwards in the Theology of Fuller*, 148-50, 168-70.

[80] West followed Edwards Sr at Stockbridge, Massachusetts, where he was pastor from 1758-1818, see Foster, *New England Theology*, 204 n.

[81] For brief biographical details of Edwards Jr, see Conforti, *Hopkins and the New Divinity*, 38, 73-74, 179, 229. Edwards Jr studied under Hopkins and Bellamy. While a pastor at Colebrook, Connecticut from 1795-99, he was involved in the 'Second Great Awakening'. See Foster, *New England Theology*, 189 n.

[82] Robert L. Ferm, *Jonathan Edwards the Younger: A Colonial Pastor* (Grand Rapids: Eerdmans, 1976), 115 n.

[83] Conforti, *Hopkins and the New Divinity*, 161.

[84] Fuller letter to John Ryland, 1 January 1795. Ryland, *Fuller*, 227-30.

[85] Fuller letter to John Sutcliff, 22 January 1795, Fuller Letters (4/5/2). See Foster, *New England Theology*, 204-205, for West's use of moral government terminology. West's *Scripture Doctrine of the Atonement* helped to popularize the governmental theory of the atonement in New England. On this, see Haykin, 'Particular Redemption in the Writings of Andrew Fuller', 121.

[86] See e.g. Fuller letter to John Sutcliff, 7 January 1801, Fuller Letters (4/5/1); See Book of Miscellaneous Writings [including Fuller's "List of Books" from 1798, and a "Meditation" by Ann Fuller] (G 95 b). The book list has a separate section for 'American pieces', although many of what Fuller appeared to consider the major

Another New England writer who was important was Joseph Bellamy, who had been close to Edwards Sr and was in many ways a transitional figure, bridging the gap between the older view of 'President Edwards' and the newer view of his son. The elder Jonathan Edwards had rejected the idea of the atonement as the literal *quid pro quo* repayment of a debt, but had nevertheless maintained that in the events of the cross God did punish Christ in order to vindicate his own character. Bellamy appeared to believe this too, but stated the Grotian view that 'God acts to uphold His Divine character', alongside it. For example, in his *True Religion Delineated* (for which Edwards wrote the original recommendatory Preface), he argued that Christ's death honoured God's moral law. As a result the benevolent moral governor of the universe could now 'pardon the whole world...consistently with his honour.'[87] Bellamy can therefore be seen as a middleman between the two positions, an 'American precursor for the governmental theory of the atonement'.[88]

The evidence connecting Bellamy and Fuller is strong. The Kettering pastor actually wrote the Preface to the English edition of *True Religion Delineated*. In his Preface Fuller stated that the 'leading principles' of Bellamy's work were 'the exceeding sinfulness of sin, the lost state of the sinner, salvation by mere grace through a mediator and acceptance with God by faith in him'. He went on to warmly commend it. 'I do from my heart,' he stated, 'wish it may meet with a candid and careful attention from the religious public. Were the doctrines here inculcated to prevail amongst us, I should hope to see more true religion than I have yet seen.'[89] Overall, there is significant evidence that Fuller was leaning on Bellamy, Hopkins and the other New England men as he used the language of 'moral government' to describe the way the atonement worked.

In his ideas on imputation, it appears Fuller owed a significant debt to Hopkins in particular. Hopkins argued that no 'real' imputation of sin to Christ took place on the cross: real imputation was not honouring to God because to mete out punishment on an innocent party smacked of injustice.[90] Oliver writes that

---

American works, such as Bellamy's *True Religion Delineated* (no. 187) and Hopkins's 2 vol. *Body of Divinity* (no. 138), appear in the main list.

[87] Conforti, *Hopkins and the New Divinity*, 164. Conforti (162-63) states that Hopkins was influenced by Bellamy's views on the atonement, 'Hopkins's *System* borrowed more heavily from Joseph Bellamy than any other of Jonathan Edwards's "improvers".'

[88] Ferm, *Edwards the Younger*, 115-16. See also Conforti, *Hopkins and The New Divinity*, 178, 'Within the New Divinity movement Bellamy represented a major link between the First and Second Great Awakenings.'

[89] Joseph Bellamy, *True Religion Delineated*, with a 'Recommendatory Preface' by Fuller, v-viii. Edwards's Preface to the 1st edn was retained, but printed after Fuller's own.

[90] For Hopkins on imputation, see *Hopkins's Works*, 1: 463-64; 467, 'The righteousness of Christ is *reckoned* in [the sinner's] favor, and avails for...justification.' (467). Italics mine.

Fuller's views on imputation seem 'very similar to those developed by Hopkins'.[91] Booth had no doubts about the provenance of Fuller's approach, attacking Hopkins directly in *Divine Justice*.[92]

If Booth was unhappy that his opponent was leaning on Hopkins, Fuller believed Booth's views were in some respects redolent of high Calvinism.[93] He further suspected that Booth had grown 'old', 'peevish' and 'jealous' and that this lay behind some of his opposition. But Booth believed he had real concerns. Morris summarises what he believed they were. The London man 'suspected that Fuller and his friends were too much attached to the sentiments of President Edwards, and other American Divines of later date, and that by importing their metaphysical refinements, there would be some danger of relaxing that muscular system of theology to which he himself was so ardently devoted.'[94] Fuller himself was quite open concerning his appreciation of the New Divinity men. The two men could not be reconciled.

The ways Fuller drew from the New England theologians further show how his thinking was shaped by some of the cultural and intellectual currents of his times. In repeatedly speaking of God as 'the infinitely wise and good Governor of the world', the New Divinity men were influenced not only by Grotius but also, as Mark Noll states, their context in the time of the American Revolution, with its concerns for 'fairness in government and personal responsibility in citizens'.[95] Their approach was moulded – in part – by the spirit of the age. There were additional reasons which made the moral government approach attractive in a European, Enlightenment context. European contemporaries who used a similar intellectual framework and language to Fuller and the New England theologians included the Utilitarian philosopher Jeremy Bentham and Cesare Beccaria (1738-94), an influential Italian thinker. Beccaria stated in his book, *On Crimes and Punishments*, that the aim of punishment was not to torture the criminal but 'to prevent others from committing the like offence'.[96] In other

---

[91] Oliver, 'Emergence of a Strict and Particular Baptist Community', 112; Foster, *New England Theology*, 185; Oliver, *History of the English Calvinistic Baptists*, 161-62.

[92] Booth, *Divine Justice*, in *Booth's Works*, 3: 50.

[93] Fuller letter to William Carey, 26 November 1802, Fuller Letters (4/5/1), 'I think [Booth's] views of imputation are too much like those of Dr Crisp, as though in the imputation of sin something more was transferred than the penal effect of it.' Cf. *Works*, 2: 710; 711-14.

[94] Morris, *Fuller*, 1st edn, 378-79.

[95] Mark A. Noll, *A History of Christianity in the United States and Canada* (London: SPCK / Grand Rapids: Eerdmans, 1992), 158. Noll continues, 'Hopkins and Bellamy did not repudiate the Calvinistic theology they had inherited from Jonathan Edwards, but the influence of contemporary notions about the imperatives of human happiness and individual rights and the need to justify all intellectual principles at the bar of reason are evident in their work.'

[96] Cesare Beccaria, *On Crimes and Punishments*,

words the purpose of penal policy was to 'deter further crime and so...ensure the welfare of society'.[97] David Bebbington comments, 'In the spirit of Beccaria, Fuller contended that the cross revealed God's view of evil and his determination to punish it.' Moreover Fuller, in a statement consistent with Beccaria, 'declared roundly' that '[t]he end of punishment is not the misery of the offender, but the general good'.[98] I have found no evidence Fuller was drawing directly from Beccaria, but they were part of the same intellectual milieu. Broader theological, philosophical and cultural streams were thus reshaping Fuller's theology of the cross as he sought to relate the gospel to the age in which he lived.

Differences Between Fuller and the New England Theologians

The importance of the New England theologians for Fuller was recognised by his contemporaries and is well brought out by Oliver. But what Oliver does not highlight so clearly is that Fuller did read these theologians critically.[99] This critical engagement can be shown in a number of ways. In his letters to Ryland and Sutcliff, although there was warm appreciation of the Americans, there were also notes of caution. Concerning Edwards Jr on *Free Grace and Atonement*, for example, he wrote to Ryland saying, 'I do not coincide with everything it contains.'[100] Fuller was quite prepared to make his caution about some aspects of the New Divinity public, stating in his 'Recommendatory Preface' to Bellamy's *True Religion Delineated* that he did not 'advocate every sentiment' written in the book.[101] Both Edwards Jr and Bellamy, in their espousal of a general, though not universal, view of the atonement, had abandoned any thought of a special design in the death of Christ. This was an important area of disagreement.[102]

The long letter Fuller wrote to Hopkins in 1798 at the height of the controversy with Booth over regeneration, from which I have already quoted, reveals

---

http://www.thefederalistpapers.org/wp-content/uploads/2013/01/Cesare-Beccaria-On-Crimes-and-Punishment.pdf [accessed 16 August 2014], 20. Cf. *On Crimes and Punishments*, trans. Henry Paolucci (Indianapolis: Bobbs-Merrill, 1963). The first English translation was published in 1767.

[97] David W. Bebbington, 'British Baptist Crucicentrism since the late Eighteenth Century: Part 1', *BQ* 44.4 (October 2011), 230.

[98] Bebbington, 'British Baptist Crucicentrism... Part 1', 230. The quotation from Fuller is found in, 'The Deity of Christ Essential to the Atonement', *Works*, 3: 693. Fuller's booklet was originally published in 1802.

[99] Oliver, 'Emergence of a Strict and Particular Baptist Community', 101; 111-15. Doubtless this is because the study of Fuller is not his primary purpose.

[100] Ryland, *Fuller*, 226.

[101] Fuller's Preface to Bellamy, *True Religion Delineated*, vii.

[102] See Foster, *New England Theology*, 116-17, for Bellamy's views.

further points of divergence between Fuller and the New Divinity.[103] In the letter, Fuller criticised Hopkins over statements the New England theologian had made, that God should be regarded as 'the author of sin'. Hopkins's view was also that of Edwards Jr and of Stephen West, who asserted 'that it was the positive design and purpose of God that moral evil should come into existence'.[104] Fuller was very wary of this way of speaking. He told Hopkins that to speak of God as 'the author of sin' would convey to most people 'that God is the friend and approver of sin; that we are the passive instruments, and that he himself, being the grand agent, ought to be held accountable for it.' He went on to cite James 1.13, and its statement that 'when tempted, no-one should say "God is tempting me"'. Fuller believed this verse challenged the teaching that God 'was the author of sin'. Of course, West never meant to convey that God 'was the friend and approver of sin' and Fuller was well aware of this. But as a man whose context for theology was an everyday pastoral ministry, Fuller saw, on a practical level, the dangers of what was being said. He went on to further criticise the New Divinity men on the basis of other verses in James chapter one, at some length. On another area of disagreement with Hopkins, Fuller contemplated the possibility of their mutual correspondence being published. Hopkins was a 'mighty reasoned,' said Fuller, 'but on this subject I feel my ground'.[105] Fuller was not afraid of Hopkins. He was willing and more than able to engage with him.

Also worthy of note are further strictures Fuller offered on some of Hopkins's fellow New Divinity thinkers. Very important, in the light of the preceding discussion on the atonement, were his detailed comments on Edwards Jr. For example, Fuller objected to the younger Edwards' account of 'public justice' as being 'too indefinite'. Tom Nettles argues that although Fuller used 'governmental language', his use of their concepts 'did not involve him in the mistakes of the governmentalists'.[106] Whatever judgment is made concerning

---

[103] There are detailed extracts from the letter in Morris, *Fuller*, 1st edn, 380-85. The following quotations are all taken from these pages.

[104] Stephen West, *An Essay of Moral Agency* (Salem, 1794), cited by Ferm, *Jonathan Edwards the Younger*; cf. the following comment by Edwards Jr also cited by Ferm, 124, 132, 'I do not deny, that God is the author of sin'.

[105] Morris, *Fuller*, 2nd edn, 298. The issue of contention was the nature of love.

[106] Thomas J. Nettles, *By His Grace and For His Glory: A Historical, Theological and Practical Study of the Doctrines of Grace in Baptist Life* (Grand Rapids: Baker, 1986), 128. Haykin's comment, 'Particular Redemption in the Writings of Andrew Fuller', 128, is that, 'Contrary to Booth's impressions, Fuller did not surrender his commitment to particular redemption. Nor did he abandon his conviction that Christ died in the stead of sinners, though, it must be admitted that his fondness for governmental language...hampered rather than helped a clear expression of this conviction.'

the value of New Divinity theology (and the verdict has often been harsh),[107] this is a better assessment than that of Philip Roberts who mistakenly states that Fuller was 'wholehearted' in his acceptance of New England views.[108] It should be emphasised again that Fuller did not copy. True, he was influenced by the New Divinity. Yet his youthful resolve 'never to be an imitator' had not left him.

Fuller's 'independence' is further highlighted by comments to Hopkins about a number of the younger New England men with whom Fuller was particularly unhappy. He confessed to enjoying some of their 'metaphysical pieces' and hoped that those who could 'throw light on evangelical subjects in this way' would continue to write. He nevertheless observed that,

> Wherever an extraordinary man has been raised up, like President Edwards...it is usual for his followers and admirers too much to confine their attention to his doctrines or manner of reasoning, as though all excellence was there concentrated. I allow that your present writers do not explicitly follow Edwards, as to his sentiments, but that you preserve the spirit of free enquiry; yet I must say, it appears to me that several of your younger men possess a rage of imitating his metaphysical manner, till some of them have become metaphysic mad. I am not without some of Mr Scott's apprehensions, lest by such a spirit, the simplicity of the gospel should be lost, and truth amongst you stand more in the wisdom of man than in the power of God.[109]

Fuller had reached a stage where he was critiquing some of the leading thinkers of his day on their own terms, faulting them for 'imitating' a man to the possible detriment of 'a spirit of free enquiry'. Fuller did not reject the approach of quoting Gill or Owen as authoritative, only to replace it by substituting new human 'authorities' which could simply be appealed to in order to decide an argument. 'Explicitly following' a man, even a man like Edwards, was just not good enough. Also characteristic of Fuller were his concerns for the 'simplicity of the gospel' and the 'power of God'. Fuller was constantly drawing people back to the 'centre', to those foundational religious truths that were simple and focused

---

[107] Perhaps best known are the criticisms of Benjamin B. Warfield, 'Edwards and the New England Theology', in *The Works of Benjamin B. Warfield. Vol 9: Studies in Theology* (Grand Rapids: Baker, 1991), 515-38; and Joseph Haroutunian, *Piety versus Moralism: The Passing of the New England Theology* (New York: Harper and Row, 1932), *passim*. See the bibliographical note in Conforti, *Hopkins and the New Divinity*, 233-36, for further works critiquing the New Divinity.

[108] As does R. Philip Roberts, *Continuity and Change: London Calvinistic Baptists and the Evangelical Revival, 1760-1820* (Wheaton, IL: R.O. Roberts, 1989), 170.

[109] Morris, *Fuller*, 1st edn, 384-85. 'Mr Scott' is, once again, the evangelical Anglican Thomas Scott. Fuller may well have had Edwards Jr and Stephen West themselves in mind when he made these comments, particularly in relation to their attempts to modify and 'improve' Edwards Sr's theory of the will. See Foster, *New England Theology*, 224-69.

on the gospel of Christ.[110] In indulging in rather esoteric metaphysical speculation, the younger New England men were departing from the evangelical emphases which Fuller held dear. Philosophy could never be set up as an 'oracle'. As he had earlier written to Ryland, philosophy was 'out of its place, when seated upon the *bench* by the side of God's word: the *bar* is the highest station to which it ought to be admitted'.[111]

In all these extracts Fuller's independence of judgment, practical 'down to earth' agenda and commitment to a 'spirit of free enquiry' (one of his favourite phrases), are all in evidence. His evangelicalism is highlighted by his commitment to the simple core truths of the gospel, truths that had to be lived as well as believed. Chief among these was his frequently stated commitment to the scriptures as the word of God. Though various human authorities, including Edwards and the very best of contemporary philosophy, could come to the 'bar' of the court – it was God's word – and God's word alone, that should sit in judgment.[112] This is important because, for Fuller, a spirit of free enquiry did not mean abandoning the Bible as the supreme standard. Bebbington has observed that in the nineteenth century some 'liberal evangelicals' drifted from their biblical roots as they advocated a completely unfettered, supposedly 'presuppositionless' pursuit of a spirit of free enquiry. He states,

> It was held that a condition of progress in scientific knowledge is a total lack of presuppositions... The belief that it is possible to operate without any presuppositions was the result of exaggerating one aspect of enlightenment teaching. An emphasis on free enquiry was exalted above one of the four evangelical characteristics, biblicism.[113]

My contention is that this was one of the traits which Fuller, in 1795, recognised in some of the New England men. It was a trait that he was determined to resist. This chapter has shown the influence of progressive American thinking on Fuller. Yet it has also shown that, as some of the 'human authorities' from a school he held dear drifted from evangelical biblicism, Fuller remained tenaciously wedded to the Bible as God's authoritative word.

---

[110] Olin C. Robison, 'The Particular Baptists in England: 1760-1820' (unpublished DPhil thesis, University of Oxford, 1963), 36.

[111] Fuller letter to John Ryland, 9 October 1795, in Ryland, *Fuller*, 229-30.

[112] Cf. Fuller letter to Timothy Dwight, 1 June 1805, in Gunton Fuller, Memoir, in *Works*, 85, in which he stated that Edwards Sr's 'sermons on justification have afforded me more satisfaction on that important doctrine than any human performance which I have read'. The qualification of Edwards's work as a 'human' performance was typical of Fuller.

[113] David W. Bebbington, *Evangelicalism in Modern Britain: A History from the 1730s to the 1980s* (London: Unwin Hyman, 1989), 76.

Fuller as a Theologian

A theological assessment of Fuller's importance and power for those doing theology today is beyond the scope of this book, although my hope is that this theological biography provides resources for others engaged in this task. The following brief assessment seeks to show Fuller's importance in the context of his times, as well as tracing out some of the ways how his theology shaped subsequent generations.

Appreciation of Fuller by his Contemporaries

As far as England and his own denomination were concerned, by the end of the eighteenth century Fuller was acknowledged by most evangelical Particular Baptists as their premier theologian. Ryland, a significant thinker in his own right, considered Fuller a man who was 'equally successful in enforcing the practical, in stating the theoretical, and discussing the polemical branches of theology.' 'He rose,' said Ryland, 'to high distinction among the religious writers of his day.'[114] Joseph Ivimey, writing soon after Fuller's death, believed that the Kettering pastor enjoyed a high and, in many ways, 'unrivalled station' as the denomination's theologian.[115] These are just two of many comments that could have been cited here.

Important as the debates covered in this present chapter were, it was the leading ideas of the *Gospel Worthy* which constituted Fuller's most important theological contribution to Particular Baptist life. The *Gospel Worthy* was the most influential text in weaning the majority of Particular Baptists away from high Calvinism. Ryland cites the example of an older minister, Joshua Thomas, who initially opposed the *Gospel Worthy*, but 'came over to Mr Fuller's views at last'.[116] He would have been one of many. In 1797 a group of Deacons in a Baptist Church in Hull wrote to the evangelical Baptist Pastor Joseph Kinghorn. The Hull church wanted Kinghorn to help them to find a minister and specified the sort of man they were looking for. Amongst other things they declared he must be a 'lively, zealous and affectionate preacher' and 'orthodox'. The letter has a marginal note explaining the meaning of 'orthodox'. It says 'of Mr Fuller's sentiments'.[117] Fuller's achievement in writing the *Gospel Worthy* and

---

[114] Ryland, *Fuller*, xii.

[115] Joseph Ivimey, *A History of the English Baptists (HEB)* 4 vols (London: Hinton, Holdsworth & Ball, 1811-30), 4: 532.

[116] Ryland, *Fuller*, 131. For Thomas, who was a minister at Leominster, see Ivimey, *HEB*, 1: 65, 73.

[117] Cited by Arthur H. Kirkby, 'Theology of Andrew Fuller in its relation to Calvinism' (unpublished PhD thesis, University of Edinburgh, 1954), 11. The letter is dated 23 March 1797, from three Deacons at George Street Baptist Church in Hull to Kinghorn who was pastor of St Mary's Baptist Church, Norwich. The original is held in the archives at St Mary's.

subsequently defending and modifying his thinking was considerable. His work would shape Particular Baptist life for generations to come.

Fuller's significance as Christian thinker was also recognised by contemporaries beyond English Particular Baptist life. For example, he was urged to accept honorary doctorates from two prestigious New England colleges in recognition of his work. Fuller declined them both. Writing to Samuel Hopkins in 1798, he expressed his gratitude at the honour he had heard the New Jersey College had conferred on him earlier that year. It was, he said, 'such a token of respect'. He continued, 'I esteem it as coming from that quarter which, beyond any other in the world, I most approve.' Despite this he did not, he believed, have the 'qualifications which are expected to accompany such titles' and in addition thought all such 'titles in religion' to be contrary to Jesus' words in Matthew 23.8, 'Do not be called Rabbi...for you are all brothers.'[118]

If Timothy Dwight (1752-1817),[119] the President of Yale from 1795 to his death, had heard of Fuller's views about titles it did not stop him writing to the Kettering pastor in 1805 informing him that '[t]he corporation of Yale College at the last public commencement conveyed on you the degree of Doctor of Divinity'. Dwight, a maternal grandson of Edwards Sr, stated that, 'As this act is the result of the knowledge of your personal character and your published works only, and as such degrees are not inconsiderately given by this body, I flatter myself that it will be regarded by you in the light of a sincere testimony of respect to you.'[120] The letter and testimony were handed to him personally by the Professor of Chemistry at Yale, Benjamin Silliman, who was in England, presumably on College business. Once again, Fuller declined. Nevertheless, in his letter to Dwight, Fuller stated that,

> The writings of your grandfather, President Edwards, and of your uncle, the late Dr Edwards, have been food to me and many others...some pieces I have met with of yours have also afforded me much pleasure... I have requested Mr Silliman to procure of my bookseller all that he can furnish of what I have published, which I

---

[118] Fuller letter to Samuel Hopkins, 17 March 1798, Fuller Letters (4/5/1). Fuller had earlier expressed his views on doctorates forcefully to Ryland, as 'John Ryland Jr Letter to Andrew Fuller', Bristol Baptist College library (G 97 B Box A [n.d but internal evidence points to late 1793]), shows. The letter is Ryland's reply to Fuller's strictures on Ryland's own honorary doctorate. Ryland regretted having received this, but he regarded being called 'Dr' as a 'nickname' and thought using it preferable to having to constantly explain that he had rejected it, leaving him open to the accusation of 'false pride'. He received the doctorate earlier in 1793 from Brown University, Rhode Island. See *The Armies of the Lamb: The Spirituality of Andrew Fuller*, ed. by Michael A.G. Haykin (Dundas, Ontario: Joshua Press, 2001), 153 n.

[119] For Dwight see *Dictionary of Evangelical Biography 1730-1860 (DEB)*, ed. by Donald M. Lewis, 2 vols (Oxford: Blackwell, 1995), 1: 336-37.

[120] Timothy Dwight letter to Fuller, 18 March 1805, in Gunton Fuller, Memoir, in *Works*, 1: 85.

hope you will accept and furnish with a place in the college library, as a token of my grateful esteem.[121]

Andrew Fuller, the self-taught boy from the Cambridgeshire Fens, had become a theologian of international standing.

Conclusion

Fuller's theology did not remain static after the publication of the *Gospel Worthy*. His thinking continued to develop and was refashioned in different ways, not only through his debate with Dan Taylor but also, as seen in this chapter, in dispute with Abraham Booth. His understanding of the atonement, especially of imputation and substitution, shifted. As he developed new approaches he was influenced by other writers, especially leading figures of the New Divinity school. Nevertheless, he did not accept their views unquestioningly; indeed, he was often critical of them, both privately and publicly. Fuller was a theologian of great merit, a pastor / scholar who grappled with large issues whilst always maintaining a practical focus. One does not have to agree with all his arguments to recognise him as one of the greatest evangelical thinkers of his age.

---

[121] Fuller letter to Timothy Dwight, 1 June 1805, in Gunton Fuller, Memoir, in *Works*, 1: 85.

CHAPTER 7

Further Ministry

A moral revolution in the hearts of men

This chapter explores further aspects of Fuller's life and ministry as it unfolded after 1792. His continuing work in Kettering is considered, together with some dimensions of his wider ministry. Some family issues are also covered. Fuller remarried in 1794 and the marriage brought him considerable joy. Yet he experienced further family trauma too, especially in respect of the eldest child from his first marriage, Robert. Finally, his role with the BMS is analysed, with most space given over to his work for the Society. Included in this section is an evaluation of an apologetic book he wrote specifically to defend cross-cultural mission work against those who opposed it. The special focus on the BMS is appropriate seeing that the Society bulked so large in Fuller's life. The theme that binds these different strands of his life and ministry together is evangelism. In each of the different dimensions of his life, his overriding concern was to work for the extension of Christ's Kingdom.

Ministry in Kettering and Beyond

Throughout Fuller's pastorate at Kettering, the work of the 'Little Meeting' grew. According to the Church Book, there were 88 members when Fuller first became pastor, a figure which had increased to 174 by the time of his death in 1815. During Fuller's pastorate 232 people were received into membership, with 146 coming off the membership list, either because they had died, had moved away or been excluded.[1] This was steady rather than spectacular growth, but account needs also to be taken of many others who were attending regularly. After 1805 a Sunday congregation at Kettering might well be over a 1000 strong, with many children and young people among them. A number of those

---

[1] Church Book, Kettering Baptist Church, 1773-1815, Fuller Baptist Church, Kettering, Entry for 23 February 1815. Of the 174 members at Fuller's death, 100 were women. Members were suspended or excluded for a variety of reasons, most commonly sexual misconduct and 'drinking to excess', e.g., 107, 136.

who came walked to the services from the villages surrounding Kettering.[2] Evidently many of these regular 'hearers' never came into membership. This fact does raise questions about the number of actual conversions and the way these attenders were (or were not) followed up.[3] Nevertheless, something significant was happening through Fuller's ministry at Kettering.

The Meeting House had already been enlarged once, in 1786,[4] to accommodate some early growth. But by the early-nineteenth century the building was again too small to accommodate the numbers of people wanting to attend. In 1805 an almost entirely new chapel was built, with only a few walls of the old structure retained. Gunton Fuller remembered being part of a small group who witnessed the foundation stone being laid when he was just six years of age. The fact that Fuller's son explicitly described the group as 'small' – just the deacons, the family and a few friends – is significant. Fuller disliked ceremonies and reacted against anything that smacked of pomp and show. The building itself was plain and simple. 'We aimed at comfort and convenience,' the pastor said, 'and such as it is we have paid for it amongst ourselves.'[5]

Church Services and Preaching Style

Services at the chapel tended to be in harmony with the building: they were simple and straightforward too. There were no musical instruments to accompany the sung worship, with the Psalms or hymns led by a precentor. Gunton Fuller, commenting from the point of view of a later nineteenth-century minister, was negative about the tunes that were often chosen, which required the 'endless repetitions' of lines, words and phrases. One hymn and tune required the congregation to repeat the words 'blast them in everlasting death'. This was sung, according to Gunton Fuller, without 'any apparent thought of [the] awful meaning' of the words.[6] There were other issues. It was the tradition to stand for the 'long prayer', with the congregation turning 180 degrees so their backs were to the minister. Pastor and people were addressing God together and it was therefore considered appropriate that everyone faced the same way. The reality was that people got distracted, especially when latecomers arrived. It appears

---

2 John Ryland Jr, *The Work of Faith, the Labour of Love, and the Patience of Hope Illustrated in the Life and Death of the Rev. Andrew Fuller*, 2nd edn (London: Button and Son, 1818), 246, 383.

3 It was not uncommon for there to be a significant difference between the numbers in membership of a church and the numbers attending. In 1818 the church at Gold Hill, Buckinghamshire, had a similar ratio of members to non-members attending services: about one in five. See David W. Bebbington, *Evangelicalism in Modern Britain: A History from the 1730s to the 1980s* (London: Unwin Hyman, 1989), 21.

4 Ryland, *Fuller*, 374.

5 Andrew Gunton Fuller, *Men Worth Remembering: Andrew Fuller* (London: Hodder and Stoughton, 1882), 52-53 (53).

6 Gunton Fuller, *Fuller*, 78.

many of the congregation were tempted to open their eyes to see who these late arrivals were! When the people were looking towards their pastor as he preached, they had to cope with two high windows either side of the pulpit. On clear days they would be almost blinded by the sun as it streamed in through the windows.[7] The building may have 'aimed at comfort and convenience', but the design was not entirely successful.

Preaching was at the heart of the worship service.[8] Some critical remarks concerning Fuller's preaching do appear in the different biographies of his life and it does seem that this was not his greatest gift. Hayden summarises some of these comments: Fuller lacked 'easy elocution' and his voice, although 'strong', could be 'heavy'.[9] In addition, he seems to have spent little time preparing for some of his regular local church preaching. His son put it delicately, stating that 'it was not often that Mr Fuller's preparations for the pulpit were elaborate'.[10] Fuller's normal practice was to jot down a few shorthand headings which he memorised, meaning he would often be without notes in the pulpit. He relied on 'the inspiration of the occasion' as he expanded on his headings.[11] Yet he was a popular speaker. Ryland commented on his friend, saying that his love for people shone through in the pulpit. Also, when Fuller spoke he had 'an evident unction from the Holy One'. Although there were some who excelled him for 'fluency' (Ryland was thinking particularly of Samuel Pearce) Fuller was an effective, extempore preacher.[12] Moreover, there were occasions when he did take more time to prepare, for example when he preached through certain books of the Bible on Sunday mornings. The practice of regular, systematic exposition was the habit of many of his friends, for instance, Robert Hall.[13] Fuller may well have been influenced by their example as he adopted this approach himself. The Kettering pastor began his expositions on Sunday mornings in April 1790, con-

---

[7] Gunton Fuller, *Fuller*, 77-78.

[8] For a very good analysis of Fuller's preaching, see Keith S. Grant, *Andrew Fuller and the Evangelical Renewal of Pastoral Theology* (Milton Keynes: Paternoster, 2013), 77-104.

[9] Roger L. Hayden, 'The Life and Influence of Andrew Fuller', in *The Kettering Connection: Northamptonshire Baptists and Overseas Mission*, ed. by Ronald L. Greenall (Leicester: Department of Adult Education, University of Leicester, 1993), 5; John Webster Morris, *Memoirs of the Life and Death of the Rev Andrew Fuller*, 1st edn (High Wycombe, 1816) 2nd edn (London: Wightman and Cramp, 1826), 1st edn, 66-67.

[10] Gunton Fuller, *Fuller*, 61.

[11] Gunton Fuller, *Fuller*, 62.

[12] Ryland, *Fuller*, 144.

[13] John Ryland Jr, *Memoirs of Robert Hall of Arnsby [sic.]. With a Brief History of the Baptist Church...* 2nd edn; rev. ed. J.A. Jones (London: James Paul, 1850), 22. Hall gave his 'expository lectures' on Sunday evenings.

tinuing until his health gave way in the closing months of his life.[14] Books he expounded included Genesis and Revelation, and his sermons on both these books were later written up and published.[15]

Fuller dedicated his volumes on Genesis and Revelation to his church and he evidently loved his people.[16] And yet, as he expounded the scriptures to believers, a concern for the spread of the gospel was never far from the surface. In his messages on Revelation, his New England influenced postmillennialism, with its concomitant belief that great success would 'attend the preaching of the gospel' even before the millennium dawned, shaped his exegesis and application.[17] Fuller believed that he and his hearers were living at the time of the 'pouring out of the seven vials' described in Revelation 16 and that this period was immediately prior to the commencement of the millennium.[18] The pouring out of the vials would be accompanied by many 'wars and struggles', but also by great spiritual victories.[19] As he preached through Revelation Sunday-by-Sunday between 1809 and 1810, he was ready to believe that a time of 'great success' was at hand as far as gospel work was concerned. In his opening dedication he declared, 'we have seen enough, amidst all the troubles of our times, to gladden our hearts; and trust that our children will see greater things than these'.[20] Some of Fuller's exposition was highly speculative and makes strange reading today, as does much written on Revelation by past (and indeed present) generations. Yet these messages on the last book of the Bible show that Fuller delighted in and looked forward to the spread of the gospel. This evangelistic note was struck in many other ways in his ministry. His work with younger people can be taken as an example.

---

[14] Ryland, *Fuller*, 382. From this date Fuller went through Isaiah, Joel, Amos, Hosea, Micah, Nahum, Habakkuk, Zephaniah, Jeremiah, Lamentations, Daniel, Haggai, Zechariah, Malachi, Job, Genesis, Matthew, Luke, John, Revelation, Acts, Romans and 1 Corinthians as far as chapter 4 Verse 5.

[15] Andrew Fuller, *Expository Discourses on the Book of Genesis: Interspersed with Practical Reflections*, 2 vols (Dunstable / London: J.W. Morris, 1806); *Expository Discourses on the Apocalypse Interspersed with Practical Reflections* (London: W. Button, 1815); *The Complete Works of the Rev. Andrew Fuller, With a Memoir of his Life by the Rev. Andrew Gunton Fuller*, ed. by Andrew Gunton Fuller, rev. ed. by Joseph Belcher; 3 vols, 3rd edn (Harrisonburg, VA: Sprinkle Publications, 1988 [1845]), 3: 1-198 (Genesis); 201-306 (Revelation).

[16] *Expository Discourses on Genesis* in *Works*, 3: 1; *Expository Discourses on the Apocalypse*, in *Works*, 3: 201.

[17] See, e.g., *Expository Discourses on the Apocalypse*, in *Works*, 3: 293-94.

[18] *Expository Discourses on the Apocalypse*, in *Works*, 3: 391.

[19] Fuller letter to John Saffery, 14 October 1811, Andrew Fuller Letters to John Saffery, Angus Library, Regent's Park College, Oxford (II/273).

[20] *Expository Discourses on the Apocalypse*, in *Works*, 3: 202. The dedication was not written until 1815, the year of Fuller's death, although the work had basically been ready for 'between four and five years'.

Work with Young People

Every year, from at least the early 1790s, Fuller would preach a new year's sermon particularly aimed at children and youth. On these occasions, according to Ryland, Fuller would 'pour forth all his heart...exhorting and charging every one, as a Father [sic.] doth his children'.[21] One of these sermons, entitled 'Advantages of Early Piety', illustrates his approach.[22]

Fuller took as his text Psalm 90.14, 'O satisfy us early with thy mercy, that we may rejoice and be glad all our days', which he believed was a prayer especially appropriate for the 'rising generation'. He began by declaring, 'I hope I need not say that this prayer...is expressive of the desires of your minister and your parents; you know it is so. Oh that it might express your own!' Fuller impressed on his hearers the importance of accepting God's saving mercy while they were young.[23] He reminded those present that during the past year there had been five funerals of young people from the congregation, 'some of them under twenty years of age, and others of them but little past that period'. 'None of them seem to have thought much of dying,' said the preacher, 'yet they are gone from the land of the living! Hark! From their tombs I hear the language of solemn warning and counsel!' He closed by pleading with his hearers to come to Christ,

> What shall I say more? Will you, my dear young people, will you drink and be satisfied at the fountain of mercy; a fountain that is wide open and flows freely through our Lord Jesus Christ? You cannot plead the want of sufficient inducements. Ministers, parents, Christians, angels, the faltering voice at death, the solemn assurance of a judgement to come, and, above all, the sounding of the bowels [i.e. heart] of Jesus Christ, all say, Come.[24]

Ryland recorded that 'many young people' who later believed in Christ 'traced their first serious impressions' to these occasions.[25] Fuller wrote to Ryland in March 1810 sharing with his friend that he had begun a weekly meeting in his vestry at Kettering for 'earnest' young people, with four of these now waiting

---

[21] Ryland, *Fuller*, 383.
[22] For the text, see 'Advantages of Early Piety: To Young People', in *Works*, 1: 421-26. The sermon is n.d. but it was preached in January 1799. See Fuller letter to the 'son of an intimate friend', 21 January 1799, in Ryland, *Fuller*, 513. The sermon was later published as *A New Year's Gift to Youth* (Boston, Newburyport [Mass.]: Maning and Loring, 1802). The earliest British edn. appears to be (Edinburgh: John Ritchie, 1805).
[23] 'Advantages of Early Piety', in *Works*, 1: 422.
[24] 'Advantages of Early Piety', in *Works*, 1: 425-26.
[25] Ryland, *Fuller*, 383.

for baptism.[26] At one stage he appears to have been meeting with them on both Mondays and Fridays, occasions that he said were 'much thronged'.[27]

Fuller also wanted to reach younger people who were beyond the immediate orbit of the church. Gunton Fuller recorded that, sometime in the 1800s (a period when Fuller had very little time for pastoral work amongst his members) his father was devising a scheme to evangelise amongst young lacemakers who worked in Kettering. This involved getting hold of some of the white wrapping paper the girls used and printing some 'little hymns' on them, some of which he planned to compose himself. In a letter to a friend he enthused about the plan, 'Every child who comes for a small quantity of thread will find it wrapped up in a paper containing a short impressive hymn addressed to its heart.'[28] Not the most plausible of Fuller's schemes, it is unlikely this was ever implemented. But the Kettering pastor's evangelistic concerns are, once again, clear.

Wider Ministry

In addition to his work at Kettering Fuller continued to travel widely, speaking at other churches both near to home and further afield. A significant proportion of these engagements, even after 1792, were separate from his work as secretary of the BMS. Fuller preached at the opening of new church buildings, to theological students at Bristol and Stepney and on behalf of various societies, for example the British and Foreign Bible Society, which was formed in 1804.[29] He was increasingly invited to give addresses at the ordinations and inductions of new ministers, with his *Works* containing many examples of this type of preaching.[30] On these occasions he often took the opportunity to encourage pastors to preach evangelistically. In a message entitled, 'The Nature of the Gospel, and the Manner in Which it Ought to be Preached', he urged the unnamed minister to be 'faithful', 'earnest' and full of love or 'great affection' as he declared the

---

[26] Fuller letter to John Ryland, 2 March 1810, Typescript Andrew Fuller Letters, transcribed by Joyce A. Booth, superintended by Ernest A. Payne, Angus Library, Regent's Park College, Oxford (4/5/1 and 4/5/2) (4/5/2).

[27] Fuller letters to John Ryland, 28 December, 1810, 27 February 1811, Fuller Letters (4/5/2).

[28] Gunton Fuller, *Fuller*, 88.

[29] See, e.g., *Works*, 1: 413, 515-21, 391, 417.

[30] See, e.g., *Works*, 1: 478-509. For a helpful survey of Fuller's ordination sermons, see Nigel D. Wheeler, 'Eminent Spirituality and Eminent Usefulness': Andrew Fuller's (1754-1815) Pastoral Theology in his Ordination Sermons (unpublished PhD thesis, Univ. of Pretoria, 2009). See also Grant, *Andrew Fuller*, esp. 53-75. I believe there is more discontinuity between Fuller's approach and that of previous generations than Wheeler allows. Nevertheless, there was significant continuity and Wheeler brings this out well.

gospel.[31] The aim was to 'set before' unbelievers the only safe 'refuge', namely Christ. It was him, and him only, that people must flee to.[32] To be called to point people to Christ was a solemn thing indeed. The message was full of weighty language as Fuller pressed home to the new minister the seriousness of his calling.[33] Another sermon, entitled 'Churches should exhibit the Light of the Gospel', shows him addressing not the pastor but the church, challenging the people as to their own evangelistic responsibilities. 'The end of your existence,' Fuller stated, 'is to hold forth the word of life'. [34] This they were to do by supporting their minister and by commending the gospel themselves, particularly by living 'blameless' lives. Holy living was, Fuller believed, a 'powerful way of preaching the gospel. It speaks louder than words – louder than thunder.'[35] Whether by word or example, Christ was to be commended.

Fuller's major role in stimulating evangelism in the churches was through the impact of his theological works, in particular the *Gospel Worthy*. But he also played a more direct personal role promoting his brand of evangelical Calvinism in local church settings. An example of this was when he travelled to give the charge at the induction of Francis Franklin, at what was to become Queens Road Baptist Church in Coventry. The church had had some struggles with issues relative to high Calvinism, but Fuller's involvement in this service was, according to the official history of the church, 'conclusive proof' as to where it now stood in 'the evangelistic spectrum'.[36] In 1803 Fuller would return to the church and preach a 'charity sermon' in support of the Sunday School, an event at which £44 was raised.[37] Thus he promoted evangelism beyond his own local church. In engaging in this sort of wider work, Fuller was making yet further contributions to the revitalisation of his denomination.

Family Issues

Remarriage and Further Children

On 18 July 1794 Fuller confided in his diary,

---

[31] 'The Nature of the Gospel, and the Manner in Which it Ought to be Preached', in *Works*, 1: 495-96

[32] 'The Nature of the Gospel...', in *Works*, 1: 495.

[33] See 'The Nature of the Gospel...', in *Works*, 1: 494-96, esp. the closing remarks, 496.

[34] 'Churches Should Exhibit the Light of the Gospel', in *Works*, 1: 532. The sermon is n.d..

[35] 'Churches Should Exhibit the Light of the Gospel', in *Works*, 1: 532-34 (533).

[36] Clyde Binfield, *Pastors and People: The Biography of a Baptist Church, Queen's Road, Coventry* (Coventry: Alan Sutton, 1984), 27. Franklin became the church's assistant minister before later succeeding the senior pastor.

[37] Binfield, *Pastors and People*, 33.

Of late my thoughts have turned upon another marriage – That passage, which has been with me in all my principal concerns thro' life – in all thy ways acknowledge him & he shall direct thy paths has recurred again – I have found much of the hand of God in this concern, both to turning me from some quarters on wh[ich] my thoughts were employed, and guiding me to others where I hope to find a helper to my soul. [38]

This extract was cited by Ryland, but only after some judicious editing. In his *Life* of Fuller the diary entry was recorded as follows,

Of late, my thoughts have turned upon another marriage. That passage, which has been with me in all my principal concerns through life – 'in all thy ways acknowledge him, and he shall direct thy paths' has recurred again. I have found much of the hand of God in guiding me to one in whom I hope to find a helper to my soul.[39]

Ryland not only tidied the grammar (his usual practice) but omitted the inference that Fuller had been looking elsewhere before he fixed on the woman he was considering when he wrote this entry. The reference to 'others' was probably an allusion to the family of the woman in question, although it was sufficiently ambiguous for Ryland to change the word in the diary entry itself to 'another' in his clear, unmistakable hand. He then changed it again to 'one' in the official version presented for public consumption.[40] Fuller had been single for two years and had not found this easy.[41] It appears he had been actively searching for a wife but, in July 1794, he believed that God had indeed led him to his future partner.

The woman was Ann Coles, the only daughter of William Coles, Baptist minister at Maulden in Bedfordshire.[42] Fuller proposed and was accepted. He and Ann were married on 30 December of that year, a service that Fuller ensured was conducted 'with as little parade as possible'.[43] He had written in his diary, 'this day will probably stamp my future life with either increasing happiness or misery'.[44] Something a little more enthusiastic might have been expected and yet, fortunately for both partners, their relationship was strong and

---

[38] Diary and Spiritual Thoughts [1784-1801] (Bristol Baptist College) (G 95 b), 18 July 1794. The reference is to Proverbs 3.6.

[39] Ryland, *Fuller*, 292.

[40] Diary and Spiritual Thoughts, 18 July 1794. Ryland, also wrote the word 'Marriage' at the head of the extract, presumably for future reference, so he could later find the section he wished to quote.

[41] Cf. Fuller letter to William Carey and John Thomas, 25 March 1794, Letters to Carey, Marshman and Ward... Angus Library, Regent's Park College, Oxford (4/3/5), 'I yet remain single...'

[42] For William Coles, see Ryland, *Fuller*, 293-94.

[43] Fuller letter to John Ryland, January 1795, in Ryland, *Fuller*, 292.

[44] Diary and Spiritual Thoughts, 30 December 1794.

loving.[45] Even so, his life with Ann was marked by tragedy, as his first marriage had been. She bore six children, of whom three died in infancy. By this point in his life Fuller was not keeping his diary in the way he had been in the 1780s – the entries for the 1790s are only very occasional. For one thing, he no longer had the time to record a lot of detail and for another, his spirituality had changed. It was less focused on self-examination and recording his inner thoughts and more concerned with outward facing gospel ministry.[46] Consequently, how Fuller coped with his children's deaths is difficult to discern with any precision. There is, however, some evidence on which to base a judgement, especially concerning Fuller's response to one of the children who died. She was called Ann after her mother, and lived until she was one year eight months old. The mother later told Ryland of a 'mournful' night when both parents had stayed up to watch over their daughter.[47] They knew in their hearts that infant Ann was dying. In the morning, physically and emotionally exhausted, the father penned some lines which included the following,

> Sweet babe! why fix they wishful eyes on us?
> We feel thy load; but cannot give thee aid!
> Didst thou know aught, we would direct thine eyes,
> To HIM from whom alone thy help must come.

> Oh! our Redeemer, and our God – our help
> In tribulation – hear our fervent prayer!
> To THEE we now resign the sacred trust,
> Which thou, erewhile, didst unto us commit.[48]

As to his emotions, they were raw. The Fullers were going through 'tribulation' and their prayers were 'fervent'. As he later said, they felt their child was being 'torn' from them.[49] As to Fuller's theology and spirituality, there was a deep trust in God's sovereignty and goodness. The emphatic HIM and THEE placed the focus on God and this focus was maintained as the poem unfolded, with the final lines of the full poem expressing the sure and certain 'hope' of eternal life to come. One senses that Fuller was reminding himself of these truths and telling himself not to lose hold of them in the midst of this new trauma. Yet despite

---

[45] Both partners wrote warmly about each other. For Andrew's thoughts, see Diary and Spiritual Thoughts, 12 May 1796; for Ann's, see Ryland, *Fuller*, 295.

[46] Cf. the example of William Carey. John Sutcliff had encouraged Carey in journal keeping, but Carey wrote to Sutcliff that he had discontinued the practice 'owing to my numerous avocations, which engross all my time.' See Carey letter to Sutcliff, 16 January 1798, in Eustace Carey, *Memoir of William Carey, DD* (London: Jackson and Walford, 1836), 322.

[47] Ryland, *Fuller*, 295.

[48] Ryland, *Fuller*, 295-96. Cf. Fuller to William Carey, 18 January 1798, Letters to Carey, Marshman and Ward.

[49] Ryland, *Fuller*, 295-96.

this inner wrestling, his faith in God and the promises of the gospel remained solid. His battle with grief was very real, yet his theological commitments meant this struggle was shot through with trust and hope. Sadly, further tragedy was to strike Fuller and the eldest son from his first marriage, Robert.

Robert Fuller

Fuller expressed some concerns about his son Robert in a diary entry for 12 May 1796. This time the issue had nothing to do with his child's physical health. The father wrote, 'This day my eldest Son Robert is gone to London, upon trial at a warehouse belonging to Mr Burles'. He continued, 'Some times he has expressed a desire after the ministry... My [heart] has been much exercised about him... I know not whether he be a real Christian as yet.'[50] 'Mr Burles' was William Burls, a wealthy Baptist merchant who supported the BMS financially and was an important agent for the Society in the capital.[51] Despite Fuller's doubts about Robert's spiritual state, he hoped his son might indeed one day become a pastor and had extracted a promise from Burls that he would release Robert from his apprenticeship if he became soundly converted and showed potential for ministerial work.[52] However, contrary to the father's hopes, Robert's life was to follow a rather different path.

The apprenticeship was a disaster, as Fuller confided to his diary later that month. His son had shown himself to be unstable and lacking application.[53] In July 1796 he lamented that, given Robert's behaviour, he 'must leave London'. 'What to do with him,' Fuller confessed, 'I know not.'[54] The solution was an apprenticeship to a joiner and cabinet maker in Kettering but this also worked out poorly, with Robert 'every few months running away'.[55] Things went from bad to worse. In 1798 Robert joined the army as a private solider, much to his father's distress. He was discharged, but in 1799 he ran away to join the Marines. Almost immediately he was pleading with his father to buy him out. This duly happened, yet by the middle of the year Robert had run off once more.

---

[50] *Diary and Spiritual Thoughts*, 12 May 1796.

[51] *Baptist Autographs in the John Rylands University Library of Manchester, 1741-1845*, trans. and ed. by Timothy Whelan (Macon, GA: Mercer UP, 2009), 362-63. Ryland, who included this diary extract, only referred to Burls as 'Mr. B.'. See Ryland, *Fuller*, 297. Fuller and Burls became firm friends and the London man saw Fuller the day before he died. See [Anon.], 'A Memoir of the Rev. Andrew Fuller', in *Baptist Magazine*, vol. 7, July 1815 (London: Button & Son, 1815), 274.

[52] *Diary and Spiritual Thoughts*, 12 May 1796.

[53] *Diary and Spiritual Thoughts*, 29 May 1796.

[54] *Diary and Spiritual Thoughts*, July 1796.

[55] *Diary and Spiritual Thoughts*, 21 July 1800. This entry is a long account of Robert's struggles, which refers to events as early as 1797.

Fuller wrote, 'The sorrows of my heart have been increased...to a degree almost insupportable.'[56]

It appears Robert wanted to go to sea and so Fuller got him a place on a merchant ship. The Captain was a respectable man and it seemed Robert would be looked after. Then disaster struck. Whilst still ashore and waiting to board his ship, Robert was press-ganged into the Royal Navy. Conditions in the navy for ordinary seaman were notoriously bad and Fuller wept for his son. His misery was compounded when a report reached him that Robert had received 300 lashes as a punishment for some misdemeanor and, as a result of his terrible punishment, had died.

Up to this point Fuller had remained hopeful for his son, but under this new blow he was close to despair.

> Oh!... this is heart-trouble! In former cases, my sorrows found vent in tears; but now, I can seldom weep. A kind of morbid heart sickness, preys upon me from day to day. Every object around me reminds me of him! Ah!...he was wicked; and mine eye was not over him, to prevent it...he was detected, and tried, and condemned; and I knew it not...he cried under his agonies; but I heard him not...he expired, without an eye to pity, or a hand to help him!...O Absalom! my son! my son! would I had died for thee, my son![57]

This extract, included by Ryland, appears to be a translation of a shorthand passage in Fuller's diary, part of an entry from 10 June 1801.[58] In his grief he pictured the terrible death, unable to do anything to stop it or offer comfort to his son. He was now almost beyond tears. Nevertheless, he continued to trust in God and not long after writing these words was overjoyed when a letter arrived from Robert. The report had in fact been 'altogether erroneous'.[59] Robert was very much alive and had not been punished in the way Fuller had supposed. Yet this was only a temporary reprieve. In 1804 Robert deserted in Ireland and was recaptured. This time he was really punished, receiving not 300 but 350 lashes.[60] He survived – just –but was invalided out of the Navy. Father and son were reunited in London, where Robert was nursed back to health by a doctor who was known to Fuller. Yet in 1805 the son disappeared once more, incredibly joining the Marines for a second time. He was never seen by his family again.[61]

---

[56] Diary and Spiritual Thoughts, 21 July 1800. For a summary of Robert's life from 1797-1800 see Ryland, *Fuller*, 299.

[57] Ryland, *Fuller*, 292.

[58] Diary and Spiritual Thoughts, 10 June 1801. Fuller's ♥ symbol appears in the right places, as does the longhand word 'David'. Ryland does not explicitly name his source.

[59] Ryland, *Fuller*, 301.

[60] Extract from Fuller letter to Ryland, July 1804, in Ryland, *Fuller*, 300.

[61] Ryland, *Fuller*, 300-302.

Did Robert suffer from some of the mental health issues that his mother had experienced? This may be hinted at in a letter from Fuller to his son, dated December 1808, in which the father declared, 'I cannot but consider you as having long been under a sort of mental derangement, piercing yourself through, as well as me, with many sorrows.' He continued, 'My prayer for you, continually, is, that the God of all grace and mercy may have mercy upon you.'[62] The father shared the gospel with his son in the letter, urging him, as he had done many times previously, to turn to Christ,

> Do not despair. Far as you have gone, and low as you are sunk in sin, yet if from hence you return to God by Jesus Christ, you will find mercy. Jesus Christ came into the world to save sinners, even the chief of sinners. If you had been ever so sober and steady in your behaviour towards men, yet without repentance towards God and faith in Christ, you could not have been saved. And if you return to God by him, though your sins be great and aggravated, yet you will find mercy.[63]

It is not known whether Robert Fuller received the letter. He died somewhere off the coast of Lisbon, Portugal in March 1809. The Sunday after his father heard the dreadful news he referred, in the course of his preaching, to Jonah, whom God had heard even as 'the billows and waves passed over him'. Unable to continue speaking, he broke down and wept in the pulpit. Ryland recorded that many of his congregation 'wept with him'.[64] An article in the *East Midland Baptist Magazine* for 1895 gave an account of a talk the writer had with an old lady in Kettering who had been eight years of age at the time of Fuller's death. 'She remembered Fuller's greatest grief; a prodigal son had gone abroad and sorrowful tidings came back respecting him.'[65] Robert's death made a deep impact. The father's grief was so great it could not be hidden.

Yet, unknown to Fuller, it appears that Robert may have made a real Christian commitment on his final voyage. Certainly this was what Gunton Fuller believed, citing the testimony of a Mr Waldy, a deacon in the Baptist church at Falkirk, whom Gunton Fuller met in 1845. Waldy claimed to have served with Robert on this last voyage. He reported that Robert 'was a very pleasing, nice youth, and became a true Christian man'.[66] This ending is not as implausible as it first appears, as letters written by Robert to his father and half-sister Sarah (which are now lost), together with a report from the ship's captain, gave Fuller himself some hope that his son had come to repentance and faith at the end of

---

[62] Fuller letter to Robert Fuller, December 1808, in Ryland, *Fuller*, 302.
[63] Fuller letter to Robert Fuller, December 1808, in Ryland, *Fuller*, 302.
[64] Ryland, *Fuller*, 304.
[65] As cited by Arthur H. Kirkby, 'The Theology of Andrew Fuller in its Relation to Calvinism' (unpublished PhD thesis, Edinburgh University, 1956), 24. Duncan P. McPherson was a North American Baptist minister serving in Britain. See *The Baptist Handbook for 1896* (London: Clarke and Co, 1895), 360.
[66] Gunton Fuller, *Fuller*, 73.

his life.[67] If Gunton Fuller's account is to be believed then Michael Haykin's words are fitting, 'Andrew Fuller's many prayers for his wayward son were answered and that verse from Psalm 126 powerfully illustrated, "They that sow in tears shall reap in joy."'[68] Yet again it appears Fuller's evangelistic work had borne fruit.

Growth of the BMS

Fuller's evangelistic priorities are seen most clearly through his work for the BMS. The Society developed steadily after 1792. Thanks in part to strenuous find-raising efforts at home Carey was joined by a number of co-workers. Some of these died soon after their arrival. For example, William Grant, who arrived in 1799, died from cholera and dysentery less than a month after landing in India.[69] But two men who had stepped ashore with Grant, Joshua Marshman (1768-1837) and William Ward (1764-1823) survived the dangerous early months and proved to be extremely significant to the developing work.[70] Carey, Marshman and Ward together became known as 'the Serampore trio', deriving their name from the missionaries' base of operations from 1800 onwards. Carey and Marshman engaged in extensive Bible translation work and Ward, a printer, was instrumental in establishing a press at Serampore so that the scriptures and other literature could be printed and distributed. The first Hindu convert was Krishna Pal (d. 1822), a carpenter converted and baptised in 1800. Although India was the primary sphere of operations for the BMS in Fuller's lifetime, work also started elsewhere. Jacob Grigg and James Rodway were sent to pioneer a mission in Sierra Leone in 1795 and BMS work in the Caribbean began in 1813/14.[71] Moreover, there were now a number of other missionary societies following where the BMS had led. The inter-denominational London Missionary Society had been formed in 1795 and the Anglican Church Missionary So-

---

[67] Ryland, *Fuller*, 303-304; cf., Gunton Fuller, *Fuller*, 72-73.

[68] *Armies of the Lamb*, 286.

[69] For information in this paragraph see Stephen Neill, *A History of Christian Missions* (Harmondsworth: Penguin, 1964), 262-4; E. Daniel Potts, *British Baptist Missionaries in India, 1793-1837* (Cambridge: Cambridge University Press, 1967), 172; Brian Stanley, *The History of the Baptist Missionary Society, 1792-1992* (Edinburgh: T. & T. Clark, 1992), 70.

[70] Ward is the one most referred to in this chapter. For an appreciative nineteenth-century account of him, see Samuel Stennett, *Memoirs of the Life of the Rev. William Ward* (London: J. Haddon: 1825). For a recent study, see A. Christopher Smith, 'William Ward, (1769–1823),' in *The British Particular Baptists, 1638–1910, Vol. 2*, ed. by Michael A.G. Haykin (Springfield, MO: Particular Baptist Press, 2000), 255–271.

[71] This work in Sierra Leone failed due to Rodway's poor health, which meant he had to return home and Grigg's radical political views, which led to him being expelled from the colony. Fuller letter to William Carey, 11 October 1796, Letters to Carey, Marshman and Ward.

ciety in 1799.[72] As already stated, the Northamptonshire Particular Baptists were at the vanguard of a movement which would have global repercussions. As secretary of the BMS from its inception to his death in 1815, Fuller made an incalculable contribution to the work of the Society. The way he conceived of his role is shown by an image that would be picked up by most biographers, both of Fuller and Carey.[73] Ryland recorded that Fuller, whilst on a journey with a 'confidential friend', had remarked,

> Our undertaking to India really appeared to me, on its commencement, to be somewhat like a few men, who were deliberating about the importance of penetrating into a deep mine, which had never before been explored. We had no one to guide us; and while we were thus deliberating, Carey, as it were, said, 'Well, I will go down, if you will hold the rope'. But before he went down...he, as it seemed to me, took an oath from each of us, at the mouth of the pit, to this effect – that 'while we lived, we should never let go of the rope'.[74]

The phrases 'as it were' and 'as it seemed to me' probably indicate that the rope holding image originated with Fuller rather than Carey. Certainly it was Fuller, out of the original founders, who took his role in supporting Carey and the other missionaries most seriously. No one in Britain made a contribution to the Mission in its early years which even approached his in terms of its significance.

What were Fuller's duties as secretary? He issued the regular *Periodical Accounts* of the Society[75] and supplied missionary news to John Rippon's *Baptist Annual Register*, as well as to the *Evangelical Magazine* and the *Baptist Magazine*. He also took the lead role in the selection of missionary personnel and corresponded regularly with those already in the field. He wrote further letters promoting the work and raised awareness and funds by visiting individuals and speaking in churches.[76] As well as 'one off' visits, he engaged in longer tours as he traversed the British Isles on behalf of the Society. He also championed the cause of Christian missions in general and the BMS in particular, defending the

---

[72] Early BMS supporter Thomas Scott was the first secretary of the CMS, which was known as 'The Society for Missions in Africa and the East' until 1812. Carey had met Scott several times when the latter was Curate at Olney between 1781 and 1785. Although interdenominational, the LMS was mainly supported by Congregationalists.

[73] See also Joseph Ivimey, *A History of the English Baptists (HEB)* 4 vols (London: Hinton, Holdsworth & Ball, 1811-30), 4: 529.

[74] Ryland, *Fuller*, 157. Cf. Gilbert Laws and the subtitle of his *Andrew Fuller: Pastor, Theologian, Ropeholder* (London: Kingsgate Press, 1942). The 'confidential friend' referred to in the extract in the main text was almost certainly Ryland himself.

[75] Although this was originally done by Samuel Pearce until his death in 1799, Ryland *Fuller*, 147.

[76] Cf. the comments of Ryland, *Fuller*, 212.

missionaries against attacks at home and abroad.[77] Consequently, there are many areas that could be followed up in detail. The focus in the rest of the chapter will be, firstly, on his journeys to promote the cause in the churches and, secondly, on his work as an apologist for the Mission.

Fuller's Journeys on Behalf of the BMS

Fuller was regularly away from Kettering for up to three months of each year, travelling huge distances on behalf of the Society, aiming to collect 'a pound a mile'.[78] He ventured to London on many occasions, and at one time or other visited most of the counties in England, even making one journey to the high Calvinist bastion of Norfolk.[79] But even more remarkable were visits to Ireland (in 1804), Wales (in 1812) and Scotland (in 1799, 1802, 1805, 1808 and 1813).[80] The extensive Scottish journeys are the best documented of all his tours on behalf of the Mission. Fuller kept a journal on his first visit to Scotland, recording details of travel arrangements, together with reflections on his preaching engagements and the people he met. He also included various observations on the life of the churches he visited. Information concerning the other trips north of the border can be extracted from various letters.[81] In Scotland his ministry produced what was described as a 'hallowed excitement' and he enjoyed great personal popularity.[82] As Stanley notes, 'by his later years Fuller was probably better known, and certainly better loved, in Scotland and the North of England than in London'.[83] After his positive first visit Fuller aimed to make his Scottish tours 'triennial', but at the very end of his life this would be something even he would fail to manage.

---

[77] The most detailed study is probably still Doyle L. Young, 'The Place of Andrew Fuller in the Developing Modern Missions Movement' (unpublished PhD thesis, Southwestern Baptist Theological Seminary, 1981).

[78] Fuller letter to James Deakin, 14 August 1812, in [Anon.], 'Letters to James Deakin', *BQ* 7 (October 1935), 365. Fuller estimated that the journey to Wales was also 'about a 600 miles excursion'. Still he raised what he usually aimed for – 'my old price, a pound a mile'. Cf. Fuller letter to William Ward, 5 September 1814, Typescript Andrew Fuller Letters, transcribed by Joyce A. Booth, superintended by Ernest A. Payne, Angus Library, Regent's Park College, Oxford (4/5/1 and 4/5/2) (4/5/2). See also Stanley, *History of the BMS*, 20.

[79] Fuller letter to James Deakin, 14 August 1812, in 'Letters to James Deakin', 365.

[80] Ryland, *Fuller*, 156. Young, 'The Place of Andrew Fuller in the Developing Modern Missions Movement', 243-54, includes much material from Fuller's tours and shorter journeys, giving a flavour of the pace at which he worked.

[81] Ryland, *Fuller*, 164-83, reproduced the bulk of the journal. He also included much primary evidence relating to the other Scottish tours. See 184-212.

[82] Ryland, *Fuller*, 156; Francis A. Cox, *History of the Baptist Missionary Society of England from 1792 to 1842* (London: T. Ward, 1842), 21.

[83] Stanley, *History of the BMS*, 20.

Fuller in Scotland

Fuller's work in Scotland can be taken as an example of his extensive travels as BMS secretary. Three broad points can be made. The first is that Fuller sought to generate support from a range of denominations and church groupings on these tours. He was positive about many non-Baptist evangelicals in Scotland and they in turn welcomed him. In Edinburgh in 1799 he had his first face-to-face meeting with his own and Ryland's correspondent, the Church of Scotland minister John Erskine, whom he described as 'an excellent old man', full of 'kindness and goodness'.[84] Fuller was also impressed with a number of other ministers 'in the Kirk',[85] as he was by the independent evangelicals Robert Haldane (1764-1842) and his brother James (1768-1851). Descended from the prestigious Haldane family of Gleneagles, the brothers were men of considerable means. Following their evangelical conversions they developed a network of itinerant evangelists, and they established churches in a number of Scottish cities. In 1799 James Haldane himself became pastor of the church which met at the former circus building in Edinburgh. The work flourished and a large purpose built 'Tabernacle' was opened in 1801 to house the growing congregation. Together the brothers stood for a lively evangelicalism which incorporated a strong commitment to mission both at home and abroad (in 1796 Robert had actually attempted to undertake a self-financed evangelistic tour to Bengal).[86] It was at the brothers' instigation that Fuller made his first visit to Scotland.[87] They and their churches were to prove fertile soil for the message of the BMS.

Fuller was welcomed into the pulpits of the Haldanes' growing connexion and preached at the Edinburgh Circus on his first visit. He recorded his initial impressions in his journal, 'Certainly these appear to be excellent men, free from the extravagance and nonsense which infect some of the Calvinistic Methodists in England; and yet trying to imbibe and communicate their zeal and affection.'[88] One of those who heard him was Christopher Anderson (1782-1852), a member of the Circus church who was 'much impressed by Fuller's powerful public appeals on behalf of the Baptist mission'.[89] Anderson gave up his mem-

---

84 Journal, 11 October 1799, in Ryland, *Fuller*, 168-69.

85 Journal, 11 October 1799, in Ryland, *Fuller*, 168.

86 For information in this paragraph and for more detail on the Haldanes, see Deryck W. Lovegrove, 'Unity and Separation: Contrasting Elements in the Thought and Practice of Robert and James Alexander Haldane, in *Protestant Evangelicalism: Britain, Ireland, Germany and America c.1750 – 1950*, ed. by Keith Robbins (Oxford: Ecclesiastical Historical Society / Blackwells, 1990), 154; *Dictionary of Evangelical Biography 1730-1860 (DEB)*, ed. by Donald M. Lewis, 2 vols (Oxford: Blackwell, 1995), 1: 500-503.

87 Ryland, *Fuller*, 164.

88 Journal, 11 October 1799, in Ryland, *Fuller*, 169.

89 A. Christopher Smith, 'Christopher Anderson and the Serampore Fraternity' in, *A Mind for Mission; Essays in Appreciation of the Rev. Christopher Anderson 1782-*

bership of the Haldanes' connexion in 1801 when he became a Baptist (although not a 'Scotch Baptist' [whose churches were led by a plurality of elders]).[90] During Fuller's second Scottish tour Anderson offered himself for cross-cultural missionary service with the BMS at a personal interview with Fuller. Anderson subsequently studied with Sutcliff in Olney and Ryland in Bristol, although it was judged that, because of health problems, it would be unwise for him to go overseas. Instead he founded a Baptist church in Edinburgh on the English single pastor model. Anderson was a convinced evangelical Calvinist, principles he had imbibed, at least in part, through his friendship with Fuller, Sutcliff and Ryland. Nevertheless, he 'had been deeply influenced by the aims and ministry of the Haldanes' as well.[91] Fuller was engaging cross-denominationally as he promoted the work of the BMS.

In contrast to his generally appreciative view of the Haldanes and their churches, Fuller was less positive about the Scotch Baptists, also sometimes known as the MacLeanite Baptists after Archibald MacLean, their most prominent figure. MacLean's 'Sandemanian' views were noted briefly in chapter six. A key feature of Sandemanianism was a very passive, intellectualized view of faith.[92] Fuller and Sutcliff – his travelling companion on his first Scottish tour – believed this understanding of faith had contributed to what they regarded as the arid nature of many of the Scotch Baptist churches. Sutcliff raised the issue directly. Fuller approvingly recorded in his journal that 'Brother S' had asked a Scotch Baptist whether his religion 'allowed a proper and scriptural place for the exercise of the affections?' Evidently neither of the Northamptonshire men thought it did.[93] Fuller had further criticisms to offer. Scotch Baptist life exhibited little tolerance and was prone to frequent schisms over matters of minor

1852, ed. by Donald E. Meek (Edinburgh: The Scottish Baptist History Project, 1992), 25.

[90] James M. Gordon, 'The Early Nineteenth Century' in *The Baptists in Scotland: A History*, ed. by David W. Bebbington (Glasgow: The Baptist Union of Scotland, 1988), 34. See Derek B. Murray, 'An Eighteenth Century Baptismal Controversy in Scotland' in, *Baptism, the New Testament and the Church: Historical and Contemporary Essays in Honour of R.E.O. White*, ed. by Stanley E. Porter and Anthony R. Cross (Sheffield: Sheffield Academic Press, 1999), 428-29, for a guide to the complexities of Scottish church life during this period.

[91] Gordon, 'The Early Nineteenth Century' in *The Baptists in Scotland*, ed. by Bebbington, 34.

[92] So Michael A.G. Haykin, 'Andrew Fuller and the Sandemanian Controversy', in *'At the Pure Fountain of Thy Word': Andrew Fuller as an Apologist*, ed. by Michael A.G. Haykin (Milton Keynes: Paternoster, 2004), 228. For a detailed study, see Thomas J. South, 'The Response of Andrew Fuller to the Sandemanian View of Saving Faith' (unpublished Th.D thesis, Mid-America Baptist Theological Seminary, 1993).

[93] Journal, 11 October 1799, in Ryland, *Fuller*, 170. Fuller and Sutcliff believed this comment was relevant to many of the Scottish Independent churches as well.

importance.[94] Most importantly, their churches were not sufficiently committed to the spread of the gospel. One might summarise by saying that for Fuller, the Scotch Baptists were not evangelical enough. For their part, on more than one occasion the Scotch Baptists refused to have Fuller preach for them.[95] This negative picture does need to be qualified, for MacLean and a number of his associates supported the work of the BMS and for this Fuller was grateful.[96] Nevertheless, his relationship with them remained uneasy.[97]

Fuller's contacts with the Haldanes and ministers in the Church of Scotland were significant, although, as Stanley notes, pan-evangelicalism had its limits for the BMS secretary.[98] He remained implacably opposed to infant baptism and, at a time when the attitudes of some other Particular Baptists were softening, was a strong supporter of closed communion – only those baptised as believers could participate in the Lord's Supper in Baptist churches. Consequently, the introduction of open communion at Serampore in 1805 was resolutely opposed by Fuller.[99] Largely because of his determined opposition, the trio reverted to a policy of closed or strict communion in 1811.[100] His denominational commitments were not lightly held and this reminds us again that Fuller was a particular type of evangelical, a staunch Nonconformist and steadfast Baptist. These commitments were not abandoned, yet – as with his Calvinism – his views were infused with an evangelicalism which reshaped them. Furthermore, despite his continuing denominational commitments his Scottish tours do show him actively practicing a form of evangelical ecumenism. Fuller's concern was not that people should become Baptists (although he welcomed Anderson's 'conversion', as well as that of the Haldanes in 1808). Rather, the pressing need was for all professing Christians – of whatever denominational stripe – to dis-

---

[94] Journal, 8 October 1799, in Ryland, *Fuller*, 168; cf. Fuller letter to James Deakin, 25 Feb 1804, in [Anon.], 'Andrew Fuller and James Deakin, 1803', *BQ* 7 (July 1935), 328, 'I do not know how it is, but there is something about the Baptists in your country that seems to *divide* and *scatter*, on almost every difference that occurs.'

[95] Fuller letter to Ann Fuller, 19 September 1802, in Ryland, *Fuller*, 188.

[96] For Maclean's support for the Mission, see Archibald MacLean letter to Fuller, 21 September 1797, Fuller Chapel Letters [Letters to Andrew Fuller], vol. 1 (1-34), vol. 2 (35-71), Fuller Baptist Church, Kettering, 2. 42. For more general Scotch Baptist support, see Fuller letter to William Carey, 2 May 1796, Letters to Carey, Marshman and Ward.

[97] Fuller critiqued Maclean's views in a book length study, *Strictures on Sandemanianism, in Twelve Letters to a Friend* (London: W. Button and Sons / Edinburgh: Oliphant and Balfour, 1810). For the text, see *Works*, 2: 561-646.

[98] Stanley, *History of the BMS*, 22-23.

[99] See, e.g., Fuller letter to William Carey, 1 Nov 1806, Fuller Letters (4/5/2).

[100] See E. Daniel Potts '"I throw away the guns to preserve the ship": A Note on the Serampore Trio', *BQ* 20.3 (July 1963), 115-117, for an account of what both Carey and Ward referred to as the 'mixt [sic] business'.

cover 'the lively affectionate spirit of Christianity'[101] and engage in 'free preaching to the unconverted'.[102] Issues of Baptist church polity were not inconsequential, far from it. Nevertheless, they were still of secondary importance.[103]

A second point to note is that Fuller achieved the aim for which he had initially set out, namely raising funds for the Mission. In fact the Scottish visits made a vital contribution to the continuing work of the BMS. Wherever Fuller preached he took collections and he also solicited money by going house-to-house, visiting ministers and prominent Christian laypeople. He often preached to thousands, for example to over four thousand at the Haldanes' Tabernacle in Glasgow on his second tour in 1802.[104] He was never shy about fund-raising.[105] Before Fuller's first visit to Scotland, Robert Haldane had arranged for £100 to be transferred to BMS funds. Ryland recorded that one evening during that first journey, in October 1799, a lady commented, "'O sir, why did you not come here before?" Fuller (with his tongue perhaps only slightly in his cheek), responded, "Why madam, every man, as Sir Robert Walpole said, has his price; and till that gentleman there [Robert Haldane] sent me a hundred pounds, I did not know it would be worthwhile to visit you.'"[106]

The sums Fuller collected (carefully recorded in his journal), could vary from £20 from a small congregation to upwards of £200 at somewhere like the Edinburgh Circus. It greatly aided the work on the ground in India, with collections often specifically earmarked for the support of Bible translation, printing and distribution. Thanks in large part to the Haldane brothers, Fuller may well have been able to exceed his pound a mile target on his Scottish tours. It is almost impossible to imagine this sort of unabashed fund raising for Christian endeavour taking place in, say, the seventeenth century. These events, once again, mark out Fuller as an eighteenth-century evangelical who played a significant role in the spread of the evangelical gospel way beyond the shores of Britain.

---

[101] Journal, 11 October 1799, in Ryland, *Fuller*, 170. Cf. Michael A.G. Haykin, 'Hazarding all for God at a Clap: The Spirituality of Baptism Among British Calvinistic Baptists', *BQ* 38.4 (October 1999), 193.

[102] Fuller letter to Ann Fuller, 25 September 1802, in Ryland, *Fuller*, 190. See the emphasis placed on the phrase 'very affecting and evangelical' in Grant, *Andrew Fuller*, 9-14 and *passim*.

[103] Cf. Fuller letter to James Deakin, 26 March 1805, in 'Letters to James Deakin', 361.

[104] Fuller letter to Ann Fuller, 19 September 1802, in Ryland, *Fuller*, 189.

[105] From the very beginning of his work for the BMS. See, e.g., Stephen Hulcoop and S. Newens, 'John Davis, Minister at Waltham Abbey 1764-1795', *BQ* 39.8 (October 2002), 410, and Davis's comment of 5 November 1794, preserved in his private papers, 'Mr Andrew Fuller from Kettering here begging for mission giving to India.' Davis's papers are now held in the Essex Record Office, Chelmsford (A/10720).

[106] Ryland, *Fuller*, 164; Alexander Haldane, *The Lives of Robert and James Haldane*, 3rd edn (London: Hamilton and Adams, 1853), 298-99. Sir Robert Walpole was an early eighteenth-century British Prime Minister.

A third and central point regarding Fuller's missionary tours through Scotland is the way they highlight his activism. As already noted, this was a central tenet of evangelicalism and one which his Scottish journal and letters illustrate perhaps more strongly than any of the material considered so far in this biography. A typical day would see him travel upwards of forty miles, visit, preach and collect (on a Sunday usually three times) and then stay up into the night talking with ministers.[107] In the short term this work was immensely enjoyable and stimulating, yet the cumulative effect of his Scottish tours was to sap his strength. Even before he began making his regular trips north of the border, his health was fragile. In 1793, just four months after the BMS had been founded Fuller suffered a 'paralytic stroke'.[108] He lost movement on one side of his face and although the paralysis passed he would be prone to severe headaches for the rest of his life.[109] In 1801 he was seriously ill again and unable to preach for several months. He wrote to Carey, 'I have for the past fortnight been very ill, having nearly lost my taste, smell, voice and hearing. Yesterday I was worked violently by an emetic – last night a blister was laid on my stomach – today I can but just move about... The pain in my stomach has been as acute, I think, as gout.'[110] The attempted cures can hardly have helped. '[W]orked violently by an emetic' meant he was given something to make him sick; the 'blister' on his stomach was caused by a caustic substance placed there. The blister was then drained, the theory being that the toxic substances causing the initial illness would be drawn away from the body.

Perhaps surprisingly given this sort of medical treatment, Fuller recovered. As soon as he was able he picked up his former hectic pace once again. His tours were just one strand of his work on behalf of the Society and he had many other duties to attend to alongside his many BMS responsibilities. He continued to write and (when he was there), pastor the church at Kettering. One of his letters captures his dilemma,

> Pearce's memoirs are now loudly called for. I sit down almost in despair... My wife looks at me with a tear ready to drop, and says, 'My dear, you have hardly time to speak to me'. My friends at home are kind, but they also say, 'You have no time to see us or know us, and you will soon be worn out'. Amidst all this there is 'Come again to Scotland – come to Portsmouth – come to Plymouth – come to Bristol'.[111]

Robert Hall Jr, having heard that Fuller had indeed recently visited Plymouth and Bristol, expressed his fears for Fuller's health in a letter to Ryland, 'If he is

---

[107] Ryland, *Fuller*, 196-97, 202, 207.

[108] Ernest A. Payne, 'Andrew Fuller as Letter Writer', *BQ* 15.7 (July 1954), 292.

[109] Fuller letter to John Ryland, 8 February 1793, in Ryland, *Fuller*, 343.

[110] Fuller letter to William Carey, 19-20 August 1801, Fuller Letters (4/5/2).

[111] Fuller letter to unnamed correspondent, March 1800, in Gunton Fuller, *Fuller*, 91-92.

not more careful he will be in danger of wearing himself out before his time. His journeys, his studies, his correspondencies [sic.] must be too much for any man.'[112] Yet in 1805, on his third journey to Scotland, Fuller was pursuing his usual exhausting schedule. The following extract is from a letter to Ann, written towards the close of his tour on 1 August as he began his journey south,

> The last letter I wrote to you, was from Glasgow, Tuesday, July 23. (This letter is wanting.) Since then, I have preached at Paisley, Greenock, Saltcoats, Kilmarnock, Kilwinning, Air [sic], and Dumfries. I am now on my way to Liverpool, I have not been in bed till tonight, since Lord's Day night, at Irvine, in Scotland. I have felt my strength and spirits much exhausted; yet hitherto the Lord hath helped and my health is good.[113]

This sort of punishing programme was not at all unusual for Fuller in Scotland. Despite his failing health it never seems to have occurred to him to ease off. It is hard to escape the conclusion that BMS secretary's job should have been full time. In many ways, Fuller was his own worst enemy. When advice to slow down was given, he felt unable to heed it. It was not until 1811 that Fuller had a proper assistant at Kettering, John Keen Hall, a nephew of Robert Hall Jr.[114] Yet the provision of this help had only a limited impact, for Fuller was not a good delegator. As far as the BMS was concerned, he wanted to keep 'hold of the rope' himself with the help of only a few longstanding friends. He feared a takeover of the Society's affairs by London Baptists, a fear that was not without foundation, as we will see. But by the 1800s the friends who Fuller did trust were stretched themselves. Ryland was in Bristol with responsibilities for Broadmead Baptist Church as well as the Bristol Academy. Sutcliff was still pastor at Olney, yet as the nineteenth century wore on he was increasingly battling health issues of his own. Pearce, who probably would have been a key man, had died in 1799. Fuller soldiered on, with failing strength and an increasing workload. Ryland declared that his friend's 'exertions proved greater than nature was able to sustain, and he sunk under them into a premature grave'. Perhaps the remarkable thing is that Fuller managed to survive until 1815.[115] What is clear is that Fuller gave himself unstintingly to the work of the mission. For him, health concerns were entirely secondary.

Political and Apologetic Work

Fuller's tours are all the more staggering given that, as already noted, they formed only one strand of his work for the BMS. What I am terming his political and apologetic work on behalf of the Mission was vitally important and, in

---

[112] Robert Hall Jr letter to John Ryland, 25 May 1801, in Geoffrey F. Nuttall, 'Letters from Robert Hall to John Ryland, 1791-1824', *BQ* 34.3 (July 1991), 127.

[113] Fuller letter to Ann Fuller, 1 August 1805, in Ryland, *Fuller*, 197.

[114] Laws, *Fuller*, 8; Gunton Fuller, *Fuller*, 85.

[115] Ryland, *Fuller*, 381.

different ways, just as taxing. Fuller was sensitive to the fact that, from the time Carey and his party slipped into Calcutta without an official permit from the British East India Company, the mission to India hung by the 'slenderest of political threads'.[116] He was anxious to avoid doing anything that would jeopardise the future of the work. In this he was helped by Anglican evangelicals such as William Wilberforce and, particularly, Charles Grant (1746-1823), who was described by Fuller as a 'faithful friend'. Grant had been the East India Company's senior merchant in India and from 1805 was the deputy chair of its Court of Directors. It was he who advised Fuller to be careful when sending goods which could be turned into money, a move which could have laid the missionaries open to an accusation that they were acting as traders.[117] The secretary was grateful for this sort of inside information, but needed no encouragement to be scrupulously thorough in his efforts to avoid inadvertently offending the colonial authorities.

It is against this background that his disdain for the radical politics of the early BMS missionary John Fountain (1767-1800) should be viewed. Fountain arrived in India in 1797 to assist Carey and alarmed and indeed angered Fuller by openly making his republican views known.[118] Fuller had been concerned about Fountain's political commitments even before the young man had set off for India.[119] As early as September 1797, just a few months after Fountain's arrival in Bengal, Fuller was warning him by letter, urging him to curb his 'great edge for politicks'.[120] Later, in 1800, he wrote to William Ward deploring the new missionary's 'rage for politics', lamenting that he 'seemed incapable of refraining from talking about them in any company'.[121] Fountain died in India in 1801, but not before he had almost been recalled by the home committee.

Despite the increasing success of the Indian Mission following the arrival of Marshman and Ward (indeed, in part because of it), the work was regularly under threat from those who wanted the missionaries recalled. This was particularly true in the period 1806-08. A mutiny amongst the East India Company's Indian troops stationed at Vellore in 1806 was attributed by some to interference with the religious views of Indian soldiers.[122] As a result, for a time the mission-

---

[116] Stanley, *History of the BMS*, p. 24.

[117] Ernest F. Clipsham, 'Andrew Fuller and the Baptist Mission', *Foundations* 10.1 (January 1967), 12, 17 n.

[118] For Fountain, see Basil Amey, 'Baptist Missionary Society Radicals', *BQ* 26.8 (October 1976), 363-76.

[119] Fuller letter to William Carey, 13 March 1796, Letters to Carey, Marshman and Ward.

[120] Fuller letter to John Fountain, 7 September 1797 in Gunton Fuller, *Fuller*, 143; cf. Stanley, *History of the BMS*, 24.

[121] Fuller letter to William Ward, 21 September 1800, Bound Volume of Fuller Letters (III/170), 136.

[122] See John Clark Marshman, *The Story of Carey, Marshman and Ward, The Serampore Missionaries* (London: Alexander Strahan, 1864), 117-18. The European garrison

aries had to operate under severe restrictions. Plans were made by the opponents of the BMS to introduce a motion in the Company's Court of Proprietors in London which would lead to the expulsion of Carey and his colleagues. Carey wrote to Fuller, urging the home committee to 'try to engage men such as Mr Grant, Mr Wilberforce and others to use their influence to procure for us the liberty we want, viz. liberty to preach the gospel throughout India.' 'Do your utmost,' Carey urged, 'to clear our way.'[123]

Fuller's response was restrained but thorough. He visited a number of the directors with his Anglican friends and he prepared a written statement defending the Indian mission. This was to be distributed at a meeting on 7 June 1807 at which the possible recall of the missionaries was to be discussed. Grant persuaded Fuller, however, that it would be better to leave the matter in the hands of himself and some others on the committee who were sympathetic.[124] This careful, restrained approach paid off and, with Fuller watching anxiously from the gallery of India House, the motion failed.[125] Some involved with the London Missionary Society had been critical of Fuller's careful approach whilst he had been in London, describing Grant as 'timid and irresolute' and urging Fuller to disregard the advice of his friend and 'act on the offensive'.[126] But Fuller's tactics were almost certainly correct, showing him to be a safe pair of hands as far as looking after the Society's interests was concerned.

By the end of 1807, however, the attacks against the missionaries had intensified yet further. The immediate catalyst was a small thirteen page tract printed by William Ward at Serampore which became known as the 'Persian pamphlet'.[127] In writing it Ward had drawn from two main sources. The first of these was an evangelistic tract by Samuel Pearce, originally written for Muslim dockworkers in England.[128] The second was a well-known English commentary

---

at Vellore, in the Madras presidency, was attacked and there was considerable loss of life.

[123] William Carey and others letter to BMS home committee, 2 September 1806, BMS MSS, Angus Library, Oxford.

[124] The statement, written by Fuller and endorsed by the Home Committee, is reproduced by Ivimey, *HEB*, 4: 94-107.

[125] Morris, *Fuller*, 2nd edn, p. 142-43; Ryland, *Fuller*, 156-57; Stanley, *History of the BMS*, 24-26.

[126] Gunton Fuller, *Fuller*, 119; Marshman, *Carey, Marshman and Ward*, 124.

[127] For an excellent treatment of the dispute surrounding the pamphlet, see J. Ryan West, 'Evangelizing Bengali Muslims, 1793-1813: William Carey, William Ward, and Islam' (unpublished PhD thesis, Southern Baptist Theological Seminary, Louisville, KY, 2014), 201-207. This is now the authoritative treatment, but see also Potts, *British Baptist Missionaries*, 183-91.

[128] For the text, see Samuel Pearce, 'Letter to the Lascars', in *The Baptist Annual Register*, ed. by John Rippon, vol. 3 (London: Button, Conder, Brown *et al*, 1801), 433-38. Pearce's tract was originally written in the autumn of 1798. See Michael A.G.

on the Qur'an from the early-eighteenth century.[129] Ward's aim was to use the tract in outreach work among Bengali Muslims. The language in the pamphlet was strong and unequivocal, insisting that people were only saved through faith in Christ and warning of the impending judgement of God.[130] Yet, as Ryan West shows, it was less confrontational than some of Ward's preaching to Muslims. Furthermore, the mission literature produced at Serampore had always dealt in clear, straightforward language.[131] Why did this new tract cause such problems? The issue was the translation of Ward's work into Bengali. The translator, who was a recent Christian convert from Islam, had inserted the word 'Tyrant' before each mention of Mohammed's name.[132] By this point vast quantities of literature were being produced by the missionaries at Serampore, with tract distribution an important part of their outreach. With his heavy workload, it appears Ward had not properly checked this particular pamphlet before running it off. Carey knew nothing of the tract and was deeply concerned when parts of it were read to him.[133] Its circulation was immediately stopped, but the damage had been done.

The newly appointed British Governor, Lord Minto, was alarmed by the pamphlet believing – not unreasonably – that it would inflame religious tension. He demanded that the missionary printing presses be handed over to him. Moreover, he insisted that preaching that had been taking place in Calcutta be 'immediately discontinued'.[134] Fuller appears to have written to the trio, advising them to refuse these demands. It would be better to go to jail than agree.[135]

Haykin, *Joy Unspeakable and Full of Glory: The Piety of Samuel and Sarah Pearce* (Kitchener, Ontario: Joshua Press, 2012), 173.

[129] George Sale, *The Koran, commonly called the Alcoran of Mohammed: translated into English immediately from the original Arabic…to which is prefixed a preliminary discourse* (London: C. Ackers for J. Wilcox, 1734). Ward culled material from Sale's 'preliminary discourse'.

[130] See the summary given in West, 'Evangelizing Bengali Muslims, 1793-1813', 203-204.

[131] Furthermore, this is how the evangelical Particular Baptists spoke to people in England. Their evangelism was both forthright and spoken with love. What drove them was a belief that men and women were eternally lost without Christ. For them, the unloving approach would have been to remain silent or somehow water down their message.

[132] West, 'Evangelizing Bengali Muslims, 1793-1813', 205. The convert is named as Hadatullah.

[133] Morris, *Fuller*, 143-44.

[134] Letter from the Governor's office to William Carey, in Marshman, *Carey, Marshman and Ward*, 315.

[135] William Ward's Journal, 12 September 1807, BMS Missionary Correspondence, Angus Library, Regent's Park College, Oxford (IN/17A). Cf. West, Evangelizing Bengali Muslims, 1793-1813', 217. Fuller's letter to the missionaries was probably destroyed.

The fact that Serampore was in Danish controlled territory afforded them some protection and bought them some time, with the Danish governor, Colonel Krefting, more sympathetic than Minto. Carey's prompt reaction in withdrawing the pamphlet and a commitment to submit future publications to both the Danish and British governors for approval helped mollify the authorities.[136] The demand for the presses to close was dropped and the tensions began to ease slightly – on the ground in India at least.

In Britain, a series of pamphlets appeared attacking Carey and his colleagues. An important publication was Thomas Twining's (1776–1861) *A Letter to the Chairman of the East India Company, on the Danger of Interfering in the Religious Observances of the Natives of India*, which had appeared earlier in 1807.[137] Twining, a member of the famous tea-trading family, believed that the activities of the missionaries could result in the expulsion of the British from India and sought to rekindle the accusation they were responsible for the Vellore massacre. Other writers such as John Scott Waring (1747-1819) criticised the missionaries in much the same terms.[138] Another pamphlet was published by a 'Bengal Officer' which contrasted the breadth and tolerance of Hinduism with the narrowness and bigotry of Christianity. Although the officer in question published his work anonymously, it was generally known that the writer was Major Charles Stuart, an orientalist and a prolific author.[139] Carey and his co-workers were also famously attacked by the Anglican Clergyman Sydney Smith in the *Edinburgh Review*. The 'Anabaptist missions', he declared, were 'pernicious' and 'extravagant'.[140] Smith's article was controversial but he was unrepentant, later describing the missionaries as a 'nest of consecrated cobblers', a snide reference to Carey's former trade as a shoemaker.[141] But these were only some of a large number of attacks.[142] Given the tide of publications, Fuller believed he had to write a public defence of the BMS operations in Bengal and as

---

[136] Morris, *Fuller*, 2nd edn, 145.
[137] The tract is wrongly attributed to Richard Twining (1749–1824), a director of the East India Company, by Clipsham, 'Andrew Fuller and the Baptist Mission', 13. Thomas Twining, who wrote four 'Letters' on the 'danger of interfering in the religious opinions of the natives in India' between 1795 and 1808, was Richard Twining's second son. See *Oxford Dictionary of National Biography (DNB)*, Oxford University Press, 2004; online edn, Oct 2009 [http://www.oxforddnb.com/view/article/27912, accessed 24 July 2014]. Thomas Twining had spoken against the BMS missionaries at India House on 7 June 1807.
[138] *DNB* [http://www.oxforddnb.com/view/article/24893, accessed 25 July 2014].
[139] *DNB* [http://www.oxforddnb.com/view/article/26465, accessed 24 July 2014].
[140] 'Publications Respecting Indian Missions', in *Edinburgh Review or Critical Journal* 12 (April 1808) (Edinburgh: Constable, 1808), 151-181 (180). 'Anabaptist', i.e., 're-baptiser', was a term of abuse.
[141] *Works of the Rev. Sydney Smith in Three Volumes*, vol. 1 (London: Longman, Orme et al, 1839), 185. This comment was actually made in 1809.
[142] See the list given in 'Publications Respecting Indian Missions', 151.

a result produced his *Apology for the Late Christian Missions to India* in 1808.[143]

Fuller's Apology for the Late Christian Missions to India

In the *Apology* Fuller sought to rebut what seemed to be the most damaging of the attacks on the missionaries. For example, he rejected the charge that Baptists were to blame for Vellore, pointing out that no credible evidence had been produced to substantiate this allegation.[144] As well as dealing with specific charges such as this, Fuller defended the integrity and general approach of the missionaries. He reproduced some written testimonies as to their character, penned by those who had known Carey and his colleagues personally in India.[145] As to the general *modus operandi* of the missionaries, he argued for their right both to proclaim the uniqueness of Christianity and to challenge the views and practices of others. At the heart of Fuller's argument were these foundational beliefs: God would judge sin in sinful humanity and the gospel of Christ was God's appointed way of escape; Christ was quite simply the Lord of all and Christianity was not a religion on the same footing as others; rather, the gospel was the only way of salvation for people whatever their culture, background or inherited faith. These commitments were fundamental to Fuller's worldview and they underpinned and shaped his whole argument. Moreover, he believed Christians were obliged to spread the gospel over the whole world. He was now ready to say with Carey that the great commission was not 'confined to the apostles'. The contemporary church was 'obliged to do its utmost' in the 'use of those means Christ has appointed for the discipling of all nations'. This, for Fuller as for his colleagues, was non-negotiable and the *raison d'être* of the BMS.[146]

As part of his argument in the *Apology*, Fuller also sought to show that the accounts of Hinduism given by Twining, Scott-Waring and particularly Stewart were highly selective. Some of Fuller's strictures on religion in India, based on information received from the missionaries, can seem harsh when read today, but he and the trio simply could not accept some of the prevailing customs. These included ritual infanticide, *ghat* murders (in which the sick and dying were exposed on the banks of the Ganges) and *sati* (the custom of widows

---

[143] Andrew Fuller, *An Apology for the Late Christian Missions to India* (London: Burditt and Button, 1808). For the text, see *Works*, 2: 763-836. This was originally issued in three parts, all appearing in 1808.

[144] *Apology*, in *Works*, 2: 768-69. The *Eclectic Review* emphasised this point in its review of some of the literature relative to the dispute, including Fuller's own work. See *Eclectic Review*, 4.1 (London: Longman, Hurst *et al*, 1808), 339-40; 346.

[145] In an Appendix to the *Apology*, in *Works*, 2: 829-31.

[146] *Apology*, in *Works*, Vol. 2, pp. 817-18.

throwing themselves on the funeral pyres of their dead husbands).[147] Fuller insisted the missionaries were right to oppose all such pracitices (they were also opposed, it should be noted, by many within Hinduism as well). As far as Fuller was concerned, the social concern that he had earlier shown in his Clipstone sermon, when he had publicly attacked slavery, was also evident here.

A further important theme of the *Apology* was its plea for toleration for the Serampore missionaries. Twining had argued that the activities of the missionaries were at variance with 'the mild and tolerant spirit of Christianity'. He believed that Carey and his colleagues should not be allowed to make converts, arguing that 'our native subjects in every part of the East' should be 'permitted quietly to follow their own religious opinions'.[148] Fuller's answer was carefully nuanced. Any attempt to coerce Indian Hindus or Muslims to follow Christ would be wrong. If any so-called 'missionary' tried to do this, or deliberately sought to disturb the 'peace of society', they could have no complaints if they were dealt with severely by the government.[149] Overthrowing another religion by force was anathema to Fuller, as were any 'measures subversive of free choice'.[150] As an English Nonconformist, grateful for the 1689 Act of Toleration but still experiencing significant social and legal discrimination at home, Fuller was committed to freedom of conscience in religion.[151]

Yet when Fuller came to define toleration positively, his approach was very different from Twining's. In a statement crucial to his argument, the BMS secretary wrote that toleration was 'a legal permission not only to enjoy your own principles unmolested, but to make use of all the fair means of persuasion to recommend them to others'. In other words, people should be free not only to hold to certain principles, but also to propagate those principles through all reasonable means. Only this view of toleration, Fuller believed, was acceptable. By contrast, Twining's views were actually corrosive of religious freedom. Turning the tables on his opponent, Fuller argued that Twining was himself being 'intolerant' by saying that Christians in India 'must not be allowed to make proselytes', or indeed circulate the scriptures in the Indian languages. This was not 'toleration' but 'persecution'.[152] Fuller argued for a distinctively Christian view of toleration, with a commitment to a free and truly tolerant society which was not incompatible with evangelistic activity or indeed claims to absolute truth.

Twining, Scott-Waring and others continued to agitate for the missionaries to

---

[147] *Apology*, in *Works*, 2: 800 (*sati*), 802-03 (*ghat*); Timothy George, *Faithful Witness: The Life and Mission of William Carey* (Leicester: IVP, 1991), 149-52.

[148] Thomas Twining, *A Letter, to the Chairman of the East India Company: On the Danger of Interfering in the Religious Opinions of Natives in India...* 2nd edn (London: Ridgeway, 1807), 30-31; cf. *Apology*, in *Works*, 2: 764.

[149] *Apology*, in *Works*, 2: 834, cf. 763.

[150] *Apology*, in *Works*, 2: 763.

[151] For Fuller's views on 'civil and religious liberty', see Gunton Fuller, *Fuller*, 197-203

[152] *Apology*, in *Works*, 2: 764.

be recalled or, at the very least, for their activities to be severely curtailed. However, to Fuller's relief, attempts to press the matter with the East India Company's London based board were rebuffed by Grant and other sympathetic governors.[153] The missionaries continued their work. They had little legal protection and were extremely vulnerable. Yet the expulsion of Carey and his colleagues that Twining and other like-minded men hoped for never materialised. Although the influence of Grant and others on the board of the East India Company was crucial in safeguarding the interests of the BMS, what Stanley describes as Fuller's 'political discretion' was important as well.[154] A more impetuous or less thorough secretary could have endangered the work. Fuller's 'political contribution' allowed the work of conversions to continue and flourish, not just in India but, as the Society grew, in other parts of the world too.

Fuller, the Indian Mission and Wider Social and Political Issues

Before concluding this chapter, it is appropriate to note how Fuller's political and apologetic work for the BMS relates to wider issues discussed by missiologists and historians. The relationship between evangelism and socio-political action in mission work, an important theme in current missiological thinking, was addressed by Fuller. To state his position bluntly: he believed the fundamental task of Christian mission was evangelism, not social action or political involvement. His dismay concerning Fountain's determination to speak of his radical politics was understandable given the volatile situation in India. If the missionary had continued to air his views unchecked he would have risked the wrath of the East India Company's officials and heightened the possibility – already strong – that Fountain and his colleagues would simply be expelled from Bengal. Yet Fuller's basic principle – missionaries should 'stand aloof' from any radical political involvement – was based on more than pragmatic necessity alone. He was a political conservative himself. His beliefs in this area can be judged from a letter to Carey, written in 1799. According to Fuller, the leaders of the French Revolution were mostly 'unprincipled infidels' and Christian pastors who were enthusiasts for democratic ideals were often autocrats in their own churches. In any case, there was little to choose between democratic and other forms of civil government. 'Jesus', Fuller insisted in another letter to Carey, 'spent His [time] in accomplishing a moral revolution in the hearts of men'.[155] Missionaries, indeed 'good men in general', should do likewise.[156] His advice to Fountain included the following, 'Well does the apostle charge us who have engaged to be soldiers of Christ, not to entangle ourselves in the affairs of

---

[153] There had been one such attempt early in 1808. See Andrew Fuller letter to Joshua Marshman, 12 February 1808, Fuller Letters (4/5/2).

[154] Stanley, *History of the BMS*, 25.

[155] Fuller letter to William Carey, 18 April 1799 (H/1/3). Cf. Gunton Fuller, *Fuller*, 196, 'The bias of Mr Fuller's politics was 'deference to the powers that be.''.

[156] Fuller letter to William Carey, 18 January 1797, Fuller Letters (4/5/1).

this life.'[157] Fuller's approach was not just a matter of expediency but one of principle.

Fuller did have a social conscience, as his aforementioned comments on slavery indicate. Moreover, the reality on the ground in India was that Carey worked for the abolition of practices that were exploitative of women, the sick and the vulnerable. Ward had been radical politically before going to India and retained a strong social conscience;[158] other BMS missionaries, for example, Hannah Marshman, engaged in social projects, in her case establishing pioneering schools which benefitted some of India's poorest and most vulnerable people.[159] Such work was done with the support of the home committee including, in his lifetime, Fuller. So he was not entirely consistent in his approach to sociopolitical questions. Nevertheless, for Fuller the overriding focus was evangelism, or 'accomplishing a moral revolution in the hearts of men'. For him, it was this that was the major work of Christian mission. Nothing was more important and nothing could stand in its way.[160]

Fuller's work defending the BMS in India also raises the issue of the connection between overseas cross-cultural mission and colonial expansion. There are two linked questions. Firstly, did Fuller and his friends arrogantly assume that European culture was superior to indigenous Indian culture? Secondly, did they collude in furthering colonial interests, doing so under the cover of 'spreading the gospel'? A detailed exploration of these questions is beyond the scope of this book. Even so, a few observations can be offered. On the first question, it is true that in dress and general approach the Serampore missionaries remained 'European'; the more thoroughgoing attempts to enculturate the gospel made by later missionaries such as J. Hudson Taylor and, for the BMS, Timothy Richard, were some years away. Still, the missionaries sought to delineate Hindu culture sympathetically.[161] The Indian religious leader Rammohun Roy (1772-

---

[157] Fuller letter to John Fountain, 7 September 1797, in Gunton Fuller, *Fuller*, 144.

[158] See, e.g., William Ward, *Farewell Letters to a Few Friends in Britain and America, on Returning to Bengal in 1821*, 2nd edn (London: S. & R. Bentley, 1821), 62–85. On Ward's radical views in the 1790s, see A. Christopher Smith, 'William Ward, Radical Reform, and Missions in the 1790s,' *American Baptist Quarterly* 10 (1991), 218–44.

[159] Hannah Marshman began a number of girls' schools. Although this work did not begin until 1820, by 1824 there were 160 Indian girls attending six schools. This work was rightly called, 'pioneering' by George Howells, *The Story of Serampore and its College* (Serampore: The College, 1927), 11.

[160] My own view is that Christians are called to integral mission which very much includes evangelism but which is not limited to this. For an extraordinarily clear and helpful expression of this approach from an evangelical perspective, see Christopher J.H. Wright, *The Mission of God: Unlocking the Bible's Grand Narrative* (Leicester: IVP, 2006).

[161] Ward's views were expressed in *An Account of the Writings, Religion, and Manners of the Hindoos*, 2 vols (Serampore, 1811). Brian Pennington argues that Ward dis-

1833) considered the Serampore missionaries to be 'the best qualified and the most careful observers of the foreign countries in which Europeans have set-tled'.[162] And in their mission they were demonstrably motivated by love. This was love for the God they believed had created the whole world and uniquely revealed himself in Jesus Christ and love for the people they believed were per-ishing without the gospel. They also insisted that practices such as *sati* were unacceptable. Interestingly, the independent Indian government produced a postage stamp in 1993 to commemorate the bicentenary of Carey's arrival in India and later Indian nationals have paid tribute to his influence.[163] So, the an-swer to the question about culture is a complex one. The missionaries, support-ed by Fuller, made mistakes—with the 'Persian pamphlet' certainly ranking as one of them. Yet the point about love is surely crucial. Whatever mistakes were made, their motivation was primarily what they said it was: the spread of the gospel of the God they loved to people they loved.

On the second question, regarding whether they furthered colonial interests, as we have seen Fuller wanted the missionaries to avoid political involvement, although he was willing for them to address social questions. Yet ironically he was unable to avoid political involvement himself as he fought for the right of the BMS to continue operations in colonial Bengal. As Ryan West shrewdly observes, 'Although he strongly objected to missionaries immersing themselves in political struggles, Fuller did not apply the same standard to himself.'[164] His own political work led to him cooperating with sympathetic friends on the Brit-ish East India Company Board whose primary aim was economic expansion and the maintenance of British rule in India. Yet Fuller did not endorse colonial expansion. If he was at fault it was in seeing colonial rule as an opportunity which created a context which made evangelistic mission possible. Fuller and the missionaries were outsiders. The trio worked in British East India Company territory without an official license and they were willing to go to jail rather than give their printing presses to the authorities. The Particular Baptists status – or more accurately lack of it – as Dissenting outsiders should not be underes-timated. They were shut out from the corridors of political power and influence and had known significant oppression in their own country. Norman Ethering-ton's general verdict about mission and Empire is fair when applied specifically to Fuller and Serampore trio: they were willing (albeit reluctantly) to use their

---

played a moral and, to a degree, cultural superiority in his writings. See Brian K. Pennington, *Was Hinduism Invented? Britons, Indians, and the Colonial Construc-tion of Religion* (Oxford: Oxford University Press, 2005), 82-84. For a balanced ap-praisal, see West, 'Evangelizing Bengali Muslims, 1793-1813', 31.

[162] As cited in Potts, *British Baptist Missionaries in India*, 7. Cf. West, 'Evangelizing Bengali Muslims, 1793-1813', 31, n 20.

[163] Ruth and Vishal Mangalwadi, *Carey, Christ and Cultural Transformation* (Carlisle: Paternoster, 1993).

[164] West, 'Evangelizing Bengali Muslims, 1793-1813', 222.

relationship with government officials to aid their evangelistic agenda. If this agenda was hindered, however, they were willing to stand against those officials as necessary.[165] The BMS missionaries' overarching goal was not the extension of the British Empire, but the extension of Christ's Kingdom through evangelism. This overarching goal was actually the keynote of the whole of Fuller's ministry.

Conclusion

This chapter gets to the heart of what drove Fuller on. He loved God and he loved people and wanted them to know Christ which was God's best for them. These core values had to be translated into action. For him, this meant being primarily concerned for the extension of Christ's Kingdom through evangelistic activity. Seeing him as chiefly concerned with this helps us make sense of the choices he made and the life he lived. In his pastorate at Kettering and in his wider ministry he prioritised evangelism and encouraged others to do the same. This fundamental commitment to evangelism can even be seen in respect of his son Robert, whose errant behaviour nearly broke his heart. Fuller's overriding concern for Robert, expressed in his last known letter to him, was that he turned to Christ.

Fuller's concern for evangelism can be seen both in miniature and on a broader canvas. His multi-faceted work for the BMS gave his evangelistic ministry a global dimension. He kept the missionaries on the field and sent out others, working round-the-clock to provide for them financially and defending their right to share the gospel in colonial Bengal. When reports of the Mission's first Indian converts reached England, Fuller was elated. He wrote to Krishna Pal and others on behalf of the home committee,

> In you we see the first fruits of Hindustan, the travail of our Redeemer's soul, and a rich reward for our imperfect labours. You know, beloved, that the love of Christ is of a constraining nature. It was this, and only this, that constrained us to mediate the means of your conversion. It was this that constrained our brethren that are with you to leave their country and all their worldly prospects, and to encounter perils, hardships and reproaches. If you stand fast in the Lord and are saved this is their and our reward.[166]

Fuller was aware that his and his friends' efforts had been 'imperfect'. Yet, he said, the love of Christ had constrained them to make great efforts to share the gospel cross-culturally. It was this love and this love alone, he insisted, which had motivated them in a venture that involved considerable sacrifice. Although

---

[165] Norman Etherington, 'Introduction', in *Missions and Empire*, ed. by Norman Etherington (Oxford: Oxford University Press, 2005), 3-5.

[166] Fuller letter to Brother Krishna, Sister Joymonee... 19 August 1801, Letters to Carey, Marshman and Ward. Fuller alluded to the text 2 Cor. 5.14, 'For the love of Christ constraineth us...'

he did not say so, it was not only Carey and the other missionaries who had experienced 'perils, hardships and reproaches', Fuller had been through these as well. Yet these new believers were themselves more than enough 'reward': he was united to them as a 'brother'. Later in the letter he declared that the Indian Christians were now 'fellow citizens' of Christ's Kingdom. 'Neither distance of situation, difference of customs, language or colour, shall prevent a union of spirit.' Love for Christ and love for others blended together. This was Fuller at his most passionate and indeed most joyful. Unsurprisingly, and as will be shown in chapter eight, he maintained this evangelistic focus to the very end of his life.

CHAPTER 8

Good Lives, Good Deaths

...going after dear brother Pearce

As already noted, Fuller struggled with health issues. The illness that struck in 1801, referred to in the previous chapter, was the most severe he had yet faced. Those close to him thought he might not recover. Writing to Joshua Marshman after the danger had passed he put it this way, 'Many of my friends apprehended me going after dear brother Pearce'.[1] The reference was to Samuel Pearce and his death two years earlier in 1799, at the age of thirty-three. Pearce has been mentioned a number of times in this book. Although he was a generation younger than Fuller, the two men became very close, a friendship grounded in a common theology and vision and forged in the context of a shared task, namely, the work of the BMS. Moreover, the older man was deeply challenged by the personal piety of his younger colleague in ministry. Consequently, Fuller wrote his *Memoirs* of Pearce not just as a memorial to his friend, but because he thought Pearce was an exemplar of true spirituality.[2] He encapsulated what was best about evangelical spirituality as it was expressed among the English Particular Baptists and provided a model of the Christian life to which others could aspire.[3] Fuller believed Pearce's *Memoirs* would show people how to live a good life and, indeed, how to die a good death. This chapter examines Fuller's

---

[1] Fuller letter to Joshua Marshman, 19 November 1801, Fuller Letters to Carey, Marshman and Ward... (4/3/5) Angus Library, Regent's Park College, Oxford. Cf. Fuller letter to John Sutcliff, 1 September 1801, in John Ryland Jr, *The Work of Faith, the Labour of Love, and the Patience of Hope Illustrated in the Life and Death of the Rev. Andrew Fuller*, 2nd edn (London: Button and Son, 1818), 345.

[2] See Andrew Fuller, *Memoirs of the Late Rev. Samuel Pearce... with Extracts from Some of his Most Interesting Letters*, 1st edn (Clipstone: J.W. Morris, 1800), 288, and cf. 203. I have cited exclusively from the first edition in this chapter. For the *Memoirs* in Fuller's *Works*, see *The Complete Works of the Rev. Andrew Fuller, With a Memoir of his Life by the Rev. Andrew Gunton Fuller*, ed. by Andrew Gunton Fuller, rev. ed. by Joseph Belcher; 3 vols, 3rd edn (Harrisonburg, VA: Sprinkle Publications, 1988 [1845]), 3: 367-446.

[3] A view that was shared by others. See, e.g., the comments of William Ward quoted in *Memoirs of Pearce*, 208-09. Ward spent several months in 1799 in Birmingham preaching for Pearce as the latter's health failed.

friendship with Samuel Pearce and analyses the major themes of the *Memoirs*, with a special focus on the spirituality that was important to Fuller. It closes by reconsidering Fuller's own spirituality as it was displayed in the final years of his life, and by describing his own final illness and death at the age of 61.

Samuel Pearce and Andrew Fuller

Pearce's Life and the Growth of a Friendship

Samuel Pearce was born on 20 July 1766, in Plymouth in the south west of England.[4] His parents were Calvinistic Baptists but, according to his own testimony, he turned from his Christian background and followed 'evil' and 'wicked inclinations',[5] although he continued attending chapel. His conversion came in 1782 when he heard a sermon from Isaiah Birt (1758-1837), a young man who was on trial as potential co-pastor of the Plymouth church he attended.[6] 'I believe,' Pearce said later, that 'few conversions were more joyful. The change produced in my views, feelings, and conduct, was so evident to myself, that I could no more doubt of its being from God, than of my existence. I had the witness in myself, and was filled with peace and joy unspeakable.'[7] On his seventeenth birthday he was baptised as a believer and became a member of the Plymouth church.[8]

Pearce was working as an apprentice silversmith but a call to pastoral and preaching ministry was soon discerned. In 1786 he was sent to the Bristol Baptist Academy to train.[9] At Bristol, Pearce's passion for evangelism grew. On one occasion he preached in a simple hut to a group of between thirty and forty coal miners, reducing them to tears and weeping himself as he spoke of the cross of Christ.[10] Understandably, he was highly regarded in the Academy.

---

[4] For another treatment of Pearce's life, see the fine biographical sketch by Michael A.G. Haykin, *Joy Unspeakable and Full of Glory: The Piety of Samuel and Sarah Pearce* (Kitchener, Ontario: Joshua Press, 2012), 1-41. The rest of Haykin's book is an edited collection of Pearce's letters, many of which appear in published form for the first time.

[5] *Memoirs of Pearce*, 73-74. For the information in this paragraph, see *Memoirs of Pearce*, 73-76.

[6] For Birt, see *Baptist Autographs in the John Rylands University Library of Manchester, 1741-1845*, trans. and ed. by Timothy Whelan (Macon, GA: Mercer UP, 2009), 356-57.

[7] *Memoirs of Pearce*, 75.

[8] Roger Hayden, *Continuity and Change: Evangelical Calvinism Among Eighteenth-Century Baptist Ministers Trained at Bristol Academy, 1690-1791* (Didcot: Baptist Historical Society, 2006), 225.

[9] *Memoirs of Pearce*, 73; 76.

[10] *Memoirs of Pearce*, 108, 247; Samuel Pearce Carey, *Samuel Pearce M.A., The Baptist Brainerd* (London: Carey Press, n.d. [1922]), 83.

It is worth pausing to note the evangelical nature of Pearce's early experiences, training and developing ministry. Pearce's conversion was due to evangelical, invitational gospel preaching: Birt was himself Bristol trained and had imbibed Caleb Evans's evangelical theology and practical, applied approach.[11] Pearce's description of his conversion, with the emphases on felt joy and assurance of faith was typical of evangelicalism too; indeed, elements of his experience are redolent of John Wesley's, who, in 1738, felt his heart 'strangely warmed' and 'felt [he] did trust in Christ', receiving full 'assurance' of salvation.[12] Pearce's experience fitted this classic evangelical mould. He followed Birt by studying under Caleb Evans himself. Finally, his approach to preaching, typified by his experiences with the miners, was evangelical, in content (the focus on the cross), in delivery (applied), and in effect (both preacher and hearers were deeply moved). The young Samuel Pearce was both Baptist and evangelical.

As he came to the end of his course at Bristol, Pearce was recommended to the Particular Baptist Church at Cannon Street, Birmingham. He was called as their pastor and ordained on Wednesday 18 August 1790. Caleb Evans preached at the ordination service and Fuller led in prayer. This was probably the first time the two men met. Pearce submitted a report of his own ordination to the *Baptist Annual Register*. In it he said that 'Mr Fuller...implored the divine blessing on the new relation which the church had then formed.'[13] Such heartfelt prayer would have resonated with the new pastor. The two men were like-minded and they became firm friends.

Pearce would remain the evangelistically-minded pastor of the Birmingham church for the rest of his life. As a minister he gave himself wholeheartedly to his work. Birmingham was England's second city and the leading industrial centre of the Midlands. Birt visited his convert in 1792 and described the country near Birmingham as full of 'coal and iron works', speaking evocatively of a land of 'burning, of smoke, and of terror'.[14] In this urban setting Pearce ministered with remarkable effectiveness. 335 new members joined the church during

---

[11] See *Dictionary of Evangelical Biography 1730-1860 (DEB)*, ed. by Donald M. Lewis, 2 vols (Oxford: Blackwell, 1995), 1: 101.

[12] *The Works of John Wesley*, ed. by Richard P. Heitzenrater and Frank Baker (Oxford: Oxford University Press, 1975-), 18: 249-50. Whether Wesley's experience can rightly be described as his 'conversion' has been hotly debated. For an extended discussion of the issues, see Henry D. Rack, *Reasonable Enthusiast: John Wesley and the Rise of Methodism* (London: Epworth, 1989), 145-57.

[13] *The Baptist Annual Register (BAR), Vol. 1, 1790-93*, ed. by John Rippon (London: Dilly, Brown and James, 1793), 517.

[14] Isaiah Birt, Diary entry, 7 June 1793, cited in John Birt, 'Memoir of the Late Rev. Isaiah Birt', *Baptist Magazine*, 30 (London: G. Wightman, 1838), 107. It should be noted that Birt was describing the industrialisation that especially marked the landscape to the north and west of the city. This was not quite so characteristic of the area immediately around Cannon Street.

his pastorate.[15] He thus enjoyed more numerical 'success' as a local church pastor than Fuller and in a shorter space of time. In one five month period he baptised almost forty people, nearly all of whom he described as 'newly awakened'.[16] One of those who came to Christ in the early days of his time at Cannon Street was Sarah Hopkins (1771–1804), and in 1791 she became his wife. She was a woman of deep piety and their marriage was a happy one.[17]

One incident which helps illustrate Samuel Pearce's ministry also relates to Fuller. Pearce was preaching in 1794 at Guilsborough, Northamptonshire, at the opening of a new meeting house. A number of other ministers were in attendance, among them Fuller himself. The sermon was so effective the preacher was asked to speak again the next day, with the service beginning at 5.00 a.m. The early start was to enable labourers to attend before they began work. After this second sermon had been given, Fuller declared how much he had appreciated the content of the message. However, he suggested there were some issues with the structure. 'I thought,' Fuller said, 'you did not seem to close when you had really finished... you seemed, as it were, to begin again at the end – how was it?' According to Francis Cox (1783-1853), who was present, Pearce was reluctant to respond but, after being pressed for an answer, he eventually said,

Well, my brother, you shall have the secret... Just at the moment I was about to resume my seat, thinking I had finished, the door opened, and I saw a poor man enter, of the working class; and from the sweat on his brow, and the symptoms of his fatigue, I conjectured that he had walked some miles to this early service, but that he had been unable to reach the place till the close. A momentary thought glanced through my mind – here may be a man who never heard the gospel, or it may be he is one that regards it as a feast of fat things; in either case, the effort on his part demands one on mine. So with the hope of doing him good, I resolved at once to forget all else, and, in despite of criticism, and the apprehension of being thought tedious, to give him a quarter of an hour.[18]

Pearce had finished his message, but continued preaching just for this man, with his desire to speak to him overriding his 'apprehension of being thought tedious'. I believe Fuller would have been deeply moved and challenged by his

[15] Joseph Ivimey, *A History of the English Baptists (HEB)* 4 vols (London: Taylor Hinton, Holdsworth and Ball, 1830), 4: 543.

[16] *Memoirs of Pearce*, 100. The evidence suggests the five month period referred to was in 1792.

[17] *Memoirs of Pearce*, 78. For more detail, see the evidence collected by Haykin, *Joy Unspeakable*, 18-24.

[18] Francis A. Cox, *History of the Baptist Missionary Society*, 2 vols (London: T. Ward and G. & J. Dyer, 1842), 1: 52–53. It should be noted that Cox was only a boy at the time of the incident, and so is unlikely to have captured Pearce's actual words in his later account. Cox went on to train at Bristol and enjoyed a significant ministry. See *DEB*, 1: 263-64.

friend's reply. Here was an example of what the writer of the *Memoirs* would later term Pearce's 'holy love', that is, a heartfelt love for God, the gospel and people.[19] This 'holy love' was central to the piety Fuller so admired.

In addition to ministry at Cannon Street and his preaching elsewhere, Pearce was closely involved in the formation of the BMS. He was present on 2 October 1792 at the Society's founding meeting at Kettering. What is more, he arrived at the second meeting later that month with a gift of £70, collected from his congregation in the intervening period.[20] This was an astonishing sum which, John Ryland said, 'put new spirits into us all'.[21] The Cannon Street pastor also came with a proposal that an auxiliary society should be formed, based in Birmingham, to help support the new venture. This was accepted and Pearce was welcomed onto the full BMS committee.[22] Fuller would say much about his friend's passion for cross-cultural mission when he came to write his *Memoirs*.

Ministry in Birmingham continued and in June 1796 Pearce also visited Ireland and preached there, having responded to an invitation from the General Evangelical Society in Dublin.[23] The Christians in Dublin were so taken with Pearce that he was urged to stay and offered a generous stipend to minister at a church in a well-to-do area of the city. When he demurred, the church proposed arrangements which would necessitate the Englishman being in Ireland for only part of each year. Again Pearce declined, this time after a short period of reflection and prayer. As we shall see, he had wanted to go to India under the auspices of the BMS, but had not been accepted. Yet, although he had been willing to go and face an uncertain future in a pioneer situation, he could not be tempted away from his Birmingham congregation by what Fuller called 'the most flattering prospects of a worldly nature'.[24] Once again, Pearce's actions had the Kettering pastor's seal of approval.

Pearce would almost certainly have been unsuitable for service with the BMS in India due to his delicate health. From the early 1790s onwards he was often unwell and in 1798 he was caught in a rainstorm, ending up soaked through. He developed a fever he could not shake off. In the final months of his life he spent some time in his home town of Plymouth in a vain attempt to recover some strength. From there he wrote a letter to his church which included the following passage, later inserted in the *Memoirs*.

> You, beloved, who have found the peace speaking blood of the atonement, must not be satisfied with what you have already known or enjoyed. The only way to be

---

[19] *Memoirs of Pearce*, 242.
[20] Anon. [Andrew Fuller?], 'An Account of the Particular Baptist Society...including a Narrative of its Rise and Plan', in *BAR*, 1: 376; *Memoirs of Pearce*, 99.
[21] Ryland *Fuller*, 150.
[22] 'An Account of the Particular Baptist Society', 377.
[23] *Memoirs of Pearce*, 146. Birt, who spent two months in Dublin with the same Society in 1792, had probably recommended his friend. See 'Memoir of Isaiah Birt', 107.
[24] *Memoirs of Pearce*, 161.

constantly happy, and constantly prepared for the most awful changes which we must all experience, is to be constantly *looking* and *coming* to a dying Savior[sic.]... if you thus live (and oh that you may daily receive fresh life from Christ so to do) 'the peace of God will keep your hearts and minds', and you will be filled with 'joy unspeakable and full of glory'.[25]

Thus Pearce quoted the same text (1 Pet. 1.8) he had cited in his earlier account of his conversion. He returned to Birmingham, but his condition continued to deteriorate. For the whole of August it seems he was unable to write although he did receive visitors and was able to communicate briefly with some of them.[26] The diagnosis was 'consumption' (that is, pulmonary tuberculosis) and it was evident he was slipping away. He died on 10 October 1799. Fuller heard the news whilst he was in Scotland. From there on 19 October he wrote Sarah Pearce a letter which included the line, 'Memoirs of his life must be published.'[27] Fuller himself was determined to make sure this happened.

Andrew Fuller's *Memoirs* of Samuel Pearce

Fuller had been thinking of writing Pearce's *Memoirs* for several months before he penned his letter to Sarah from Scotland. In a letter to his dying friend on 30 August, he declared his intentions, reassuring Pearce,

[Y]ou need not fear that I will puff off your character, any more than you would mine. We are all of us, God knows it, poor unworthy creatures. Yet the truth may be told to the glory of sovereign grace; and I long to express my inextinguishable affection for you in something more than words, I mean by doing something that shall be of use to your family.[28]

In his final comment, Fuller indicated he would donate the profits from the sales of any work to Sarah, as indeed happened.[29] Despite his eagerness to write Pearce's life and the benefits he thought would accrue from it (financial in the case of Sarah, spiritual in the case of the reading public) he did not find the book easy to produce due to the other pressures he was under; hence the comment already mentioned in the previous chapter, 'Pearce's memoirs are now loudly called for. I sit down almost in despair...'. [30] Yet, as already noted, Pearce's *Memoirs* did appear later that year. It was the only book-length biography Fuller ever wrote. It is to four of the central themes of these *Memoirs* we

---

[25] *Memoirs of Pearce*, 224-25. The spelling of Savior is original to the English 1st edn.
[26] *Memoirs of Pearce*, 238-39.
[27] Cited in Carey, *Samuel Pearce*, 216.
[28] As cited in Ernest A. Payne, 'Some Sidelights on Pearce and his Friends', *BQ* 7 (1934–1935), 275.
[29] See the 'Advertisement' immediately after the title page of the *Memoirs of Pearce*.
[30] Andrew Gunton Fuller, *Men Worth Remembering: Andrew Fuller* (London: Hodder and Stoughton, 1882), 91-92.

now turn, themes that tell us as much about the author as they do about his subject.

A Biblical, Calvinistic, Evangelical Theology

Fuller included much material which emphasised that, with regard to outlook, Pearce was biblical, Calvinistic and evangelical. Regarding the essential biblicism of his subject, Fuller included a letter from Pearce to a young man 'whose mind...was bewildered by fruitless speculations'. In this the Cannon Street pastor declared that the Bible was an 'inspired book'. It should be received, he insisted, 'not as the word of man, but as the word of God'.[31] This commitment was deeply held. As part of a day of fasting and prayer which he kept in October 1794 he read the whole of Psalm 119. As he did so he found its focus on God's 'law' resonated – had much 'congruity' – with the 'breathings of [his] own heart'.[32] His particular approach to the Bible was christocentric. For him, both the Old and New Testament scriptures pointed to Christ. Some lines he composed around the time he started work as a pastor serve to highlight this, as well as illuminating other dimensions of his theology. The verses were entitled 'On the Scriptures'. The second, third and fifth stanzas were as follows,

> Here in those lines of love I see
> What Christ my Savior did for me;
> Here I behold the wondrous plan,
> By which he saves rebellious man.
>
> Here we may view the Savior, God.
> Oppress'd by pain, o'erwhelm'd with blood;
> And if we ask the reason, why?
> He kindly says, 'For you I die.'
>
> O boundless grace! O matchless love!
> That brought the Savior from above,
> That caus'd the God for man to die,
> Expiring in an agony.[33]

The scriptures, the 'lines of love', pointed to Christ, in particular to Christ crucified. The cross was the fulcrum of God's 'wondrous plan' of salvation. The horror of the cross was not sidestepped: Christ was 'Oppress'd by pain' and 'o'erwhelm'd with blood'. But it was the theology of the atonement rather than Christ's physical suffering that was the central concern. The 'boundless grace' of God led Christ to die for 'rebellious' sinners; indeed, Pearce has Christ saying, 'For you I die', applying the message of the cross in a way that emphasised

---

[31] *Memoirs of Pearce*, 269-70.

[32] *Memoirs of Pearce*, 129

[33] *Memoirs of Pearce*, 97-98.

substitution and which was intensely personal. In the aforementioned letter to the 'bewildered' young man, Pearce stated his belief in the atonement as the 'leading truth of the New Testament'.[34] Fuller commented approvingly on his friend, 'Christ crucified was his...theme, from first to last.'[35]

Further theological emphases can be discerned in the lines of 'On the Scriptures'. Pearce's Calvinism is hinted at by the emphasis on God's sovereignty. God put *his* 'plan' of salvation into effect; salvation was all dependent on God's grace. If his biblicism and crucicentrism were typical of evangelicalism generally, Pearce here revealed himself to be a particular stripe of evangelical, namely a Calvinistic one. His predecessor as pastor of Cannon Street had left having embraced Wesleyan convictions,[36] but this did not happen with Pearce. Elsewhere in the *Memoirs* there is material indicating his firm rejection of Arminianism,[37] although he could still appreciate and be influenced by the preaching of Arminians, for example the Wesleyan Methodist Thomas Coke.[38] Moreover, he always sought to distinguish between principles and personalities.[39] This was typical of the evangelical Calvinism – sometimes described as 'moderate' Calvinism[40] – which characterised late eighteenth-century Particular Baptists including, as we have seen, Fuller himself.

The striking christological statements in Pearce's stanzas should also be noted. The language is explicit. Christ came 'from above'; indeed, it was God himself who could be viewed hanging on the cross. In the atonement 'God' was dying for 'man'. For the author of 'On the Scriptures' there was no ambiguity, he held to the full deity of Christ. Elsewhere, Pearce also emphasised Christ's humanity, speaking of him as the 'friend of sinful man' whose 'humble love' and commitment to do his 'duty' were examples to all.[41] Yet in 'On the Scriptures' it was the divinity of Christ which was boldly stated, and this in the context of eighteenth-century debates in which Christ's deity was questioned. As already noted, one of the effects of the eighteenth-century Enlightenment was a growth in Unitarianism, a doctrine which ravaged many English General Baptist churches. Pearce himself was not completely impervious to such currents, confessing to a friend that he had been 'perplexed' about christology for a short period. This coincided with his reading of several 'Socinian' authors,[42] includ-

---

[34] *Memoirs of Pearce*, 269.
[35] *Memoirs of Pearce*, 247.
[36] Ivimey, *HEB*, 4: 542.
[37] *Memoirs of Pearce*, 84-86.
[38] *Memoirs of Pearce*, 108. For Coke, see *DEB*, 1: 238-39.
[39] A trait also evident in his relationships with Anglicans. See *Memoirs of Pearce*, 253.
[40] See, e.g., Brian Stanley, *The History of the Baptist Missionary Society, 1792-1992* (Edinburgh: T. & T. Clark, 1992), 13.
[41] See the verses, 'Excitement to Early Duty: Or, The Lord's-day Morning', *Memoirs of Pearce*, 96.
[42] So called after the sixteenth-century Italian theologian Faustus Socinus who adopted, amongst other unorthodox beliefs, Unitarian views.

ing Joseph Priestley (1733-1804), who between 1780 and 1791 had been based in Birmingham. But Fuller stated that after this brief internal struggle his subject decisively rejected Priestley's theology.[43] Indeed, according to Fuller (who himself engaged in print with Priestley),[44] Pearce's wrestling with this issue led to him holding even more 'firmly' to orthodox views on the person of Christ.[45] In an age when Unitarianism was culturally attractive, he remained wedded to an orthodox christology and to Trinitarianism. Thus, the *Memoirs* contain much material which illuminates their subject's evangelical theology.

The relationship between Pearce and currents associated with the Enlightenment was never explicitly noted by Fuller, but there is much material in the *Memoirs* which suggests the link. He rejected the rationalism of the Socinians, but this was only one strand of Enlightenment thinking. There is substantial evidence indicating he was influenced by other dimensions of this complex cultural movement. For example, in a letter to an unnamed young man in Edinburgh, Pearce discoursed in 'enlightened' language about truth and happiness.[46] He also owned and enjoyed using a microscope and appreciated philosophy[47] and, most importantly for this section, he defended the authority of the Bible in distinctly enlightened terms. He believed the Bible to be God's word 'not as the religion of our ancestors, but on the invincible conviction which attends an impartial investigation of its evidences'.[48] The rejection of tradition as a sufficient authority, together with the emphases on 'evidence' and 'impartial investigation', were typical of the spirit of the age; indeed, here was enlightenment empiricism writ large.

Nevertheless, for Pearce these cultural influences never led him away from Christ as God's Son or the Bible as God's word. He was happy to 'amuse' himself with philosophy, he said to a friend, but Jesus would always be his 'teacher'.[49] He rejected out of hand the rationalist deism he described as 'the fashion

---

[43] *Memoirs of Pearce*, 84-85; cf. 247. There is an abundance of secondary literature on Priestly, who was a major Enlightenment figure on both sides of the Atlantic. The authoritative study is the two volume work by Robert E. Schofield, *The Enlightenment of Joseph Priestley: A Study of His Life and Work from 1733 to 1773* (University Park, PA: Pennsylvania State UP, 1997); *The Enlightened Joseph Priestley: A Study of His Life and Work from 1773 to 1804* (University Park, PA: Pennsylvania State UP, 2004).

[44] See, esp. the aforementioned *Calvinistic and Socinian Systems...Compared* (London: T. Hamilton *et al*, 1810), in *Works*, 2: 108-242. For explicit references to Priestley, see, e.g., Fuller's 'Preface', 108-111.

[45] *Memoirs of Pearce*, 247.

[46] *Memoirs of Pearce*, 276-77.

[47] *Memoirs of Pearce*, 261.

[48] *Memoirs of Pearce*, 270. The way he described his conversion also smacks of 'enlightened' thinking, e.g. in its stress on evidence ('so evident to myself') and certainty.

[49] *Memoirs of Pearce*, 261; cf. 273.

of the day'.[50] Most importantly, the Bible was ultimately God's 'revelation' to sinful humanity and should be received as such.[51] These attitudes were all admiringly recorded by Fuller. In an age when enlightened cultural currents ebbed and flowed, with challenges to biblical faith swirling all around him, Pearce held firmly to an essential biblical orthodoxy which was focused on Christ. This is what Fuller himself aimed for and he was happy to hold up Pearce and his evangelical beliefs as an example for others to follow.

A Spiritual Theology

Yet the *Memoirs* reveal something further. Pearce's theology was not only orthodox, it was deeply 'spiritual'. We might say that his was an approach which encompassed both 'head' and 'heart'. So, whilst doctrinal orthodoxy was foundational to his spirituality, the truth had to be prayed and sung and lived. In his reading of Psalm 119 on the aforementioned fast day, he took care to pray slowly through the Psalm, meditating on particular verses. 'Often with holy admiration I paused and read, and thought, and prayed over the verse again,' he declared.[52]

This same commitment to reflect on truth in order for it to become deeply embedded in his own experience is evident in 'On the Scriptures', with the appreciation of Christ's 'kindness' and the emotional exclamations, 'O boundless grace! O matchless love!' brought on by meditation on the atonement.[53] Study and devotion were closely integrated in his approach to theology. In a letter dated 19 August 1793 he wrote of the need both for more 'light' (i.e. truth) and 'heat' (i.e. 'sincerity and ardour'). Whilst pursuing these twin goals himself he sought to commend them to others. In the letter he also spoke of his preaching to his people 'urging the necessity of *heart* religion'.[54] Here was what evangelicals habitually called an 'experimental' faith. It was not enough to know about some aspect of doctrinal truth, important as that was. That truth had to be imbibed and experienced in ways that fired the heart and shaped the inner and outer dimensions of Christian discipleship. This was a trait exemplified by Pearce as he appears in the pages of the *Memoirs*. For Fuller, his friend's 'religion was that of the heart'.[55]

The corporate dimensions of learning and devotion were important to Pearce. He was not only committed to 'secret', private prayer but also to family prayer.[56] Moreover, he engaged wholeheartedly in the corporate prayer meetings of his church. On 10 October 1794 he wrote,

---

[50] *Memoirs of Pearce*, 276.
[51] *Memoirs of Pearce*, 277.
[52] *Memoirs of Pearce*, 129.
[53] *Memoirs of Pearce*, 97.
[54] *Memoirs of Pearce*, 88.
[55] *Memoirs of Pearce*, 242.
[56] See, e.g., *Memoirs of Pearce*, 120.

Whilst at the prayer meeting tonight, I learned more of the meaning of some passages of Scripture than ever before. Suitable frames of soul are like good lights in which a painting appears to its full advantage. I had often meditated on Phil. iii. 7, 8. and Gal. vi. 14: but never *felt* crucifixion to the world, and disesteem for all that it contains as at that time.[57]

A number of points can be made in respect of this diary entry. Firstly, here is further evidence of the importance of 'experimental' religion to Pearce. '[C]rucifixion to the world' was a truth the importance of which he had known previously, but never 'felt' in the way he did at this meeting. Secondly, prayerful meditation on the scriptures was his practice (this had also been his approach to Psalm 119). Thirdly, and perhaps most strikingly, corporate worship and prayer were the contexts in which a deeper learning was experienced. The meeting had got him into a 'suitable frame of soul', thus shedding 'light' on verses of scripture so they could be seen more clearly. Here was 'investigation' into the scriptures that was far from 'impartial'. Rather, the setting of committed congregational worship allowed the truth of the Bible to be seen more clearly and appreciated more deeply. In summary, Pearce's theology as presented by Fuller was doctrinal, 'experimental' and applied. For Pearce, the ideal was for God's truth as revealed in Christ to penetrate deeply into heart and mind through the operation of the Holy Spirit.

Outwardly Focused

Already Pearce and Fuller's emphasis on the application of scripture to the Christian life has been seen. Truth had to make a difference to the way life was lived. There were some in Pearce's congregation who were, as Fuller expressed it, 'infected' with an 'antinomian spirit' and who did not believe Christians were called to obey the moral law. 'Soothing doctrine was all they desired.' By contrast, Pearce exhorted his Christian hearers to press on in 'practical godliness'.[58] The antinomianism which had been present at Fuller's first church in Soham and many other places in the mid-eighteenth century continued to be a significant problem in Particular Baptist life, with antinomian preachers such as William Huntington enjoying much popularity.[59] Yet this was a movement evangelicals in the Pearce / Fuller circle were determined to resist.

Given that the Christian life had to be lived with passion, a vital dimension of 'practical godliness' was activity in the cause of Christ. On the day of prayer and fasting during which Pearce meditated on Psalm 119, he also gave time to

---

[57] *Memoirs of Pearce*, 120.

[58] *Memoirs of Pearce*, 86-87.

[59] *Memoirs of Pearce*, 248. For some helpful material on Huntington and antinomianism in its late-eighteenth / early-nineteenth century context, see Robert Rix, *William Blake and the Cultures of Radical Christianity* (Aldershot: Ashgate, 2007), 26-34, esp. 28-29. For Huntington, see also *DEB*, 1: 586-67.

'visiting the wretched, and relieving the needy'.[60] His activity included a strong social element –'relieving the needy' – but evangelism was the overriding concern of the Pearce presented to us in the *Memoirs*. He engaged in vigorous evangelistic ministry at home and had an abiding concern for such work overseas. On 10 October 1794 he wrote, 'Enjoyed much freedom today in the family [i.e., family devotions]. Whilst noticing in prayer the state of the millions of heathen who know not God, I felt the aggregate value of their immortal souls with peculiar energy.'[61] Pearce threw himself into the work of the BMS and, as already stated, wanted to go overseas himself. In fact, a significant amount of space in the *Memoirs* is taken up with letters relating to this desire, together with entries from the diary he kept as he waited for the decision of the rest of the BMS committee.[62] Even when he was turned down by the BMS, he continued to give himself zealously to the cause. Indeed, one reason he was rejected as a missionary candidate was his importance to the Society as a promoter of its work at home.[63] Pearce's piety was an active piety.

At one point in the *Memoirs* Fuller made an important observation, declaring, 'Mr Pearce has been uniformly the spiritual and the active servant of Christ; but neither his spirituality nor [sic.] his activity would have appeared in the manner they have, but for his engagements in the *introduction of the gospel among the heathen.*'[64] Fuller here distinguishes between 'spiritual' and 'active', appearing to use the former term to describe the 'spiritual exercises' such as prayer, fasting and meditative Bible reading, together with Pearce's 'heart' relationship with God. In common with a number of recent writers, I define the term 'spirituality' differently. It certainly includes the interior life of the soul, but it is more than this, also encompassing the way the interior life is expressed and, crucially, lived out.[65]

Having established this difference in meaning, Fuller's comments can be analysed. They are deeply revealing of the type of life that was important to both men. Firstly, he recognised that both the 'spiritual' (as he understood it) and the 'active' were crucial to Pearce. Activity which did not flow out of a deep relationship with God was fruitless, and a relationship with God which did not lead to active pursuit of holiness, ministry and mission was a sham. Secondly, Fuller saw that both the 'spiritual' and 'active' dimensions of Pearce's life had been decisively shaped by the context of the foundation and development of the BMS, specifically by his own 'engagements' in this work. Mission was the

---

[60] *Memoirs of Pearce*, 129.

[61] *Memoirs of Pearce*, 120.

[62] *Memoirs of Pearce*, ch. 2, 98-141. Fuller's comments are interspersed with these.

[63] *Memoirs of Pearce*, 103; 114.

[64] *Memoirs of Pearce* 98.

[65] For a discussion, see Peter J. Morden, '*Communion with Christ and His People': The Spirituality of C.H. Spurgeon* (Oxford: Regent's Park, 2010 / Eugene, OR: Wipf and Stock, 2014), 2-4.

outworking of his prayer and devotion but it was also the essential context which shaped that devotion, providing the content for his prayers and moulding the different ways he related to God. The broader but still focused understanding of spirituality I am working with actually fits Pearce very well. He insisted on the importance of both the retired and the active, the devotional and the evangelistic. If we want to understand both Pearce's and Fuller's conception of the ideal Christian life, we need to see them not only as they reflect on the Bible and engage in private and corporate prayer, but also as they solicit funding for the BMS, preach for conversions and throw themselves wholeheartedly into a whole range of gospel activity. As far as Fuller's judgement of Pearce was concerned, there were 'few men' who had managed to unite 'a greater portion of the contemplative and active'.[66] The two dimensions of spirituality repeatedly informed and shaped one another. Here was perhaps the central reason Fuller wanted to commend Pearce's piety as a model for others.

'Faithful Unto Death'

Finally, Pearce's true spirituality was shown by the way he faced death. Fuller devoted a whole chapter to detailing Pearce's 'last affliction, and the holy and happy exercises of his mind under it.'[67] He included a number of letters Pearce wrote to him in the last year of his life. In one of these the Cannon Street pastor declared, '[T]hanks be to God, who giveth my heart the victory, let my poor body be consumed, or preserved. In the thought of *leaving*, I feel a momentary gloom; but in the thought of *going*, a heavenly triumph.'[68] He then quoted the line, 'Oh to grace how great a debtor!' from Robert Robinson's hymn, 'Come thou fount of every blessing'.[69] Pearce continued, 'Praise God with me, and for me, my dear brother, and let us not mind dying any more than sleeping. No, no; let every Christian sing the loudest, as he gets the nearest to the presence of his God.' He signed off, 'Eternally yours in Him who hath washed us both in his blood.'[70]

In death as in life Pearce was, for Fuller, a faithful exemplar of true spirituality. His spirituality was genuine (bearing up under this great and final test), biblical (the use of 1 Corinthians 15.57 in the opening lines cited). It also emphasised 'heart' religion (the insertion of the word 'heart' into the Bible quotation and his use of Robinson's warm, evangelical hymn), submitted to the sovereignty of God ('let my poor body be consumed, or preserved') and, above all, focused on the grace of God and on Christ and his cross. Because he and his

---

[66] *Memoirs of Pearce*, 245.
[67] *Memoirs of Pearce*, ch. 4, 195-242 (195).
[68] Samuel Pearce letter to Fuller, 23 March 1799, in *Memoirs of Pearce*, 212.
[69] 'Oh to grace how great a debtor / Daily I'm constrained to be!' are the opening lines of the fourth stanza of the original version of the hymn, which was written in 1757 when Robinson was just 22 years of age.
[70] Samuel Pearce letter to Fuller, 23 March 1799, in *Memoirs of Pearce*, 212-13.

friend were alike 'washed' in the 'blood' of Christ, they were eternally secure. Pearce could no longer actively serve a cause such as the BMS, but his trust in God as he faced death was set forth as an example to all who read the *Memoirs*, not least to the author of those *Memoirs* himself.

Andrew Fuller's Final Years

Continuing Work for the BMS

Pearce's *Memoirs* were extremely popular. Morris went so far as to say it was 'perhaps the most useful of all of Mr Fuller's writings.'[71] The work was revised twice in Fuller's lifetime and he may have been working on changes for the fourth edition in the years running up to his death.[72] But he was also occupied with much else in the closing years of his life.

In February and March of 1813 he was in London again, pressing for a clause in the British East India Company's new charter which would provide some legal protection for missionaries.[73] In the summer he was in Scotland on what would be his final tour there, often preaching in the open air in bad weather.[74] In 1814, he was forced to stay closer to home, but still he wanted to work at a demanding pace. In a letter dated 11 May 1814, Fuller set out his projected itinerary for the next few months,

> I have much journeying before me; first, to Olney and Bedford next week; then to the Association at Leicester, in Whitsun-week; then into Essex, on June 6th, where I must be at a missionary meeting, of that county, at Bocking, on June 8th; and collect what I can between that and our London annual meeting, which I suppose is on June 22. I must then return and be at Kettering by the 26th, which is our Lord's supper day. Then I must set off and be out all July in the north of England: – the first sabbath at Liverpool, the second at Manchester, third at Leeds, fourth at Newcastle, and fifth at Hull.

---

[71] Morris, *Fuller*, 2nd edn, 163.

[72] The 2nd edn appeared almost immediately (Clipstone: J.W. Morris, 1801). The 3rd edn (Dunstable: J.W. Morris, 1808) was the last over which Fuller had full control. For the 4th edn, which was published posthumously, see (London: W. Baynes *et al*, 1816).

[73] Fuller letter to William Ward, 5 March 1813, Letters to Carey, Marshman and Ward... Angus Library, Regent's Park College, Oxford (4/3/5). The clause was inserted, but its terms were not such as to please Baptists and other Nonconformists. The new charter set up an Anglican establishment and Dissenters still had to apply to the East India Company for a licence. See Stanley, *History of the BMS*, 26.

[74] Cf. Fuller letter to Ann Fuller, 25 July 1813, 'Letters to and from Andrew Fuller and Others of the Fuller Family', Bristol Baptist College Library (G 95 B), 13.

Given this punishing schedule, it is unsurprising he added the comment, 'May the Lord strengthen me for these labours.'[75] Yet by now his physical strength was fading fast. He was unable to make the journey into Essex,[76] and, unsurprisingly, the ambitious tour of the north of England was cancelled too.[77] He was vomiting frequently, losing weight and susceptible to fever. What was wrong? He may have been suffering from tuberculosis, as Pearce had been. But some form of cancer is also a possibility with the liver seemingly affected, although this may not have been the primary site.[78] Perhaps he was suffering from both these complaints or, indeed, a number of others. Whatever the precise physical cause, it was becoming obvious that the end of his life was near. Then, on 22 June 1814, John Sutcliff died. This was both an emotional blow to Fuller – another close friend had gone – and something which increased yet further his workload.[79] He wrote what appears to have been his last letter to Carey in February 1815. In it he declared,

> I scarcely know how to get on from week to week: The death of dear brother Sutcliff adds to my labours, and my strength decreases and the years are come in which I have but little pleasure in them. It is some comfort to me, however, that the Cause of God lives and prospers.[80]

Fuller was so worn out that even the work of his beloved BMS gave him little pleasure. Yet the 'cause of God' lived and prospered and still he kept going, sometimes spending twelve hours a day at his desk in these final few months.[81] The active piety Fuller had lauded in Pearce found no less an exemplar in Fuller himself.

---

[75] John Webster Morris, *Memoirs of the Life and Death of the Rev Andrew Fuller*, 1st edn (High Wycombe, 1816), 2nd edn (London: Wightman and Cramp, 1826), 2nd edn, 148.

[76] Fuller letter to John Ryland, 11 June 1814, in Ryland, *Fuller*, 350.

[77] Ryland, *Fuller*, 352.

[78] See the comment of Fuller's Doctor, recorded in Ryland, *Fuller*, 355. Cf. Fuller letter to Ryland, 2 April 1815, in Ryland, *Fuller*, 351, in which he mentioned a 'liver complaint'.

[79] On the emotion he felt on Sutcliff's passing, see, e.g., Fuller letter to Jabez Carey (William Carey's son), 18 August 1814, in *The Armies of the Lamb: The Spirituality of Andrew Fuller*, ed. by Michael A.G. Haykin (Dundas, ON: Joshua Press, 2001), 263, 'My dear young people, the fathers are dying. Sutcliff is no more!'

[80] Fuller letter to William Carey, 11 February 1815, Typescript Andrew Fuller Letters, transcribed by Joyce A. Booth, superintended by Ernest A. Payne, Angus Library, Regent's Park College, Oxford (4/5/1 and 4/5/2) (4/5/2).

[81] Fuller letter to John Ryland, 11 January 1815, Fuller Letters (4/5/2).

Continuing Theological Commitments

By March 1815 he was increasingly conscious he was dying. His 'ghastly, ca-daverous appearance' as he preached at the ordination of John Mack on 29 March at Clipstone shocked his friends. On descending from the pulpit Fuller said, 'I am very ill – a dying man.'[82] But as he faced this ultimate test of faith his theological commitments and his spirituality remained firm. On 2 April he preached for the last time, from Isaiah 66.1-2, 'Thus saith the Lord, the heaven is my throne, and the earth is my footstool...' As he presided at communion with his people, speaking slowly and haltingly, he appeared caught up contemplation of Christ crucified and risen. As he approached death he submitted to the sover-eignty of God and depended on God's grace as it was revealed in Jesus, espe-cially his cross.[83] He was confined to bed soon after this final communion ser-vice. In Gunton Fuller's words, his father had come 'into the house to die'.[84]

Fuller's last letter to Ryland, who he addressed as his 'dearest friend', was composed on 28 April 1815. He was too weak to write, but was able to dictate the letter to his brother, John Fuller, who was with him. Some of what he wrote ran as follows,

> We have some, who have been giving out, of late, that if 'Sutcliff, and some oth-ers, had preached more of Christ, and less of Jonathan Edwards, they would have been more useful.' If those who talk thus, preached Christ half as much as Jona-than Edwards did, and were half as useful as he was, their usefulness would be double what it is. It is very singular that the Mission to the East should have orig-inated with men of these principles; and without pretending to be a prophet, I may say, if it ever falls into the hands of men who talk in this strain, it will soon come to nothing.[85]

Some of Fuller's last words were in defence of the Edwardsean evangelical Calvinism of which he had become the principal British advocate. He also asked Ryland to speak at his funeral service, on Romans 8.10, 'And if Christ be in you, the body is dead because of sin; but the Spirit is life because of right-eousness.' As he looked forward the emphases were characteristic. He declared,

> I am a poor, guilty creature; but Christ is an almighty Saviour. I have preached and written much against the *abuse* of the doctrine of grace; but that doctrine is all my salvation and all my desire. I have no other hope than from salvation by mere sovereign, efficacious grace, through the atonement of my Lord and Saviour. With this hope, I can go into eternity with composure. Come, Lord Jesus! Come when thou wilt! Here I am; let him do with me as seemeth him good![86]

---

[82]   Gunton Fuller, *Fuller*, 187-88.
[83]   For further evidence, see Fuller letter to Jabez Carey, in *Armies of the Lamb*, 264.
[84]   Gunton Fuller, *Fuller*, 188.
[85]   Fuller letter to John Ryland, 28 April 1815, Ryland, *Fuller*, 355-56.
[86]   Fuller letter to John Ryland, 28 April 1815, Ryland, *Fuller*, 355.

If his body was riddled with cancer he would have been in agony with no effective pain relief. He spoke movingly to his son of the 'bodily misery' he was enduring [87] and his assistant, John Keen Hall, wrote that, 'his pain and restlessness were extreme'.[88] Earlier in his life this physical pain would most likely have been accompanied by spiritual depression, but now he was calm. He told someone who was attending him, 'I do not recollect before to have had such depression of animal spirits accompanied with such calmness of mind.' To his wife he said, 'We shall meet again. All will be well.'[89] On 7 May 1815 his pain finally ended. It was a Sunday, and Fuller was roused from semi-consciousness when he heard the sound of singing from the Meeting House, to which the Manse was attached. He tried to join in worship from his bed, but all his strength was gone. His last words, as recorded by his son, were 'Help me!' He died before the service was over. When the congregation were told the news an 'audible wail went up'. Keen Hall abandoned his sermon, led briefly in prayer and then closed the meeting.[90] When news of Fuller's death reached India, William Ward spoke of Fuller having had 'as large a share as any man on earth' in the establishment and promotion of the mission, and of having 'left no living person who can fill his place'.[91] It is no exaggeration to say that Fuller had given his life for the BMS. Ward's words were a fitting epitaph, as was the comment of John Webster Morris, 'He lived and died a martyr to the Mission.'[92]

Conclusion

In many ways, Fuller and Pearce were very similar. They were both Baptist and Calvinistic, with those convictions infused with evangelicalism. They were both influenced by eighteenth-century cultural currents which moulded who they were and how they communicated their faith, without eroding their Christian commitments. Most of all they both loved God and people and gave themselves to gospel mission. Morris's epitaph for Fuller might have served for Pearce as well. Both were willing to be martyrs for the cause of Christian mission. Both had received grace, and were sure it was their duty to live for God and for others with a passion.

Fuller and Pearce, then, had parallel commitments and concerns. Yet they can hardly be said to have lived parallel lives. Their journeys through life were very different. One area of difference can be noticed here. Pearce, was, almost

---

[87] Gunton Fuller, *Fuller*, 188.

[88] John Keen Hall letter to Isaac James, 9 May 1815, in Ryland, *Fuller*, 359.

[89] Gunton Fuller, *Fuller*, 189: 'I have no raptures, but no despondency. My mind is calm.'

[90] Gunton Fuller, *Fuller*, 188-91.

[91] William R. Ward, *A Sketch of the Character of the Late Rev Andrew Fuller* (Bristol: J.G. Fuller, 1817), 16. The sermon was originally preached at the Lal Bazaar Chapel, Calcutta, 1 October 1815.

[92] Morris, *Fuller*, 2nd edn, 352.

from the moment of his conversion, schooled in the warm-hearted evangelical Calvinism which was the hallmark of the revival of eighteenth-century Baptist life. By contrast,

Fuller's theology and praxis shifted considerably, developing significantly during his early years as a Christian and pastor. He had to break free from the high Calvinism which had shaped his theology, ministry and spirituality. His evangelical priorities had not been inherited. He had worked out his commitments for himself, wrestling with a range of issues and coming to conclusions which, once reached, were fixed and immovable, precisely because they had been so hard won. Fuller has emerged in this biography as a complex man whose life exhibited many insecurities and struggles. But in his mature theological commitments and ministry priorities his convictions were unshakeable. And, at the last, his trust in God was unshakeable too.

CHAPTER 9

Conclusion: Fuller's Legacy

so valuable a life...

A letter from a member of the Kettering congregation to Ryland, dated 19 August 1801, contains the following lines, 'Mr F.'s exertions are too much for his health... Dear sir, pray for us, that so valuable a life may yet be continued.'[1] Of course, to declare a life 'valuable' is to make a subjective judgement. The factors which might have led to the anonymous church member describing his pastor in this way – Fuller's work for the BMS, his theological and apologetic writing, his preaching and pastoral ministry, his modelling of an evangelical spirituality – would not necessarily count as 'valuable' with every observer. Yet I hope this theological biography has shown that his life was an extremely important one. As a local church pastor, denominational leader, published author and, especially, missionary statesman he was a significant figure. Summing up this multi-dimensional life and ministry is no easy task. This brief final chapter attempts to draw together some of the most prominent threads that were woven through his sixty-one years, before considering aspects of his legacy.

Journey

The motif of journey which I have deployed on a number of occasions in this book, not least at the close of the previous chapter, is a helpful one, for Fuller's life can be viewed as a series of journeys. Firstly, there are the physical journeys he made. Most notable was the move from Soham to Kettering, but there were also many other excursions to preach at Sunday services, ordinations and the opening of Meeting Houses. There were journeys on behalf of the BMS as well, to Scotland, Ireland and Wales and throughout England. Fuller's well-worn map of London remains as a symbol of these excursions to the four corners of the British Isles and Ireland. The countryman whose ancestors had lived and died in a small area of the Cambridgeshire Fens had broken the mould of

---

[1] John Ryland Jr, *The Work of Faith, the Labour of Love, and the Patience of Hope Illustrated in the Life and Death of the Rev. Andrew Fuller*, 2nd edn (London: Button and Son, 1818), 344.

generations, spending much of his working life covering mile after wearying mile on behalf of his beloved BMS.

Secondly, Fuller also went on a journey of suffering. That suffering was physical. From 1793 onwards his health was rarely good and he was often extremely unwell, for example in 1801. The final illness (or illnesses) which led to his death left him in excruciating pain in the last months of his life. His suffering was also mental. This was linked to the suffering and death of various children and to the illness and death of his first wife, Sarah. Fuller himself was depressed – I have argued that at times he was clinically depressed. As already noted in this biography, his story was one of triumph but it was not one of triumphalism.

Thirdly, there were the journeys in his thinking about life and faith. Primary among these was his journey from high Calvinism to evangelicalism, a journey that had a number of different stages. To begin with, his theology changed, then his practice of ministry and, finally, his spirituality. By 1793, a year after the BMS was founded, Fuller had moved away from an introspective piety to an outward looking focus on Christ and Christian mission. This is not to say his thinking and practice remained static after this date. Theologically he continued to develop until at least 1806, especially through his debates with Dan Taylor and Abraham Booth. Overall, by the end of his life Fuller had travelled far.

Influences

Having said there was significant movement in his life and thought, it needs to be emphasised there was there was much continuity as well. Much of his inherited tradition remained important and was never rejected. This tradition continued to influence him. Fuller remained Dissenting and Baptist as to ecclesiology and Calvinistic as to theology. In fact I have found no evidence that he ever wavered in any of these commitments. What did happen was that his commitments to Baptist polity and to Particular Redemption were reshaped and renewed by the evangelicalism he embraced. These continuing theological and ecclesiological commitments also determined the type of evangelical he was. Although he had friendships with a range of evangelicals such as the Anglican Charles Grant and the Congregationalist Thomas Toller he was not the same as them and his enduring commitment to closed communion meant they could not have shared the Lord's Supper at his church. He felt a common bond with the Baptist evangelicalism of Dan Taylor's New Connexion but even here, active cooperation was limited. This can be illustrated by Fuller's reaction to a proposal made to him by John G. Pike, a New Connexion General Baptist. Pike had been deeply impressed with Fuller's *Memoirs* of Pearce. Partly through reading these he developed a keen missionary interest.[2] In 1812 Pike, who by

---

[2] Ernest A. Payne, *The First Generation: Early Leaders of the Baptist Missionary Society in England and India* (London: Carey Press, n.d. [1937]), 135-34.

that stage was a minister in Derby, wrote to Fuller on behalf of the New Connexion General Baptist Conference to ask if they could send a missionary of their own, a man who would cooperate with those BMS workers already in the field. Fuller was happy to receive money from the General Baptists for BMS work, but he firmly rejected Pike's proposal. As he reported to William Ward, to proceed in the way Pike suggested was inappropriate given the continuing 'disputes' between the two groups of Baptists around the subject of particular versus general redemption. 'Unanimity' on this issue, he insisted, 'was of great importance'.[3] Evangelical ecumenism had clear boundaries for Fuller. Specific theological and ecclesiological commitments remained very important to him and he remained influenced by them right to the end of his life.

Yet one of the central arguments of *The Life and Thought of Andrew Fuller* has been that its subject was transformed by evangelicalism and I want to restate that foundational argument here. True, he was wedded to Baptist principles and to Calvinistic decrees, but the way these commitments were articulated and worked out was remoulded by the inflow of evangelicalism. Jonathan Edwards was the primary extra-biblical source reshaping him in this way. The *Freedom of the Will* was of first importance, but the significance of the *Life of Brainerd* and the *Humble Attempt*, with their strong practical message, should not be downplayed. The New Divinity theologians were also very important, although Fuller engaged with them critically and overall was less positive about them than he was about Edwards. Friendship with likeminded people was vital. These friendships – with Hall, Sutcliff, Ryland, Carey and Pearce especially – flourished in the context of shared undertakings. These undertakings usually took the form of evangelistic ventures and pride of place has to go to the BMS. The excitement of working collaboratively with others in evangelism was deeply attractive to Fuller and he was continually drawn to this type of work. Such involvement convinced him yet further of the value of 'gospel work'. He was also shaped by culture but he always sought to be faithful to the biblical witness. Indeed, one of the arguments of this book has been that scripture was primary for Fuller. Human theologians shaped him, friends influenced him, culture shaped him (in a number of ways he was doubtless unaware). Yet it was the Bible, which he regarded as the very 'oracles of God', that he sought to be faithful to as it bore witness to the gospel of Christ. He was aware he was not entirely successful in his aim to be faithful to what God had revealed, for he was only too aware of his fallibility. Nevertheless, Fuller was an exemplar of the biblicism that was characteristic of the Evangelical Revival.

---

[3] Fuller letter to William Ward, 7 Jan 1813, in Letters to Carey, Marshman and Ward... Angus Library, Regent's Park College, Oxford (4/3/5).

Legacy

Fuller's legacy can especially be seen in his work with the BMS and in his theology. The BMS did not have an easy time immediately after his death. Fuller had so much concentrated in his own hands he was nigh on impossible to replace as secretary. His own chosen successor, from as early as 1807, was Christopher Anderson, the Scotsman he had first met in the Haldanes' connexion and who had adopted Baptist principles. However, Anderson was not acceptable to some of the BMS constituency and was not appointed in 1815.[4] He became the Serampore missionaries' primary supporter during their struggles with the London based home committee in the late 1820s.[5] The BMS had to navigate some stormy seas in the years following the founding secretary's passing. Nevertheless, the Society prospered, became the template for other groups and continued to help fire a movement which had global repercussions.

As to theology, 'Fullerism' had become the theological orthodoxy for the majority of Particular Baptists before Fuller's death and this legacy continued to be hugely significant after 1815. As David Bebbington has stated, 'Fuller's convictions formed the touchstone of Baptist orthodoxy for the rest of the century', as well as being highly influential for others.[6] Fuller's triumph was not quite complete, however. Older high Calvinists would continue to reject 'duty faith', and their criticisms would be taken up by a new generation. Key leaders of the nineteenth-century Strict Baptist movement such as William Gadsby and Joseph C. Philpot were scathing in their condemnation of Fuller. For Gadsby, Fuller was 'the greatest enemy the church of God ever had, as his sentiments were so much cloaked in the sheep's clothing'. Fuller was blamed for the erosion of true Calvinistic principles amongst the Particular Baptists, for opening the door to mixed communion and, along with it, Arminianism.[7] Moreover, as the nineteenth-century wore on, Particular Baptists became far less committed to Calvinism. Was this due to Fuller's influence? Kenneth Dix's verdict is fair, and deserves to be quoted at length,

> The Strict Baptists did not treat Fuller with the respect he deserved as the leading
> Baptist theologian of his day. There was a failure to accept Fuller's testimony of

---

[4] Brian Stanley, *The History of the Baptist Missionary Society, 1792-1992* (Edinburgh: T. & T. Clark, 1992), 3-4, 29-35; A. Christopher Smith, 'Christopher Anderson and the Serampore Fraternity' in, *A Mind for Mission; Essays in Appreciation of the Rev. Christopher Anderson 1782-1852*, ed. by Donald E. Meek (Edinburgh: The Scottish Baptist History Project, 1992), 25-27.

[5] See Stanley, *History of the BMS*, 61-67, for the disputes; 65, for Anderson's involvement.

[6] David W. Bebbington, 'SBJT Forum', *Southern Baptist Journal of Theology* 17.1 (2013), 48. Other nineteenth-century figures influenced by Fuller and Fullerism include the Scottish 'Common-sense' philosopher Thomas Chalmers.

[7] As noted by Kenneth Dix, *Strict and Particular: English Strict and Particular Baptists in the Nineteenth Century* (Didcot: Baptist Historical Society, 2001), 37 n, 103.

his commitment to 'strict Calvinism', or of the very gracious way he wrote of his opposition to mixed communion principles. There were certainly times when Fuller made statements which might have been construed as a departure from the particularist position, but this was not the case. His belief in an atonement that was sufficient for all men but efficacious only for the elect, offended high-Calvinists, but he never gave up the seventeenth-century confessions. Andrew Fuller was no more responsible for any shift from orthodox Calvinism in the nineteenth century than the men who framed the 1677 Confession could be held responsible for the path taken by some of their opponents into the chilling winds of high-Calvinism.[8]

This is an assessment with which I heartily concur. It is true that nineteenth-century Strict Baptists regarded Fuller as their 'greatest enemy' and so an analysis of his theology is important in any description of the emergence of the Strict and Particular Baptist Community.[9] But the nineteenth-century shift away from 'strict Calvinism' was far more attributable, as Ian Sellers states, to 'the tide of nineteenth-century opinion [which] was running against religious particularism of any form'.[10] Those who laid the 'blame' for the erosion of Calvinistic distinctives amongst the Particular Baptists at Fuller's door were wrong. Rather than abandoning Calvinism and opening the door to Arminianism, Fullerism actually opened the door to expansive gospel ministry by allowing increasing numbers within the Particular Baptist denomination to hold together strict Calvinism with invitational gospel preaching. That he was able to do this so successfully was part of his genius as a theologian.

A further dimension of that genius was his ability to adapt theology to new cultural currents without turning from central biblical teaching. As we have seen, his mature thinking was adapted to the spirit of the age but he always prioritised the biblical revelation. He made some significant adjustments in his thinking but there was much he did not change. David Bebbington comments,

> Fuller was prepared to make bold alterations to the system of beliefs he inherited for the sake of making the Christian message intelligible to his contemporaries, but he was acutely conscious that the spirit of the age could lead to a distortion of sound teaching. He was an expert in the adjustment of the relations of gospel and culture.[11]

---

8   Dix, *Strict and Particular*, 269-70.
9   Robert W. Oliver, 'The Emergence of a Strict and Particular Baptist Community Among the English Calvinistic Baptists, 1770-1850' (unpublished PhD thesis, CNAA [London Bible College], 1986), 119.
10 Ian Sellers, 'John Howard Hinton, Theologian', *Baptist Quarterly* 33.3 (July 1989), 123. For more detail, see Dix, *Strict and Particular*, 70. Evangelical Calvinism would enjoy a notable resurgence at the end of the nineteenth century in the person of Charles Haddon Spurgeon.
11 Bebbington, 'SBJT Forum', 48.

Once again, I heartily concur. In relating gospel and culture in careful, thoughtful and bold ways he was influential in his own time and beyond. He also provides a model for modern theologians, missiologists and all thinking Christians, a model of bold engagement with the culture held together with a commitment to remain faithful to the biblical witness.

Moreover, he leaves a legacy of thought turned into action. His influence as far as this is concerned is nicely illustrated by an anecdote regarding a student attending Charles Haddon Spurgeon's Pastors' College in the 1870s. Thomas L. Johnson was an African American who came to London in 1876 to study at the College.[12] In his memoirs, Johnson related his first experience of preaching at 'Sermon Class'. Understandably nervous, he put much effort into preparing his message. Whilst still in America he had been given a number of books by Andrew Fuller which he had brought with him to London. Re-reading these works, he was particularly struck by some of Fuller's comments on the subject of being 'born again'. After some hesitation he decided to use these – it appears verbatim and unattributed – in his message. He reasoned, 'Notwithstanding that I was told not to 'plagiarise', I felt that I could not say the thing better myself... I thought that the book, being old, no-one would detect it.' However, he was wrong. After the student had preached, the College's principal, George Rogers, rose to give his feedback. In the course of his comments, he said of Johnson, 'I see in him an Andrew Fuller!' This was high praise indeed and the listening students 'cheered and clapped and thumped [their] desks' in support. But Johnson knew his unacknowledged use of another's work had been discovered.[13] He had not been aware that the College principal knew and appreciated Fuller's writings. Indeed, Spurgeon himself regarded Fuller as the 'greatest theologian' of the eighteenth century.[14] Johnson's time at the Pastors' College was extremely positive and he looked back on it with great fondness, but on this occasion he was crestfallen. Rather harsh on himself (given that many preachers have done something similar at one time or another) he concluded that his sin had found him out and that he had learnt a great lesson.[15]

---

[12] There is some uncertainty about the date Johnson became a student. Johnson himself states he entered the College in December 1876, but the College registers – probably mistakenly – say he began study in 1875.

[13] Thomas L. Johnson, *Twenty-Eight Years a Slave*, 7th edn (Bournemouth: Mate and Sons, 1909), 94.

[14] See Spurgeon letter to Andrew Gunton Fuller, in Gilbert Laws, *Andrew Fuller: Pastor, Theologian, Ropeholder* (London: Kingsgate Press, 1942), 127. For Spurgeon's use of Fuller, see Peter J. Morden, *'Communion with Christ and His People:' The Spirituality of C.H. Spurgeon* (Oxford: Regent's Park, 2010 / Eugene, OR: Wipf and Stock, 2014), 132, 225-26.

[15] Johnson, *Twenty-Eight Years a Slave*, 94. For Johnson's time at the Pastors' College and his reflections on it, see 86-104. See also, Ian M. Randall, *A School of the Prophets: 150 years of Spurgeon's College* (London: Spurgeon's College, 2005), 52, 79-80, 98-90.

Thomas Johnson became part of the larger story of evangelical mission; indeed he went on to serve with the BMS itself. At the close of his time at the Pastors' College, he, together with his wife Henrietta and another missionary couple, went to West Africa and began ministry in the Cameroonian village of Bakundu under the auspices of the BMS. As was all too common, the work of this pioneering husband and wife was tragically cut short by death and illness: Henrietta died of a fever and Thomas was soon forced to leave Africa due to his own severe ill-health, returning to England after little more than a year of active ministry.[16] Nevertheless, he remained an enthusiastic advocate of overseas mission for the rest of his life, in a sense fulfilling Rogers' words that he would become 'an Andrew Fuller'. Others would step forward to take the Johnsons' place in the field, sponsored by one of the plethora of missionary societies which had come into existence by the second half of the nineteenth century, seeking nothing less than world evangelisation. Fuller's influence was not just confined to the western world; his significance as a pioneer of modern cross-cultural mission was, and remains, global. He had been closely involved in the beginnings of a movement which had an impact that was both deep and broad. As men and women engage in such work today, Fuller's legacy and influence live on.

---

[16] The Johnsons sailed for West Africa in November 1878; Thomas's return ship landed in Liverpool in January 1880. See Johnson, *Twenty-Eight Years a Slave*, 107; 142. Thomas Johnson's story is a powerful one. His motto, 'Christ for Africa', was one he carried to his grave. In later years he engaged in itinerant evangelism in England, with much success.

Bibliography

Primary Sources – Manuscripts

Angus Library, Regent's Park College, Oxford

Letters of William Carey, William Ward, Joshua Marshman, and Others to the Baptist Missionary Society Committee, 1800-1827 (IN/21)

Fuller, Andrew, Bound Volume of Andrew Fuller Letters to W. Carey, J. Marshman, W. Ward and other BMS Missionaries, 1795-1815, transcribed in India, with an index compiled by A. Gunton Fuller (3/170)

—, Letter to William Carey, 18 April 1799 (H/1/3)

—, Letters to Carey, Marshman and Ward... (4/3/5)

—, Letters to John Saffery (II/273)

—, Letter to William Wilberforce, 5 December 1801 (II/200)

—, Typescript Andrew Fuller Letters, transcribed by Joyce A. Booth, superintended by Ernest A. Payne (4/5/1 and 4/5/2)

William Ward's Journal (IN/17A)

Bristol Baptist College Library

Book of Miscellaneous Writings [including Fuller's "List of Books" from 1798, and a "Meditation" by Ann Fuller] (G 95 b)

Fuller, Andrew, Commonplace Book [first entry 22 June 1798] (95 a)

—, Diary and Spiritual Thoughts [1784-1801] (G 95 b)

—, Letter to an un-named missionary and his colleagues at Serampore [7 January 1813] (G 96 Box D)

—, Shorthand Sermons with some Meditations in Longhand, Books I-V, Bristol Baptist College (G 95 A)

—, Subscribers' list and notes about collection for BMS, plus some Greek grammar (G 95 b)

Letters to and from Andrew Fuller and Others of the Fuller Family (G 95 B)

Ryland Jr, John, Letter to Andrew Fuller (G 97 B Box A)

Cambridgeshire County Archives, Cambridge

Annual Letters on the State of the Ch[urch] sent to the Association from the year 1776 (N/B - Soham R70/20)

Fuller, Andrew, A Narration of the dealings of God in a way of Providence with the Baptist Church at Soham from the year 1770 (NC/B - Soham R70/20)

Soham Baptist Church Book, 1752-1868 (N/B - Soham)

Fuller Baptist Church Archive, Kettering, Northamptonshire
Church Book of Kettering Baptist Church (The 'Little Meeting'), 1773-1815
Fuller Chapel Letters [Letters to Andrew Fuller], vol. 1 (1-34), vol. 2 (35-71)
Remaining page of Wallis Church Book

Southern Baptist Theological Seminary, Louisville, Kentucky
Fuller, Andrew, Thoughts on the Power of Men to do the Will of God, Wrote [sic.] in 1777, or 1778

Primary Sources – Magazines and Periodicals
Baptist Magazine
Eclectic Review
Evangelical Magazine
Periodical Accounts of the Baptist Missionary Society
Theological and Biblical Magazine

Primary Sources – Books and Booklets
Baptist Handbook for 1896 (London: Clarke and Co, 1895)
Beccaria, Cesare, *On Crimes and Punishments*, trans. Henry Paolucci (Indianapolis: Bobbs-Merrill, 1963)
Bellamy, Joseph, *True Religion Delineated; or, Experimental Religion... Set in a Scriptural and Rational Light*, 3rd edn (London: T. Hamilton, 1809)
Bennett, James and David Bogue, *The History of Dissenters During the Last Thirty Years: from 1808 to 1838* (London: Hamilton and Adams, 1839)
Booth, Abraham, *The Works of Abraham Booth... With Some Account of his Life and Writings*, 3 vols (London: W. Button and Son, 1813)
Brooks, Thomas, *Heaven on Earth* (London: Banner of Truth, 1961 [1654])
Bunyan, John, *Grace Abounding to the Chief of Sinners...* (Harmondsworth: Penguin, 1987 [1666])
—, *The Pilgrim's Progress, From This World to That Which is to Come, Delivered Under the Similitude of a Dream* (London: The Book Society, 1876 [1678])
Burroughs, Jeremiah, *Evil of Evils; or, the Exceeding Sinfulness of Sin* (London: Goodwin, Nye *et al*, 1654)
Button, William, *Remarks on a Treatise Entitled The Gospel of Christ Worthy of All Acceptation* (London, 1785)
Calamy, Edmund and Samuel Palmer, *The Nonconformists' Memorial...* vol. 1 (London: W. Harris, 1775)
Carey, Eustace, *Memoir of William Carey, DD* (London: Jackson and Walford, 1836)

Carey, William, *An Enquiry into the Obligations for Christians to use Means for the Conversion of the Heathens* (London: Kingsgate Press, 1961 [1792])

Church Book: St Andrew's Street Baptist Church, Cambridge: 1720-1832 [typescript by Leonard G. Champion; Introduction by Len Addicott] (Didcot: Baptist Historical Society, 1991)

Coleman, Thomas, *Facts and Incidents in the Life and Ministry of the late Rev. Thomas Northcote Toller* (London: John Snow, 1865)

Cox, Francis A., *History of the Baptist Missionary Society from 1792 to 1842*, 2 vols (London: T. Ward and G. & J. Dyer, 1842)

Jonathan Edwards, *Freedom of the Will*, in *The Works of Jonathan Edwards*, vol. 1, ed. by Paul Ramsey (New Haven: Yale University Press, 1985 [1754])

—, *The Life of David Brainerd*, in *The Works of Jonathan Edwards*, vol. 7, ed. by Norman Pettit (New Haven: Yale University Press, 1985 [1749])

—, *The Works of Jonathan Edwards*, 2 vols, ed. by Edward Hickman (Edinburgh: Banner of Truth, 1974 [1834])

The Sermons and Other Practical Works of the Later Reverend Ralph Erskine, A.M., vol. 7 (London: Wm. Tegg, 1865)

Fawcett Jr, John, *An Account of the Life, Ministry and Writings of the late Rev John Fawcett, DD* (London: Baldwin, Craddock and Joy, 1818)

Fletcher, Jonathan, *A Vindication of the Rev. Mr Wesley's Minutes* (Bristol: Pine, 1771)

Fuller, Andrew, *The Complete Works of the Rev. Andrew Fuller, With a Memoir of his Life by the Rev. Andrew Gunton Fuller*, ed. by Andrew Gunton Fuller, rev. ed. by Joseph Belcher; 3 vols, 3rd edn (Harrisonburg, VA: Sprinkle Publications, 1988 [1845])

—, *The Gospel Worthy of All Acceptation*, 1st edn (Northampton: Thomas Dicey, 1785)

—, *The Last Remains of the Rev. Andrew Fuller: Sermons, Essays, Letters, and Other Miscellaneous Papers, Not Included in His Published Works*, ed. by Joseph Belcher (Philadelphia: American Baptist Publication Society, 1856)

—, *Memoirs of the Late Rev. Samuel Pearce... with Extracts from Some of his Most Interesting Letters*, 1st edn (Clipstone: J. W. Morris, 1800)

—, *Miscellaneous Pieces on Various Religious Subjects, being the last remains of the Rev. Andrew Fuller*, ed. by John Webster Morris (London: Wightman and Cramp, 1826)

—, 'Recommendatory Preface' to Joseph Bellamy, *True Religion Delineated; or, Experimental Religion... Set in a Scriptural and Rational Light*, 3rd edn (London: T. Hamilton, 1809)

Fuller, Andrew Gunton, *Men Worth Remembering: Andrew Fuller* (London: Hodder and Stoughton, 1882)

Fuller, John G., *A Brief History of the Western Association* (Bristol, I. Hemmans, 1843)

Fuller, Thomas E., *A Memoir of the Life and Writings of Andrew Fuller: By His Grandson* (London: Heaton and Son, 1863)

Gill, John, *A Complete Body of Doctrinal and Practical Divinity*, 1839 edn (London: repr. Paris, Arkansas: Baptist Standard Bearer, 1989)

—, *The Doctrines of God's Everlasting Love to His Elect... Stated and Defended. In a Letter to Dr Abraham Taylor* (London, 1732)

—, *An Exposition of the Old Testament*, 4 vols (London: Matthews and Leigh, [1763-65] 1810)

—, 'Recommendatory Preface' to Richard Davis, *Hymns Composed on Several Subjects, and on Divers Occasions*, 7th edn (London: J. Ward, 1748), printed in George T. Streather, *Memorials of the Independent Chapel at Rothwell* (Rothwell: Rothwell United Reformed Church, 1994)

Wise Counsel: John Newton's Letters to John Ryland Jr, ed. by Grant Gordon (Edinburgh: Banner of Truth, 2009)

Haldane, Alexander, *The Lives of Robert and James Haldane*, 3rd edn (London: Hamilton and Adams, 1853)

Hall Jr, Robert, *The Works of Robert Hall*, ed. by Olinthus Gregory, vol. 6 (London, 1833)

Hall Sr, Robert, *The Complete Works of the Late Robert Hall*, ed. by John Webster Morris (London, 1828)

Hopkins, Samuel, *The Works of Samuel Hopkins, DD...With a Memoir* [by Edwards Amasa Park] *of his Life and Character*, 3 vols (Boston: Doctrinal Tract and Book Society, 1852)

Hupton, Job, *A Blow Struck at the Root of Fullerism. In a Letter to a Friend* (London: L.J. Higham 1804)

Hussey, Joseph, *God's Operations of Grace, But No Offers of His Grace* (London: D. Bridge, 1707)

Ivimey, Joseph, *A History of the English Baptists (HEB)* 4 vols (London: Hinton, Holdsworth & Ball, 1811-30)

Johnson, Thomas L., *Twenty-Eight Years a Slave*, 7th edn (Bournemouth: Mate and Sons, 1909)

Protestant Nonconformist Texts: Vol. 1: 1550-1700; ed. by R. Tudor Jones *et al* (Aldershot: Ashgate, 2007)

Lewis, Charles B., *The Life of John Thomas* (London: MacMillan, 1873)

Baptist Confessions of Faith, ed. by William L. Lumpkin (Valley Forge: Judson Press, 1969)

Marshman, John Clark, *The Story of Carey, Marshman and Ward, The Serampore Missionaries* (London: Alexander Strahan, 1864)

Martin, John, *Thoughts On The Duty Of Man Relative To Faith In Jesus Christ, In Which Mr Andrew Fuller's Leading Propositions On This Subject Are Considered* (London: W. Smith, 1788-91)

Molyneux, Thomas, *An Introduction to Byrom's Universal English Short-hand*, 4th edn [London: J. Wilson, 1813])

Church Book of the Independent Church...Isleham 1693-1805, ed. by Kenneth C. Parsons (Cambridge Antiquarian Records Society: Cambridge, 1984)

Pearce, Samuel, 'Letter to the Lascars', in *The Baptist Annual Register*, ed. by John Rippon, vol. 3 (London: Button, Conder, Brown *et al*, 1801)

The Baptist Annual Register, ed. by John Rippon, vol. 1 (London: Dilly, Button and Thomas, 1793)

Rippon, John, *A Brief Memoir of the Life and Writings of the late Rev. John Gill, DD* (London: John Bennett, 1838)

Ryland Jr, John, *Memoirs of Robert Hall of Arnsby [sic.]. With a Brief History of the Baptist Church...* 2nd edn; rev. ed. J.A. Jones (London: James Paul, 1850)

—, *The Work of Faith, the Labour of Love, and the Patience of Hope Illustrated in the Life and Death of the Rev. Andrew Fuller*, 1st edn (London: Button and Son, 1816), 2nd edn (London: Button and Son, 1818)

Sale, George, *The Koran, commonly called the Alcoran of Mohammed: translated into English immediately from the original Arabic...to which is prefixed a preliminary discourse* London: C. Ackers for J. Wilcox, 1734)

Scott, John, *The Life of Thomas Scott* (London: Seeley, 1836)

Scott, Thomas, *Warrant and Nature of Faith in Christ Considered...* 2nd edn (Buckingham: J. Seeley, 1801 [1797])

Protestant Nonconformist Texts, Vol. 2: The Eighteenth Century; ed. by Alan F. Sell *et al* (Aldershot: Ashgate, 2006)

Smith, Sydney, 'Publications Respecting Indian Missions', in *Edinburgh Review or Critical Journal* 12 (April 1808) (Edinburgh: Constable, 1808)

—, *Works of the Rev. Sydney Smith in Three Volumes*, vol. 1 (London: Longman, Orme *et al*, 1839)

Stennett, Samuel, *Memoirs of the Life of the Rev. William Ward* (London: J. Haddon: 1825)

Stonehouse, George, *Fullerism Defended; or Faith in Christ Asserted to be a Requirement of the Moral Law...* (Cranbrook, Kent: S. Waters, 1804)

Spurgeon, Charles Haddon, *Autobiography: Compiled from his Diary, Letters, and Records by his Wife and his Private Secretary*, 4 vols (London: Passmore and Alabaster, 1897–99)

Taylor, Adam, *Memoirs of the Rev. Dan Taylor* (London: Baynes and Son, 1820)

Taylor, Dan [writing as 'Philanthropos'], *Observations on the Rev Andrew Fuller's late pamphlet entitled The Gospel of Christ Worthy of All Acceptation* (London: J. Buckland, 1788)

—, *Observations on the Rev Andrew Fuller's Reply to Philanthropos* (St Ives, Cambridgeshire: T. Bloom, 1788)

—, *The Friendly Conclusion Occasioned by the Letters of 'Agnostos'* (London: W. Ash, 1790)

Twining, Thomas, *A Letter, to the Chairman of the East India Company: On the Danger of Interfering in the Religious Opinions of Natives in India...* 2nd edn (London: Ridgeway, 1807)

Wallin, Benjamin, *The Christian Life, In Divers of its Branches Described and Recommended*, 2 vols (London: Ward, 1746)

Ward, William, *Farewell Letters to a Few Friends in Britain and America, on Returning to Bengal in 1821*, 2nd edn (London: S. & R. Bentley, 1821)

—, *A Sketch of the Character of the Late Rev Andrew Fuller* (Bristol: J.G. Fuller, 1817)

The Works of John Wesley, ed. by Richard P. Heitzenrater and Frank Baker (Oxford: Oxford University Press, 1975-)

—, *Exhortations, Relating to Prayer and the Lord's Supper* (London: Ward, 1752)

Williams, Richard, *Y Pregethwr a'r Gwrandawr; sef, Calfinistiaeth a Ffwleriaeth yn Cael ei Hystyried, ar Ddull Ymddyddan Rhwng Dau Gyfaill* [The Preacher and the Listener: Namely Calvinism and Fullerism Considered, by Means of a Conversation between Two Friends] (Machynlleth: T. Hughes, 1840)

Secondary Sources – Books and Booklets

Bebbington, David W., *Baptists Through the Centuries* (Baylor UP: Waco, TX, 2010)

—, *Evangelicalism in Modern Britain: A History from the 1730s to the 1980s* (London: Unwin Hyman, 1989)

—, *Holiness in Nineteenth-Century England* (Carlisle: Paternoster, 2000)

Binfield, Clyde, *Pastors and People: The Biography of a Baptist Church, Queen's Road, Coventry* (Coventry: Alan Sutton, 1984)

Brewster, Paul, *Andrew Fuller: Model Pastor – Theologian* (Nashville, Tennessee: B. & H., 2010)

Box, Bart D., *The Atonement in the Thought of Andrew Fuller* (New Orleans: ProQuest, 2009)

Briggs, John H.Y., *The English Baptists of the Nineteenth Century* (Didcot: Baptist Historical Society, 1994)

Broome, John R., *A Bruised Reed: The Life and Times of Anne Steele* (Harpenden: Gospel Standard Trust, 2007)

Brown, Raymond, *The English Baptists of the Eighteenth Century* (London: Baptist Historical Society, 1986)

—, *Spirituality in Adversity: English Nonconformity in a Period of Repression, 1660-1689* (Milton Keynes: Paternoster, 2012)

Dictionary of Scottish Church History and Theology, ed. by Nigel M. de S. Cameron (Edinburgh: T & T Clark, 1993)

Chadwick, Owen, *The Spirit of the Oxford Movement* (Cambridge: Cambridge University Press: 1990)

Chun, Chris, *The Legacy of Jonathan Edwards in the Theology of Andrew Fuller* (Leiden: Brill, 2012)

Conforti, Joseph A., *Samuel Hopkins and the New Divinity Movement* (Grand Rapids: Eerdmans, 1981)

Coppenger, Raymond A., *A Messenger of Grace: A Study of the Life and Thought of Abraham Booth* (Joshua Press: Dundas, ON, 2009)

Crawford, Michael J., *Seasons of Grace, Colonial New England's Revival Tradition in its British Context* (Oxford: Oxford University Press, 1991)

Darby, Henry C., *The Draining of the Fens*, 2nd edn (Cambridge: Cambridge University Press, 1968)

De Jong, James A., *As the Waters Cover the Sea: Millennial Expectations in the Rise of Anglo-American Missions, 1640–1810* (Kampen: J.H. Kok, 1970)

Dix, Kenneth, *Strict and Particular: English Strict and Particular Baptists in the Nineteenth Century* (Didcot: Baptist Historical Society, 2001)

Dudley Smith, Timothy, *John Stott: The Making of a Leader* (Leicester: IVP, 1999)

Elwyn, Thornton S.H., *The Northamptonshire Baptist Association* (London: Carey Kingsgate Press, 1964)

New Dictionary of Theology, ed. by Sinclair Ferguson and David F. Wright (Leicester: IVP, 1988)

Ferm, Robert L., *Jonathan Edwards the Younger: A Colonial Pastor* (Grand Rapids: Eerdmans, 1976)

Foster, Frank H., *A Genetic History of the New England Theology* (Chicago: Univ. Chicago Press, 1907)

George, Timothy, *Faithful Witness: The Life and Mission of William Carey* (Leicester: IVP, 1991)

Grant, Keith S., *Andrew Fuller and the Evangelical Renewal of Pastoral Theology* (Milton Keynes: Paternoster, 2013)

The Kettering Connection: Northamptonshire Baptists and Overseas Mission, ed. by Ronald L. Greenall (Leicester: Department of Adult Education, University of Leicester, 1993)

Grigg, John A., *The Lives of David Brainerd: the Making of an American Evangelical Icon* (Oxford: Oxford University Press, 2009)

Gunton, Colin, *The Actuality of the Atonement: A Study of Metaphor, Rationality and the Christian Tradition* (Edinburgh: T. & T. Clark, 1988)

Haroutunian, Joseph, *Piety versus Moralism: The Passing of the New England Theology* (New York: Harper and Row, 1932)

Haskell, Thomas J., *Objectivity is Not Neutrality: Explanatory Schemes in History* (Baltimore: John Hopkins University Press, 1998)

Hayden, Roger, *Continuity and Change: Evangelical Calvinism Among Eighteenth-Century Baptist Ministers Trained at Bristol Academy, 1690–1791* (Didcot: Baptist Historical Society, 2006)

Haykin, Michael A.G., *Joy Unspeakable and Full of Glory: The Piety of Samuel and Sarah Pearce* (Kitchener, Ontario: Joshua Press, 2012)

—, *One Heart and One Soul: John Sutcliff of Olney, his friends and his times* (Durham: Evangelical Press, 1994)

The Armies of the Lamb: The Spirituality of Andrew Fuller, ed. by Michael A.G. Haykin (Dundas, Ontario: Joshua Press, 2001)

'At the Pure Fountain of Thy Word': Andrew Fuller as an Apologist, ed. by Michael A.G. Haykin (Milton Keynes: Paternoster, 2004)

The British Particular Baptists, 1638-1910, 2 vols, ed. by Michael A.G. Haykin (Springfield, Missouri: Particular Baptist Press, 1998-2000)

The Emergence of Evangelicalism: Exploring Historical Continuities, ed. by Michael A.G. Haykin and Kenneth J. Stewart (Leicester: IVP, 2008)

The Life and Thought of John Gill (1697-1771): A Tercentennial Appreciation, ed. by Michael A.G. Haykin (Leiden: Brill, 1997)

The Atonement Debate: Papers from the London Symposium on the Theology of Atonement ed. by David Hilborn, Justin Thacker and Derek Tidball (Grand Rapids: Zondervan, 2008)

Hindmarsh, D. Bruce, *The Evangelical Conversion Narrative: Spiritual Autobiography in Early Modern England* (Oxford: Oxford University Press, 2005)

—, *John Newton and the English Evangelical Tradition* (Oxford: Clarendon Press, 1996)

Hodge, Charles, *Systematic Theology*, 3 vols (London: James Clarke & Co., 1960 [1865])

Holmes, Stephen R., *God of Grace and God of Glory: An Account of the Theology of Jonathan Edwards* (Edinburgh: T. & T. Clark, 2000)

—, *The Wondrous Cross: Atonement and Penal Substitution in the Bible and History* (Paternoster: Milton Keynes, 2007)

Howells, George, *The Story of Serampore and its College* (Serampore: The College, 1927)

Hylson-Smith, Kenneth R., *The Churches in England from Elizabeth I to Elizabeth II. Vol. 2: 1689-1833* (London: SCM Press, 1997)

Lambert, Frank, *Pedlar in Divinity* (Princeton: Princeton University Press, 1994)

Laws, Gilbert, *Andrew Fuller: Pastor, Theologian, Ropeholder* (London: Kingsgate Press, 1942)

Dictionary of Evangelical Biography 1730-1860, ed. by Donald M. Lewis, 2 vols (Oxford: Blackwell, 1995)

Lloyd Jones, D. Martyn, *Spiritual Depression: its Causes and Cures* (Glasgow: Pickering & Inglis, 1965)

Mangalwadi, Ruth and Vishal, *Carey, Christ and Cultural Transformation* (Carlisle: Paternoster, 1993)

Marsden, George M., *Jonathan Edwards: A Life* (New Haven and London: Yale University Press, 2003)

Morden, Peter J., *C.H. Spurgeon: The People's Preacher* (Farnham: CWR, 2009)

—, 'Communion with Christ and His People': The Spirituality of C.H. Spurgeon (Oxford: Regent's Park, 2010 / Eugene, OR: Wipf and Stock, 2014)

—, *John Bunyan: The People's Pilgrim* (Farnham: CWR, 2013

—, *Offering Christ to the World: Andrew Fuller (1754–1815) and the Revival of Eighteenth Century Particular Baptist Life* (Carlisle: Paternoster, 2003)

Murray, Iain H., *Jonathan Edwards: A New Biography* (Edinburgh: Banner of Truth, 1987)

Naylor, Peter, *Picking up a Pin for the Lord: English Particular Baptists from 1688 to the Early Nineteenth Century* (Durham: Grace Publications Trust, 1992)

Neill, Stephen, *A History of Christian Missions* (Harmondsworth: Penguin, 1964)

Nettles, Thomas J., *By His Grace and For His Glory: A Historical, Theological and Practical Study of the Doctrines of Grace in Baptist Life* (Grand Rapids: Baker, 1986)

Noll, Mark A., *A History of Christianity in the United States and Canada* (London: SPCK, 1992)

—, *The Rise of Evangelicalism: The Age of Edwards, Whitefield and the Wesleys* (Leicester: IVP, 2004)

— *Turning Points, Decisive Moments in the History of Christianity* (Leicester: IVP, 1997)

Nuttall, Geoffrey F., *Studies in English Dissent* (Weston Rhyn: Quinta, 2002)

Oliver, Robert W., *History of the Calvinistic English Baptists, 1771-1892* (Edinburgh: Banner of Truth, 2006)

Payne, Ernest A., *Baptists of Berkshire: Through Three Centuries* (London: Carey Kingsgate Press, 1951)

—, *The Prayer Call of 1784* (London: Kingsgate Press, 1941)

—, *The First Generation: Early Leaders of the Baptist Missionary Society in England and India* (London: Carey Press, n.d. [1937])

Pearce Carey, Samuel, *Samuel Pearce M.A., The Baptist Brainerd* (London: Carey Press, n.d. [1922])

—, *Memoir of William Carey, DD* (London: Hodder and Stoughton, 1923)

Pennington, Brian K., *Was Hinduism Invented? Britons, Indians, and the Colonial Construction of Religion* (Oxford: Oxford University Press, 2005)

Porter, Roy, *Enlightenment: Britain and the Creation of the Modern World* (London: Penguin, 2000)

Potts, E. Daniel, *British Baptist Missionaries in India, 1793-1837* (Cambridge: Cambridge University Press, 1967)

Rack, Henry D., *Reasonable Enthusiast: John Wesley and the Rise of Methodism* (London: Epworth, 1989)

Randall, Ian M., *A School of the Prophets: 150 years of Spurgeon's College* (London: Spurgeon's College, 2005)

Rinaldi, Frank W., *The Tribe of Dan: The New Connexion of General Baptists, 1770-1891* (Carlisle: Paternoster, 2008)

Rix, Robert, *William Blake and the Cultures of Radical Christianity* (Aldershot: Ashgate, 2007)

Roberts, R. Philip, *Continuity and Change: London Calvinistic Baptists and the Evangelical Revival, 1760-1820* (Wheaton, IL: R.O. Roberts, 1989)

Schofield, Robert E., *The Enlightenment of Joseph Priestley: A Study of His Life and Work from 1733 to 1773* (University Park, PA: Pennsylvania State UP,1997)

—, *The Enlightened Joseph Priestley: A Study of His Life and Work from 1773 to 1804* (University Park, PA: Pennsylvania State UP, 2004)

Sell, Alan P.F., *The Great Debate: Calvinism, Arminianism and Salvation* (Worthing: H. E. Walter, 1982)

Sorkin, David, *The Religious Enlightenment: Protestants, Jews, and Catholics from London to Vienna* (Princeton, NJ, and Oxford: Princeton University Press, 2008)

Stanley, Brian, *The History of the Baptist Missionary Society, 1792-1992* (Edinburgh: T. and T. Clark, 1992)

Stout, Harry S., *The Divine Dramatist: George Whitefield and the Rise of Modern Evangelicalism* (Grand Rapids: Eerdmans, 1991)

Toon, Peter, *The Emergence of Hyper-Calvinism in English Nonconformity, 1689–1765* (London: Olive Tree, 1967)

Tyerman, Luke, *The Life of the Rev. George Whitefield*, 2nd edn, 2 vols (London: Hodder and Stoughton, 1890)

Ward, Bruce K., *Redeeming the Enlightenment: Christianity and the Liberal Virtues* (Grand Rapids: Eerdmans, 2010)

Watts, Michael R., *The Dissenters. Vol 1: From the Reformation to the French Revolution* (Oxford: Clarenden Press, 1978)

Baptist Autographs in the John Rylands University Library of Manchester, 1741-1845, trans. and ed. by Timothy Whelan (Macon, GA: Mercer UP, 2009)

Whitley, William T., *A History of English Baptists* (London: Charles Griffin, 1923)

Wilson, Linda, *Constrained by Zeal: Female Spirituality among Nonconformists 1825–1875* (Carlisle: Paternoster, 2000)

Withers, Charles W.J., *Placing the Enlightenment: Thinking Geographically about the Age of Reason* (Chicago, IL: The University of Chicago Press, 2004)

Wright, Christopher J.H., *The Mission of God: Unlocking the Bible's Grand Narrative* (Leicester: IVP, 2006)

Wright, Stephen, *The Early English Baptists, 1603-1649* (Woodbridge: Boydell, 2006)

Yeager, Jonathan M., *Enlightened Evangelicalism: The Life and Thought of John Erskine* (Oxford: Oxford University Press, 2011)

Secondary Sources – Chapters in Edited Volumes

Bebbington, David W., 'Response', in Michael A.G. Haykin and Kenneth J. Stewart (eds), *The Emergence of Evangelicalism: Exploring Historical Continuities* (Leicester: IVP, 2008)

—, 'Towards an Evangelical Identity', in *For Such a Time as This*, ed. by Steve Brady and Harold H. Rowden (London: Scripture Union, 1996)

Briggs, John H.Y., 'Baptists in the Eighteenth Century', in *Pulpit and People: Studies in Eighteenth-Century Baptist Life and Thought*, ed. by John H.Y. Briggs (Milton Keynes: Paternoster, 2009)

Brodie, Alexander, 'Introduction – What was the Scottish Enlightenment?' in *The Scottish Enlightenment: An Anthology*, ed. by Alexander Brodie (Edinburgh: Canongate, 1997)

Coffey, John and Paul C.H. Lim, 'Introduction', in *The Cambridge Companion To Puritanism*, ed. by John Coffey and Paul C.H. Lim (Cambridge: Cambridge University Press, 2008)

—, 'Puritan Legacies', *The Cambridge Companion To Puritanism*, ed. by John Coffey and Paul C.H. Lim (Cambridge: Cambridge University Press, 2008)

Etherington, Norman, 'Introduction', in *Missions and Empire*, ed. by Norman Etherington (Oxford: Oxford University Press, 2005)

Gordon, Grant, 'John Ryland, Jr. (1753-1825)', in *The British Particular Baptists, 1638-1910*, ed. by Michael A.G. Haykin (Springfield, Missouri: Particular Baptist Press, 2000)

Gordon, James M., 'The Early Nineteenth Century', in *The Baptists in Scotland: A History*, ed. by David W. Bebbington (Glasgow: The Baptist Union of Scotland, 1988)

Hayden, Roger L., 'The Life and Influence of Andrew Fuller', in *The Kettering Connection: Northamptonshire Baptists and Overseas Mission*, ed. by Ronald L. Greenall (Leicester: Department of Adult Education, University of Leicester, 1993)

Haykin, Michael A.G., 'Andrew Fuller and the Sandemanian Controversy', in *'At the Pure Fountain of Thy Word': Andrew Fuller as an Apologist*, ed. by Michael A.G. Haykin (Milton Keynes: Paternoster, 2004)

—, 'Particular Redemption in the Writings of Andrew Fuller (1754–1815)' in *The Gospel in the World: International Baptist Studies*, ed. by David W. Bebbington (Carlisle: Paternoster, 2002)

Hindmarsh, D. Bruce, 'The antecedents of evangelical conversion narrative: spiritual autobiography and the Christian tradition', in *The Emergence of Evangelicalism: Exploring Historical Continuities*, ed. by Michael A.G. Haykin and Kenneth J. Stewart (Leicester: IVP, 2008)

—, 'The Politically Correct Evangelicalism of John Newton', in *Amazing Grace, Evangelicalism in Australia, Britain, Canada and the United States*, ed. by George A. Rawlyk and Mark A. Noll (Grand Rapids: Baker, 1993)

Holmes, Stephen R., 'Ransomed, Healed, Restored, Forgiven: Evangelical Accounts of the Atonement', in *The Atonement Debate*, ed. by Derek Tidball, David Hilborn and Justin Thacker (Grand Rapids: Zondervan, 2008)

Jarvis, Clive, 'The Myth of High Calvinism?', in *Recycling the Past or Researching History?* ed. by Philip E. Thompson and Anthony R. Cross (Carlisle: Paternoster, 2005)

Larsen, Tim, 'The Reception given to *Evangelicalism in Modern Britain* since its Publication in 1989', in *The Emergence of Evangelicalism: Exploring Historical Continuities*, ed. by Michael A.G. Haykin and Kenneth J. Stewart (Leicester: IVP, 2008)

Lovegrove, Deryck W., 'Unity and Separation: Contrasting Elements in the Thought and Practice of Robert and James Alexander Haldane, in *Protestant Evangelicalism: Britain, Ireland, Germany and America c.1750 – 1950*, ed. by Keith Robbins (Oxford: Ecclesiastical Historical Society / Blackwells, 1990)

Morden, Peter J., 'Andrew Fuller: A Biographical Sketch' and 'Andrew Fuller as an Apologist for Missions', in *'At the Pure Fountain of Thy Word': Andrew Fuller as an Apologist*, ed. by Michael A.G. Haykin (Carlisle: Paternoster, 2004)

—, 'Andrew Fuller and the *Gospel Worthy of All Acceptation*', in *Pulpit and People: Studies in Eighteenth-Century Baptist Life and Thought*, ed. by John H.Y. Briggs (Milton Keynes: Paternoster, 2009)

—, 'John Bunyan: A Seventeenth-Century Evangelical?', in *Grounded in Grace: Essays to Honour Ian M. Randall and Renewal Evangelicalism*, ed. by Peter J. Lalleman, Peter J. Morden, Anthony R. Cross (London: Baptist Historical Society / Spurgeon's College, 2013)

—, 'Nonconformists and the Work of Christ: A Study in Particular Baptist Thought', in *T. & T. Clark Companion to Nonconformity*, ed. by Robert Pope (Edinburgh: T. & T. Clark, 2013)

Murray, Derek B., 'An Eighteenth Century Baptismal Controversy in Scotland', in *Baptism, the New Testament and the Church: Historical and Contemporary Essays in Honour of R.E.O. White*, ed. by Stanley E. Porter and Anthony R. Cross (Sheffield: Sheffield Academic Press, 1999)

O'Brien, Susan, 'Eighteenth Century Publishing in Transatlantic Evangelicalism', in *Evangelicalism: Comparative Studies in Popular Protestantism in North America, The British Isles and Beyond, 1700-1990*, ed. by Mark A. Noll, David W. Bebbington and George A. Rawlyk (Oxford: Oxford University Press, 1994)

Oliver, Robert W., 'Andrew Fuller and Abraham Booth', in *'At the Pure Fountain of Thy Word': Andrew Fuller as an Apologist*, ed. by Michael A.G. Haykin (Milton Keynes: Paternoster, 2004)

—, 'John Gill (1697-1771)' in *The British Particular Baptists,* vol.1, ed. by Michael A. G. Haykin (Springfield, MO: Particular Baptist Press, 1998)

Sell, Alan P.F., 'The Gospel its Own Witness: Deism, Thomas Paine and Andrew Fuller', in *"You Shall Be My Witnesses": A Festschrift in Honor of Reverend D. Allison A. Trites on the Occasion of his Retirement*, ed. by R. Glenn Wooden *et al* (Macon, GA: Mercer University Press, 2003)

Sheehan, Clint, 'Great and Sovereign Grace: Fuller's Defence of the Gospel Against Arminianism', in *'At the Pure Fountain of Thy Word': Andrew Fuller as an Apologist*, ed. by Michael A.G. Haykin (Milton Keynes: Paternoster, 2004)

Smith, A. Christopher, 'Christopher Anderson and the Serampore Fraternity', in *A Mind for Mission; Essays in Appreciation of the Rev. Christopher Anderson 1782-1852*, ed. by Donald E. Meek (Edinburgh: The Scottish Baptist History Project, 1992)

Warfield, Benjamin B., 'Edwards and the New England Theology', in *The Works of Benjamin B. Warfield. Vol 9: Studies in Theology* (Grand Rapids: Baker, 1991)

Secondary Sources – Journal Articles

[Anon.], 'Andrew Fuller and James Deakin, 1803', *Baptist Quarterly* 7 (July 1935), 326-33

[Anon.], 'Letters to James Deakin', *Baptist Quarterly* 7 (October 1935), 361-73

Amey, Basil, 'Baptist Missionary Society Radicals', *Baptist Quarterly* 26.8 (October 1976), 363-76

Baines, Arnold H.J., 'The Pre-History of Regents Park College', *Baptist Quarterly* 36.4 (October 1995), 191-201

Bebbington, David W., 'British Baptist Crucicentrism since the late Eighteenth Century: Part 1', *Baptist Quarterly* 44.4 (October 2011), 223-37

—, 'SBJT Forum', *Southern Baptist Journal of Theology* 17.1 (Spring 2013), 47-48

Clipsham, Ernest F., 'Andrew Fuller and the Baptist Mission', *Foundations* 10.1 (January 1967), 4-18

—, 'Andrew Fuller and Fullerism: A Study in Evangelical Calvinism', *Baptist Quarterly* 20.1-4 (1963): '1. The Development of a Doctrine'; 99-114; '2. Fuller and John Calvin', 147-54; '3. The Gospel Worthy of All Acceptation', 215-25; '4. Fuller as a Theologian', 269-76

Davies, Ronald E., 'Robert Millar – An Eighteenth-Century Scottish Latourette', *Evangelical Quarterly* 62.2 (1990), 143-56

—, 'The Great Commission from Christ to Carey', *Evangel* 14.2 (1996), 46-49

Ella, George M., 'John Gill and the Charge of Hyper-Calvinism', *Baptist Quarterly* 36.4 (October 1995), 166-77

Elwyn, Thornton S.H., 'Particular Baptists of the Northamptonshire Association as Reflected in the Circular Letters, 1765-1820', Part 1, *Baptist Quarterly* 36.8 (October 1996), 368-81; Part 2, 37.1 (January 1997), 3-19

Finn, Nathan A., 'The Renaissance in Andrew Fuller Studies: A Bibliographic Essay', in *Southern Baptist Journal of Theology* 17.2 (Summer 2013), 44-61

Forsaith, Peter S., Review of Doreen Rosman, *Evangelicals and Culture*, 2nd edn, in *Wesley and Methodist Studies* 4 (2012), 175-76

Haste, Matthew, 'Marriage and Family Life of Andrew Fuller', *Southern Baptist Journal of Theology* 17.1 (Spring 2013)

Hastings, F.G., 'Andrew Fuller and Ministerial Removals', *Baptist Quarterly* 8.1 (January 1936), 11-17

Haykin, Michael A.G., '"A Habitation of God, through the Spirit": John Sutcliff (1752-1814) and the Revitalization of the Calvinistic Baptists in the Late-Eighteenth Century', *Baptist Quarterly* 34.7 (July 1992), 304-19

—, 'The Baptist Identity: A View From the Eighteenth Century', *Evangelical Quarterly* 67.2 (1995), 137-152

—, 'Hazarding all for God at a Clap: The Spirituality of Baptism Among British Calvinistic Baptists', *Baptist Quarterly* 38.4 (October 1999), 185-95

—, '"To Devote Ourselves to the Blessed Trinity": Andrew Fuller and the Defense of 'Trinitarian Communities, *Southern Baptist Journal of Theology* 17.2 (Summer 2013), 4-19

—, '"Very affecting and evangelical': A Review of Keith S. Grant, Andrew Fuller and the Evangelical Renewal of Pastoral Theology', *Southern Baptist Journal of Theology* 17.1 (Spring 2013), 42-45

Hulcoop, Stephen and S. Newens, 'John Davis, Minister at Waltham Abbey 1764-1795', *Baptist Quarterly* 39.8 (October 2002), 409-410

James, Sharon, 'Revival and Renewal in Baptist Life: The Contribution of William Steadman (1764-1837)', *Baptist Quarterly* 37.6 (April 1998), 263-82

Kirkby, Arthur H., 'Andrew Fuller, Evangelical Calvinist', *Baptist Quarterly* 15.5 (January 1954), 195-202

Langley, Arthur S., 'Baptist Ministers in England About 1750 A.D.', *Transactions of the Baptist Historical Society*, 6 (1910-11), 138-57

Morden, Peter J., 'Andrew Fuller and the BMS', *Baptist Quarterly* 41 (July 2005), 134-157

—, 'Biblical Renewal for Mission: Andrew Fuller and Eighteenth-Century Baptist Life', *Bulletin of the Strict Baptist Historical Society* (Autumn, 2011), 1-20

—, '"So valuable a life...': A Biographical Sketch of Andrew Fuller (1754-1815)', *Southern Baptist Journal of Theology* 17.1 (Spring 2013), 4-14

Nettles, Thomas J., 'The Passion and Doctrine of Andrew Fuller in *The Gospel Worthy of All Acceptation*' *Southern Baptist Journal of Theology* 17.1 (Summer 2013), 20-42

Nuttall, Geoffrey F., 'Letters from Robert Hall to John Ryland, 1791-1824', *Baptist Quarterly* 34.3 (July 1991), 127-31

—, 'The State of Religion in Northamptonshire (1793) by Andrew Fuller', *Baptist Quarterly* 29.4 (October 1981), 177-79

O'Brien, Susan, 'A Transatlantic Community of Saints: The Great Awakening and the First Evangelical Network, 1735-1755', *American Historical Review* 91 (1986), 812-24

Oliver, Robert W., 'George Whitefield and the English Baptists', *Grace Magazine* 5 (October, 1970) 9-12

Payne, Ernest A., 'Andrew Fuller and James Deakin, 1803', *Baptist Quarterly* 7 (1934-35), 326-33

—, 'Andrew Fuller as Letter Writer', *Baptist Quarterly* 15.7 (July 1954), 290-96

—, 'Some Samuel Pearce Documents', *Baptist Quarterly* 18.1 (January 1959), 26-34

—, 'Some Sidelights on Pearce and his Friends', *Baptist Quarterly* 7 (1934–1935), 270-75

—, 'John Dyer's Memoir of Carey', *Baptist Quarterly* 22.6 (April 1968), 326-27

Pocock, John G.A., 'Historiography and Enlightenment: A View of their History', *Modern Intellectual History* 5.1 (April 2008), 83-96

Potts, E. Daniel, '"I throw away the guns to preserve the ship:" A Note on the Serampore Trio', *Baptist Quarterly* 20.3 (July 1963), 115-117

Randall, Ian M., 'The Low Condition of the Churches': Difficulties faced by General Baptists in England – the 1680s to the 1760s', *Pacific Journal of Baptist Research* 1.1 (October 2005), 3-19

Robison, Olin C., 'The Legacy of John Gill', *Baptist Quarterly* 24.3 (July 1971), 11-25

Sellers, Ian, 'John Howard Hinton, Theologian', *Baptist Quarterly* 33.3 (July 1989), 119-32

Smith, A. Christopher, 'The Spirit and Letter of Carey's Catalytic Watchword: A Study in the Transmission of Baptist Tradition', *Baptist Quarterly* 33.5 (January 1990), 226-37

—, 'William Ward, Radical Reform, and Missions in the 1790s', *American Baptist Quarterly* 10 (1991), 218–244

Ward, W. Reginald, 'Baptists and the Transformation of the Church, 1780–1830', *Baptist Quarterly* 25.4 (1973), 167–84

Whitley, William T., 'Baptist Board Minutes, 1750-1820', *Transactions of the Baptist Historical Society* 7 (1918-19), 72-127

—, 'The Baptist Interest under George I', *Transactions of the Baptist Historical Society* 2 (1910-11), 95-109

Yeager, Jonathan, 'The Letters of John Erskine to the Rylands', *Eusebia* 9 (Spring 2008), 183-95

Secondary Sources – Theses

Kirkby, Arthur H., 'Theology of Andrew Fuller in its relation to Calvinism' (unpublished PhD thesis, University of Edinburgh, 1956)

Mitchell, Christopher W., 'Jonathan Edwards's Scottish Connection and the Eighteenth-Century Scottish Evangelical Revival, 1735-1750' (unpublished PhD thesis, University of St Andrews, 1997)

Morden, Peter J., 'Andrew Fuller (1754-1815) and the Revival of Eighteenth Century Particular Baptist Life' (unpublished MPhil thesis, University of Wales / Spurgeon's College, 2000)

Oliver, Robert W., 'The Emergence of a Strict and Particular Baptist Community Among the English Calvinistic Baptists, 1770-1850' (unpublished DPhil thesis, CNAA / London Bible College, 1986)

Pollard, Richard, 'To Revive Experimental Religion or Primitive Christianity in Faith and Practice: The Pioneering Evangelicalism of Dan Taylor (1738-1816)' (unpublished PhD thesis, University of Wales / Spurgeon's College, 2014)

Robison, Olin C., 'The Particular Baptists in England: 1760-1820' (unpublished DPhil thesis, University of Oxford, 1963)

Smith, Karen, 'The Community of Believers: A Study of Calvinistic Baptist Spirituality in Some Towns and Villages of Hampshire and the Borders of Wiltshire, c. 1730-1830' (unpublished DPhil thesis, University of Oxford, 1987)

South, Thomas J., 'The Response of Andrew Fuller to the Sandemanian View of Saving Faith' (unpublished Th.D thesis, Mid-America Baptist Theological Seminary, Cordova, TN, 1993)

Sugden, Keith, 'The Occupational and Organizational Structures of the Northamptonshire Worsted and Shoemaking Trades, circa 1750-1821' (unpublished MA thesis, University of Cambridge, 2011)

West, J. Ryan, 'Evangelizing Bengali Muslims, 1793-1813: William Carey, William Ward, and Islam' (unpublished PhD thesis, Southern Baptist Theological Seminary, Louisville, KY, 2014)

Author Index

Names Index

Anderson, Christopher, 165-66, 167, 203

Beccaria, Cesare, 142, 143
Bedome, Benjamin, 21
Bellamy, Joseph, 63, 90, 141, 141n.87, n.88, 142n.95, 143
Bentham, Jeremy, 142
Birt, Caleb Evans, 23
Birt, Isaiah, 23, 183, 184
Booth, Abraham, 121, 124, 125-39, 140-142, 143, 149, 201
Brainerd, David, 60
Brine, John, 17, 19, 20, 53, 67, 85
Brooks, Thomas, 107
Bunyan, John, 1, 29, 32, 53, 54, 67, 107
Burls, William, 159
Burroughs, Jeremiah, 107
Button, William, 82-86, 93, 95

Carey, William, 2, 6, 105n.47, 109, 116, 117, 118, 120, 120, 122, 126, 127, 158n.46, 162, 163, 169, 171, 172, 173, 174, 175, 176, 177, 181, 196, 202
Cecil, Richard, 121
Chalmers, Thomas, 203n.6
Charnock, Stephen, 53
Clarkson, David, 12
Coke, Thomas, 189
Coles, William, 157
Cook, Captain James, 116
Cox, Francis, 185, 185n.18
Crisp, Tobias, 132, 142n.93

Davis, Richard, 16, 17, 18, 111
Diver, Joseph, 34, 35, 36
Doddridge, Philip, 52
Dutton, Anne, 19
Dwight, Timothy, 148

Edwards, Jerusha, 59
Edwards, John, 60
Edwards, Jonathan, 4, 10, 26, 37, 57-65, 72, 84, 90, 112-13, 128, 131n.37, 135, 139, 141, 142n.95, 145, 146, 148, 197, 202
Edwards, Jonathan Jr., 140, 143, 144, 145n.109
Elliott, John, 59, 59n.122, 60
Emery, John, 36, 37
Erskine, John, 58, 59, 112, 165
Erskine, Ralph, 29
Evans, Caleb, 24, 56, 63, 80, 84, 111, 184
Evans, John, 20, 21
Eve, John, 15, 16, 18, 20, 29, 33, 34, 35, 37, 41, 43, 50

Fawcett, John, 28, 111, 117, 120
Fawkner, Robert, 74, 77
Fletcher, Jonathan, 66
Fountain, John, 171, 177
Franklin, Francis, 156, 156n.36
Fuller, Andrew Gunton, 5, 7, 12, 14, 33, 42, 43n.34, 121, 151, 155, 161, 162, 169, 177, 187
Fuller, Ann (née Coles), 157, 158, 170
Fuller, Bathoni, 102
Fuller, John, 13, 22, 43n.34, 197
Fuller, Robert, 11, 13, 14, 44-45
Fuller, Robert ('Bobby'), 98, 102, 150, 159-162, 180
Fuller, Sarah (née Gardiner), 42, 70, 78, 201
Fuller, Sarah ('Sally'), 98, 103, 106, 109, 161
Fuller, Thomas, 6, 7

Gadsby, William, 203
Gifford, Andrew, 24, 27

225

Scripture Index

Subject Index

A Blow at the Root of Fullerism, 1
Act of Toleration, the, 22
Act of Uniformity, the, 12
Anglican Church Missionary
  Society, the, 162-63
antinomianism, 34, 35, 85, 192
Arminianism, 64, 72, 84, 85,
  129, 189, 203, 204
atonement, the, 124, 131-39,
  143, 149, 186, 188, 189

Baptist Annual Register, the,
  163, 184
Baptist Magazine, the, 6
Baptist Missionary Society, the
  (BMS), 2, 8, 28, 109-21, 124,
  155, 159, 162-70, 175, 180, 182,
  186, 193, 194, 195, 198, 200-
  201, 203, 206
Baptist Quarterly, the, 3, 55
believers' baptism, 12, 23, 28,
  86
Bengal, 165, 171, 174, 177, 179,
  180
Bible translation, 162, 168
biblical Christianity, 1, 188, 189
biblical exposition, 2
Bristol Baptist Academy, the,
  19, 24, 56, 183
British and Foreign Bible Society,
  the, 155
British East India Company,
  171, 177, 179, 195

Calcutta, 171
Calvinistic theology, 13, 15-16
Careful and Strict Enquiry, A,
  61
Christ, 20, 24, 30, 32, 33, 42, 44,
  45, 48, 57, 66, 71, 78, 81, 83,
  89-91, 116, 128, 129, 133, 134,

138, 139, 141, 154, 156, 161,
  173, 173n.131, 175, 179, 180,
  188, 189, 192, 194, 195, 197,
  201, 202
church order, 26-27
colonial expansion, 178-79
Congregationalism, 13
conversion(s), 55, 128, 177, 184,
  190n.48
cross, the, 131-132, 136, 138,
  139, 141, 143, 183, 188, 194,
  197

Divine Justice Essential, 133-34

*East Midland Baptist Magazine,
  the*, 161
Eclectic Review, the, 175n.144
Edwards, Jonathan,
  *Faithful Narrative of Surprising
  Conversions, A*, 57
  Freedom of the Will, The, 58, 60-
  65, 90, 95, 202
  Humble Attempt, An, 112, 202
  Life of David Brainard, A, 59, 202
English Calvinistic Baptists, 1, 2
Edinburgh Review, the, 174
Enlightenment, the, 66-67, 142,
  189, 190; thinking, 92-96,
  190
Enquiry, An, 118-19
eschatology, 113, 153
Evangelical Magazine, the, 6,
  29, 60, 129, 163
Evangelical Revival, the, 18, 25-
  28, 31, 37, 39, 86, 202
evangelicalism, 33, 37, 74, 165,
  167, 184, 189, 198, 201
evangelism, 2, 24, 73, 117, 150,
  156, 173n.131, 177, 178, 179,
  180, 183, 193, 202